Harvard Business Review
On Management

Harvard Business Review

On Management

Volume 2

Classic
Advice on
Managing
Systems

PERENNIAL LIBRARY

Harper & Row, Publishers
New York, Cambridge, Philadelphia, San Francisco
London, Mexico City, São Paulo, Singapore, Sydney

Library of Congress Cataloging in Publication Data
Main entry under title:

Harvard business review—on management.

   "Originally published as part of a larger volume under same title"—V. 2, t.p. verso.
   "Best selling articles from the Harvard business review's reprint Service"—V. 2, p.
   Includes index.
   1. Management—Addresses, essays, lectures.
I. Harvard business review. II. Title: On management.
HD31.H3497 1986   658.4   85-45411
ISBN 0-06-091286-3 (pbk. : v. 2)

86 87 88 89 90 MPC 10 9 8 7 6 5 4 3 2 1

Contents

Foreword

The *Harvard Business Review* is a medium for the continuing education of executives in business, industry, and government. Drawing on the talents of many of the most creative people in modern business and business teaching, it attempts to bridge the gap between academic planning and business practice.

Harvard Business Review—On Management, containing articles selected from the thousands published in the past 25 years of *HBR*, has been designed for managers and would-be managers who want to improve their skills and to learn more about the role of the executive.

The book contains some of *HBR*'s most outstanding presentations of management philosophies and strategies; approaches which, we believe, every well-informed practicing businessman should understand. We have tried to cover in a systematic fashion many management functions and problems of special importance—a fairly good range of topics but, of course, still only a sample of all the ones possible. The selection of articles has been limited to include only methods and ideas which will not go out-of-date.

We hope that this book will be useful to the business community for a long time.

The Editors
Harvard Business Review

Part I

Planning and Strategy

Preface

Whether it is a "mom-and-pop" grocery anticipating next week's demand for bologna, a multibillion-dollar conglomerate determined to meet growing competition in the Common Market, or a social welfare agency anticipating economic trends in its service area, every organization finds planning and formulation of strategy necessary. It is obvious that a manager must plan his action before he takes it (and then observe the results). But it is not obvious to many how planning—particularly corporate planning—has changed in the last two decades or so as a result of changing economic, societal, and market forces.

Time was when almost every business concentrated on a single product or a group of related products or services. Planning was essentially a matter of making sure that the products moved out of the factory, that the demand for them was present (sometimes created, if not already present), and that the demand was met at a profit. Long-term strategy often was confined to such questions as whether to extend the market territory west of the Mississippi or whether to expand the product line to more fully meet the needs of customers. Usually, the objectives of the organization were more or less fixed; its management carried on the planning process, most often informally, to make sure that those objectives were being met.

Then came World War II. The dislocations it caused in operational and in managerial terms, coupled with the economic boom that followed it, made the old way of conducting business hopelessly inadequate and obsolete. New markets opened up, first in the United States, then elsewhere; competition stiffened as new rivals sprang up and the imaginary limits of spheres of activity vanished; and the surging stock market set a premium on performance translated into earnings per share. The informal, single-minded planning process had to adjust accordingly. As Frank Gilmore wrote in his contribution to this section, the managers of business organizations "recognized that—

. . . concern for short-term problems would have to shift to plans for capitalizing on long-term opportunities;

. . . sizing up the situation as a basis for a new course of action would have to give way to reappraising existing strategy in the light of the changing environment;

... sporadic diagnosis would have to be replaced by constant surveillance; ... concern for immediate profits and for adaptability to meet changes in current conditions needed to shift to focusing on long-range ROI, growth, flexibility, and stability.

In the most progressive corporations—in the most progressive large non-business organizations too—planning departments were established. As top executives increasingly became aware of the value of this function, planners gained access to their offices. By 1970 a leader in the upgrading of this function, George A. Steiner, was able to write in the Harvard Business Review, *"As recently as 1965, [the corporate planner] was viewed in many corporations as, at best, a fad and, at worst, a necessary overhead. . . . This view . . . is disappearing and is not prevalent at all in the advanced larger companies."*

A principal task for the planner became scanning the external environment. Increasing government regulation and surveillance of business, the more demanding and more strident voice of consumers, the accelerating pace of technology, the increasing interdependence of national economies—these factors and many more added greater complexity and difficulty to the task of strategic planning. The pricing of a product made by a German subsidiary, for example, might depend to an extent on the valuation in inventory of its components, and that value would hinge in part on the fluctuating worth of the Deutschmark against the dollar.

In different ways, the three articles in this section reflect the enlarged scope of planning and strategy formulation. Myles Mace's contribution stresses the active role which the top officer of the organization must play in the process on a continuous basis. The second article demonstrates the importance of including both "reach" and "realism"—that is, what might be as well as what should be—in the planning activity. Finally, Frank Gilmore outlines a procedure for developing strategy in smaller organizations, where resources are limited and where busy executives often tend to focus on tomorrow's imperatives at the expense of problems and opportunities on the horizon.

1. The President and Corporate Planning

Myles L. Mace

What is effective planning? Here a person who has both participated in the exercise in a large corporation and studied it as a scholar and teacher outlines the steps to be taken to ensure that corporate objectives are defined, communicated, adhered to, reviewed, and redefined. The most essential ingredient in the process is the active involvement of the chief executive; he cannot delegate to subordinates his role as the leader.

Throughout the early 1960's, many top executives were concerned about the need for more formalized corporate planning in their respective organizations. Some chief operating executives searched for the "best system" and the "best methods" with the hope that the installation of another company's successful approach would achieve more effective results in their own corporate planning function. This situation is somewhat similar to that of the early 1950's, when many company executives were searching for the best system to provide for the growth and development of key personnel.

As in the 1950's, preoccupation with the forms, procedures, and techniques of a best system produces lip service to an important management function, but accomplishes little toward achievement of real, honest-to-goodness plans for the future direction of corporations. To mechanically adopt the methods and procedures which appear to be useful in the ABC Corporation does not assure fulfillment of the planning function in the XYZ Corporation. Such thinking is analogous to believing that the adoption of a "suggestion system" automatically builds employee morale.

Administrative Focus

Effective corporate planning does not consist simply of a system. Rather, it is an administrative process and a critically important job which should concern the management of every corporation. Forms and procedures may

5

be employed as convenient and useful tools. But the success of corporate planning is not measured by the writing of procedures, the addition of a new box on the organization chart, or the production of an impressive-looking book entitled "Corporate Goals and Plans—Confidential."

Some executives have indicated that corporate planning is required only in large and diverse enterprises and that managements of small and medium sized companies need not be concerned. Planning as an essential business function is as important to the small company as it is to the large. Indeed, individual planning is important for each person who has aspirations for success in a business organization.

In 1961 and 1962, George G. Montgomery, Jr., now a vice president of White Weld Company in New York, and I made a research study of the problems involved in the acquisition of one company by another.[1] A segment of that study was concerned with planning for growth through acquisition. With this background, which has been augmented by continued interest and experience, especially with regard to the planning function, I shall undertake to deal in this article with what seem to be some of the most important and practical steps involved in the attainment of effective and useful corporate planning.

PRESIDENT'S INVOLVEMENT

Probably the single most important problem in corporate planning derives from the belief of some chief operating executives that corporate planning is not a function with which they should be directly concerned. They regard planning as something to be delegated, which subordinates can do without responsible participation by chief executives. They think the end result of effective planning is the compilation of a "Plans" book. Such volumes get distributed to key executives, who scan the contents briefly, file them away, breathe a sigh of relief, and observe, "Thank goodness that is done—now let's get back to work."

George Montgomery and I found in the course of the acquisition research mentioned above that effective corporate planning is not possible without the personal involvement and leadership of the chief operating executive. Subsequent study confirmed this conclusion. Involvement and leadership mean spending the time and energy to manage the function—to see that something concrete is done. They mean personally putting into action what is too often abrogated by general words and phrases. In specific terms, there are two fundamental functions which absolutely demand the chief executive's active involvement:

(1) *Leadership in the tough and laborious process of realistically evalu-*

1. *Management Problems of Corporate Acquisitions* (Boston, Division of Research, Harvard Business School, 1962).

ating existing product lines, markets, trends, and competitive positions in the future.

(2) *Leadership in the establishment of corporate objectives.*

After examining each of these critically important leadership functions, I shall discuss the basic elements of a planning program.

Realistic Evaluation

Among many corporate executives, the concept of planning is believed necessary only to find new areas of product opportunity. Planning programs organized to achieve this limited scope completely overlook the possibility of augmenting or strengthening existing product lines or product divisions.

Analysis of the history of sales, margins, and profits by product or product line discloses significant trends which are frequently unnoticed in the course of the day-to-day management of companies. For example:

A five-year history was compiled of the products which comprised 80% of a company's sales. It became clear that some product margins had steadily declined, others had remained stable, and the increase in total company sales and profits was attributable to a few high gross-margin items. The company's success had camouflaged what was happening to products which once had been substantial contributors to profits.

This relatively simple analysis led to further study of market prospects for the less profitable items. It was concluded that an inability to raise market prices or reduce costs required the addition of new, higher margin products if the sales and profits of the corporation were to be maintained or grow in the future.

Some chief operating executives find it difficult to recognize that product lines which have produced generous profits over many years are in jeopardy. Competitive facts of life encroach on markets, but a sentimental attachment to the past leads to a euphoric attitude about the future. Reluctance to face up to the situation is characterized by such statements as, "We have been through tough times before and we can do it again," or, "This business has been mighty good to us in the past and we are going to stick with it," or, "Sooner or later the competitor's prices have got to come back in line, and when that happens, we will be on our way again."

Admittedly it is painful to accept the unpleasant fact that uncontrollable outside competitive forces have depleted long-standing markets and margins. But a chief operating executive who procrastinates in adopting an action-planning program to adjust to changing conditions jeopardizes profits and, in some cases, the company's solvency. For example:

In a situation where competitors had moved in and taken over a certain company's once very profitable market, the chief operating executive of the company recognized the fact that the market was completely gone. However, sentimentally aware of the score of key people whose careers were identified only with that market, he refused to make the hard decision to reduce sharply or eliminate outright the jobs of the people working on the lost cause. The last several years have been characterized by increasing annual deficits, and the inevitable decision remains to be made.

When chief operating executives do not, as an integral part of their planning role, recognize realistically the status of their existing operations and fulfill the leadership role by adapting to changing conditions, they jeopardize current profits as well as the capacity of the organization to prosper in the future.

Corporate Objectives

In some companies a distinction is made between corporate objectives and corporate goals. Here I regard objectives and goals as synonymous, because corporate planning consists of creating the goals and defining in detail the corporate plans to achieve those goals.

I have found that the phrase "creation of corporate objectives" is regarded by some chief operating executives as rather meaningless, academic language—they think creating objectives is something professors talk about, and that such goals have little real value in the management of a business enterprise. Discounting the value of defining corporate objectives probably arises in part from the many published statements which describe the goals in broad general terms—such as increased sales, increased profits, a broader base of operations, a better environment for the growth of personnel, and so forth. Such expressions of objectives are, indeed, neither meaningful nor useful.

DIRECTION NEEDED

In some companies I have found no explicit or implicit concepts of corporate goals. One consequence of this lack of direction is that product and division managers more often than not create their own goals, and the result is a hodgepodge of unrelated, unintegrated, and expensive internal research and product development programs. Consider this example:

In one company, the division managers were urged by the chief operating executive to "do something about increasing sales and broadening the base of operations." Each of four division managers embarked on independent and uncoordinated product development projects. Later, capital appropriations and operating budgets were approved by headquarters management, and after a four-year period and a loss of $3 million, the four division managers were engaged in liquidating their respective abortive ventures.

A product development program with carefully defined goals certainly is no guarantee that the product produced and marketed will be successful. But a product development program with goals certainly is financially more economical and less wasteful of management talent at the division level.

Discussions with chief executives about the concept of creating corporate goals indicate that many think there is something mysterious about the process. There is concern about the method or approach to be used in outlining corporate objectives. How does one go about deciding the mission of an organization? Do statements of goals spring full blown from the minds of presidents? Should we hire consultants to tell us what our objectives should be? Or perhaps hire an economist who can forecast the most promising markets of the future? How do we know what business conditions will be like two years or five years from now? How can we plan effectively when our business is so fast moving that the creation of long-range goals means anticipating what we will do next week?

THINKING REQUIRED

Some companies neglect corporate planning because the process intrinsically requires thinking about the future and the future is always uncertain. Anticipating all the factors which affect a company's sales and profits means dealing intellectually with mercurial and intangible elements. This is especially difficult for the action-minded, decision-oriented executive who enjoys and derives great satisfaction from "doing things." Also, and this is one of the most common reasons for deferring thinking about the future, day-to-day crises need decisions right now, and there are usually enough crises to occupy most or all of each business day.

One president stated that "the tyranny of the moment prevents me from paying attention to the important future of the company." Another president said:

"Thinking seems to have lost respectability in some companies. If a vice president is caught sitting at his desk without papers, people, or telephone calls and, in response to a query by the president as to what he is doing, says 'thinking,' the typical reaction of the president is likely to be, 'Thinking! If you are going to think, think on your own time.'"

But despite the obstacles, real and imagined, to corporate planning, many chief executives regard the function as one of their principal duties and are actively engaged in planning the future paths of their organizations.

SIMPLE PROCESS

Yet the process of corporate planning is relatively simple and straightforward. Much of the mystery of planning comes from the many general admonitions provided by students of management who describe planning as a composite of abstract elements made up of strategy, tactics, purpose, specifications, alternatives, and so on. Chief executives who are doing effective planning jobs describe the process in more practical and meaningful terms. From conversations with them, I shall summarize and illustrate briefly the five basic elements of a planning program, including the creation of corporate goals.

Analyzing the Present

Planning for the future starts with an intimate and realistic understanding of existing products, divisions, markets, margins, profits, return on investment, cash flow, availability of capital, research and development abilities, and skills and capacities of personnel. These significant aspects of operations can be looked at in an orderly manner, and there is nothing mysterious about an analysis of the company's strength and weakness in each of these areas. Basic to consideration of a mission for the company in the future is a clear recognition of how well the organization is doing today.

Analysis of present operations can be done effectively by reviewing the past few years' performance as part of the evaluation of the current year's operating and capital budget forecasts. In some cases, top managements ask division or functional managers to submit the proposed annual budgets together with budgets for the next three to five years. The headquarters review of the short-term forecast is thus combined with the long-term forecast, which otherwise would be a separate, second step. This method of reviewing and evaluating both forecasts simultaneously has the apparent advantage of economy of management time and effort.

However, many top executives find that the discussion invariably focuses on the short-term prospect because of its imminence, and that the long-term problems are deferred or given only brief attention. Current operating problems should be distinguished from the longer-term goals and plans. The purposes of evaluating short-term forecasts and long-term projections— both extremely important—are so different that two separate presentations and evaluations need to be made. Short-term budgets require headquarters modification and approval for financial commitments, whereas long-term forecasts are not subject to authority to spend or commit.

Predicting the Future

Forecasts for each of the next three to five years, based on current operations and existing plans for improving operations, are an important element of a sound planning program. If the company continues to do what it is doing and planning to do today, what will be its future sales, profit, market position, and so on?

Many different approaches produce useful forecasts. These vary from elementary dollar results to more detailed and complex breakdowns of business functions. In one company, which is organized on the basis of decentralized, autonomous divisions for which profit and loss are measurable, each of the seven division managers is asked to submit five-year plans based on an eight-point outline. (A detailed breakdown of this type of outline is given in the Appendix for the reader who would like a more concrete picture of such a forecast.)

In another company, as an illustration, division managers are asked to supply the following information for a three-year forecast:

◻ Sales by product line.
◻ Gross profits by product line.
◻ Personnel requirements.
◻ Capital expenditure needs.

Normally, the data prepared by division or functional managers is submitted in writing two or three weeks in advance of a review date so that the president and other headquarters executives can thoroughly examine the forecasts prior to the meeting.

Reviewing the Forecasts

Here again, practices vary among the companies I have observed. In one, for example, eight divisional managers meet for two days at headquarters, and each manager is allowed two hours to make a presentation of his present operations and his plans for the future. The president and key headquarters executives listen to each presentation and typically ask general, unchallenging questions. It is an essentially meaningless exercise for all concerned.

In contrast, in a certain company where the president regards corporate planning as his most important job, full-day reviews are made of each division manager's report on his goals and his plans to achieve those goals for each of the next three years. Here the president and key headquarters executives study the written portions of the presentation prior to the meeting and are well armed with perceptive and challenging questions about the validity of their managers' forecasts. Several years' experience with this approach has resulted in increasingly effective, realistic forecasts by the division managers and complete recognition by executives in the company that, while the president is the leader in planning, all key personnel have a share in making the planning function real and meaningful.

Critical evaluation of forecasts prepared by division or functional managers is also required to prevent subordinates from regarding the process of preparing forecasts as an exercise and not an integral part of responsible planning. For example:

□ In some companies managers supply financial forecasts by product line by mechanically projecting 5% increases in sales and profits for each year. Such an approach observes the amenities of corporate procedures but, if unchallenged by top executives, adds little effectiveness to statements of what can be expected in the future.

□ In other companies managers purposely overstate their expectations with the hope of manifesting to headquarters executives what fine performances can be expected in the future.

□ Still other managers employ the strategy of understating forecasts for the purpose of establishing financial goals relatively easy to achieve. Thus approbation will come from headquarters if the forecasts are subsequently exceeded. Hopefully, this will be expressed in higher salaries and bonuses.

Careful and thoughtful review, therefore, is required to validate the reasonableness of managers' forecasts and to provide a realistic composite picture of the future achievement of the entire enterprise.

Critical evaluation by top executives of division or functional managers' longer-range goals and plans has another important advantage. A discussion by able, experienced, and interested executives about the operations of a division inevitably results in the disclosure of some new opportunity not thought of previously. The interplay of active minds dedicated to greater growth and success stimulates new avenues of thought which can be enormously helpful to the division and to the company.

When all of the division or functional managers' goals and plans have been reviewed, a composite report representing the totals for the entire company should be prepared. Some companies accept the forecasts of divisions as presented, and the total becomes the program. In others, the chief executive and his key subordinates review again all the separate programs and adjust the division figures according to their previous experience with the respective division managers. History indicates that some managers are unreformed optimists and others are perpetual pessimists. If discussion during the review does not result in adjustment, the chief executive must make appropriate increases or decreases in order to arrive at a realistic overall forecast.

Evaluating the Program

When all managers' forecasts have been reviewed critically and adjusted to represent more appropriately the judgment of the company's top executives, the total program can be evaluated for the purpose of (1) accepting the forecasted performance as reasonable, or (2) deciding that the stated program does not comprise a suitable growth rate for the company.

DOMINANT CONSIDERATIONS

A significant and controlling determinant in arriving at a conclusion as to the adequacy of proposed division or functional plans is the attitude, personal desire, and aspiration of the chief operating executive. It is frequently assumed that every chief executive aspires to head a growing and increasingly profitable enterprise—that by taking into account the interests of stockholders, employees, customers, and the communities within which the company operates, he will make thoughtful decisions to grow, prosper, and fulfill social and public responsibilities. While this is generally true, some chief executives are motivated by other primary considerations which dominate many major policy decisions. For example:

In a western consumer products company the president and his key subordinates recognized that their major strengths were in the research, development, and manufacturing of potentially profitable new products, but the company's marketing organization had proved to be ineffective in establishing distribution to thousands of outlets in the United States. Several unsuccessful attempts were made to strengthen the marketing group.

Meanwhile, a competitor with a superb marketing staff continued to increase its share of the market. The president of the competing company, in planning the future growth of his enterprise, perceived that continued growth in sales and profits would be possible only with more effective product research, development, and manufacturing facilities. Dissatisfied with the time which would be required to build a stronger development and manufacturing group, he explored the alternative of acquiring another company with the necessary strengths to complement his organization.

A study of possible acquisitions resulted in the identification of the western company described above, and the two presidents initiated negotiations to merge the two companies. Continued discussions disclosed that the fit was even better than originally conceived—stock prices and dividend policies were substantially alike, terms of exchange were agreed on, antitrust laws were not an obstacle—and a plan for the integration of the two organizational structures was evolved which met the desires and aspirations of both groups.

The one snag was: Who would be the chief operating executive of the merged enterprises? It was clear that joining the two companies would substantially benefit the stockholders, the employees, and the communities where the companies had operations. Negotiations continued intensively for several weeks, but were terminated when it was apparent that both presidents wanted to be the chief operating executive of the merged companies. Neither was willing to take the second position, although many possible divisions of authority and re-

sponsibility were considered and rejected in turn. The personal desire of each
president to retain the position as chief executive prevented the merger, and
the two companies continued to operate competitively.

I have found similar examples of dominant personal considerations in
other situations, but the real reasons for termination of merger discussions
are rarely publicized. The usual explanation is that differences on price or
differences on major policies have led both parties to conclude that each
company should remain independent and autonomous.

HIDDEN MOTIVES

In other cases, the chief operating executives disguise their personal desires
and goals for their companies. They profess the conviction that their companies should adjust to changed conditions in their respective industries,
that new areas of activity should be searched for and entered. But personal,
and usually unexpressed, reasons control the decisions not to take the
risks involved in moving into promising market opportunities.

At a research seminar conducted at the University of California, Los
Angeles, to discuss long-range planning, one of the participants, Rex Land,
described his experience with a company which tried to hide its basic
objectives, but eventually was found out. Land said:

"I know of a company, very closely held, the executives of which (after
a great deal of probing action) finally admitted they were primarily interested in maintaining the prestige of other members of the family. The top
executive was not going to take certain risks that would jeopardize his
income or that of four or five members of his family. His could have been
a growing and healthy company if it had brought in and held executives,
but he could not keep people for very long. It took people five years to
realize what the real objectives of this company were."[2]

In another company, the president made a review of a five-year forecast
of sales and profits based on the continuation of status quo operations. It
seemed possible with existing products, he reasoned, to maintain the same
flat curve of sales and profits achieved over the last several years. He
concluded, therefore, that the company's plan would be to maintain this
level of performance and not to try to grow in size or profitability. In a
lengthy discussion of his plan and planning process, he conceded that he
felt personally comfortable heading the organization at its present size.
"If I grow and take on more people, I am not too sure I could do it. And
even if I could, I am not willing to pay the price of the extra effort
required."

2. Reported in *Managerial Long-Range Planning*, edited by George A. Steiner (New
York, McGraw-Hill Book Company, 1963), p. 38.

PERSONAL FEARS

Other chief operating executives, after reviewing forecasts of gradually declining sales and profits based on present operations and plans, resignedly accept the anticipated results because of personal fears of risking substantial sums of development or capital expenditure money. Consider this example:

The president of a large family corporation in the East regarded his role as that of a conservator. Several members of the family held corporate executive titles, and the value of the company constituted the principal of the family trust created for them by their deceased father, who had founded the company.

Technological changes in the industry resulted in a gradual erosion of the company's sales and profits which, for years, had enjoyed the dominant position in a segment of the industrial instruments business. None of the company's top executives could foresee anything except continued declines in sales, profit, and market position unless the company risked an estimated $3 million investment in product development.

The policy dilemma of whether to risk $3 million of what was regarded as the assets of the family trust or whether to accept the forecasted future of further declines was resolved by the president when he chose to "ride out this temporary decline trend." The company president has continued to reject the alternative risk, and the company sales and profits have continued to deteriorate.

While these foregoing examples illustrate the importance and influence of attitudes, personal desire, and aspirations of chief operating executives, indeed they are not at all typical of the majority of companies.

TYPICAL EXECUTIVES

Usually presidents are found to be searching for ways to increase the size and profitability of their respective corporations. And if the forecasted performance of existing operations fails to produce expectations of profitable growth, plans are initiated to build on the business of the present. In my studies the more common president is one who is rarely satisfied with nominal growth rates, who stretches the forecasts of divisional or functional managers, and who establishes new and challenging standards of performance for the organization to achieve. Such presidents regard lack of growth as stagnation, an attribute they abhor.

When chief operating executives review and evaluate the forecasted performance for three to five years and conclude that the financial figures are reasonable and plans for their realization feasible, the composite documents constitute the corporate plan for the stated period of years ahead. Sometimes these "working papers" are regarded as "company goals and plans." In other cases the significant elements of them are formalized into "corporate goals," and the various segments of the corporate plans for achievement are spelled out in great detail. The mission and the plan for achievement are thus clearly defined.

However, when the chief operating executives conclude that the anticipated results are not adequate, it becomes imperative to think through and construct a new or modified set of goals and a new plan to fulfill these desired objectives.

Creating the Goals

In my discussions with presidents who are concerned about the anticipated lack of growth in their companies, the query recurs, "Just how do I go about creating a new set of corporate goals?"

While I have found several successful approaches in the many companies studied, my major conclusions will be discouraging to those who are looking for a quick and easy method. There is no mechanical or expert "instant answer method." Rather, defining corporate goals—and modifying those goals as the future becomes the present—is a long, time-consuming, and continuous process. Each president in each company must regard the construction and adjustment of goals as an important, absolute, and—in a sense—unique requirement of his job.

There are, however, several ways of defining company goals that may suggest a modus operandi to those concerned with this requirement.

REORGANIZE WORK HABITS

With the background and essential information resulting from (1) a realistic analysis of existing operations, including opportunities for growth, (2) adjusted forecasts by division or functional managers of their anticipated performance, and (3) an evaluation of the three-, four-, and five-year forecasts, the chief operating executive can embark on the difficult process of creating a structure of corporate goals.

The process is particularly difficult for some chief executives because accepting corporate planning as an important function means not engaging in parts of the satisfying activities which have kept them completely occupied in the past. Planning takes time, and time becomes available for busy men largely through modification of their work habits. The president of a large eastern company stated recently, "The creation and manning of three new group vice presidential positions to cover nine domestic divisions and our international subsidiaries ought to enable me to give more attention to our corporate goals."

Another said, "In the past I did not take the time as skipper of this corporate ship to plot our course. The absence of direction created a vacuum into which rushed improvisation. The resulting chaos and hodge-podge forced me to recognize that I must take the time to think through where we want to go."

ENLIST KEY PEOPLE

While the main responsibility for defining corporate goals rests on the chief executives, they can enlist the minds and imaginations of other key people in their organizations. To do this, some chief operating executives ask the top eight or ten executives to join them in a three- or four-day retreat to help them start thinking through together what the corporate goals should be. Preferably, such a meeting should be held away from "headquarters" to avoid the diversions of telephones, problems, and decisions. Such "think" or "skull" sessions are found to be most effective when tentative drafts of ideas are prepared prior to the meeting to serve as the focus of discussion. Such preliminary drafts can, but need not, delimit the considerations, since thoughtful and imaginative executives usually extrapolate quickly. One president observes that these sessions should also provide for a break of an hour or two in the afternoon for exercise; otherwise everyone gets to thinking in circles.

Some company presidents look for more from such skull sessions than can be reasonably expected. The thinking and planning process, as indictated earlier, is a long, continuing, and tough process. It is long because answers are not easily come by; continuing because the corporate goals are subject to change, adapting to new conditions; and tough because the process of thinking about the future means dealing with intangibles and assumptions. If an organization is formalizing its planning program for the first time, the most that can be expected from such a meeting is the beginning of an understanding of the magnitude of the problems and the start of the process of formulating possible elements of a statement of goals.

Some presidents assign the job of defining corporate goals to a task force made up of three or four key members of the organization. Others ask an experienced line or staff executive to study the problems and recommend a statement of mission for the company. But, irrespective of the approach used, I find that no real and meaningful goals are outlined without the direct involvement of the chief operating executive. Without his active leadership in the function, resulting concepts are usually interesting but irrelevant products of an academic exercise. With his leadership, it is possible to analyze, to think through alternatives, and to arrive at a practical, workable, and useful outline of the mission of the enterprise.

HIRE RESPONSIBLE CONSULTANTS

Other presidents employ management consultants to advise on what the goals of their corporation should be. Responsible consultants, unbiased and unprejudiced by the way things have been done, can bring to the task the benefit of outside objectivity. Most organizations include undisclosed sacred cows which executives of the company have learned not to molest. Sometimes the unmolested sacred cow is the reason for lack of interest in growth, and the consultant feels a responsibility to report his conclusions objectively. Many times suggestions by consultants on sacrosanct subjects have opened them up for re-examination and, sometimes, even change. New points of view injected by consultants often stimulate corporate top management to audit anew many policies, practices, and other matters which have continued unchallenged over the years. Here is an example:

In one company in the East a substantial part of its sales and profits over the last 20-year period had been derived from one product line in the electronics industry. More recently, competitive Japanese products had entered the United States and pre-empted a large portion of the market. The eastern company sought protection through increased tariffs and intercountry agreements on the amounts to be imported, but neither approach stemmed the increasing market share taken over by the Japanese products. The company management was slow in recognizing the business facts of life and continued to maintain a large and expensive manufacturing facility and a high-salaried marketing group.

A consultant was employed to analyze the company's operations and to recommend a program of remedial action. A few months after he began his analysis of the company, he asked the president and the executive committee, "Why do you stay in that part of the electronics industry when you have been losing money steadily for three years and there are no prospects you can ever make profits there again?"

The directness of the question on a clearly vulnerable point jarred the executives into facing up to a decision not previously even discussed—liquidation of the unprofitable product line with no potential for improvement.

In addition to a hard-nosed look at sacrosanct subjects, the consultant (with wider experience in different companies and industries than corporate executives whose careers may have been limited to one company, one industry, or one geographical area) can often bring to the task new insights. In one company, the president and nine out of ten of the other top executives had devoted their entire careers to the same company. Their understanding of business was limited to a single industry with its small tangential and related activities. Here the consultant—knowing that the world of business is larger than the manufacture and sale of umbrellas, or file cabinets, or maple furniture—was able to suggest possibilities for a broadened base of operations.

No consultants are known, however, who have instantaneous, magic answers as to what goals a particular company might adopt. Surprisingly, some presidents think, "There must be someone, somewhere, who can tell us quickly what we ought to do." Here again, no such consulting sources can be found. The responsible consultant will take the time—and this does take time—to analyze objectively a company's existing operations before he is prepared to recommend programs of action and goals.

ADOPT A STATEMENT

The form and detail of the actual statements which define company goals vary from very simple to elaborate verbal descriptions. In one company, for example, the corporate goals were briefly stated:

1. To increase the return on investment from 4% to 6% by next year.

2. To increase earnings from $3 per share this year to $5 per share in two years.

Another company's objectives are stated in a more detailed way:

1. To raise after-tax earnings from $12 million to $18 million within two years without diluting the equity.

2. To change the proportion of the company's military business from 65% to 40% in two years. (In another company a goal was expressed "to raise the percentage of military business from 40% to 65%.")

3. To liquidate in an orderly manner Division A and those parts of Division B which are unprofitable as soon as possible.

4. To search for and acquire one or more companies in the United States with sales of at least $10 million in the XYZ industry.

5. To establish in the Common Market at least three bases of operations, either by acquisition or by starting our own operations, within two years.

DESIGN A PLAN

The creation of a statement of reasonable goals, in turn, leads to the need for a plan to realize those goals. Here, again, the plan may be a written description or exist only in the minds of top executives, and it may be relatively simple or exceedingly detailed and complex. Many companies of substantial size write descriptions of their goals and an over-all company plan to arrive at those goals, and support these with a marketing plan, a technical plan, a manufacturing plan, a personnel plan, and a financial plan which includes a cash-flow plan.

Planning Staff

The importance of involvement by the chief operating executive has been stressed throughout this article to underline my conviction of the need for his participation. But clearly much of the data collection, procedures for the collection of data, and analysis can and should be done by subordinates in the organization or by a corporate planning office. The need for a separate planning staff is determined largely by the capacities, interests, and time of line and staff executives available. Sometimes the vice president of finance is given the responsibility of heading the planning function because the number aspects constitute a common language of plans.

I find, however, that the most effective way of accomplishing corporate planning is to create a new staff group—reporting to the president—free from the diversion of day-to-day crises and charged with the responsibility of assisting the president. The assistance includes, among other things, helping the chief operating executive "to crystallize goals in the leadership and direction of the company."

FUNCTIONS AND QUALIFICATIONS

The functions of a planning group vary, but the vital ones are included in the following statement adopted by a large western company:

1. To assure that divisions and subsidiaries prepare annual and five-year plans for growth.

2. To assist divisions and subsidiaries in the preparation of annual and five-year projections.

3. To identify areas of product opportunity for divisions and subsidiaries, and for corporate investment.

4. To perform market research as requested by divisions and subsidiaries.

5. To coordinate and monitor the preparation of a written, company-wide, five-year plan.

6. To analyze the economic future of existing operations and to recommend programs of growth or divestment.

7. To make analyses of business, economic, and political conditions bearing on existing or prospective areas of operations.

8. To be responsible for all negotiations with possible companies to be acquired.

During the past few years, many company managements have come to recognize the need for more formalized planning activities. This often leads to the creation of new units, ranging in size from one man to a dozen or more. Frequently, the personnel assigned to the function are transferred from existing line or staff activities. In some cases, these people perform admirable jobs. In a New York chemical company, for example, when the need for intensive planning was recognized, a statement was drafted of the ideal personal qualifications and experience for the job. Here are the important elements of that statement:

☐ Technical knowledge of organic and inorganic chemistry.

☐ Ability to manage people.

☐ Ability to inculcate division managers and headquarters staff officers with the importance of planning as an essential part of their jobs.

☐ Analytical capacity.

☐ Knowledge of financial data, including ability to analyze balance sheets, profit and loss statements, cash-flow forecasts, and operating and capital budgets.

☐ Imagination—ability to perceive new applications for corporate competence.

A review of personnel employed within the company disclosed that the manager of the research and development laboratory possessed most of the desired qualities, and he was moved to the new post, "Director of Product Development and Corporate Planning."

JOB REQUIREMENTS

Often, however, chief operating executives do not think through the job requirements of the important role to be performed by the head of planning. Consequently, they assign somebody who just happens to be available. In some companies, retired, about-to-retire, pseudo-retired, or quasi-retired executives are asked to take on this function during their remaining years with the company. The rationale is: "Joe has been with the company for 40 years, and he knows it inside and out. The planning responsibility will keep him busy for three or four years, and, besides, we need a younger man in his important operational job." When the planning group is regarded so lightly that it becomes a dumping ground for the aging or less competent, it is likely to achieve nothing of consequence. Planning today is a critically important function in management, and it requires the best talent, not the infirm of mind or body.

The need for additional personnel is dictated by the magnitude of the corporate tasks and the availability of staff help in the organization. For example:

☐ In one company, the director of budgets had had extensive experience in another company with financial operating forecasts and cash flows, and their analyses. He was able and interested in serving the needs of the director of plans, and it was not necessary to assign a financial analyst to the plans office.

☐ In another company, the market research department, part of the marketing group, regarded assignments from the plans department as an important part of its responsibilities and was equipped to handle them.

Many companies have assigned only a few personnel to the planning task initially and added others only when the job requirements indicated need for additional help.

Planners' Problems

Two critical problems which are sometimes encountered by the director
of plans call for special attention and close monitoring by the chief executive to assure the success of the corporate planning function. Let's look at
what can be done about each one.

INCULCATING AWARENESS

One difficult problem of a director of plans is to inculcate line managers
of divisions, subsidiaries, or other company operations with an awareness
of the importance of planning as a vital part of *their* jobs. In some situations, long-range planning means nothing more to a division manager than
going through the needless task of preparing an annual operating budget,
getting it done, sending it to the vice president of finance, and forgetting
about it until the next year.

In one eastern company with five years' experience with formalized corporate planning, the vice president for plans summarized his concepts of
what remained to be done on this problem in future planning meetings:

1. *Create an awareness in division managers of the need for planning
beyond the next 12 months into the following two years and beyond.* This
can be done by directing the questions and discussion away from the current
year whenever possible and talking about objectives for the following two
years.

2. *Assess how well the divisions have integrated all the elements of
planning in their programs (including timing) to make sure that programs
have been thought through.* The use of a checklist in this connection may
be helpful, of which the key elements should be:

   ☐ Analysis (e.g., product line breakdowns).
   ☐ Potentials—available skills, and available and needed resources.
   ☐ Problems—deficiencies evident.
   ☐ Establishment of best alternatives—suggested economic goals.
   ☐ Coordination-implementation-timing—the results expected, both financial
and nonfinancial.

3. *Create a means of implementing* continued *planning so that the divisions will complete any unfinished plan or revise any inadequate parts of
it during the coming year.* As the discussion progresses, it is wise to examine areas in which planning is not complete and ask that a timetable and
action plan be set up for putting together the missing elements after the
meeting. Such a plan can be worked up between the division and the
director of plans. In this instance, it is necessary to cover (a) the need for
planning responsibility to be centered in a capable individual, and (b) the

importance that management attaches to this function—which might require additional expenditure.

4. *Determine what standards for measurement, if any, the divisions have in setting goals.* For example, have the divisions set some over-all goal to strive for in sales, profits, investment, and return, as a measuring stick of their own performance? Do they feel that the goals are adequate? What restrictions are holding them back from enlarging these goals?

5. *Determine whether the divisions have compared the amount of technical effort (either at the division level or at the company's headquarters laboratory) on their long-range projects with the profit potential in these projects.* In addition, it is important to determine whether they have considered the degree to which they should be investing profits from existing business in technical effort for potential future rewards. (Similar consideration can be given to marketing's planning for future sales by strengthening or adding to the market organization.)

6. *Get across to the divisions that they should be striving to add more projects to their existing base than they or the corporation can absorb in terms of research and development and capital facilities, so that the most desirable projects can be selected from a wide list.*

7. *Assess the reasonableness of the goals, so as to come up with a consolidated, long-term corporate goal, adjusted to take into account undue optimism or pessimism in the divisions.* The plans should be weighed against past ability to get the job done, how tight a timetable is possible, and how capable the organization is, or can rapidly become, to accomplish the task.

8. *Determine the degree to which the headquarters staff, including marketing, planning, research laboratory, market research, manufacturing, can help implement the divisions' programs.*

9. *Make sure a program is established to see that the advice given by the headquarters staff is followed up.*

10. *Identify the ways in which the divisions can work together in projects requiring complementary skills.*

UNPLANNED PLANS

Another critical—and frustrating—problem of directors of corporate planning evolves from the actions of the chief operating executive who accepts and approves a carefully worked out set of corporate goals and plans for achievement and then, by his arbitrary decisions, moves the company into activities neither related nor contemplated. Indeed, the most carefully thought-out corporate goals and plans must yield to the emergence of some new and previously unthought-of opportunity. Any planning program must be flexible. But, on fundamental plan principles, deviation from agreed-upon programs ought to be restudied before commitments are made. Consider:

In a company where a substantial part of its total investment was subject to the risks of operations abroad, the chief operating executive stated that the ratio of domestic to foreign investment should be increased and that no new money should be exposed to risks from abroad. Shortly after the corporation goals were discussed and adopted by the executive committee, the president learned of a possible acquision in Italy. He flew to Rome and, within a relatively short time, negotiated and arranged for the purchase of a company. The foreign investment commitment increased by several million dollars, and the stated ratio goals became meaningless standards for the organization.

Concluding Note

Corporate planning is an inseparable part of the job of all chief operating executives; the futures of their companies depend upon the corporate courses prescribed by them. The only constant in the management of business organizations is change. The leadership in adapting corporate operations to the changing business world must come from the chief executives. Unless company presidents who have heretofore shunned the role give hard and fast attention to the future of their enterprises by personal involvement in planning, only the most fortuitous circumstances will enable their companies to avoid declines in sales, profits, and market positions.

Appendix to Chapter 1

Outline of a Five-Year Forecast

I. *Product-Line and Customer-Class Planning*

A. Reports on major long-term, high-priority product-line or customer-class programs. Each such report should be a 15-30 minute summary giving the highlights of the technical marketing and production aspects of the program with a general timetable and financial projections. These reports should cover the two or three most important programs aimed at any one of these:

1. Markedly expanding the division's participation in present product lines.

2. Expanding present customer classes.

3. Entering a new product area.

B. A report on the compilation of information needed to do an effective job of long-range planning. Such information might include:

1. Lists of appropriate product lines in which the division is now making products and product lines which might be considered for the division in the future.

2. Lists of appropriate customer classes now being served by the division and new ones that might feasibly be served by it in the future.

3. Market data on:
    a. Size of market—past, present, future.
    b. Rate of growth of market.
    c. Our sales to the market, if any.
    d. Rate of growth of our sales, if any.

4. Financial data to cover these questions:
    a. In each product line and customer class in which we now participate, what is our *net* profit, investment, and return on investment?
    b. To the extent that it is possible to say, what are our competitors' profits in the same fields?
    c. In new areas, what level of profitability can be expected?

5. Analyses of:

    a. Resources (technical, marketing, production) available and required to expand our position.

    b. Competitive situation.

II. *Marketing Planning*

Obviously the previous section has included much of marketing planning, but more general subjects should be discussed under this heading. Possible examples are—

    A. Marketing organization planning, including possible changes in:

        1. Assignment of responsibilities by product line vs. customer class vs. geographical areas.

        2. Greater use of product managers, market managers, or specialists.

    B. Increase or decrease in the use of dealers or distributors to sell the division's products.

    C. Possibility of distributing products manufactured by others.

    D. Statement of pricing policy and pricing practices and discussion of possible changes.

    E. Salesmen's compensation plan—evaluation, expense control, incentives.

III. *Technical Planning*

Insofar as possible give a breakdown of this year's actual and next year's estimated expenses of the division's technical program, both in division laboratories and at central research, by the classes of work listed below. Cite the principal projects now being worked on and being considered for the future.

    A. Long-range offensive research—work requiring more than one year to complete that will be aimed at creating new or improved products for markets in which the division either does not participate or has such a small share as to be negligible.

    B. Long-range defensive research—work requiring more than one year to complete that will be aimed at maintaining or expanding the division's business in its present markets.

    C. Offensive development work—work requiring more than a few days, but usually less than a year, to complete that will be aimed at developing products for markets in which the division either does not participate or has a very small position.

    D. Defensive development work.

    E. Production service—short-range work aimed at troubleshooting in plant, routine formulation changes, routine process improvements, and the like.

F. Customer service—work required to help the customer use the division's products.

G. Quality control—inspection of incoming raw materials, in-process materials, and finished goods.

IV. Production Planning

A. What major new facilities are being considered?

B. What, if any, possibilities are there for major improvements in processing efficiency, and what plans are being made to investigate them?

C. Report on status of program to obtain data on the capacity of each plant, preferably by major departments, covering:

1. What percent of capacity is now being utilized.

2. What further capacity will be required.

3. What steps must be taken to provide more capacity where needed or to utilize excess capacity where available.

V. Export Planning

A. Summary of past export sales by product line.

B. Plans, if any, for expanding these sales or adding new product lines.

VI. Acquisition Suggestions

A. In which geographical areas, product lines, and/or customer classes does the division think that acquisition of allied businesses should be considered as a route toward future growth?

B. What specific companies, if any, might be desirable acquisitions?

VII. Manpower Planning

A. Projection of manpower requirements in the next three years for:

1. Key salaried employees.

2. Other salaried employees.

3. Production (manufacturing) labor.

B. In forecasting manpower requirements consider the present number in the group modified by:

1. Turnover (including anticipated requirements).

2. Needs anticipated for future growth of organization.

[An expanded outline must be prepared to assist the divisions in estimating manpower requirements, and mailed to division heads in advance.]

C. Brief summary of recruiting and training program.

VIII. *Financial Statements*

    A. Last two years actual; next three years projected.
    B. Sales by product line.
    C. Gross profit by product line.
    D. Sales, administrative, and general expense.
    E. Profit.
    F. Investment—working and fixed.
    G. Return on investment.
[Sample forms must be provided for these items.]

2. Balance "Creativity" and "Practicality" in Formal Planning

John K. Shank, Edward G. Niblock, and William T. Sandalls, Jr.

This article contends that to be effective every formal long-range planning system must achieve a compromise between "creativity" and "practicality"—goals for planning that are often in conflict. The authors also argue that the problem of maintaining a satisfactory balance can be directly addressed by varying the design features of the planning/budgeting interface. After specifying the set of design features, they go on to show how six companies have used various combinations of them to achieve an appropriate degree of creativity that is consistent with practicality.

Every company engaged in long-range planning would like its efforts to attain two fundamental but often conflicting goals. On the one hand, management wants the planning function to reflect pragmatic judgments based on what is possible. On the other hand, it wants planning to reflect forward-looking, assertive, and creative thinking.

The primary way of enhancing "realism" is to give the planning function a clear action orientation. Generally, this is done by relating long-range planning closely with short-term budgetary control. And this is where the difficulty lies. While close linkage between planning and budgeting puts the stress on the desired action, it also promotes a focus that can be disastrous to mind-stretching "reach."

We are making the assumption, of course, that for the formal planning system to operate effectively it must achieve a balanced compromise between realism and reach. In this article, we shall argue that these dual objectives need not be mutually exclusive. In fact, our purpose is to illustrate that the long-range planning system can be structured to achieve both an action orientation and a focus on mind stretching. Our discussion will proceed in two steps.

In the first stage, it is important for long-range planners to begin thinking about the realism-reach trade-off as a problem they can do something about. That "something" involves varying those aspects of the long-range planning system which relate to its interface with the short-range budgeting process. In this regard, we shall summarize the general features of the

29

planning system which relate to plan-budget linkage, illustrating both the "tight" and "loose" form of each "linkage device."

Then, in the second step, we shall illustrate some of the most interesting devices actually being used. These reflect the experiences of six companies which we selected because they (a) are successful in terms of compound earnings growth and (b) have long-range planning systems with both action-oriented and mind-stretching characteristics.

In short, we believe that management can control the focus a planning system will exhibit with respect to the realism versus reach problem. It may not always be possible to achieve a totally satisfactory trade-off, but we shall describe the mechanisms being used by a sample of successful companies to achieve what for each of them is a satisfactory compromise.

Plan-Budget Design

On close examination, it quickly becomes apparent that the different aspects of plans and budgets can be linked in three distinct ways:

1. *Content linkage* relates to the correspondence between the data presented in the plan document and that presented in the budget.

2. *Organizational linkage* focuses on the relationship between the units responsible for planning and budgeting.

3. *Timing linkage* concerns the sequencing of the annual planning and budgeting cycles.

Within each of these categories, there are several specific features of the planning system that can be manipulated to influence the extent of plan-budget linkage. Let us take a closer look at each of these linkage devices.

FINANCIAL FEATURES

One important feature of content linkage is the amount of detail in the financial statements included in the plan document. The tightest linkage would be to include statements with the same level of detail as in the monthly reporting package which compares budgeted with actual results. The loosest linkage would be not to include financial statements at all.

Another design feature related to the financial content is the level of rounding in the plan document. Although it may not seem particularly significant at first blush, there is evidence that rounding to a much higher level in the plan than in the budget (e.g., millions of dollars in the plan versus thousands in the budget) can foster a kind of mental distinction between plan and budget numbers which reduces the tendency to view the plan as solely a long-range budget. This can in turn facilitate a much more creative planning effort by making it clear that the managers do not have to commit themselves (in a budgetary sense) to delivering the planned financial results.

Still another important content feature is the conformity between plan and budget numbers for those years which are common to both documents. If the numbers differ, planning may face a credibility gap. Many companies, however, feel that allowing such differences is critical to maintaining the aggressive forward thrust of the planning effort.

For example, one conglomerate includes in the first year of its five-year plan the earnings from acquisitions that are projected to be closed during the next twelve months but which are not yet finalized. The company does not include these earnings in the budgeted results for the next year which line managers are asked to commit themselves to deliver.

Several other companies show differences between planned and budgeted profit for the next year because the two documents are prepared at different times. The one prepared later in the year would reflect the latest thinking and this might differ from projections made earlier in the year.

Situations like these may or may not be desirable, but they certainly reflect loose content linkage. If numerical differences are permitted, one way of moving back toward tightness is to require that some kind of formal reconciliation of them be included in the plan. Many companies which permit differences require such reconciliation.

Related to plan-budget conformity for years common to both documents is the issue of the uniformity of the numbers for any given year as they appear in succeeding annual plan documents. If the planned figures for any one future period change significantly each time a plan is put together, the perceived realism of the planning effort can suffer.

Our evidence suggests, however, that rarely do companies require the numbers for a given year to be "cast in concrete" the very first time that year appears in a plan document. This degree of linkage is probably unrealistically tight.

As we shall illustrate later, a few companies do require formal explanations in the plan for any changes in the projections related to a given future year. This clearly reflects a tighter linkage form of this planning-system variable than would otherwise be reflected by complete freedom to change future years' projections at each iteration of the planning cycle. At least a few companies feel that some tightness at this point is desirable.

A final important design feature is the structure of the content of the plan. In most companies, the budget is structured in terms of the organizational units which will be responsible for carrying it out. Such an approach is a fundamental part of what is often referred to as "responsibility accounting."

Given this situation, it is possible to restructure the plan to focus on programs rather than on the organizational units. The total expenditures for a given year are the same in either case, but there is nevertheless a distinctly looser impact on the way in which the plan document is interpreted.

ORGANIZATIONAL RELATIONSHIPS

The major design feature in this category is the relationship between
the organizational units responsible for the long-range planning and those
responsible for the budgetary-control processes. The loosest form is to
lodge planning and budgeting in separate organizational channels reporting
to different top-level executives. The tightest form is to have the two functions combined in one department.

Even in those situations in which planning and budgeting are separated
in terms of formal organizational relationships, there is wide latitude in
the extent to which the controller is formally involved in the long-range
planning effort. Naturally, the loosest linkage situation is to have scant
involvement on the part of the controller. However, because of his expertise in analyzing and communicating financially oriented data, it is probably neither possible nor desirable to exclude him completely from the
formal planning effort.

Between this extreme of separate planning and budgeting channels and
the complete integration of these functions lies a very broad middle ground
which can be probed to achieve an appropriate level of involvement for
any given company. Among the relevant questions to ask in this regard are
the following:

☐ Does the controller provide staff support for the preparation of the
financial data in the plan document?

☐ Does the controller review the plan document before it is finalized?

☐ Does the controller have any direct or indirect responsibility for ap-
proving the plan?

☐ Does the controller have any direct or indirect responsibility for
monitoring planned financial results against actual results?

The more questions of this kind that can be answered *yes,* the tighter
the plan-budget linkage, even though the functions may officially be
separate.

TIMING CONSIDERATIONS

The most important design feature here is concerned with the sequencing
of the annual planning and budgeting cycles. If the two cycles are carried
out sequentially, which one is done first? How much time elapses between
the completion of the first cycle and the beginning of the one which follows it? If the two cycles are undertaken concurrently, what is the relationship between initiation dates, completion dates, and approval dates?

The loosest timing linkage is to have the planning cycle done before the
budgeting cycle and to have several months elapse between the two. One
major food products manufacturer, for example, completes the annual

planning cycle in February and does not begin the budgeting phase until November. Situations like this are least inhibiting to the achievement of "reach" in the planning effort.

The tightest form of the design feature related to sequencing would be to complete the budgeting cycle first and to have the planning cycle follow it with minimal elapsed time in between. Since the budgeting cycle almost always concludes in the last quarter of the fiscal year, it is rare to find a company in which the planning cycle comes last. There are, however, many companies that undertake the two cycles concurrently.

In general, the more the budget process precedes the plan preparation—in terms of initiation, completion, and approval dates—the tighter the linkage, since the budgeting focus will tend to dominate the joint planning-budgeting effort.

One final timing-related design feature is the time horizon for the long-range planning effort. Usually, the shorter this span, the closer the relationship between the budget and the planning process and thus the tighter the plan-budget linkage. Conversely, the longer the time frame, the easier it becomes to clearly distinguish the process from budgeting and thus the looser the plan-budget linkage.

Nowhere in the whole range of system-design features is the trade-off between realism and reach more clearly defined than in the choice of a planning horizon. The longer the time frame, the wider the range of factors which can be varied and thus the broader the range of strategies which can be considered in moving the company toward its long-range objectives.

At the same time, a longer time span increases the uncertainty regarding environmental assumptions, corporate strengths, and the financial parameters which shape the strategy formulation and evaluation process. At some point, uncertainty overcomes the gain in flexibility.

What constitutes an appropriate time horizon certainly varies from industry to industry. It is probably easier, for example, for most public utilities to do fifteen-year planning than it is for defense-aerospace companies to do five-year planning. Within the reasonable range for any given industry, however, the longer the time considerations, the looser the plan-budget linkage. Furthermore, in our opinion, a planning horizon of three or four years reflects a heavy emphasis on realism at the expense of reach, regardless of the industry.

Linkage Examples

In the preceding section of this article, we concentrated on a general framework for considering the plan-budget problem. Now, we shall turn our attention to some of the interesting devices actually being used by the six manufacturing companies that we selected as a small but representative sample of those which have (a) participated in formal planning studies, (b) earned the reputation for having both action-oriented and creative planning systems, and (c) been highly successful in terms of compound EPS growth. Since we believe it unlikely that their records of sustained performance could have been achieved without the help of good planning, it should be revealing to examine in some detail how these companies cope with the linkage problem.

The six companies we observed were Cincinnati Milacron, General Mills, Quaker Oats, Raytheon, Toro, and Warnaco. In them, we encountered such a large number of different linkage devices that we concluded the variety of specific links is limited only by the imagination of the personnel. We shall use the same categories as in the preceding section in reviewing the most interesting linkage practices in these sample companies.

But, first, a note of caution. It is not our intent to propose *the* right answer to the linkage problem, but only to identify some of the more important factors to be considered in determining *a* right answer for a given company at a specific point in time.

CONTENT-RELATED APPROACHES

One of the most innovative attempts to use structure as a mechanism to overcome the creativity-practicality problem is the distinct separation between group and division planning at Warnaco. Each division manager prepares a three-year plan, while each group vice president plans five years out.

Warnaco's objective here is to encourage the group vice presidents to think in more general and longer range terms. They then carry this framework with them to meetings with their division managers. This encourages them to do more creative planning.

It is important to note that the formats of these two plans are much different, with the divisional plans being done in much greater detail than the group plans. This serves to focus the group manager's attention on the strategy of the group itself rather than on the specific details of the divisions' operating programs.

A mechanism we mentioned earlier to overcome the problem of loose linkage is the comparison of a plan with its predecessor from a year earlier. Consider, for example, this situation taken from the planning records of a large paper manufacturer. Here are this company's profit projections for 1971 as shown in—

Five-year plan done in 1966	$60 million
Five-year plan done in 1967	$50 million
Five-year plan done in 1969	$36 million
1971 budget prepared in 1970	$16 million

At the very least, a plan-to-plan comparison would have called the company's attention to the increasing lack of realism the further the projections extended into the future. The threat of having to formally justify this ever-receding bonanza might have served as a sobering influence to the planners.

It is also possible to use plan-to-plan comparisons to overcome the problems of overly conservative forecasting. Thus, if the paper company's profit projections had demonstrated an ascending pattern, the happy surprise of realizing more profits than expected might also have been accompanied by the undesirable development of capacity shortages and missed market opportunities. In such a case, a plan-to-plan comparison could serve as an impetus for more expansive projections.

Of the six companies we visited, only General Mills requires the reporting and justification of significant changes from the preceding year's plan. At General Mills, management feels that this checking device is sufficiently useful in preventing blue-sky fantasizing to justify its risk in terms of discouraging open-ended mind stretching.

A third content-related mechanism worth noting is the relationship between the plan and budget formats. As we noted earlier, if the two documents differ in form and style, it is more difficult to directly transpose the plan to the budget. Both Toro and Raytheon approach a program format for planning and a functional format for budgeting, but they also retain the program and project breakout in the budget as well as the functional allocation. In the other companies we sampled, this split is less distinct since the divisions are largely organized by program area or product line. We view this loosening device as a very significant one that has potential applicability in many companies.

Finally, all six of the sample companies vary the level of detail between the plan and the budget. It is interesting to note, however, that the absolute level of details in the plan also varies significantly among the six companies. Cincinnati Milacron shows only very highly aggregated summary data, whereas Raytheon's plans approach the same level of detail as its budgets. The other four companies fall in between these extreme approaches.

ORGANIZATION COORDINATION

At the corporate level, it is important to understand who is coordinating the planning and who is coordinating the budgeting. The basic question here is whether the company wants to split the two processes. The splitting of this coordination function has the effect of loosening the linkage between planning and budgeting. Both Toro and Cincinnati Milacron provide excellent examples of this.

At Toro, planning is coordinated by the Corporate Planner and budgeting by the Controller. No formal attempt is made to ensure that these two functions proceed in a similar fashion. Cincinnati Milacron handles this in much the same way that Toro does.

At General Mills, the end result is the same but the mechanisms are much more complex, with coordination being handled by groups instead of individuals.

Different handling at the division level can also affect the linking process. The basic split here is between strategy formulation and the quantified explication of that strategy. While in almost all instances both are coordinated by the division manager, the degree of delegation of the quantification phase can vary significantly.

It is noteworthy that there is very little divergence in the way quantification of plan results is handled by the six sample companies. All of them largely delegate this phase to the divisional controller. This has a loosening effect by focusing the division manager's attention on policy rather than on detailed profit and loss information.

Although it is not a "device" in the usual sense, a company's informal communication process can function in a way that tightens the linkage between planning and budgeting. A great deal of informal information transfer across the corporate/divisional interface increases top management's cognizance of what is in the plan and how it relates to the budget. The presence of informal channels of communication may make top management appear to have an omniscient awareness of these issues, even if this is actually not the case.

At Cincinnati Milacron, where the planning and budgeting systems are very closely linked, one division manager stated that he really felt strongly committed to delivering the performance projected in his five-year plan. At Quaker Oats and Toro, where there are loose linkage systems, two division managers reported similar feelings of commitment. It is difficult for us to assess what precise influence the informal communication processes in the foregoing companies had in forging the personal commitments of these three division managers to delivering the planned results. However, the counter-intuitive coincidence of loose systems and strong commitments at least offers circumstantial evidence that this influence does exist and should not be overlooked.

TIME HORIZONS

A separation in time between the end of the planning cycle and the beginning of the budgeting cycle, as we noted earlier, has the effect of loosening the linkage between the two processes. When the time to worry about next year's performance commitment is still several months away, it is easier to be expansive about the future. In addition, since forecast conditions are always changing, the more time that elapses subsequent to submission of the plan, the easier it is to justify a revision in the budget.

Of the six sample companies, only Raytheon pursues its planning and budgeting cycles concurrently. Cincinnati Milacron has a six-month separation between the end of planning and the beginning of budgeting. General Mills, Quaker Oats, Toro, and Warnaco all have at least a two- to three-month separation.

In general, as the number of years in the budget is extended, or the number of years in the plan contracted, the similarity between the plan and the budget increases. Different time horizons for the two processes tend to emphasize the different purposes of each. Five of the six companies we sampled have either a four- or five-year planning range and a one- or two-year budget span. The exception is Warnaco, which we noted previously.

Appropriate Equilibrium

Individual linkage devices impact on the planning system by facilitating an overall planning effort which is either more creative or action oriented. As is evident from the preceding discussion, some devices serve to promote a stronger action orientation in planning while others encourage more creativity.

Since a single planning system will utilize several devices which may have opposing effects on the plan-budget balance, an "algebraic" sum of the devices is needed to determine where the planning system is located on the linkage continuum. This plays a pivotal role in achieving an appropriate equilibrium between divergent requirements for both creative and action-oriented planning.

Whether or not a particular planning balance is appropriate for a given company hinges on the corporate setting. Thus, if the underlying essence of planning is to improve a company's ability to cope with changes, it follows that, as the changes are realized, the need for specific forms of planning will also change. In other words, a dynamic corporate setting may call for heavy emphasis on creativity at one point in time and heavy emphasis on practicality at another. The implication is that, as a company's needs change, devices must be added or subtracted in order to adjust the balance between these planning objectives.

The concept of a dynamic corporate setting seems particularly relevant to the four of the six sample companies which are now diversifying extensively beyond the boundaries of their traditional industries. Consider:

□ The Toro Company has changed from a manufacturer of lawn

mowers and snow blowers to a broad-based participant in the environmental beautification market.

□ General Mills's Fashion Division, which was established only recently,
already contributes significantly to the company's sales and earnings and
competes in markets dramatically different from those served by Cheerios
and other ready-to-eat cereals.

□ Quaker Oats, in one recent fiscal year, derived 25% of its sales from
nongrocery product sources, including 12% from Fisher-Price Toys. The
company has since further diversified in nongrocery areas through
acquisition of Louis Marx & Co. Toys and the Needlecraft Corporation
of America.

□ Cincinnati Milacron, the largest manufacturer of machine tools in
the world, is seeking points of entry into the minicomputer and semi-
conductor markets.

A dynamic corporate setting, however, is not necessarily dependent on
the diversification activity of a company. For example:

□ Cincinnati Milacron, with 80% of its sales in the machine tool industry, contends with market cycles which brought machine tool sales
volume in one recent year down 50% to 60% below the peak reached two
years earlier.

□ The Raytheon Equipment Division, a defense contractor, faces rapid
turnover in eletronics technology—a contract bidding process that sometimes makes a ticket in the Irish Sweepstakes look like a sure bet—and
concomitant uncertainties and headaches in dealing with mercurial government customers.

□ Warnaco, competing with 30,000 other companies in the apparel industry, finds that although total sales volume is relatively stable, individual
markets are highly volatile as fashions come and go in quick succession.

Whether the result of extensive diversification programs or corporate
response to the challenges of traditional markets, all six companies are in
a state of perpetual change.

Given this state of flux, it is significant to note that the planning systems in five of the companies have recently been changed, are in the process
of being changed, or will be changed in the near future (the exception is
Raytheon Equipment). To illustrate:

□ At Toro, David M. Lilly, Chairman and Chief Executive Officer,
recently projected the development of looser linkage between the planning
and budgeting systems.

□ At General Mills, one recent year's planning instructions announced
a procedure to highlight where that year's plan deviated from the previous
year's plan; the same instructions reemphasized a year-old procedure which

required "new" businesses to be differentiated from "present" businesses.

◻ At Quaker Oats, the corporate planner foresees the emergence of tighter linkage as the company becomes acclimated to its new divisionalized structure.

◻ At Cincinnati Milacron, a new planning system is in operation; this system is very loosely linked to budgeting and shifts the burden of planning from the division managers to the group managers.

◻ At Warnaco, as we noted earlier, a systems modification has been implemented; this requires group vice presidents to plan five years into the future and their subordinate division managers three years ahead.

In seeking a comprehensive explanation of the planning system changes just described, we find particularly pertinent the observation that management control systems must be consistent with top management's objectives in order to be truly effective. If the same can be said of formal planning systems, then it follows that a change in an effective planning system is usually triggered by a change in top management's objectives.

The implication here is that whether or not a given change improves a planning system may be beside the point. To paraphrase Marshall McLuhan, the planning system and the changes made in it may be "the medium that is the message"—i.e., the message from top management.

CRITERION OF CONSISTENCY

In this section of the article, we shall examine more closely two of the planning system changes previously mentioned to see what inferences about top management's objectives we can draw from them.

Since 1971, Cincinnati Milacron has been pulling out of a severe recession that afflicted the entire machine tool industry. Operating management's ordeal during the past two years has been something akin to a day-to-day struggle. As the company has begun to emerge from this traumatic experience, top management has installed a new planning system to allow maximum opportunity for broad-level mind stretching. Furthermore, the burden of planning has been shifted upward to a level of management where there exists the opportunity and authority to implement a diversification program.

The message of Cincinnati Milacron's two planning-system changes appears to be rather straightforward: top management wants aggressive diversification planning.

In his memorandum covering General Mills's 1971 planning instructions, James P. MacFarland, Chairman and Chief Executive Officer, indicated the need for a more aggressive capital investment program in the years ahead to achieve the company's sales and earnings objectives. He also referred to progress in the control of capital use and to a change in the planning procedures which would allow top management to focus easily on the changes made subsequent to the previous planning cycle. His general instructions described this procedural change in more detail and reiterated a year-old procedure which separated the planning for new businesses from that for current businesses.

In our judgment, it is a fair guess that it will be a tougher task to revise estimates upward in order to justify additional capital for a current business than to submit new estimates in order to justify seed capital for a new business. The message of the announcement of both a new procedure and reemphasis on an old one appears to be that the encouragement of heavier investments is intended for new and not for current businesses.

(This message, incidentally, is clearly reflected in the chairman's and president's letter to General Mills's stockholders and employees in the 1971 Annual Report.)

The procedure at General Mills of separating current and new businesses is particularly noteworthy in that it creates an opportunity to differentiate the planning perspectives, and to apply different standards of expectation to each type of business. In this manner, top management can encourage a division manager to be creative in planning for his new businesses and action oriented in planning for his current businesses.

Future-oriented businesses will be best suited for loosely linked planning/budgeting systems. As the potential of a business begins to be realized, tighter linkage will be desirable in order to transform promises into results. At that point, a balance between creative planning and action-oriented planning would be especially appropriate. Later, as the business exhausts its growth potential and evolves into a "cash generator," even tighter linkage will be desirable to accommodate the corporation's capital needs for the next generation of new businesses.

In short, recognition of divergent corporate objectives for both the mature and the future-oriented business is manifested in different degrees of linkage in their respective planning/budgeting systems. As evident at Quaker Oats, for example, a divisionalized company can find itself at several points—up and down—on the linkage continuum at the same time. In evaluating whether or not any point on the continuum is "right" or "wrong," the sole criterion must be its consistency with corporate objectives.

Conclusion

To be effective, every formal long-range planning system must achieve a workable compromise between creativity and practicality—twin goals that are often in conflict. This problem of maintaining a satisfactory balance between "reach" and "realism" can be directly addressed by varying those design features of planning which relate to its interface with budgeting. However, in order to put in perspective the importance of loosening the plan/budget linkage, it is important to consider the role of informal communications and the personalities of management.

At the corporate/division interface, companies that have a great deal of informal communication transfer are likely to be constantly aware of what was written in the plan and how that relates to the budget. This has the effect of very tightly linking the plan and the budget, even in structurally loose systems, unless management makes a conscious effort to demonstrate that this is not wanted. Even if this intent is demonstrated at the corporate level, there still may be tight linkage built in at the division level because of the division manager's personality.

Generally speaking, the divisional planning and budgeting are either both done by the division manager himself or at least coordinated by him. As he coordinates the preparation of the budget, he often feels—either consciously or subconsciously—an obligation to justify the value of the plan by reflecting much of it in the budget which represents his short-term game plan for the division.

Briefly, loosening devices have much broader applications than to just those companies which have structurally tight linkage systems. In fact, some of them may be needed in any action-oriented planning system.

We believe that managers should consider these devices as variables they can and should manipulate in the interest of more effective planning. Viewed in this context, the linkage continuum can be considered as a powerful interpreter of the top-management objectives implicit in the planning system.

Although at first this may seem to be counter-intuitive, we believe that it is not the planning system which generates corporate objectives but rather the corporate objectives which dictate the appropriate planning system. We are neither proposing that there is a "correct" form for any of these design features, nor that it is always possible to structure a planning system so that "realistic creativity" is ensured.

We do believe, however, that "realistic reach" in planning is not just an illusory phenomenon which exists independent of management's actions. Rather, it is well within management's control to influence the focus of the efforts by changing the structure of the planning system. That, we feel, is all any manager can ask.

3. Formulating Strategy in Smaller Companies

Frank F. Gilmore

While many sophisticated concepts of formulating corporate strategy are being studied with interest by large corporations, they hold little promise for medium-sized and smaller companies—at least, in the foreseeable future. For the latter, strategic planning is still more of an art than a science. A conference table approach to strategy, based on executive judgment and intuition, is outlined in this article. The author describes six major steps in the process and lists the types of questions the chief executive should ask his management team to consider.

Corporate planning, aimed at strategy formulation for the company, has now become so generally accepted that many executives are having second thoughts about their approaches. Indeed, the top management group of one major corporation has concluded that, since each of its members has at one time or another been in charge of his company's corporate planning department, there is little need to go through the formal planning cycle that characterized its approach for the past decade. Inasmuch as all of them think like planners, they feel that they have outgrown their initial planning approach and are groping for something better.

In other large companies, consideration is being given to possible ways in which management science and the computer may be applied to the strategy formulation problem. A suggestion offered by Russell L. Ackoff in the form of an adaptive approach appears to hold promise as a frame of reference within which such improvements may be developed over time.[1]

But for the medium-sized or small company that does not have planning departments, operations research groups, or large-scale computing capacity, and that simply cannot afford to engage in planning research, a more modest approach must be sought. This does not mean that the managers of such companies can afford to neglect their planning responsibilities. Today's widespread adoption of strategic planning will not permit such a course. What is needed is a simple, practical approach that is within the

1. *Concept of Corporate Planning* (New York, Wiley-Interscience, 1970).

reach of these smaller companies. I shall try to meet that need in this article.

Evolution of Approach

Prior to the middle 1950's, the major task of the chief executive was viewed as that of adapting the company to changing conditions. This traditional approach developed during the period between World Wars I and II, when unpredictable and violent fluctuations meant adaptation or failure.

In this traditional top management approach, determination of objectives presupposed a size-up of the situation of the company as a whole. The objectives could then provide direction and unity of purpose for the development of a program of action covering the various activities of the company.

Size-ups were made in various ways, depending on the background of the management involved, the organization of the company, and the position of the company in terms of its growth and its place in its industry. Any one of several approaches could serve the purpose. Size-ups were most commonly conducted along departmental lines because most companies were more or less centralized then and were therefore organized by major functions, such as marketing, production, and finance. For this reason, the functional size-up approach will be examined more closely.

Exhibit I shows this traditional approach. It indicates the process required to reach a diagnosis of the company's prospects and problems:

1. An analysis was made of the total picture. Its components were analyses of the competitive situation and of the various functions. (Some executives found it useful to look at the competitive situation first, and then analyze the financial and operating picture. They felt that a size-up of these two areas often provided measuring sticks or raised pertinent questions that served to sharpen the analysis of other functional areas. Moreover, many analysts found it helpful to defer the size-up of the executive organization to the last because of the light that was shed on management performance by the examination of the functional areas.)

2. Under each topic in the breakdown, significant findings were noted and classified, and an effort was made to reach a conclusion on each major topic.

3. The separate conclusions were then combined, and an attempt was made to arrive, inductively, at the overall diagnosis. Particular attention was paid to interrelationships that might be significant for the company as a whole.

This painstaking, sizing-up, inductive process became the basis for

Exhibit I. Example of traditional approach to strategy formulation

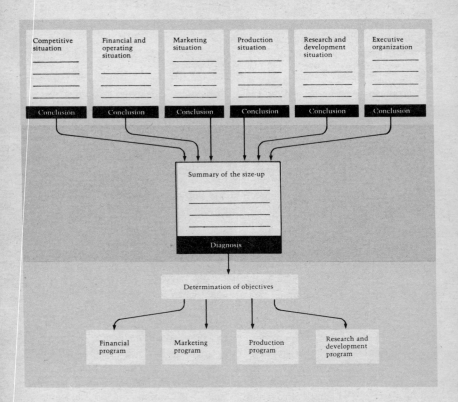

determining objectives for the future. The chief executive then faced the task of deciding on a course of action and, in the light of the objectives, choosing between alternative ways of solving the problem diagnosed in the size-up.

This approach was actually incomplete, since the process remained open-ended, as shown in Part A of *Exhibit II*. There was a definite tendency for top management to size up the situation, starting at the very base; formulate objectives and programs of action; organize to carry out the plans; and exercise executive control; but then drift along until serious problems made it necessary to size up the situation again.

FORMALIZING THE ANALYSIS

During the 1950's, it became increasingly clear that a new approach to policy formulation was urgently needed. It was recognized that—

44

Exhibit II. Formulating strategy

A. Traditional open-loop process

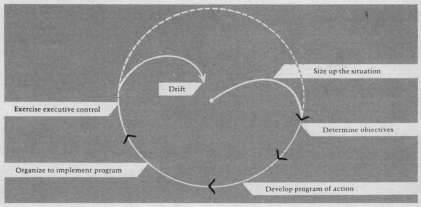

B. Modern closed-loop process

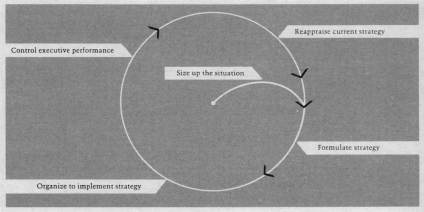

. . . concern for short-term problems would have to shift to plans for capitalizing on long-term opportunities;

. . . sizing up the situation as a basis for a new course of action would have to give way to reappraising existing strategy in the light of the changing environment;

. . . sporadic diagnosis would have to be replaced by constant surveillance;

. . . concern for immediate profits and for adaptability to meet changes in current conditions needed to shift to focusing on long-range ROI, growth, flexibility, and stability.

In other words, occasional preoccupation with such questions as "Where are we?" and "Where are we going?" needed to be replaced by frequent consideration of such questions as "Are we making satisfactory progress with respect to plan?" and "Are our plans still valid?"

Not surprisingly, therefore, since the 1950's there has been a significant shift to formal, long-range, strategic planning. The most significant distinguishing characteristic of this approach has been that executives are now managing in accordance with a constantly updated strategic plan. Instead of just sizing up the situation at a given point of time, they schedule reappraisals of current strategy. The effect of this change is a shift from an open-loop, short-range approach to a closed-loop, long-range approach, illustrated in Part B of *Exhibit II*.

As this conceptual scheme shows, the size-up of the situation can be thought of as a spring-board; and as long as reappraisal of present strategy closes the loop, the system continues to cycle. Feedback and regular surveillance serve to keep the company's strategy constantly before management. Thus, after the first cycle, reappraisal of current strategy takes the place of the size-up of the situation. Such reappraisal examines the same areas, but analysis is focused on the possible consequences of continuing the current strategy, given trends and developments in the external environment, and existing internal operating conditions and results.

Accompanying the change from sporadic size-up to frequent, and in many cases regular, reappraisal, there has been a shift in emphasis from size-up to formulation. In keeping with Peter F. Drucker's advice in the early 1950's, management attention has been focused more on the discovery of opportunities than on the solution of problems.[2] As a result, more emphasis has been placed on the evaluation of alternative courses of action and on maximization of performance.

In the formulation of strategy, management may, in time, have the assistance of tools and techniques from management science. But before significant progress along these lines can be made (as I shall discuss in the next section), there must be a better understanding of the structure of the problem itself.

STRUCTURE OF RELATIONSHIPS

One approach to structuring the problem of strategy formulation is summarized in *Exhibit III*. In this model, which was developed during a Cornell research project, the relationship between the company and its competitive environment is expressed by the strategy of the enterprise, which has three basic components:

2. *The Practice of Management* (New York, Harper & Brothers, 1954).

Exhibit III. Model of new approach

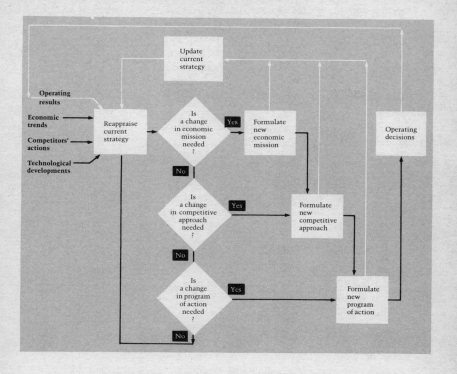

1. *Economic mission*—This is concerned with the kind of business the company should be in, and what its performance objectives should be.

2. *Competitive approach*—This is concerned with finding the product-market-sales approach that will accomplish the economic mission, and with deriving pertinent goals in the various areas of the business.

3. *Program of action*—This involves a search for efficient means of implementing the competitive approach.

In summary form, the process works as follows: Current strategy is reappraised from time to time in the light of internal operating results, economic trends, competitors' actions, and technological developments. When opportunities or threats have been disclosed, management proceeds to ask questions designed to indicate when and in what respect strategy should be changed. If a new economic mission is called for, the planners proceed to formulate a revised approach. This, in turn, calls for revision of the competitive approach and of the program of action. If the economic mission is considered sound, the competitive approach is questioned. If the competitive approach seems appropriate, the process continues until the appropriate area for revision is identified and a new strategy is formulated.

Of course, it might be concluded that the overall current strategy is sound. Then no revision would take place, and another reappraisal would be made at a later date. The white lines in *Exhibit III* indicate the feedback of operating results (part of the control process) and the updating of current strategy as a result of formulation.

Management Science?

At first thought, it would appear that management science would offer several possible approaches to strategy formulation. However, the few approaches that might prove useful are in such an early stage of development that they hold little promise at this time. While a number of operations research (OR) approaches are useful in decision making at the operations level, most of these are of limited use in strategy formulation because of the large number of variables involved. For example, consider mathematical programming and simulation:

□ Of the various forms of mathematical programming, the best known is linear programming, which is applicable to those situations where relationships are linear and there is no uncertainty (or it may be assumed away). Under these conditions, linear programming results in optimization, but the limitations may be too restrictive for strategy formulation. Other forms of mathematical programming avoid some of the difficulties of linear programming, but computation becomes considerably more difficult and often necessitates trial-and-error approaches.

□ Simulation may be useful in strategy situations that do not fall within the limitations of linear programming. For example, such nonlinear relationships as those due to economies of scale may be easily incorporated, and probabilistic data reflecting the presence of uncertainty may be used. But whereas mathematical programming requires only that data be provided for an already established model, simulation requires that the model itself be constructed. This is a formidable task, involving many assumptions as to the interaction of the various components within the company and of the company with its environment. A simulation model thus requires a great deal of time and effort to construct and test, and is extremely difficult to validate. And, even if these tasks are successfully completed, there is little assurance that the same model will continue to be valid.

Other OR approaches are not relevant to the overall decision, but are applicable to parts of the strategy decision process. Among these are capital budgeting, inventory theory, scheduling theory, and so forth. They are useful as components in strategy formulation, but they cannot handle all the major aspects of the problem.

Thus, OR is only appropriate for the solution of well-defined problems where the relevant relationships can be specified and the objectives have been decided on. Under such conditions, calculations are dominant, and mathematics is often almost a substitute for judgment.

Actually, "systems analysis"—or the "systems approach," as it is often called—may offer more promise in strategy formulation than OR. Systems analysis has been defined as an approach to solving complex problems of choice under uncertainty by systematic examination of the costs, effectiveness, and risks of various alternatives. It is appropriate for use in poorly structured problems, where the relationships are not clear and where decisions must be made among alternative objectives. It became a major instrument in governmental decision making during the 1960's, and is attracting increasing attention in business as a useful way of analyzing top management planning problems.

All in all, however, the potentials of management science for strategic purposes seem limited to use in large companies that possess considerable technical resources for their development and use. For the foreseeable future, managements in medium-sized and small companies will have to use the generalizing, inductive, empirical method which has evolved out of the old, size-up approach. And this approach remains more an art than a science.

Simple, Practical Method

I shall describe now a simple, practical planning method that can be employed by top executives in medium-sized and small companies. Several influences have shaped the sequence of steps to be suggested. John Dewey's concepts of how people think provide a useful rationale for the approach as a whole: the process of strategy formulation may be viewed as a form of reflective thinking, where one progresses step by step from recognition of the problem to solution.[3] The experience of management, teachers, and consultants during the past half century has also had a strong impact: the older, size-up approach has contributed to early steps in the sequence, while recent developments in strategy formulation have helped shape later steps. Finally, the need for top management to advocate its proposals, when formulated, to the board of directors has influenced the scheme to be described.

The process of strategy formulation may be carried out in six progressive steps. I shall describe them in detail and illustrate them with notes made at a series of top management meetings in a small company that was applying this approach. The company, a manufacturer of insulated wire and cable, will be identified as "IWAC Co."

3. *How We Think* (Boston, D. C. Heath & Co., 1933).

1. RECORD CURRENT STRATEGY

The recording of current strategy is an important foundation for sub-sequent steps. In a company that is managing according to a well-defined strategy, it will be easy for the manager to record his plans. Typically today, the strategy of large corporations is a matter of record. But many medium-sized and small companies operate informally with a loosely defined strategy. In these cases, the task of recording current strategy becomes more difficult. Nevertheless, it is usually possible to infer from trends and executive behavior what strategy is impicit in the company's operations. If efforts to record current strategy fail, one can fall back on the size-up approach for the first step.

In recording current strategy, it is important to clarify top management's criteria as to the kind of company it wants to operate. These criteria will be expressed in terms of values held by the top management group. Also, what kind of company does top management think it *should* operate? Criteria for this answer will be expressed in terms of management's concept of social responsibility.

Such criteria will be important in later steps, when the core of the strategy problem is discovered, and alternative strategies are formulated and evaluated. To illustrate, in the case of IWAC Co., the top manage-ment group described the strategy that had characterized its operations for some years as follows:

"The company develops, manufactures, and sells standard telephone wire and cable to independent telephone companies. It is attempting to diversify into such products as electronic connectors, printed electronic circuits, heavy-duty lighting cords, and retractile cords. The company markets all its products through distributors."

2. IDENTIFY PROBLEMS

The current strategy must be reappraised to determine whether problems exist. A strategy problem is one which may have a significant influence on the future success of the enterprise as a whole.

Management must first look at the company's environment. In order to estimate the consequences of continuing the current strategy, it needs to study external trends and developments and to make assumptions about the economic outlook, the shape of future technology, and competitors' actions. In short, it needs to establish premises about the environment on which analysis of company operations can be based. In effect, it asks, "Given the environmental outlook, is our strategy still valid? Are any opportunities or threats disclosed by this outlook?"

Then management must examine the operating situation of the company as disclosed by financial results and progress made under the current strategy in the various areas of operations. As with the old, size-up approach, a useful next step is to analyze the financial and operating picture. Meaningful reappraisal of current strategy is facilitated by a careful analysis of financial and operating trends, since, as noted earlier, useful measuring sticks for appraising other aspects of the company's operations can be derived from the financial phase of the analysis.

Executives can then proceed to reappraise the marketing, production, and research and development policies, and the management organization of the company. In particular, they must be on the alert for significant weaknesses or unutilized strengths. Throughout this part of the analysis they ask, "Is the company making satisfactory progress according to plan?"

Cutting through symptoms: Strategy problems may take the form of threats or opportunities in the environment; failure to meet plans; signs of organizational strife; adverse trends with respect to share of market, competitive advantage, or financial results or condition; or other indications of loss of health or vigor. These problems are likely to be symptoms of a more deep-seated difficulty. To illustrate in terms of a real-life situation, let us turn back to the IWAC case.

When the top executives began analyzing the problems, risks, and opportunities of the company, they were surprised by the shape of the picture that began to emerge. I shall mention just some of the highlights of the findings management considered:

"Changes in industry structure are intensifying competition. The number of independent telephone companies is declining largely because of acquisitions by General Telephone. Vertical integration into wire and cable insulation is taking place among both suppliers and end users. Some of the larger wire and cable companies are owned by major suppliers of wire and insulation material.

"In the last five years, the number of companies making plastic-insulated telephone wires and cables has increased from 5 to 13. A slump in wire demand, along with falling copper prices early in the current year, led to price cutting in the industry. With the economy experiencing a recession, the wire and cable industry is faced with overcapacity.

"Our competitors are moving toward direct selling; of 25 competing companies, 20 have sales offices, 10 have warehouses, and 13 have no distributors at all. General Cable attributes its great success to the establishment of sales offices and stock distribution centers. Yet our company continues to leave its sales effort largely in the hands of exclusive distributors. Indeed, our company is unique in its nonaggressive, competitive approach in sales.

"In addition to the increase in competition as a result of changes in industry structure and the trend toward direct selling, other competitive pressures are becoming evident. Competitors are underselling us in connection with broadcast wires and cord sets because of our insistence on excessively high quality.

"Despite the fact that competition is growing more intense, the company's immediate position is sound. Our sales have declined less this year (12%) than has been true for the insulated wire and cable industry as a whole (15%). Return on stockholders' investment, while sporadic, has been generally favorable. The company is financially liquid and has a reasonable long-term debt/equity ratio.

"Some moves have been made to offset the impact of increased competition. First, a new works manager has been brought into the company, and already he has achieved significant operating economies. Inventory investment has been reduced 30%, and purchasing costs have declined significantly.

"A promising outlook exists for some of the company's special products. The company holds patents on commercial applications of heavy-duty lighting cords, a recent addition to the product line. There are few competitors in this field, but the company is limiting its opportunity by selling the systems through one exclusive distributor.

"The product line is being broadened through the addition of color-sheathed cords, oilproof cords, large flexible cables, and secondary power cables. But the market potential of these new products is not known by the company. Prospects in the power cable field look attractive, with only a few manufacturers currently competing. But the company is moving very slowly in this area.

"Although some changes have been made in the executive organization, among them the appointment of the new works manager, several long-term employees are still entrenched in established ways of doing business which will have to be changed in light of competitive trends. Particularly notable are broadly held values about the desirability of extremely high-quality products and the feeling that the present method of selling through distributors can be changed only at great cost."

3. DISCOVER THE CORE ELEMENTS

If the reappraisal discloses that major problems exist, it is necessary to discover their core. The basic difficulty may take many forms. For example, the current strategy may require greater competence and/or resources than the company possesses; the strategy may fail to exploit adequately the company's distinctive competence; the company may lack sufficient competitive advantage, or it may fail to exploit opportunities and/or meet threats in the environment; or the strategy may not be internally consistent. Diagnosis with respect to the company's performance against plan and prognosis as to the future consequences of continuing the current strategy are both involved in this step. To return to IWAC:

Management concluded that a shift in strategy was needed. It saw that IWAC could not continue on its traditional course and keep growing profitably. Two major considerations were involved. "First, the company can no longer concentrate on *standard* wire and cable products," it was reported. "All signs point to a loss of market share in this area. There appear to be better opportunities in *specialized* wire and cable products, where the company possesses distinctive competence. Second, the current policy of selling through distributors no longer appears appropriate. It is neither consistent with industry practice nor compatible with specialization."

4. FORMULATE ALTERNATIVES

Once the core of the strategy problem has been discovered, management can formulate alternative ways of solving the problem. It is characteristic of modern planning approaches that one must try to conceive of all alternatives that might offer some possibility of providing a solution. Then consideration must be given in a preliminary way to limitations imposed by the company's competence and resources. Also, management's values and sense of social responsibility will set some boundaries.

But this is more the time for imagination and innovation than for logic. More rigorous evaluation can come in the next step. In the IWAC case, the thinking of executives was summarized as follows:

"The company has three alternative strategies it might follow. First, it could merge with a supplier or end user of insulated wire and cable. Second, it could specialize in insulated wire and cable products that require strict quality specifications and technological expertise, and at the same time improve its marketing effectiveness by distributing its products directly through its own sales force. Third, it could become an aggressive marketer of a relatively full line of insulated wires and cables with an extensive direct-sales organization.

"The first alternative is a distinct possibility. Current trends toward vertical integration in the industry make the company a possible investment opportunity for an end user or supplier. The company's research capabilities, manufacturing know-how, and capacity to produce telephone wire and cable might make it an attractive acquisition for a company such as General Telephone.

"The second alternative would require a closer relationship with our customers. In particular, a technical sales force would be needed that could work directly with customers in determining the end user's needs, product quality, technical characteristics of the product, and new systems applications.

"The third alternative would emphasize an aggressive competitive approach embracing a full line of products and extensive marketing organization, not unlike that used by General Cable. The company would become a manufacturer of a wide line of insulated wires and cables, utilizing its technological know-how to develop new products. Increased marketing expenditures would be required in advertising and in the development of a sizable sales organization, establishment of warehouses, maintenance of inventories in the field, and development of sales branch offices."

5. EVALUATE ALTERNATIVES

In this step, management looks at the bearing of the various vital factors on the choice of a strategy. The alternatives must be compared in terms of:

□ Relative effectiveness in solving the strategic problem.

□ The degree to which each matches the company's competence and resources.

□ Their relative competitive advantage.

□ The extent to which they satisfy management's preferences and sense of social responsibility.

□ Their relative ability to minimize the creation of new problems.

In strategy problems, more than in other types of problems, executives would like to be able to optimize with respect to *several* relevant factors. Therefore, trade-offs are necessary, for optimization with respect to one factor will be at the expense of another. This is a characteristic of business strategy problems which, along with the premium placed on discovering the core elements, makes them the most difficult challenges facing management. Probably the best one can hope to do at this time is to choose that alternative which, in his judgment, offers the best blend of advantages. If the reasoning of the IWAC executives were to be reconstructed, it might run as follows:

"All three alternatives would meet the strategic challenge presented by the increasing competition in the industry. The merger route might involve the risk of lengthy and costly litigation under antitrust laws. Merger would also raise a question as to how much basic research the company as a 'captive shop' would be encouraged to do. It would probably limit the scope of technological problems considered by the laboratory. This alternative would meet the threat of the declining market in telephone wires and cables more effectively than the other two alternatives, but would provide less of an outlet for management's innovativeness or entrepreneurship.

"The success of the second alternative, the specialization approach, would depend largely on the company's ability to continue as an innovator. It would capitalize on the organization's capabilities in solving customers' needs. To be successful under this approach, the company would have to carve out a special niche in the insulated wire and cable market. This approach could constitute a good match between the company's capabilities and resources and the opportunities in the industry. But considerable expenditure would be needed for the development of the technically expert sales force that would be required.

"The third alternative, an aggressive marketing approach involving a full line of products and a greatly enlarged marketing organization, would tax the innovative capabilities of the laboratory and would set the company into direct competition with larger companies, such as General Cable. Compared with the other two alternatives, this would require the largest additional investment. The risk involved in this alternative would center on financial problems, with the possibility of overextension with respect to long-term debt or loss of control through sale of common stock to outsiders.

"We conclude that the second alternative is superior to the third, but the choice between merger and specialization is less apparent. The merger alternative might be rejected largely on the basis of management's implied emphasis on quality, innovation, and entrepreneurship."

6. CHOOSE THE NEW STRATEGY

In this last step, management identifies those factors which are of overriding importance. These are the factors on which the decision turns. In a strategy problem, where there may appear to be five or six relevant factors of significance, one or two of them may seem pivotal, and the relative standing of the alternatives with respect to these factors provides the basis for the final choice. Here is what happened in the IWAC case:

Management concluded that the best strategy was the second of the three possibilities considered—specializing in insulated wire and cable products which required high-quality specifications, and marketing its products directly through its own sales force. This meant eliminating products that did not utilize the company's distinctive competence in insulation, such as printed circuits and electronic connectors, and ceasing at the earliest practical moment to rely on distributors. Under this strategy, the company would undertake aggressive development and marketing of power cable and heavy-duty lighting cords.

Exhibit IV. Questions to use in formulating strategy

1. Record current strategy:
   a. What is the current strategy?
   b. What kind of business does management want to operate (considering such management values as desired return on investment, growth rate, share of market, stability, flexibility, character of the business, and climate)?
   c. What kind of business does management feel it ought to operate (considering management's concepts of social responsibility and obligations to stockholders, employees, community, competitors, customers, suppliers, government, and the like)?

2. Identify problems with the current strategy:
   a. Are trends discernible in the environment that may become threats and/or missed opportunities if the current strategy is continued?
   b. Is the company having difficulty implementing the current strategy?
   c. Is the attempt to carry out the current strategy disclosing significant weaknesses and/or unutilized strengths in the company?
   d. Are there other concerns with respect to the validity of the current strategy?
   e. Is the current strategy no longer valid?

3. Discover the core of the strategy problem:
   a. Does the current strategy require greater competence and/or resources than the company possesses?
   b. Does it fail to exploit adequately the company's distinctive competence?
   c. Does it lack sufficient competitive advantage?
   d. Will it fail to exploit opportunities and/or meet threats in the environment, now or in the future?

e. Are the various elements of the strategy internally inconsistent?
   f. Are there other considerations with respect to the core of the strategy problem?
   g. What, then, is the real core of the strategy problem?

4. Formulate alternative new strategies:
   a. What possible alternatives exist for solving the strategy problem?
   b. To what extent do the company's competence and resources limit the number of alternatives that should be considered?
   c. To what extent do management's preferences limit the alternatives?
   d. To what extent does management's sense of social responsibility limit the alternatives?
   e. What strategic alternatives are acceptable?

5. Evaluate alternative new strategies:
   a. Which alternative *best* solves the strategy problem?
   b. Which alternative offers the *best* match with the company's competence and resources?
   c. Which alternative offers the *greatest* competitive advantage?
   d. Which alternative *best* satisfies management's preferences?
   e. Which alternative *best* meets management's sense of social responsibility?
   f. Which alternative *minimizes* the creation of new problems?

6. Choose a new strategy:
   a. What is the *relative significance* of each of the preceding considerations?
   b. What should the new strategy be?

Conclusion

The approach described in this article is most valuable for medium-sized and small companies. Top executives of these companies, working at the conference table, can approach strategy formulation as a joint effort. In such group problem solving, one of the principal tools contributing to effective leadership by the president is a carefully prepared outline for guiding the discussion. The six-step approach I have described can be the starting point for such an outline. *Exhibit IV* exemplifies the kinds of questions that might be asked. The president, as chairman of the meeting, can phrase the questions in terms of the situation under discussion, note pertinent additional questions at appropriate points, and thus guide the meeting. Each of the six main tasks becomes a milepost to be passed in the progress toward a solution.

The chairman can advance group thinking by offering interpretative summaries, and, using transitional statements, he can lead the group from one major step to the next. The constant challenge for him is to maintain that balance between freedom and control which makes for progress and yet does not act to stifle creative thinking.

Since 1960 the job of top executives has undergone substantial change. Corporate strategy has become their dominant concern. But strategy is not yet a science even in large corporations, despite recent developments in management science and computers. And for the medium-sized or small company which cannot afford OR, planning departments, or large-scale computer capacity, the task is likely to remain an art during the foreseeable future. In such circumstances, strategy should be formulated by the top management team at the conference table. Judgment, experience, intuition, and well-guided discussions are the key to success, not staff work and mathematical models.

Part II

Marketing

Preface

Marketing is often called a function of management, but it is more than that. For many companies it is practically synonymous with corporate strategy, and for most it is at least the keystone in the strategic arch. In this section, therefore, marketing is discussed in fairly broad management terms. Marketing goals are seen not as the goals of a department or division in the organization but as corporate-wide goals. Sales executives are seen not as experts in salesmanship but as company planners and policy makers. Marketing and sales techniques are seen not as tools of specialists but as methods that many managers should know about.

In "Marketing Myopia," one of the most influential articles ever published in HBR, the focus is on the way businessmen think of their companies' roles and missions. Conceiving an organization's mission as selling particular products or services, rather than meeting certain customer needs, is a form of tunnel vision that has got many businesses into serious trouble. "Marketing Planning for Industrial Products," based on a study of 50 industrial marketers, analyzes the three principal causes of problems in putting marketing planning concepts into practice in industrial companies. "Get the Most Out of Your Sales Force," also based on a survey, offers guidelines to executives who want to tailor hiring and managing practices to the job the company is trying to do. "Manage the Customer, Not Just the Sales Force" is an application of the "Marketing Myopia" concept to the activities of sales managers in particular. "Demarketing—Yes, Demarketing" discusses a need that a growing number of companies are becoming aware of—how to relate to customers during times of shortages, excess demand, or unwanted demand. "Grass Roots Market Research" focuses on the opportunities for field sales forces to do research tasks traditionally reserved to centralized market research departments.

4. Marketing Myopia

Theodore Levitt

Today's growth product is tomorrow's buggy whip—and often management does not seem to realize it. A company must learn to think of itself not as producing goods and services but as buying, creating, and satisfying customers. This approach should permeate every nook and cranny of the organization; if it doesn't, no amount of efficiency in operations can compensate for the lack. Marketing myopia is not easy to overcome, but unless it is, an organization cannot achieve greatness. This is the lesson learned by many companies in many industries, including the most glamorous "growth" industries.

Every major industry was once a growth industry. But some that are now riding a wave of growth enthusiasm are very much in the shadow of decline. Others which are thought of as seasoned growth industries have actually stopped growing. In every case the reason growth is threatened, slowed, or stopped is *not* because the market is saturated. It is because there has been a failure of management.

Fateful Purposes

The failure is at the top. The executives responsible for it, in the last analysis, are those who deal with broad aims and policies. Thus:

☐ The railroads did not stop growing because the need for passenger and freight transportation declined. That grew. The railroads are in trouble today not because the need was filled by others (cars, trucks, airplanes, even telephones), but because it was *not* filled by the railroads themselves. They let others take customers away from them because they assumed themselves to be in the railroad business rather than in the transportation business. The reason they defined their industry wrong was because they were railroad-oriented instead of transportation-oriented; they were product-oriented instead of customer-oriented.

◻ Hollywood barely escaped being totally ravished by television. Actually, all the established film companies went through drastic reorganizations. Some simply disappeared. All of them got into trouble not because of TV's inroads but because of their own myopia. As with the railroads, Hollywood defined its business incorrectly. It thought it was in the movie business when it was actually in the entertainment business. "Movies" implied a specific, limited product. This produced a fatuous contentment which from the beginning led producers to view TV as a threat. Hollywood scorned and rejected TV when it should have welcomed it as an opportunity—an opportunity to expand the entertainment business.

Today TV is a bigger business than the old narrowly defined movie business ever was. Had Hollywood been customer-oriented (providing entertainment), rather than product-oriented (making movies), would it have gone through the fiscal purgatory that it did? I doubt it. What ultimately saved Hollywood and accounted for its recent resurgence was the wave of new young writers, producers, and directors whose previous successes in television had decimated the old movie companies and toppled the big movie moguls.

There are other less obvious examples of industries that have been and are now endangering their futures by improperly defining their purposes. I shall discuss some in detail later and analyze the kind of policies that lead to trouble. Right now it may help to show what a thoroughly customer-oriented management *can* do to keep a growth industry growing, even after the obvious opportunities have been exhausted; and here there are two examples that have been around for a long time. They are nylon and glass—specifically, E. I. Du Pont de Nemours & Company and Corning Glass Works:

Both companies have great technical competence. Their product orientation is unquestioned. But this alone does not explain their success. After all, who was more pridefully product-oriented and product-conscious than the erstwhile New England textile companies that have been so thoroughly massacred? The Du Ponts and the Cornings have succeeded not primarily because of their product or research orientation but because they have been thoroughly customer-oriented also. It is constant watchfulness for opportunities to apply their technical know-how to the creation of customer-satisfying uses which accounts for their prodigious output of successful new products. Without a very sophisticated eye on the customer, most of their new products might have been wrong, their sales methods useless.

Aluminum has also continued to be a growth industry, thanks to the efforts of two wartime-created companies which deliberately set about creating new customer-satisfying uses. Without Kaiser Aluminum &

Chemical Corporation and Reynolds Metals Company, the total demand for aluminum today would be vastly less than it is.

Some may argue that it is foolish to set the railroads off against aluminum or the movies off against glass. Are not aluminum and glass naturally so versatile that the industries are bound to have more growth opportunities than the railroads and movies? This view commits precisely the error I have been talking about. It defines an industry, or a product, or a cluster of know-how so narrowly as to guarantee its premature senescence. When we mention "railroads," we should make sure we mean "transportation." As transporters, the railroads still have a good chance for very considerable growth. They are not limited to the railroad business as such (though in my opinion rail transportation is potentially a much stronger transportation medium than is generally believed).

What the railroads lack is not opportunity, but some of the same managerial imaginativeness and audacity that made them great. Even an amateur like Jacques Barzun saw what is lacking when he said:

"I grieve to see the most advanced physical and social organization of the last century go down in shabby disgrace for lack of the same comprehensive imagination that built it up. [What is lacking is] the will of the companies to survive and to satisfy the public by inventiveness and skill."[1]

Shadow of Obsolescence

It is impossible to mention a single major industry that did not at one time qualify for the magic appellation of "growth industry." In each case its assumed strength lay in the apparently unchallenged superiority of its product. There appeared to be no effective substitute for it. It was itself a runaway substitute for the product it so triumphantly replaced. Yet one after another of these celebrated industries has come under a shadow. Let us look briefly at a few more of them, this time taking examples that have so far received a little less attention:

□ *Dry cleaning*—This was once a growth industry with lavish prospects. In an age of wool garments, imagine being finally able to get them safely and easily clean. The boom was on.

Yet here we are only a few decades after the boom started and the industry is in trouble. Where has the competition come from? From a

1. Jacques Barzun, "Trains and the Mind of Man," *Holiday*, February 1960, p. 21.

better way of cleaning? No. It has come from synthetic fibers and chemical additives that have cut the need for dry cleaning. But this is only the beginning. Lurking in the wings and ready to make chemical dry cleaning totally obsolescent is that powerful magician, ultrasonics.

□ *Electric utilities*—This is another one of those supposedly "no-substitute" products that has been enthroned on a pedestal of invincible growth. When the incandescent lamp came along, kerosene lights were finished. Later the water wheel and the steam engine were cut to ribbons by the flexibility, reliability, simplicity, and just plain easy availability of electric motors. The prosperity of electric utilities continues to wax extravagant as the home is converted into a museum of electric gadgetry. How can anybody miss by investing in utilities, with no competition, nothing but growth ahead?

But a second look is not quite so comforting. A score of nonutility companies are well advanced toward developing a powerful chemical fuel cell which could sit in some hidden closet of every home silently ticking off electric power. The electric lines that vulgarize so many neighborhoods will be eliminated. So will the endless demolition of streets and service interruptions during storms. Also on the horizon is solar energy, again pioneered by nonutility companies.

Who says that the utilities have no competition? They may be natural monopolies now, but tomorrow they may be natural deaths. To avoid this prospect, they too will have to develop fuel cells, solar energy, and other power sources. To survive, they themselves will have to plot the obsolescence of what now produces their livelihood.

□ *Grocery stores*—Many people find it hard to realize that there ever was a thriving establishment known as the "corner grocery store." The supermarket has taken over with a powerful effectiveness. Yet the big food chains of the 1930's narrowly escaped being completely wiped out by the aggressive expansion of independent supermarkets. The first genuine supermarket was opened in 1930, in Jamaica, Long Island. By 1933 supermarkets were thriving in California, Ohio, Pennsylvania, and elsewhere. Yet the established chains pompously ignored them. When they chose to notice them, it was with such derisive descriptions as "cheapy," "horse-and-buggy," "cracker-barrel storekeeping," and "unethical opportunists."

The executive of one big chain announced at the time that he found it "hard to believe that people will drive for miles to shop for foods and sacrifice the personal service chains have perfected and to which Mrs. Consumer is accustomed." As late as 1936, the National Wholesale Grocers convention and the New Jersey Retail Grocers Association said there was nothing to fear. They said that the supers' narrow appeal to the price buyer limited the size of their market. They had to draw from miles around. When imitators came, there would be wholesale liquidations as volume fell. The current high sales of the supers was said to be partly due to their novelty. Basically people wanted convenient neighborhood grocers. If the neighborhood stores "cooperate with their suppliers, pay attention to their costs, and improve their service," they would be able to weather the competition until it blew over.

It never blew over. The chains discovered that survival required going into the supermarket business. This meant the wholesale destruction of their huge investments in corner store sites and in established distribution and merchandising methods. The companies with "the courage of their convictions" resolutely stuck to the corner store philosophy. They kept their pride but lost their shirts.

SELF-DECEIVING CYCLE

But memories are short. For example, it is hard for people who today confidently hail the twin messiahs of electronics and chemicals to see how things could possibly go wrong with these galloping industries. They probably also cannot see how a reasonably sensible businessman could have been as myopic as the famous Boston millionaire who unintentionally sentenced his heirs to poverty by stipulating that his entire estate be forever invested exclusively in electric streetcar securities. His posthumous declaration, "There will always be a big demand for efficient urban transportation," is no consolation to his heirs who sustain life by pumping gasoline at automobile filling stations.

Yet, in a casual survey I recently took among a group of intelligent business executives, nearly half agreed that it would be hard to hurt their heirs by tying their estates forever to the electronics industry. When I then confronted them with the Boston streetcar example, they chorused unanimously, "That's different!" But is it? Is not the basic situation identical?

In truth, *there is no such thing* as a growth industry, I believe. There are only companies organized and operated to create and capitalize on growth opportunities. Industries that assume themselves to be riding some automatic growth escalator invariably descend into stagnation. The history of every dead and dying "growth" industry shows a self-deceiving cycle of bountiful expansion and undetected decay. There are four conditions which usually guarantee this cycle:

1. The belief that growth is assured by an expanding and more affluent population.

2. The belief that there is no competitive substitute for the industry's major product.

3. Too much faith in mass production and in the advantages of rapidly declining unit costs as output rises.

4. Preoccupation with a product that lends itself to carefully controlled scientific experimentation, improvement, and manufacturing cost reduction.

I should like now to begin examining each of these conditions in some detail. To build my case as boldly as possible, I shall illustrate the points with reference to three industries—petroleum, automobiles, and electronics —particularly petroleum, because it spans more years and more vicissitudes. Not only do these three have excellent reputations with the general public and also enjoy the confidence of sophisticated investors, but their managements have become known for progressive thinking in areas like financial control, product research, and management training. If obsolescence can cripple even these industries, it can happen anywhere.

Population Myth

The belief that profits are assured by an expanding and more affluent population is dear to the heart of every industry. It takes the edge off the apprehensions everybody understandably feels about the future. If consumers are multiplying and also buying more of your product or service, you can face the future with considerably more comfort than if the market is shrinking. An expanding market keeps the manufacturer from having to think very hard or imaginatively. If thinking is an intellectual response to a problem, then the absence of a problem leads to the absence of thinking. If your product has an automatically expanding market, then you will not give much thought to how to expand it.

One of the most interesting examples of this is provided by the petroleum industry. Probably our oldest growth industry, it has an enviable record. While there are some current apprehensions about its growth rate, the industry itself tends to be optimistic. But I believe it can be demonstrated that it is undergoing a fundamental yet typical change. It is not only ceasing to be a growth industry, but may actually be a declining one, relative to other business. Although there is widespread unawareness of it, I believe that within a fairly short time the oil industry may find itself in much the same position of retrospective glory that the railroads are now in. Despite its pioneering work in developing and applying the present-value method of investment evaluation, in employee relations, and in working with backward countries, the petroleum business is a distressing example of how complacency and wrongheadedness can stubbornly convert opportunity into near disaster.

One of the characteristics of this and other industries that have believed very strongly in the beneficial consequences of an expanding population, while at the same time being industries with a generic product for which there has appeared to be no competitive substitute, is that the individual companies have sought to outdo their competitors by improving on what they are already doing. This makes sense, of course, if one assumes that sales are tied to the country's population strings, because the customer can compare products only on a feature-by-feature basis. I believe it is significant, for example, that not since John D. Rockefeller sent free kerosene lamps to China has the oil industry done anything really outstanding to create a demand for its product. Not even in product improvement has it showered itself with eminence. The greatest single improvement, namely, the development of tetraethyl lead, came from outside the industry, specifically from General Motors and Du Pont. The big contributions made by the industry itself are confined to the technology of oil exploration, production, and refining.

ASKING FOR TROUBLE

In other words, the industry's efforts have focused on improving the *efficiency* of getting and making its product, not really on improving the generic product or its marketing. Moreover, its chief product has continuously been defined in the narrowest possible terms, namely, gasoline, not energy, fuel, or transportation. This attitude has helped assure that:

□ Major improvements in gasoline quality tend not to originate in the oil industry. Also, the development of superior alternative fuels comes from outside the oil industry, as will be shown later.

□ Major innovations in automobile fuel marketing are originated by small new oil companies that are not primarily preoccupied with production or refining. These are the companies that have been responsible for the rapidly expanding multipump gasoline stations, with their successful emphasis on large and clean layouts, rapid and efficient driveway service, and quality gasoline at low prices.

Thus, the oil industry is asking for trouble from outsiders. Sooner or later, in this land of hungry inventors and entrepreneurs, a threat is sure to come. The possibilities of this will become more apparent when we turn to the next dangerous belief of many managements. For the sake of continuity, because this second belief is tied closely to the first, I shall continue with the same example.

Idea of Indispensability

The petroleum industry is pretty much persuaded that there is no competitive substitute for its major product, gasoline—or if there is, that it will continue to be a derivative of crude oil, such as diesel fuel or kerosene jet fuel.

There is a lot of automatic wishful thinking in this assumption. The trouble is that most refining companies own huge amounts of crude oil reserves. These have value only if there is a market for products into which oil can be converted—hence the tenacious belief in the continuing competitive superiority of automobile fuels made from crude oil.

This idea persists despite all historic evidence against it. The evidence not only shows that oil has never been a superior product for any purpose for very long, but it also shows that the oil industry has never really been a growth industry. It has been a succession of different businesses that have gone through the usual historic cycles of growth, maturity, and decay. Its over-all survival is owed to a series of miraculous escapes from total obsolescence, of last-minute and unexpected reprieves from total disaster reminiscent of the Perils of Pauline.

PERILS OF PETROLEUM

I shall sketch in only the main episodes:

◻ First, crude oil was largely a patent medicine. But even before that fad ran out, demand was greatly expanded by the use of oil in kerosene lamps. The prospect of lighting the world's lamps gave rise to an extravagant promise of growth. The prospects were similar to those the industry now holds for gasoline in other parts of the world. It can hardly wait for the underdeveloped nations to get a car in every garage.

In the days of the kerosene lamp, the oil companies competed with each other and against gaslight by trying to improve the illuminating characteristics of kerosene. Then suddenly the impossible happened. Edison invented a light which was totally nondependent on crude oil. Had it not been for the growing use of kerosene in space heaters, the incandescent lamp would have completely finished oil as a growth industry at that time. Oil would have been good for little else than axle grease.

◻ Then disaster and reprieve struck again. Two great innovations occurred, neither originating in the oil industry. The successful development of coal-burning domestic central-heating systems made the space heater obsolescent. While the industry reeled, along came its most magnificent boost yet—the internal combustion engine, also invented by outsiders. Then when the prodigious expansion for gasoline finally began to level off in the 1920's, along came the miraculous escape of a central oil heater. Once again, the escape was provided by an outsider's invention and development. And when that market weakened, wartime demand for aviation fuel came to the rescue. After the war the expansion of civilian aviation, the dieselization of railroads, and the explosive demand for cars and trucks kept the industry's growth in high gear.

◻ Meanwhile centralized oil heating—whose boom potential had only recently been proclaimed—ran into severe competition from natural gas. While the oil companies themselves owned the gas that now competed with their oil, the industry did not originate the natural gas revolution, nor has it to this day greatly profited from its gas ownership. The gas revolution was made by newly formed transmission companies that marketed the product with an aggressive ardor. They started a magnificent new industry, first against the advice and then against the resistance of the oil companies.

By all the logic of the situation, the oil companies themselves should have made the gas revolution. They not only owned the gas; they also were the only people experienced in handling, scrubbing, and using it, the only people experienced in pipeline technology and transmission, and they understood heating problems. But, partly because they knew that natural gas would compete with their own sale of heating oil, the oil companies pooh-poohed the potentials of gas.

The revolution was finally started by oil pipeline executives who, unable to persuade their own companies to go into gas, quit and organized the spectacularly successful gas transmission companies. Even after their success became painfully evident to the oil companies, the latter did not go into gas transmission. The multibillion dollar business which should have been theirs went to others. As in the past, the industry was blinded by its narrow preoccupation with a specific product and the value of its reserves. It paid little or no attention to its customers' basic needs and preferences.

☐ The postwar years have not witnessed any change. Immediately after World War II the oil industry was greatly encouraged about its future by the rapid expansion of demand for its traditional line of products. In 1950 most companies projected annual rates of domestic expansion of around 6% through at least 1975. Though the ratio of crude oil reserves to demand in the Free World was about 20 to 1, with 10 to 1 being usually considered a reasonable working ratio in the United States, booming demand sent oil men searching for more without sufficient regard to what the future really promised. In 1952 they "hit" in the Middle East; the ratio skyrocketed to 42 to 1. If gross additions to reserves continue at the average rate of the past five years (37 billion barrels annually), then by 1970 the reserve ratio will be up to 45 to 1. This abundance of oil has weakened crude and product prices all over the world.

UNCERTAIN FUTURE

Management cannot find much consolation today in the rapidly expanding petrochemical industry, another oil-using idea that did not originate in the leading firms. The total United States production of petrochemicals is equivalent to about 2% (by volume) of the demand for all petroleum products. Although the petrochemical industry is now expected to grow by about 10% per year, this will not offset other drains on the growth of crude oil consumption. Furthermore, while petrochemical products are many and growing, it is well to remember that there are nonpetroleum sources of the basic raw material, such as coal. Besides, a lot of plastics can be produced with relatively little oil. A 50,000-barrel-per-day oil refinery is now considered the absolute minimum size for efficiency. But a 5,000-barrel-per-day chemical plant is a giant operation.

Oil has never been a continuously strong growth industry. It has grown by fits and starts, always miraculously saved by innovations and developments not of its own making. The reason it has not grown in a smooth progression is that each time it thought it had a superior product safe from the possibility of competitive substitutes, the product turned out to be inferior and notoriously subject to obsolescence. Until now, gasoline (for motor fuel, anyhow) has escaped this fate. But, as we shall see later, it too may be on its last legs.

The point of all this is that there is no guarantee against product obsolescence. If a company's own research does not make it obsolete, another's will. Unless an industry is especially lucky, as oil has been until now, it can easily go down in a sea of red figures—just as the railroads have, as the buggy whip manufacturers have, as the corner grocery chains have, as most of the big movie companies have, and indeed as many other industries have.

The best way for a firm to be lucky is to make its own luck. That requires knowing what makes a business successful. One of the greatest enemies of this knowledge is mass production.

Production Pressures

Mass-production industries are impelled by a great drive to produce all they can. The prospect of steeply declining unit costs as output rises is more than most companies can usually resist. The profit possibilities look spectacular. All effort focuses on production. The result is that marketing gets neglected.

John Kenneth Galbraith contends that just the opposite occurs.[2] Output is so prodigious that all effort concentrates on trying to get rid of it. He says this accounts for singing commercials, desecration of the countryside with advertising signs, and other wasteful and vulgar practices. Galbraith has a finger on something real, but he misses the strategic point. Mass production does indeed generate great pressure to "move" the product. But what usually gets emphasized is selling, not marketing. Marketing, being a more sophisticated and complex process, gets ignored.

2. *The Affluent Society* (Boston, Houghton Mifflin Company, 1958), pp. 152-160.

The difference between marketing and selling is more than semantic. Selling focuses on the needs of the seller, marketing on the needs of the buyer. Selling is preoccupied with the seller's need to convert his product into cash; marketing with the idea of satisfying the needs of the customer by means of the product and the whole cluster of things associated with creating, delivering, and finally consuming it.

In some industries the enticements of full mass production have been so powerful that for many years top management in effect has told the sales departments, "You get rid of it; we'll worry about profits." By contrast, a truly marketing-minded firm tries to create value-satisfying goods and services that consumers will want to buy. What it offers for sale includes not only the generic product or service, but also how it is made available to the customer, in what form, when, under what conditions, and at what terms of trade. Most important, what it offers for sale is determined not by the seller but by the buyer. The seller takes his cues from the buyer in such a way that the product becomes a consequence of the marketing effort, not vice versa.

LAG IN DETROIT

This may sound like an elementary rule of business, but that does not keep it from being violated wholesale. It is certainly more violated than honored. Take the automobile industry:

Here mass production is most famous, most honored, and has the greatest impact on the entire society. The industry has hitched its fortune to the relentless requirements of the annual model change, a policy that makes customer orientation an especially urgent necessity. Consequently the auto companies annually spend millions of dollars on consumer research. But the fact that the new compact cars are selling so well indicates that Detroit's vast researches have for a long time failed to reveal what the customer really wanted. Detroit was not persuaded that he wanted anything different from what he had been getting until it lost millions of customers to other small car manufacturers.

How could this unbelievable lag behind consumer wants have been perpetuated so long? Why did not research reveal consumer preferences before consumers' buying decisions themselves revealed the facts? Is that not what consumer research is for—to find out before the fact what is going to happen? The answer is that Detroit never really researched the customer's wants. It only researched his preferences between the kinds of things which it had already decided to offer him. For Detroit is mainly product-oriented, not customer-oriented. To the extent that the customer is recognized as having needs that the manufacturer should try to satisfy, Detroit usually acts as if the job can be done entirely by product changes.

Occasionally attention gets paid to financing, too, but that is done more in order to sell than to enable the customer to buy.

As for taking care of other customer needs, there is not enough being done to write about. The areas of the greatest unsatisfied needs are ignored, or at best get stepchild attention. These are at the point of sale and on the matter of automotive repair and maintenance. Detroit views these problem areas as being of secondary importance. That is underscored by the fact that the retailing and servicing ends of this industry are neither owned and operated nor controlled by the manufacturers. Once the car is produced, things are pretty much in the dealer's inadequate hands. Illustrative of Detroit's arm's-length attitude is the fact that, while servicing holds enormous sales-stimulating, profit-building opportunities, only 57 of Chevrolet's 7,000 dealers provide night maintenance service.

Motorists repeatedly express their dissatisfaction with servicing and their apprehensions about buying cars under the present selling setup. The anxieties and problems they encounter during the auto buying and maintenance processes are probably more intense and widespread today than 30 years ago. Yet the automobile companies do not *seem* to listen to or take their cues from the anguished consumer. If they do listen, it must be through the filter of their own preoccupation with production. The marketing effort is still viewed as a necessary consequence of the product, not vice versa, as it should be. That is the legacy of mass production, with its parochial view that profit resides essentially in low-cost full production.

WHAT FORD PUT FIRST

The profit lure of mass production obviously has a place in the plans and strategy of business management, but it must always *follow* hard thinking about the customer. This is one of the most important lessons that we can learn from the contradictory behavior of Henry Ford. In a sense Ford was both the most brilliant and the most senseless marketer in American history. He was senseless because he refused to give the customer anything but a black car. He was brilliant because he fashioned a production system designed to fit market needs. We habitually celebrate him for the wrong reason, his production genius. His real genius was marketing. We think he was able to cut his selling price and therefore sell millions of $500 cars because his invention of the assembly line had reduced the costs. Actually he invented the assembly line because he had concluded that at $500 he could sell millions of cars. Mass production was the *result* not the cause of his low prices.

Ford repeatedly emphasized this point, but a nation of production-oriented business managers refuses to hear the great lesson he taught. Here is his operating philosophy as he expressed it succinctly:

Our policy is to reduce the price, extend the operations, and improve the article. You will notice that the reduction of price comes first. We have never considered any costs as fixed. Therefore we first reduce the price to the point where we believe more sales will result. Then we go ahead and try to make the prices. We do not bother about the costs. The new price forces the costs down. The more usual way is to take the costs and then determine the price, and although that method may be scientific in the narrow sense; it is not scientific in the broad sense, because what earthly use is it to know the cost if it tells you that you cannot manufacture at a price at which the article can be sold? But more to the point is the fact that, although one may calculate what a cost is, and of course all of our costs are carefully calculated, no one knows what a cost ought to be. One of the ways of discovering . . . is to name a price so low as to force everybody in the place to the highest point of efficiency. The low price makes everybody dig for profits. We make more discoveries concerning manufacturing and selling under this forced method than by any method of leisurely investigation.[3]

PRODUCT PROVINCIALISM

The tantalizing profit possibilities of low unit production costs may be the most seriously self-deceiving attitude that can afflict a company, particularly a "growth" company where an apparently assured expansion of demand already tends to undermine a proper concern for the importance of marketing and the customer.

The usual result of this narrow preoccupation with so-called concrete matters is that instead of growing, the industry declines. It usually means that the product fails to adapt to the constantly changing patterns of consumer needs and tastes, to new and modified marketing institutions and practices, or to product developments in competing or complementary industries. The industry has its eyes so firmly on its own specific product that it does not see how it is being made obsolete.

The classical example of this is the buggy whip industry. No amount of product improvement could stave off its death sentence. But had the industry defined itself as being in the transportation business rather than the buggy whip business, it might have survived. It would have done what survival always entails, that is, changing. Even if it had only defined its business as providing a stimulant or catalyst to an energy source, it might have survived by becoming a manufacturer of, say, fanbelts or air cleaners.

What may some day be a still more classical example is, again, the oil industry. Having let others steal marvelous opportunities from it (e.g., natural gas, as already mentioned, missile fuels, and jet engine lubricants), one would expect it to have taken steps never to let that happen again.

3. Henry Ford, *My Life and Work* (New York, Doubleday, Page & Company, 1923), pp. 146-147.

But this is not the case. We are now getting extraordinary new developments in fuel systems specifically designed to power automobiles. Not
only are these developments concentrated in firms outside the petroleum
industry, but petroleum is almost systematically ignoring them, securely
content in its wedded bliss to oil. It is the story of the kerosene lamp versus
the incandescent lamp all over again. Oil is trying to improve hydrocarbon
fuels rather than to develop *any* fuels best suited to the needs of their
users, whether or not made in different ways and with different raw materials from oil.

Here are some of the things which nonpetroleum companies are working
on:

□ Over a dozen such firms now have advanced working models of energy
systems which, when perfected, will replace the internal combustion engine
and eliminate the demand for gasoline. The superior merit of each of these
systems is their elimination of frequent, time-consuming, and irritating
refueling stops. Most of these systems are fuel cells designed to create
electrical energy directly from chemicals without combustion. Most of
them use chemicals that are not derived from oil, generally hydrogen and
oxygen.

□ Several other companies have advanced models of electric storage
batteries designed to power automobiles. One of these is an aircraft producer that is working jointly with several electric utility companies. The
latter hope to use off-peak generating capacity to supply overnight plug-in
battery regeneration. Another company, also using the battery approach,
is a medium-size electronics firm with extensive small-battery experience
that it developed in connection with its work on hearing aids. It is col-
laborating with an automobile manufacturer. Recent improvements arising
from the need for high-powered miniature power storage plants in rockets
have put us within reach of a relatively small battery capable of withstand-
ing great overloads or surges of power. Germanium diode applications and
batteries using sintered-plate and nickel-cadmium techniques promise to
make a revolution in our energy sources.

□ Solar energy conversion systems are also getting increasing attention.
One usually cautious Detroit auto executive recently ventured that solar-
powered cars might be common by 1980.

As for the oil companies, they are more or less "watching developments,"
as one research director put it to me. A few are doing a bit of research on
fuel cells, but almost always confined to developing cells powered by hydrocarbon chemicals. None of them are enthusiastically researching fuel cells,
batteries, or solar power plants. None of them are spending a fraction as
much on research in these profoundly important areas as they are on the
usual run-of-the-mill things like reducing combustion chamber deposit in
gasoline engines. One major integrated petroleum company recently took a

tentative look at the fuel cell and concluded that although "the companies actively working on it indicate a belief in ultimate success . . . the timing and magnitude of its impact are too remote to warrant recognition in our forecasts."

One might, of course, ask: Why should the oil companies do anything different? Would not chemical fuel cells, batteries, or solar energy kill the present product lines? The answer is that they would indeed, and that is precisely the reason for the oil firms having to develop these power units before their competitors, so they will not be companies without an industry.

Management might be more likely to do what is needed for its own preservation if it thought of itself as being in the energy business. But even that would not be enough if it persists in imprisoning itself in the narrow grip of its tight product orientation. It has to think of itself as taking care of customer needs, not finding, refining, or even selling oil. Once it genuinely thinks of its business as taking care of people's transportation needs, nothing can stop it from creating its own extravagantly profitable growth.

"CREATIVE DESTRUCTION"

Since words are cheap and deeds are dear, it may be appropriate to indicate what this kind of thinking involves and leads to. Let us start at the beginning—the customer. It can be shown that motorists strongly dislike the bother, delay, and experience of buying gasoline. People actually do not buy gasoline. They cannot see it, taste it, feel it, appreciate it, or really test it. What they buy is the right to continue driving their cars. The gas station is like a tax collector to whom people are compelled to pay a periodic toll as the price of using their cars. This makes the gas station a basically unpopular institution. It can never be made popular or pleasant, only less unpopular, less unpleasant.

To reduce its unpopularity completely means eliminating it. Nobody likes a tax collector, not even a pleasantly cheerful one. Nobody likes to interrupt a trip to buy a phantom product, not even from a handsome Adonis or a seductive Venus. Hence, companies that are working on exotic fuel substitutes which will eliminate the need for frequent refueling are heading directly into the outstretched arms of the irritated motorist. They are riding a wave of inevitability, not because they are creating something which is technologically superior or more sophisticated, but because they are satisfying a powerful customer need. They are also eliminating noxious odors and air pollution.

Once the petroleum companies recognize the customer-satisfying logic of what another power system can do, they will see that they have no more choice about working on an efficient, long-lasting fuel (or some way of delivering present fuels without bothering the motorist) than the big food chains had a choice about going into the supermarket business, or the vacuum tube companies had a choice about making semiconductors. For their own good the oil firms will have to destroy their own highly profitable assets. No amount of wishful thinking can save them from the necessity of engaging in this form of "creative destruction."

I phrase the need as strongly as this because I think management must make quite an effort to break itself loose from conventional ways. It is all too easy in this day and age for a company or industry to let its sense of purpose become dominated by the economies of full production and to develop a dangerously lopsided product orientation. In short, if management lets itself drift, it invariably drifts in the direction of thinking of itself as producing goods and services, not customer satisfactions. While it probably will not descend to the depths of telling its salesmen, "You get rid of it; we'll worry about profits," it can, without knowing it, be practicing precisely that formula for withering decay. The historic fate of one growth industry after another has been its suicidal product provincialism.

Dangers of R & D

Another big danger to a firm's continued growth arises when top management is wholly transfixed by the profit possibilities of technical research and development. To illustrate I shall turn first to a new industry—electronics—and then return once more to the oil companies. By comparing a fresh example with a familiar one, I hope to emphasize the prevalence and insidiousness of a hazardous way of thinking.

MARKETING SHORTCHANGED

In the case of electronics, the greatest danger which faces the glamorous new companies in this field is not that they do not pay enough attention to research and development, but that they pay *too much* attention to it. And the fact that the fastest growing electronics firms owe their eminence to their heavy emphasis on technical research is completely beside the point. They have vaulted to affluence on a sudden crest of unusually strong general receptiveness to new technical ideas. Also, their success has been shaped in the virtually guaranteed market of military subsidies and by military orders that in many cases actually preceded the existence of facilities to make the products. Their expansion has, in other words, been almost totally devoid of marketing effort.

Thus, they are growing up under conditions that come dangerously close to creating the illusion that a superior product will sell itself. Having created a successful company by making a superior product, it is not surprising that management continues to be oriented toward the product rather than the people who consume it. It develops the philosophy that continued growth is a matter of continued product innovation and improvement.

A number of other factors tend to strengthen and sustain this belief:

1. Because electronic products are highly complex and sophisticated, managements become top-heavy with engineers and scientists. This creates a selective bias in favor of research and production at the expense of marketing. The organization tends to view itself as making things rather than satisfying customer needs. Marketing gets treated as a residual activity, "something else" that must be done once the vital job of product creation and production is completed.

2. To this bias in favor of product research, development, and production is added the bias in favor of dealing with controllable variables. Engineers and scientists are at home in the world of concrete things like machines, test tubes, production lines, and even balance sheets. The abstractions to which they feel kindly are those which are testable or manipulatable in the laboratory, or, if not testable, then functional, such as Euclid's axioms. In short, the managements of the new glamour-growth companies tend to favor those business activities which lend themselves to careful study, experimentation, and control—the hard, practical realities of the lab, the shop, the books.

What gets shortchanged are the realities of the *market*. Consumers are unpredictable, varied, fickle, stupid, shortsighted, stubborn, and generally bothersome. This is not what the engineer-managers say, but deep down in their consciousness it is what they believe. And this accounts for their concentrating on what they know and what they can control, namely, product research, engineering, and production. The emphasis on production becomes particularly attractive when the product can be made at declining unit costs. There is no more inviting way of making money than by running the plant full blast.

Today the top-heavy science-engineering-production orientation of so many electronics companies works reasonably well because they are pushing into new frontiers in which the armed services have pioneered virtually assured markets. The companies are in the felicitous position of having to fill, not find markets; of not having to discover what the customer needs and wants, but of having the customer voluntarily come forward with specific new product demands. If a team of consultants had been assigned specifically to design a business situation calculated to prevent the emergence and development of a customer-oriented marketing viewpoint, it could not have produced anything better than the conditions just described.

STEPCHILD TREATMENT

The oil industry is a stunning example of how science, technology, and mass production can divert an entire group of companies from their main task. To the extent the consumer is studied at all (which is not much), the focus is forever on getting information which is designed to help the oil companies improve what they are now doing. They try to discover more convincing advertising themes, more effective sales promotional drives, what the market shares of the various companies àre, what people like or dislike about service station dealers and oil companies, and so forth. Nobody seems as interested in probing deeply into the basic human needs that the industry might be trying to satisfy as in probing into the basic properties of the raw material that the companies work with in trying to deliver customer satisfactions.

Basic questions about customers and markets seldom get asked. The latter occupy a stepchild status. They are recognized as existing, as having to be taken care of, but not worth very much real thought or dedicated attention. Nobody gets as excited about the customers in his own backyard as about the oil in the Sahara Desert. Nothing illustrates better the neglect of marketing than its treatment in the industry press:

The centennial issue of the *American Petroleum Institute Quarterly*, published in 1959 to celebrate the discovery of oil in Titusville, Pennsylvania, contained 21 feature articles proclaiming the industry's greatness. Only one of these talked about its achievements in marketing, and that was only a pictorial record of how service station architecture has changed. The issue also contained a special section on "New Horizons," which was devoted to showing the magnificent role oil would play in America's future. Every reference was ebulliently optimistic, never implying once that oil might have some hard competition. Even the reference to atomic energy was a cheerful catalogue of how oil would help make atomic energy a success. There was not a single apprehension that the oil industry's affluence might be threatened or a suggestion that one "new horizon" might include new and better ways of serving oil's present customers.

But the most revealing example of the stepchild treatment that marketing gets was still another special series of short articles on "The Revolutionary Potential of Electronics." Under that heading this list of articles appeared in the table of contents:

"In the Search for Oil"
"In Production Operations"
"In Refinery Processes"
"In Pipeline Operations"

Significantly, every one of the industry's major functional areas is listed, *except* marketing. Why? Either it is believed that electronics holds no revolutionary potential for petroleum marketing (which is palpably wrong), or the editors forgot to discuss marketing (which is more likely, and illustrates its stepchild status).

The order in which the four functional areas are listed also betrays the alienation of the oil industry from the consumer. The industry is implicitly defined as beginning with the search for oil and ending with its distribution from the refinery. But the truth is, it seems to me, that the industry begins with the needs of the customer for its products. From that primal position its definition moves steadily backstream to areas of progressively lesser importance, until it finally comes to rest at the "search for oil."

BEGINNING AND END

The view that an industry is a customer-satisfying process, not a goods-producing process, is vital for all businessmen to understand. An industry begins with the customer and his needs, not with a patent, a raw material, or a selling skill. Given the customer's needs, the industry develops backwards, first concerning itself with the physical *delivery* of customer satisfactions. Then it moves back further to *creating* the things by which these satisfactions are in part achieved. How these materials are created is a matter of indifference to the customer, hence the particular form of manufacturing, processing, or what-have-you cannot be considered as a vital aspect of the industry. Finally, the industry moves back still further to *finding* the raw materials necessary for making its products.

The irony of some industries oriented toward technical research and development is that the scientists who occupy the high executive positions are totally unscientific when it comes to defining their companies' over-all needs and purposes. They violate the first two rules of the scientific method —being aware of and defining their companies' problems, and then developing testable hypotheses about solving them. They are scientific only about the convenient things, such as laboratory and product experiments. The reason that the customer (and the satisfaction of his deepest needs) is not considered as being "the problem" is not because there is any certain belief that no such problem exists, but because an organizational lifetime has conditioned management to look in the opposite direction. Marketing is a stepchild.

I do not mean that selling is ignored. Far from it. But selling, again, is not marketing. As already pointed out, selling concerns itself with the tricks and techniques of getting people to exchange their cash for your product. It is not concerned with the values that the exchange is all about. And it does not, as marketing invariably does, view the entire business process as consisting of a tightly integrated effort to discover, create, arouse, and satisfy customer needs. The customer is somebody "out there" who, with proper cunning, can be separated from his loose change.

Actually, not even selling gets much attention in some technologically minded firms. Because there is a virtually guaranteed market for the abundant flow of their new products, they do not actually know what a real market is. It is as if they lived in a planned economy, moving their products routinely from factory to retail outlet. Their successful concentration on products tends to convince them of the soundness of what they have been doing, and they fail to see the gathering clouds over the market.

Conclusion

Less than 75 years ago American railroads enjoyed a fierce loyalty among astute Wall Streeters. European monarchs invested in them heavily. Eternal wealth was thought to be the benediction for anybody who could scrape a few thousand dollars together to put into rail stocks. No other form of transportation could compete with the railroads in speed, flexibility, durability, economy, and growth potentials. As Jacques Barzun put it, "By the turn of the century it was an institution, an image of man, a tradition, a code of honor, a source of poetry, a nursery of boyhood desires, a sublimest of toys, and the most solemn machine—next to the funeral hearse—that marks the epochs in man's life."[4]

Even after the advent of automobiles, trucks, and airplanes, the railroad tycoons remained imperturbably self-confident. If you had told them 60 years ago that in 30 years they would be flat on their backs, broke, and pleading for government subsidies, they would have thought you totally demented. Such a future was simply not considered possible. It was not even a discussable subject, or an askable question, or a matter which any sane person would consider worth speculating about. The very thought was insane. Yet a lot of insane notions now have matter-of-fact acceptance —for example, the idea of 100-ton tubes of metal moving smoothly through the air 20,000 feet above the earth, loaded with 100 sane and solid citizens casually drinking martinis—and they have dealt cruel blows to the railroads.

What specifically must other companies do to avoid this fate? What does customer orientation involve? These questions have in part been answered by the preceding examples and analysis. It would take another article to show in detail what is required for specific industries. In any case, it should be obvious that building an effective customer-oriented company involves far more than good intentions or promotional tricks; it involves profound matters of human organization and leadership. For the present, let me merely suggest what appear to be some general requirements.

VISCERAL FEEL OF GREATNESS

Obviously the company has to do what survival demands. It has to adapt to the requirements of the market, and it has to do it sooner rather than later. But mere survival is a so-so aspiration. Anybody can survive in some

4. Op. cit., p. 20.

way or other, even the skid-row bum. The trick is to survive gallantly, to feel the surging impulse of commercial mastery, not just to experience the sweet smell of success, but to have the visceral feel of entrepreneurial greatness.

No organization can achieve greatness without a vigorous leader who is driven onward by his own pulsating *will to succeed*. He has to have a vision of grandeur, a vision that can produce eager followers in vast numbers. In business, the followers are the customers. To produce these customers, the entire corporation must be viewed as a customer-creating and customer-satisfying organism. Management must think of itself not as producing products but as providing customer-creating value satisfactions. It must push this idea (and everything it means and requires) into every nook and cranny of the organization. It has to do this continuously and with the kind of flair that excites and stimulates the people in it. Otherwise, the company will be merely a series of pigeonholed parts, with no consolidating sense of purpose or direction.

In short, the organization must learn to think of itself not as producing goods or services but as *buying customers*, as doing the things that will make people *want* to do business with it. And the chief executive himself has the inescapable responsibility for creating this environment, this viewpoint, this attitude, this aspiration. He himself must set the company's style, its direction, and its goals. This means he has to know precisely where he himself wants to go, and to make sure the whole organization is enthusiastically aware of where that is. This is a first requisite of leadership, for *unless he knows where he is going, any road will take him there.*

If any road is okay, the chief executive might as well pack his attaché case and go fishing. If an organization does not know or care where it is going, it does not need to advertise that fact with a ceremonial figurehead. Everybody will notice it soon enough.

5. Marketing Planning for Industrial Products

B. Charles Ames

Why should the marketing concepts that work so well in consumer goods companies be so difficult to apply successfully in the industrial products field? Is it fair to blame the marketing function when planning results fall short of expectations? What lessons can be learned from the experience of the industry leaders who can point to concrete results from their marketing planning activities? Drawing on a study of the planning practices and results of 50 industrial companies, the author answers these questions and discusses the three principal causes of problems in putting marketing planning concepts into practice.

Corporate life would be a lot easier if management could forget or wish away the whole idea of formal marketing planning. For no one yet has been able to figure out how to get marketing plans into written form without a lot of hard work. But, if anything, this process is likely to become a more important management tool in the future as companies continue their scramble to add new products and markets to their base.

Consumer goods companies have relied increasingly on a formal marketing planning approach to focus and coordinate product strategies, and to map the tactics for sales and profit growth. Going through this discipline helps avoid the dumbbell mistakes that are bound to occur when one tries to ad lib his way to the marketplace with a complex product line.

Not surprisingly, many industrial goods companies have tried to follow suit. If marketing planning can sell more products to housewives, it ought to sell more tractors, more chemicals, or more electronic components to industrial customers. So reasoning, makers of industrial goods have set up sophisticated planning systems designed to gear their business more closely to the requirements of the marketplace.

Yet many—and perhaps even most—of these companies have found that this approach, which works so well for consumer goods makers, somehow loses its magic in the industrial marketing context. Too often, their top executives are sadly disappointed in the results of costly and time-consuming planning efforts. The comment of one vice president is typical:

"We knock ourselves out every year with a major time commitment and massive paper flow to put a plan for the business together that is heavily based on marketing input. But we can't really point to any substantive benefits that are directly traceable to all the extra effort. As I see it, our marketing group has not done the planning job it should. If it had, we'd have a lot stronger edge in the marketplace. At this point I am not sure whether it is something important that we ought to do better or whether it is just a fad that we ought to get rid of."

Why should his reaction be the rule rather than the exception? Why should the concepts that work so well in consumer goods companies be so difficult to apply successfully in the industrial field? Is it really fair to blame the marketing function when planning results fall short of expectations? Most important, what lessons can be learned from the experience of those few industrial companies which can honestly point to concrete results from their marketing planning activities?

These are the questions that a project team from McKinsey & Company set out to answer through a study of the planning practices and their effectiveness in 50 industrial companies. The names of these companies cannot be disclosed, but since they are all large, multidivision businesses listed in *Fortune's* "500," they can be presumed to have all the necessary skills and sophistication to do an effective planning job. In carrying out this project, the team worked directly with general managers and marketing executives of each of the participating companies to get a comprehensive picture of where marketing planning fits into the management process, what approaches are being followed, which are working, and which are not.

Practitioners' Pitfalls

Ignorance of planning theory or mechanics is not the cause of the disappointments so many companies are experiencing. Most of the executives we talked to—in both line and staff positions—were well aware that effective planning (a) depends on market and economic facts, (b) focuses on points of leverage, and (c) results in operating programs, not just budgets. Few executives appeared to be at all mystified by formal planning concepts. These concepts have of course received their share of emphasis in business literature and the academic world in past years, and apparently most executives have learned their lessons well.

Yet major problems crop up when companies set about putting these concepts into practice. Our study findings strongly suggest that these problems fall into three categories:

▢ Failure to fit the concept to the industrial context.
▢ Overemphasis on the system at the expense of content.

□ Nonrecognition of alternative strategies.

Let us examine each of the problem categories a bit more closely before moving on to see what vital steps have been taken by those participating companies which have successfully applied marketing planning in the industrial context.

FAILURE TO FIT CONCEPT

To a large extent, the disappointing results encountered by industrial companies reflect their failure to realize that the concept of marketing planning cannot be borrowed intact from consumer goods companies and applied successfully to their particular situation. Large industrial companies have two distinguishing characteristics that set them apart and dictate the need for a different planning approach.

The first is the multiplicity of markets and channels in which they operate, each requiring a discrete marketing strategy. A consumer goods company typically markets its several brands through one or two channels, but a multiproduct industrial manufacturer is likely to sell in a wide range of different markets through a variety of channels. For example, one electrical equipment company which participated in our study sold one of its major product lines in 30 distinct markets through several different channels. The company had been trying to cover this complex network of markets and channels with a single marketing plan; what was actually needed was 30 separate marketing plans.

Juggling a large number of markets and channels is not the only feat an industrial marketing department must perform. The second distinguishing characteristic is that the marketing department must also plan around the constraints imposed by other functions, since marketing simply does not control the factors that make or break performance in the marketplace. In the industrial world, marketing success depends largely on the activities of other functions, such as engineering, manufacturing, and technical service. This means, in turn, that changes in marketing strategy are likely to be based on product design, cost, or service innovations. Contrast this with a consumer goods company, where advertising, promotion, and merchandising are generally the core elements of the marketing plan.

Since the success of marketing plans is dependent on activities in other functional areas and on the share of total company resources each product/market business receives, it is unrealistic to expect product managers, market managers, or even the head of marketing to handle the job without the full participation of corporate and operating managers throughout the process.

Thus the role of the marketing planner in an industrial company is significantly different from that of his counterpart in consumer goods.

Rather than developing self-contained marketing plans, he analyzes and interprets market requirements so that top and operating management can decide how best to respond.

Obvious as this point might seem, it is frequently overlooked in industrial companies. Having embraced formal marketing planning as a sophisticated way of running the business, many executives try to implement the concept by turning the entire job over to marketing. After a couple of years of frustration, they are ready to write off marketing planning as a monumental waste of time. The real cause of their disappointment lies not in the concept, however, but in the way it has been applied.

For example, one major chemical company added a group of six industry planning managers to its marketing organization. Once on board, each was given a marketing planning format to follow and was told to develop a written plan for achieving a stronger and more profitable position in his assigned markets. All six men, eager to earn their spurs, embarked on a massive fact-gathering and writing effort. After several months, hundreds of pages of plans and supporting documentation had been written, but no one in top management was much impressed. The president put it this way:

"I'm being generous when I say the end products are only slightly better than useless. Admittedly, we have some better market facts now, but the plans are based on a lot of ideas for product and market development that just aren't in line with my idea of the direction this business should take. On top of that, they've left out a lot of technical and capital considerations that really count. I've concluded that our industry managers are simply too far out of the mainstream of the business to do an intelligent job of planning for us."

Not surprisingly, the industry managers felt that they too had good cause for complaint. As one of them put it:

"The first month of effort was worthwhile. We were putting a fact base together that is essential for intelligent planning. But after that we were flying blind. We never had any idea from top management on the kind of business the company wanted or didn't want, the minimal return it expected, or the kind of support it would be willing to throw into various markets. Worse still, we had no cooperation from the development group or the plants, where decisions are made that really control the business. The planning we did was bound to be a bust."

Unfortunately, this kind of situation has occurred in a great many otherwise well-managed companies. And instead of building marketing planning solidly into the management process, far too much of it is carried on as a parallel activity that gets plenty of lip service but little real attention from the decision makers.

OVEREMPHASIS ON SYSTEM

During the past several years, makers of industrial goods have put more and more effort into committing plans to writing for their various product/ market businesses. Many companies have developed comprehensive planning systems that lay out formats and procedures in great detail. Although some of this structure is unquestionably necessary, we saw a number of cases where the system was so detailed and so highly structured that it acted as a hindrance rather than a help to the planning process. In effect, the system serves as the end product rather than the means to an end.

Of all the problems described to us, this one drew the most vehement reactions from executives. They recognize that good planning is hard work and cannot be done without a certain amount of pencil pushing. But they bitterly resent demands for excessive writing that serves no practical business purpose. A product manager for an electronic equipment manufacturer voiced this complaint:

"As part of my planning responsibility, I have to follow a format prescribed by the corporate planning group that calls for a point-by-point discussion of history and a laundry list of problems and opportunities. I'm 'gigged' if I don't cover every point in the format, and there's no way to do it in less than 10 pages of text. That takes a lot of time—mostly wasted time. All the product managers are sore about it. Much of what we have to write is a rehash of the same old things year after year. In effect, we're being discouraged from concentrating on the aspects of the business that are really critical. What they want to see, apparently, is a nice, neat set of plans that all look alike. It just doesn't make sense."

The study team encountered a great number of similar situations and comments. As a rule, someone or some group had designed an overstructured and overdetailed planning system that was out of phase with the realities of the business. Typically, the resulting paper work chewed up great blocks of precious time without producing anything more than a codification of what would have been done anyway.

NONRECOGNITION OF ALTERNATIVES

In company after company, when we compared the plans that were developed for a particular product or market over several years, we were surprised to see how many planners had tunnel vision in thinking about how the business should be run. In fact, so many plans were based on nothing more than straight-line extrapolation of the past and on repetition of prior programs that they seemed hardly worth the paper they were written on.

This tendency to base current plans on past programs was forced into the open in one company when each planner was asked by top management to outline alternative strategies for developing his assigned market area and to summarize the commitments (e.g., financial, manpower, facilities) required and the payoff expected (sales, profits, ROI). The request drew a complete blank. The planners were so locked into their accustomed way of thinking about their markets that they could not conceive of a different approach that made any commercial sense at all.

Insufficient or less-than-candid analysis is a prime cause of unimaginative planning. Many planners either misjudge or fail to understand the underlying economics of the business or the changes going on in the marketplace (e.g., competitive moves, shifts in usage or demand patterns) that call for alternative strategies. Many planners also appear reluctant to face up to unpleasant truths about their competitive situation—such as high price, low product quality, or poor service—that place the company in an untenable marketing position. Without a thorough, candid appraisal of the business climate, the need for fresh ways of running the business goes unrecognized. Thus, instead of getting a choice among alternatives, top management has to content itself with a single recommendation which usually calls for the continuation of stale or imitative strategies.

Imaginative Insights

Considering that the whole purpose of formal planning is to conceive more imaginative ways of developing the business, the record so far is pretty dismal. Yet the experience of the handful of participating companies which have successfully applied marketing planning in the industrial context provides some encouragement and some useful insights. Without exception, these companies have taken the necessary steps to avoid the pitfalls just described. And they are now concentrating on developing marketing-oriented plans for their businesses that are part and parcel of the management process of each company. Our study indicates that they have reached this level of sophistication primarily because of three factors:

◻ Better definition and direction from the top.
◻ Development of fact-founded product/market strategies.
◻ Superior programming for strategy implementation.

The balance of this article will consider each of these vital factors and how they can lead to better ways of doing things and to improved results when applied in the industrial marketing context.

BETTER DEFINITION AND DIRECTION

The marketing planning done in leader companies produces results because it is carried out with full recognition of the multiplicity of products, markets, and channels, and the need for a technical, rather than a sales or merchandising, orientation. As one president in our survey commented:

"It took me three years to realize that our marketing people couldn't come up with the kind of plans I wanted for our products and markets unless I worked closely with them. They have always been able to develop a picture of where our markets are heading, identify the opportunities that exist, and interpret what we have to do to build the business. But so many considerations and options require a general management perspective that marketing can't be expected to come up with recommendations that make sense from my point of view. Unless I set the basic direction for our business, specify who is to plan what, see to it that engineering and manufacturing really work with marketing to provide what is needed, and then challenge and contribute any ideas I can on how our business can be developed, the whole planning effort is nothing more than a paper-work exercise."

Let us look at this comment more closely, for it underscores the four ways in which top management must participate in marketing planning to make it pay off.

1. *Specify corporate objectives:* Throughout our study, inadequate direction from the top was a common complaint from planners. "If only top management would tell me what they want!" I am sure we heard a hundred variations on this theme. A few of these men no doubt would like top management to spell everything out for them in detail, and they are using its failure to do so as an excuse for their own inability to do the planning job.

Nevertheless, top management guidelines that spell out the rules of the game are unquestionably a necessity for anyone who holds a marketing planning responsibility. At a minimum, these guidelines should include definite long-range growth targets or a statement of corporate objectives that expresses in specific terms how fast top management wants the business to grow, what products and markets should be emphasized, what kinds of businesses should be avoided, and what profit returns are acceptable. These guidelines do not have to be expressed with precision, and they are certainly not immutable. But without some definition like this, product/market planners will be working in a vacuum, and they will almost inevitably come up with marketing plans that are out of phase with top management's interests and objectives.

2. *Determine organization arrangements:* It is an important step in any company to determine organization arrangements, but it is particularly vital in a large-scale industrial complex with its numerous product/market

Exhibit I. Organization shift to provide capital goods company with better planning focus

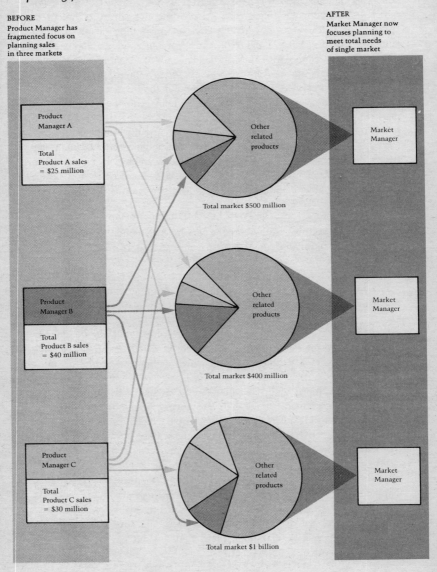

BEFORE

Product Manager has fragmented focus on planning sales in three markets

AFTER

Market Manager now focuses planning to meet total needs of single market

Product Manager A

Total Product A sales = $25 million

Product Manager B

Total Product B sales = $40 million

Product Manager C

Total Product C sales = $30 million

Other related products

Total market $500 million

Other related products

Total market $400 million

Other related products

Total market $1 billion

Market Manager

Market Manager

Market Manager

businesses. Since marketing planning requirements vary so widely from business to business, there is no one organization that is valid for all companies. Nor is the same organization necessarily valid for all time. Leader companies understand the importance of appraising and reappraising organization arrangements to make sure that the planners have the right focus and that their roles are clearly understood by everyone in the organization.

For example, the marketing organization in a capital goods company had traditionally been structured around products—that is, the product managers were responsible for planning the growth and profits of each of their major product lines (see left column in *Exhibit I*). Obliged to sell to three distinct markets, each product manager was spread so thin that he could not do a thorough job of planning for any one of them. Also, since his focus was on his product lines, he was blinded to the broader needs of the individual markets.

Management soon recognized that this traditional organization arrangement greatly restricted the company's ability to plan for development of the total market. Therefore, to provide the market orientation it wanted, the company restructured its organization around the market managers, who were responsible for identifying and planning to meet all the needs of their assigned markets (see right column in *Exhibit I*).

This example is not meant to suggest that market managers will do a better job of planning for a company than product managers. But it does demonstrate how important it is for top management to think through the planning objectives and requirements for each business, and then to design an organization structure that will provide the right focus.

3. *Provide interfunctional coordination:* Even the most carefully conceived marketing organization structure will fail unless the marketing planners (a) work effectively with the other functions that influence the performance of a business in the marketplace, and (b) command the respect of their functional counterparts. And all concerned must have a clear understanding of how they are expected to work together. This is especially important in industrial companies, for without interfunctional coordination the planners do not stand a chance.

A manufacturer in the building products field set up a product planning group in its marketing organization to spearhead the marketing planning for each product area. During the first two years of the group's existence, the plans developed fell far short of everyone's expectations, and there was much friction between the planning group and other functions.

One of the product planning managers put his finger on the problem when he pointed out the many functions other than marketing and sales he had to work with to do a good planning job. Much of the difficulty he encountered, he said, stemmed from misunderstanding on the part of many functional managers about how the marketing planning job was to be done. Even the product planning managers themselves, he added, were unsure about their responsibilities.

Recognizing the need to put the product planning group on a more sound footing for dealing with other functions, the marketing vice president took three steps. He decided first to replace four of the five product planning managers, who were basically sales-oriented, with men who had stronger technical backgrounds and better grasp of the business as a whole. He then eliminated the position of group product planning managers—putting the product planning managers on an organization par with their major contacts in other functional areas. Since they had a broader understanding of the business, they were able to communicate more effectively. Even more important, as a result of the reorganization, they now reported directly to the head of marketing and, therefore, were in close touch with top management thinking.

Finally, the marketing head persuaded the president of the company to hold a meeting with the executives of all major functions to explain what the product planning managers were trying to accomplish and how the different functions should work with them. At this meeting, the president made it clear that he was looking to the product planning managers to develop plans geared to the characteristics and requirements of the marketplace:

"We are going to bank everything on their interpretation of where the market is heading and what we must do internally to respond to market needs. I expect all functions to cooperate with our marketing planners and follow their lead completely. If we don't operate along these lines, all of our talk about being a market-oriented company is just a lot of hot air."

This no-nonsense statement on the role of marketing cleared away any misconceptions blocking effective interaction between the product planning managers and other functions.

4. *Contribute to marketing plans:* If top management truly wants to find ways of improving profits and growth, it must actively participate in the development of marketing plans by challenging their underlying assumptions and by contributing alternative ideas on strategy and programs. To be sure, most top executives try to do this; but the way they do it often stifles rather than encourages new ideas. They must take pains to avoid any atmosphere of an inquisition and, instead, must stimulate open exchange of ideas and opinions.

In such an environment one idea leads to another, and the management team soon finds itself exploring new and imaginative ways of developing the business. An interfunctional give-and-take discussion like this led a heavy machinery manufacturer to adopt a new market strategy that gave its parts operation a chance for survival. Consider:

In this company, as in many others, parts sales had traditionally been a major source of profits. Now management was concerned because "parts pirates" (local parts producers) were cutting sharply into their business. Asked to develop a marketing strategy that would reverse the trend, the parts manager first came up with a plan that called for adding three salesmen and cutting prices on a large number of parts to be more competitive. As he acknowledged, his plan was essentially no more than a holding action.

During the planning review session in which all functions took part, the company president encouraged everyone to take an entrepreneurial look at the parts business and to try to think of ways to preserve or even enlarge it. Predictably, fresh ideas were hard to come by in a business that had been run the same way for years. But eventually three embryonic ideas emerged that were considered worthwhile: (1) Build a service organization and sell contracts for maintenance service instead of just parts; (2) decentralize the parts business and set up local parts and repair shops to compete head to head with local competitors; and (3) start to buy and sell parts for other manufacturers' equipment in order to spread overhead costs.

The parts manager was naturally somewhat reluctant to do any of these things, since they would revolutionize his end of the business. But with top management backing and encouragement, he did the required analytical work and came back with alternative strategies, based on the first two ideas, that offered a much more attractive outlook.

Of course, to think that this process always leads to a more viable product/market strategy would be a foolhardy assumption. It is not always possible to overcome the scarcity of fresh ideas characteristic of a business run the same way for years. Moreover, alternative strategies are not always available. But the more successful companies insist that their planners seek out alternative strategies and avoid getting locked into a self-defeating "business as usual" pattern of thinking.

This kind of give-and-take among marketing, top management, and other functions is really the heart of the planning process. For it is during these discussions that marketing presents the requirements of the marketplace and the other functions discuss feasible ways of responding to them. With all the opportunities and constraints out in the open, top management has a good basis for deciding how to allocate corporate resources. Once the best combination of ideas is agreed on, the various functions are

Exhibit II. Forces likely to affect industrial company's market position and outlook

A. Identifying points of leverage

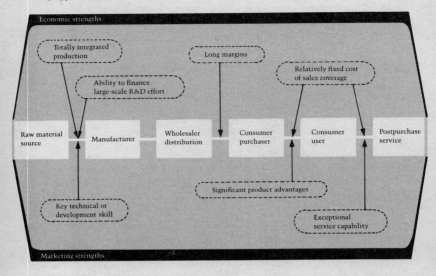

B. Identifying points of vulnerability

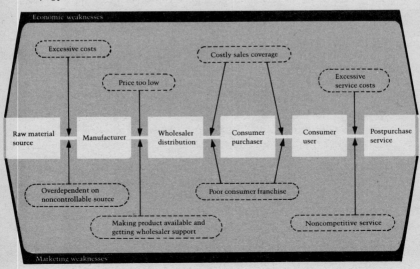

then in a position to make commitments on the timing and costs of the alternative actions that underlie the marketing plan. Leader company executives insist this is the best vehicle for triggering fresh ideas and ensuring interfunctional coordination.

FACT-FOUNDED STRATEGIES

The marketing planning done by leader companies is aimed at the development of strategies for each product/market business realistically tied to market and economic facts. Once developed, these strategies point the way for each present business, serve as underpinning for overall corporate long-range planning, and provide direction for programming key activities and projects in all functional areas.

Strategy development is an art few companies have mastered. Those that have this expertise stress the need for comprehensive knowledge of the economics of the business and the trends of the market. More specifically, this means that planners need to know the economics of their competitors as well as of their own businesses—that is, where value is added, how costs behave with changes in volume, where assets are committed, and so on. To complete their understanding, planners must also know how the market is structured and what forces are likely to affect the company's market position and outlook.

With this understanding, planners can recognize points of leverage where the company can exercise an advantage, as well as points where the company might be vulnerable to competitive thrusts. *Exhibit II* illustrates what some of these points of leverage or vulnerability might be in a typical industrial operation.

One outstanding company built a marketing strategy for its major product line on just this sort of understanding. The planners in this company, which I shall call Company A, recognized that they were operating in a slow-growth business, offering a commodity product for which demand was highly inelastic. They therefore concluded that (a) it would not make sense to sacrifice short-term profits to build a larger share position, since the value of a share point would not increase enough to pay off such an investment, and (b) although price is an important consideration in market share, it would not influence total demand.

This market analysis brought a further important trend to light: Company A was losing market position to the strong second-place factor in the industry, Company B. As no other important shifts in market share had occurred, Company A concluded that its marketing strategy should be aimed first and foremost at reversing its losses to Company B.

Next, the planners at Company A compared their own profit structure with that of Company B to find the weaknesses and strengths of the

Exhibit III. *Comparative analysis of two competitive companies*

[Dollar figures in millions]

Economic indicators	Companies A	Companies B	Conclusions
Current dollar sales	$403	$146	A's sales volume is roughly twice B's
Breakeven point	$217	$121	B's breakeven point is lower, but B is operating much closer to breakeven than A
Contribution margin rate (sales dollars less variable costs)	48%	45%	Contribution margin rates are about the same
Contribution loss from 5 percentage point drop in unit margin	$20	$7.3	However, because of differences in dollar volume, Company A stands to lose far more marginal income than B by lowering unit margin
Volume gain to offset 5 percentage point drop in unit margin	$46.5	$18.2	Thus, the volume needed to offset a 5 percentage point drop in unit margin would be much greater for Company A
Equivalent share point gain	7.0 pts.	2.8 pts.	

two companies. Their analysis produced the information shown in *Exhibit III.* (Admittedly, obtaining information of this sort about competitors is unquestionably tough. No one is going to hand it to you, and it is not likely to be available in published material. But bits of data on competitor sales and capacity levels can be pieced together from annual reports, newspaper articles, and trade and government publications. By combining such data with one's own experience, conservative assumptions can be made about competitor costs and efficiency to complete the picture.)

By the time the planners in Company A had completed this comparative analysis, they were in a position to predict what Company B's strategy was likely to be. This is what they thought Company B would do, assuming that B knew its own market and economic position:

□ Cut prices on the products competitive with Company A's highest volume products to upset price stability and to force Company A to retaliate or give up volume.

□ Add new industrial distributors by giving larger discounts, and go after Company A's distributors in prime markets.

□ Emphasize development of lower-cost products, thereby gaining more flexibility to compete on a price basis.

Starting from these assumptions, the planners in Company A proceeded to develop a counter-strategy. These were its key points:

□ Avoid going for volume on a price basis or by adding to unit costs.

□ Hold a firm price line with distributors—even at the risk of losing share in the most price-sensitive markets.

□ Build the marketing program around the changes in costs which are nonvariable with volume—e.g., upgrading and enlarging the sales force, strengthening distributor programs, and improving the physical distribution and warehousing network.

A superficial review of the situation would undoubtedly have led the planners to come up with quite a different strategy. For, in view of the high contribution rate and apparent profit leverage on volume, the most obvious strategy would have been to cut price to counteract any aggressive pricing actions of Company B. Instead, Company A planners decided to avoid price concessions or any actions that would raise unit costs. They recommended concentrating on marketing programs where costs could be amortized over their much larger unit volume and on other programs that would reduce their cost base. Management agreed, reasoning that this strategy would enable the company to lead from strength rather than play into the hands of its major competitor.

The details of Company A's strategy may be open to dispute. In themselves, however, they are not important. The purpose of the example is to show how a penetrating analysis of market and economic facts can provide a reasoned basis for strategy development. This is the process by which sophisticated planners are gaining significant advantages over their competitors, and it is easy to see the three reasons why:

1. Planners can help focus management attention on actions that really count in the marketplace and make sure that these are based on facts and judgment, not hunch or opinion.

2. They can adopt an aggressive posture instead of having to rely on retaliation or defensive maneuvers.

3. They can minimize the impact of surprise competitive moves by developing alternative contingency plans.

SUPERIOR PROGRAMMING

Everybody goes through the motions of programming, but leader companies follow three ground rules that enable them to do a superior job of strategy implementation.

First, management will approve no major program or project that is not inextricably linked to a product/market strategy. This approach may sound a little stuffy, but it makes eminently good sense, for there is really no way to evaluate a program's usefulness without the background of a product/market strategy. Moreover, the linkage keeps the functional areas of a business working together for a common purpose and prevents them from being sidetracked on functionally interesting activities that lack commercial relevance.

Second, management makes some sort of organization provision for follow-through on major programs, particularly those that cut across functional lines. In some cases, they have enlarged the role of their product managers. In others, they have set up a task force with responsibility for following a program through to completion.

Take, for example, the case of an industrial controls producer we surveyed. When it became clear that the company's product line had slipped behind competitors', the management team saw that holding market position would require a complete redesign of the product line, both to improve performance characteristics and to take out cost.

Even though the bulk of the actual work had to be done by engineering and manufacturing, the president pulled the responsible product manager out of the marketing department, placed him directly under his wing, and made him fully accountable for coordinating and pushing the program through to completion. As the president told us:

"This program can make or break us in the marketplace. It's so vital to us I'd watch over it myself if I could let some other things slip. Since I can't, I want someone to do it for me, and the product manager is the logical one to do it. I know I'm stretching his role somewhat in giving him this assignment, and I know some noses are going to be out of joint in engineering and manufacturing, but the job is too important not to have a full-time program manager."

This is one way of shepherding a crucial program. As discussed, there are others; but the objective is always to ensure interfunctional coordination for all major programs and to break through any obstacles to successful completion.

Third, leader companies see to it that the detailed steps involved in major programs are mapped out in such a way that performance can be measured against these individual steps. For some time, of course, companies in the aerospace, military electronics, construction, and other industries have been using network scheduling techniques (e.g., PERT, RAMPS) to control large and complex projects. Now, however, a few industrial goods makers are applying similar techniques to ensure interfunctional coordination on a wide variety of programs that affect market performance, since they permit management to flag potential problem areas and initiate corrective action before the program slips or gets off track.

In one company, the program for introducing a new line of flow meters was broken down into 25 steps over an 18-month span. The first step was a kick-off meeting between R&D, engineering, manufacturing, and marketing to define performance and cost requirements. Subsequent steps tracked the new product idea through development, manufacture, and market launching. Each week management received a report showing whether scheduled steps had been completed and, if not, where the bottleneck was. This feedback made it much easier to trace problems to their source for corrective action. Said the president: "The program is too important to us to rely for control on typical accounting reports. They simply tell us after the fact whether we won or lost. They're no help when it comes to making sure the program doesn't collapse."

It would be absurd to structure every program in so much detail. But detailed planning is essential for effective control over major programs that involve many functions and require tight scheduling and careful adherence in order to achieve profit and market objectives.

In Summary

Formal marketing planning can undoubtedly make a real contribution to the performance of any industrial company, just as it has in consumer goods companies. But if marketing planning is to have real impact on the industrial side, it will have to be adapted much more closely to the particular requirements of the business. This demands much less emphasis on the system—that is, format, sophisticated techniques, and lengthy writing assignments. Instead, the whole focus must be on achieving substantive improvements in thinking and actions through tough-minded analysis, continual interchange between marketing and technical executives, and more top management inputs. This is the only approach that can really lead to better ways of doing things and to improved results, thus making the formal marketing planning process something more than a costly facade.

6. Get the Most Out of Your Sales Force

Derek A. Newton

Sales management practice is like Topsy—it just grew. Each sales executive tends to work out his own style of managing from the assortment of principles he inherits from his predecessor, the customs of the industry in which he is operating, his own ideas, the expressed preferences of his corporate superiors, and so on. There has been a signal lack of method in this vital and challenging area of management. The research results presented in this article represent a considerably more scientific approach to the problem. By querying a large sample of companies on their practices and then matching the responses with indicators of high success, the author has derived a useful set of management guidelines for each of the major kinds of selling activity he has considered.

The typical sales executive does a lot of wondering about his sales force, not only about what they are doing "out there," but about his own management practices. Is he deploying his men correctly? How good are the selection and training procedures? Are controls sufficient? Is he paying his men too little or too much? His goals are good performance and low turnover on the selling staff; in order to achieve them he must find the right men and get the most out of them, and obtain their loyalty so that he can keep them. How can he best do this?

Advice for the sales executive in that dilemma has had to be pretty vague up to now. I have completed a research project, however, which sheds considerable light on the problem of improving performance and reducing turnover in the sales force. This study was designed to answer four specific questions:

1. How does the selling task to be performed differ for each of the main kinds of selling that are done today; and do these differences call for differences in management approach?

2. What management practices increase performance for each kind of selling?

3. What practices decrease turnover?

4. How are performance and turnover related to one another?

The study reports the responses of 1,029 sales executives to a questionnaire designed to probe management practices and to measure performance and turnover. Of the 1,029 respondents, 75% identified themselves as working at the level of general sales manager or higher. The sample comprised many kinds of manufacturing, wholesaling, and service businesses.

Four Kinds of Selling

In one sense, the very variety of companies represented in this sample constitutes a stumbling block. A specialized sample, on the other hand, would probably lead only to specialized conclusions. As it happens, pretests of the questionnaire indicated that one can effectively isolate four basic styles of selling that cut across industry boundaries to a large degree, and I shall present the results in this article in the context of these four basic styles:

1. Trade selling.
2. Missionary selling.
3. Technical selling.
4. New-business selling.

Each sales executive queried was asked to specify the primary responsibility of his force—whether it was trade, missionary, technical, or new-business selling. The responses showed that the breakdown of the total sample was fairly even among these four categories.

But before I discuss each of these four kinds of selling in detail, I shall explain the indexes that were used to measure performance and turnover, and present eight findings that apply to the entire sample, regardless of classification.

MEASUREMENTS

The questionnaire gathered data for a two-year period. From these data, several quantitative measurements were derived for each of the responding organizations.

Turnover rate: This quantity is the number of salesmen who quit or were discharged from a company divided by the average size of the company's sales force during the two-year period. (This is the same formula as that used by the Bureau of Labor Statistics.) While this formula has some disadvantages, it has the signal advantages of being simple, easily understood, and widely used.

Performance index: This quantity is the rate of growth of sales divided by the rate of growth of sales force. It represents the increase in sales volume per salesman over the two-year period—if you will, the increase in per-man productivity.

The reader may wonder why I did not measure performance directly, by change in sales volume. The reason for this ought to be obvious: factors other than sales force performance bear on changes in sales volume—industry growth rates, mergers and acquisitions, market conditions, management efficiency and marketing efficiency, and so on—and these factors are largely beyond the control of the sales force executive. The executive *does* control the rate of growth of his sales force, however, and I have therefore used this rate as the divisor in the index to counteract the effects of "outside" influences on changes in sales volume. This index reflects the quality of management practices more accurately than mere change in sales volume.

This performance index has its advantages and limitations. For example, while it does reward companies that increase sales faster than they increase manpower, it has the effect of penalizing the company that must temporarily deploy many salesmen to achieve an increase in market coverage. Still, the responses to the questionnaire show that the sales executive judges his own performance along a dimension parallel to this index; that is, the index was high for those companies whose executives thought that their forces were performing well, and the index was low for those companies that thought their forces were performing poorly.

Compensation rates: Compensation rates were tabulated for each company within each of the four sales classifications for the average-, highest-, and lowest-paid salesman. By comparing these data with performance and turnover rates for each company, it was possible to determine how much a salesman working on a given kind of sales force ought to be paid. Conversely, it indicated how high a level of performance and how low a rate of turnover the sales executive ought to expect for paying his men a given amount. The questionnaire also elicited information on methods of compensation—the mixture of straight salary, commission, and bonus that produces the best results in each kind of selling task.

Span of control: This quantity is the average number of salesmen on a force divided by the average number of field supervisors. As we shall see, high performance and low turnover correlate with different spans of control for each of the four sales classifications.

Opportunity rate: The percentage of men transferred out and promoted from the sales force measures advancement opportunity. The specific findings indicate that the sales executive should be careful to see that this rate of opportunity is neither too high nor too low, and the data collected suggest the optimal range for each sales classification.

Earnings opportunity ratio (EOR): This is the ratio of the compensation of the highest-paid salesman on a sales force to that of the average-paid salesman. Extremely high or low ratios correlate with high turnover. For a reason I shall explain later, the executive ought to keep an eye on this quantity as well.

Eight Major Findings

The digested data from the study exhibit eight strong conclusions that apply to all the sales force classifications alike.

1. *The turnover rate of a sales force does not directly influence its performance index.*

High performance, in other words, is just as likely to be accompanied by high turnover as by low; and the same is true for low performance.

2. *A turnover rate of 10% or more is excessively costly in all classifications, and should be avoided if possible.*

The extra costs associated with turnover, such as interruption of customers' ordering routines, and its less tangible costs, such as the disruption of customer-salesman rapport, are obvious evils. But the executive ought to look beyond these obvious considerations to a much more important one: according to the data, the factor discriminating most strongly between sales forces that are expensive to operate and those that are economical is the level of hiring activity. Hence low turnover is likely to mean a low-cost sales force, and the executive who wants a low-cost force should therefore devote a good deal of his attention to his hiring practices.

3. *The turnover rate is directly influenced by the opportunity rate.*

Sales forces which exhibit opportunity rates in excess of 6% are likely to be plagued by high turnover. I think this fact is explained easily enough: an opportunity rate of 6% or more suggests that the company is using the sales force as a convenient training ground for future marketing managers and supervisory sales personnel, and many applicants will be drawn to such sales forces by the prospect of advancement rather than by the appeal of sales work per se. But selling per se is their main function; and when management becomes aware of any lack of commitment to sales work on the part of its salesmen, it is likely to pass them over, thus inducing them to quit in disgust. In some cases, no doubt, management simply fires them.

4. Turnover is also directly influenced by compensation level.

Sales forces that have low average pay scales exhibit high turnover. It is not equally true, on the other hand, that high pay means low turnover. Paying one's best salesman overgenerously is ineffective in reducing turnover (of course, there may be other, valid reasons for tolerating a high EOR). The data show that an EOR greater than 2.0 in any sales force tends to drive up costs without reducing turnover.

5. The compensation level, however, does not directly influence the performance index, although the method of compensation does.

Once the executive has satisfied himself that his force's compensation level is on a par with the competition's, he ought to check carefully to see that the balance of fixed salary, commission, and bonus is "right" for the psychological temper of his crew. We shall look into the various payment mixes which are appropriate to each of the sales force classifications later in the article.

6. The performance index is directly influenced by the character and effectiveness of the reporting system used to control the force.

The universal characteristic of the high-performance force is that its management *insists* on receiving the frequent and regular reports that are critical to controlling sales force behavior. Because different kinds of reporting are critical to different kinds of forces, and because insistence on excessive reporting boosts the turnover rate rapidly, the sales executive must be extremely careful to identify the truly critical and necessary reports and play down or eliminate all others. The study identifies the specific reports that are critical for success in trade and technical selling; for the rest, the executive must use his own good judgment.

These six results are augmented by some discoveries about two other key quantities investigated by the questionnaire.

7. Average chronological age differs among the four sales force classifications, but for each classification there is an optimal average age.

For example, a "younger" force typically has high turnover, but also has abundant energy. Hence it may perform highly where energy is a major requisite. On the other hand, an "older" force has more maturity and stability, and is likely to perform best where these characteristics are most useful.

8. Job content is a critical factor affecting performance and turnover.

The kind of challenge in a particular selling job and the actual work which the salesman is called on to do determine the kind of man the executive ought to hire. This is primary. Once he has the kind of men that he wants, he must then *match his management practice to the men in their jobs.*

Let's take a careful look, now, at each of the four basic kinds of selling jobs that I studied and see (a) what kinds of men are required for each, and (b) how the executive ought to handle his men once he has them.

Trade Selling

The primary responsibility of the trade sales force is to build up the volume of a company's sales to its customers by providing them with *promotional assistance.* This generally amounts to improving the company's distribution channels, or, where the customer is himself a manufacturer, helping him to become a more effective seller. The trade sales force therefore "sells *through,*" rather than "sells *to,*" its customers.

Trade selling is a feature of many industries, but it predominates in food, textiles, apparel, and wholesaling. Products sold in this way tend to be well established; hence a company's selling effort, as such, is often less important than its advertising and promotion efforts. Much of this kind of selling is low-key, and the trade salesman is not as highly pressured from above as are his cousins in new-business sales, for example; but his job can easily become dull and repetitious if he has to do too much shelf-stocking or too much order-taking. The good trade salesman must be helpful and persuasive, and must thoroughly understand how the customer runs his business. Aggressiveness is less important than maturity, and technical competence is often less important than "wearing well" with customers.

Managers of high-performance forces appear to recognize many of the requirements and limitations of this kind of sales activity. For example, the high-performance groups in trade selling are older. *Exhibit I* compares the average ages of salesmen in the four classifications, and shows the average age of the highest- and lowest-performance quintiles in each. Maturity is quite evident in the highest-performance quintile in trade selling, as it is in the highest-performance quintile in new-business sales.

While maturity may be desirable here, seniority is not necessarily so. The study data exhibit no such useful correlation between seniority and turnover, for example. Turnover is largely a phenomenon of the first few years on the job; in other words, the longer a man has been with a company, the less likely he is to quit or be discharged. But turnover is also a function of chronological age: the younger the force, the higher the turnover. Age and job turnover are in fact so strongly interrelated that observations about the impact of seniority on turnover are pointless.

Exhibit I. The impact of average age on performance

Age of salesmen	Trade force performance by quintile			Missionary force performance by quintile		
	Highest	Average	Lowest	Highest	Average	Lowest
Less than 30 years old	18.8%*	19.7%	23.7%	22.2%	17.8%	13.1%
30-39 years old	32.4	35.0	39.6	31.9	34.4	37.9
40 years old or older	48.8	45.3	36.7	45.9	47.8	49.0

*Read: salesmen under 30 years of age account for 18.8% of the sales force personnel of firms within the highest-performance quintile, and so on.

The kind of comparison made in *Exhibit I*, when applied to other data from the study, provides a number of useful findings. In sketching out the guidelines presented in this article, my general method of analysis has been to find out what is "standard operating procedure" (i.e., average age of existing sales forces, average compensation, standard methods of pay, and so forth) and then to judge what variations in standard procedure conduce to a sales force showing performance in the highest quintile and turnover in the lowest quintile.

GUIDELINES

Obviously, the trade sales executive should do what he can to improve performance. Also, although turnover does not directly influence performance, it is expensive when it is excessive, and he should do what he can to hold it down. Note that the following recommendations do not involve any trading-off between performance goals and turnover goals; that is, the executive can apply them all without being forced to choose between improving performance and reducing turnover.

To begin with, the executive ought to give considerable thought to job content. Any action he can take to reduce drudgery or the salesman's lurking feeling that he is nothing but a pawn in a giant chess game will improve performance and reduce turnover. Therefore, the executive should:

□ Transfer salesmen among territories as infrequently as possible—except, of course, at their own request.

□ Design the sales-call pattern so that the salesman feels he is making important sales-related calls and not merely putting in appearances for

	Technical force performance by quintile				New-business force performance by quintile			Total-sample average
	Highest	Average	Lowest		Highest	Average	Lowest	
	18.1%	17.8%	13.9%		18.5%	22.1%	22.4%	19.2%
	39.4	37.2	39.4		32.7	34.8	39.9	35.6
	42.5	45.0	46.7		48.8	43.1	37.7	45.2

the sake of the company's image. On the average, the salesman should be given three to five chances a day to actually make a sale. Requiring more than five calls a day, even on regular accounts, is associated with high turnover.

□ Avoid asking the salesman to peddle "easy-to-buy" products—it makes him feel like a deliveryman. If a product line requires no persistence to sell it, then it may well not require a salesman at all.

The source of employees has more influence on turnover than the methods used to select applicants. Whereas the number of interviews, tests administered, and so forth do not appear to be associated with performance or turnover, companies that place heavy reliance on employment agencies and advertisements exhibit higher-than-average rates of turnover as well as disproportionately high sales force costs.

Compared with the industry grapevine and company initiative, for example, these methods of procuring applicants tend to be highly impersonal. Hiring applicants "off the street," so to speak, invites turnover trouble— which suggests that executives ought to know more than they do about their salesmen *before* they hire them.

So far as the composition of the sales force is concerned, as I have said, the balance tips in favor of the older salesman. Therefore, the executive should:

□ Use company contacts to seek out and hire salesmen in their forties or late thirties, and avoid placing heavy reliance on advertisements and employment agencies for recruitment.

The *amount* a salesman is paid appears to be an important factor in turnover, and the *method* by which he is paid appears to be an important factor in performance. The desirability of having the trade salesman view himself and his job as important to the company's marketing efforts and the influence of the size of a man's paycheck on his perception of himself indicate that generosity is called for in making compensation decisions about the trade sales force. Therefore, the executive should:

□ Make sure that, unless industry pay scales dictate otherwise, his lowest-paid salesman earns about $8,000 a year, his average salesman about $13,000, and his highest-paid salesman between $20,000 and $26,000.[1]

Quite surprisingly, the study data bearing on optimal methods of payment show that paying a low ratio of salary to commission works best. The practice of the high-performance, low-turnover forces suggests that the executive should:

□ Pay only about 60% of the average salesman's compensation in the form of fixed salary. (For every other sales force classification this proportion is 80%. That 60% works best here may surprise those executives who believe that, of the four classifications of salesmen, the salesman on the trade force has the least direct influence on sales volume. I was not prepared for this result myself. After all, trade sales volume is very heavily influenced by "outside" factors like promotion and advertising efforts; and it seems to follow that the trade salesman ought to receive a high proportion of his pay in fixed form. But consider the salesman's point of view. If he knows that a larger proportion of his pay is variable, this helps to offset his natural perception that his efforts are unimportant in comparison with his company's promotion and advertising; this increases his job satisfaction and thus improves his performance. Also, if he has the impression that he himself can really influence sales volume, he is less likely to get discouraged and quit. Thus a high proportion of variable pay tends to depress turnover as well.)

Close personal supervision, particularly for experienced salesmen, does little to improve performance and may—as a source of job dissatisfaction—encourage high turnover. Also, many salesmen appear to perceive quotas and paper work as childish or unnecessary. The study data support the conclusion that use of quotas merely boosts turnover and reduces performance. On the other hand, using an intelligent system of reporting to control the critical functions of the sales job improves performance and substitutes for close personal supervision. The data indicate that the executive should:

1. Dollar figures, here and elsewhere in the article, reflect what was reported at the time of the study; hence represent 1967 values.

□ Maintain a ratio of salesmen to field supervisors of around 12 to 1, depending on the proportion of inexperienced men in his sales force. (With a high proportion of experienced men, I would increase this span of control to 16 to 1.)

□ Avoid the use of personal sales quotas for salesmen.

□ Avoid requesting reports from salesmen except for those reports critical to controlling sales force behavior. (In these latter instances, the executive should *insist* on receiving them. For example, the *customer inventory report* is critical in trade sales.)

The company's training programs also significantly affect performance. Hence the executive should:

□ Compare in-house training effects with those of the successful competition. (In my study, high-performing forces use: less initial training and less classroom training, probably because they seek out better-qualified applicants; more on-the-job training for new men, to make sure of a smooth launching; and less on-the-job training for experienced men, a condition which probably reflects more acute management reporting controls.)

A company that uses the salesman's job as a training ground for marketing management careers may be inviting a turnover problem, as I have already stated. Therefore, the executive should:

□ Refrain from viewing the sales force assignment as a form of purgatory necessary for further advancement in the company. (Specifically, the executive should strive to keep the opportunity rate below 4%, perhaps partly by broadening the supervisory span of control and partly by reducing the number of management levels so as to make the sales organization as "horizontal" as possible.)

The general thrust of these recommendations for trade force management is twofold:

□ The executive must make the salesman perceive himself as an important element in his company's marketing strategy. To some extent, current trade force practice follows these recommendations. Trade sales executives, compared to executives in the other three classifications, emphasize commission compensation, and tend to design territories for equal earnings opportunities; they play down close personal supervision and opportunities for promotion, and avoid recruiting members of the sales force from agencies.

□ On the other hand, the executive must avoid some current trade force management practice which tends to defeat the goals as they have been stated here (and which, as a matter of fact, accounts for much of the lack of correlation between high performance and low turnover in the sample).

This practice—emphasizing use of personal sales quotas, maximizing the number of selling calls per day, and selling the easiest-to-buy items in the line—tends to undercut the importance of the total compensation that the salesman receives.

Following all these recommendations may pose problems for certain sales executives. To begin with, it is not always possible to have salesmen perceive themselves as important elements in the marketing strategy. In many companies, particularly the large, mass-distribution organizations, the salesman just is not very important, and no amount of telling him that he *is* important will offset his observation that advertising and promotion move the merchandise and he merely keeps the shelves stocked. If a company just needs someone to call on the dealers, if marketing management personnel need trade sales experience as training, and if the *real* sales activity must be restricted to a few executive salesmen who call on key customers—well, there may be no justification for making the changes necessary to attract and keep high-caliber trade salesmen.

In other companies, particularly the smaller ones for which the cost of operating the sales force is a significant percentage of the sales dollar, it may be difficult to invest the necessary money in salesman compensation to attract and keep high-caliber salesmen. High costs, however, appear to be more closely associated with high hiring levels than with high compensation levels. Here the small-company executive should pay very serious attention to his applicants.

Missionary Selling

The primary responsibility of the missionary force is to increase its company's sales volume by providing its direct customers with *personal selling assistance*. It performs this function by persuading its indirect customers to purchase company products through these direct customers—distribution channels, wholesalers, and so forth. The familiar "medical detail man," who calls on doctors as the representative of a pharmaceutical house, is a typical example of the missionary.

Like trade selling, missionary selling is low-key, but it differs in its primary objective; the missionary force "sells *for*" its direct customers, whereas the trade force "sells *through*" them. Responses to the questionnaire indicate that this type of selling is common in many industry categories—especially so in foods, chemicals, transportation and warehousing, wholesaling, and the utilities.

Good coverage of the market and the ability to make a succinct, yet persuasive, presentation of product benefits is vitally important in missionary

Exhibit II. Average performance index by frequency of transfer and by number of calls to produce an order from a new customer

	Number of companies	Average performance index
Frequency of transfer		
Never	33	102.9
Seldom	105	108.2
Occasionally	54	109.3
Calls required		
One	12	110.3
Two or three	57	108.0
Four or five	56	109.2
Six to ten	27	99.6
Eleven or more	17	105.8

sales. One missionary executive refers to his salesmen as "animated direct mail." This term is perhaps a bit harsh. Nevertheless, the missionary salesman tends to be more a communicator and persuader than a problem-solver.

This observation is supported by the relationships between the performance index and (a) the number of calls the missionary makes, (b) the number of calls he must make to produce a sale, and (c) the frequency of territorial transfer. First, the more calls the missionary is required to make, the higher his performance is likely to be. Second, as *Exhibit II* shows, the performance index rises as the number of calls required to make a sale declines. This implies that frequent call-backs are less likely to be productive in missionary selling than fresh calls, underscoring the fact that close customer-salesman relationships are relatively unimportant in this classification. Third, *Exhibit II* shows that the performance index also rises as the number of territorial transfers increases. This indicates that occasional transfers may have a mildly salutary effect on both the customers and the salesmen.

Clearly the situation here is quite different from the trade selling situation, and clearly it calls for a different kind of man.

A BASIC DILEMMA

The good missionary salesman, then, is energetic and articulate. He need not be a good "closer," because his primary audience does not buy directly from him. His personality is very important, but the cultivation of long-term customer relationships is less important than it is for the trade sales force. The major drawback in this kind of selling is that the salesman is not challenged intellectually and lacks the opportunity to develop personally satisfying relationships with his customers.

The successful missionary sales force sidesteps these drawbacks by hiring young men with the physical stamina to make a lot of calls and then making them "run like Yellow Dog Dingo," to use Kipling's phrase. (Note the age spreads for this classification in *Exhibit I*.) Little premium is placed on applicants' previous sales experience. Because of their relative youth and inexperience, their compensation package includes a high proportion of fixed salary, and the general level of pay tends to be low. Because the job may not be basically difficult and because the influence of supervision on performance may be hard to detect, the *amounts* of training and supervision are kept at minimum levels, commensurate with getting the job done.

High performance results from keeping the salesman busy; low turnover results from hiring an older sales force. The low-turnover force is relatively well paid; the high-performance sales force is not. The missionary sales executive is thus forced to choose between an older, more stable, higher-paid, relatively low-performing sales force and a younger, more volatile, lower-paid, but relatively high-performing sales force. This dilemma is reflected in the guidelines for missionary sales management that I have drawn from the study.

GUIDELINES

The missionary sales executive can afford to pay less attention to making the salesman's job activities satisfying, since the impact of this factor on turnover is low. On the other hand, he needs to devote *more* attention to making his men's call routines as efficient as possible, since the impact of this factor on performance is high. Therefore, he should:

◻ Deploy salesmen to maximize sales volume at minimum sales force cost.

As I have said, the young sales force outperforms the older, and the need for a high degree of selling skill is not so important, since much of the closing activity is left to resellers. Therefore, the executive should:

◻ Seek out and hire inexperienced men in their twenties or early thirties.
◻ Avoid judging an applicant by his previous sales experience.
◻ As in trade selling, avoid relying on agencies and advertisements for applicants.

Compensation higher than the industry average does little to improve performance, but it does reduce turnover. In addition, a high proportion of fixed earnings is a positive factor in controlling operating costs. Therefore, the executive should:

◻ Make sure that, unless industry pay scales dictate otherwise, his lowest-paid salesman earns about $8,000, his average salesman between $11,000 and $12,000, and his highest-paid salesman between $17,000 and $18,000.

◻ Use a compensation method whereby at least 80% of the average salesman's earnings comes to him in the form of salary.

To improve sales-call efficiency, the executive can encourage his supervisors to plan more thoroughly to achieve maximum volume at minimum cost. Since the span of control appears to influence performance very little and has a mixed influence on turnover, the average span exhibited by the highest-performance quintile is a good guide. Thus he should:

◻ Maintain a ratio of salesmen to supervisors of about 10 to 1.

Although high advancement opportunity may induce costly turnover problems without necessarily improving performance, the executive must permit enough advancement opportunity to attract the energetic young man. The forces in the highest-performance quintile seem to have achieved this balance, and the executive might well be guided by their practice. Accordingly, he should:

◻ Keep the opportunity rate below 6%.

Current practice in the missionary sector agrees with many of these guidelines. It emphasizes cold-calling, many calls per day, and many accounts per man; and it plays down call-back and the importance of high compensation. Current practice diverges from these guidelines by emphasizing maturity and previous sales experience as an applicant-selection criterion, and pays excessive attention to close personal supervision. The missionary sales executive can readily check his own practices against these criteria.

Implementing these recommendations poses problems for many companies, particularly the smaller ones that assign a dual role to the sales force. Although missionary selling may be the sales force's primary responsibility, trade, technical, or new-business selling is often an important secondary role, and certain sales management practices better suited to these latter roles conflict with my recommendations for missionary sales management. One possible alternative is to split the sales force, but this action is either impractical or uneconomical for many companies.

If important secondary selling activities require a different kind of selling from the "animated direct mail" function suggested by the data on the missionary sales force, a company may downgrade the total selling capabilities of its current sales force by following these recommendations too closely. If, on the other hand, a careful review of the job content reveals that the sales-force function can be performed by younger, less-experienced, and lower-paid personnel making more calls per day, the increase in per-man productivity may offset the added costs caused by the higher rate of turnover that these procedures will induce.

Technical Selling

The primary responsibility of the technical sales force is to increase the company's volume of sales to its existing customers by providing them with technical advice and assistance. The industral-products salesman who sells to the customer's purchasing agents is a good example of this type. Unlike the trade or missionary salesman, the technical salesman sells directly to the user or buyer. The technical sales force is well represented in chemicals, machinery, and the heavy-equipment categories.

In this area, the ability to identify, analyze, and solve customers' problems is vitally important, and in this sense technical selling is very much like professional consulting. As in consulting, both technical competence and personality are important qualities in the salesman—he must be able to penetrate deeply into customers' problems and persuasively present his products' benefits as the partial or complete solution to them. Too much aggressiveness, on the one hand, can undermine this delicate relationship; too little, on the other, will result in lost sales opportunities.

The executive who manages a successful technical sales force provides his men with a good deal of support, especially by emphasizing training and retraining activities and encouraging a close, continuing rapport between salesman and supervisor. The executive selects his men primarily for their ability to achieve technical competence, and then provides them with the assistance they need to master this difficult kind of selling job.

The high-performance sales force is relatively young. This reflects the need for recent education; indeed, the proportion of college graduates is higher in this classification than in any of the others. Pay scales must therefore be high enough to attract the intelligent, educated, and personable young men who are suited for this kind of work.

In the high-performance force, close personal supervision is supplemented by the judicious use of salesmen's reports. The critical report here is the *competitive* or *market information report*. This is just as important to high performance here as the customer inventory report is to high trade sales performance.

GUIDELINES

The technical sales executive faces the same dilemma as the missionary sales executive: the younger force outperforms the older one, but the younger one exhibits excessive—and hence costly—turnover. In advancing the following recommendations, I am not disregarding this conflict but, rather, am making the assumption that high performance accompanied by a mild degree of turnover is more desirable than low performance accompanied by vitrification of the sales force.

The executive should control those aspects of the work—cold-calling, most notably—that are likely to jar the nerves of the man who has the basic talents and qualities to succeed in technical sales; otherwise, turnover will rise. He must also key his deployment decisions to building up customer-salesman relations, or performance will suffer. These relations are particularly critical in technical sales, where the salesman is frequently responsible for coordinating or supplying customer services, solving customers' problems, and negotiating contracts and the like. Therefore, the executive should:

□ Design sales territories so as to optimize the customer's satisfaction with the sales-call pattern.

□ Avoid requiring excessive cold-call activity, unless the salesman receives very generous compensation for it.

□ Transfer salesmen among territories as infrequently as possible (except, of course, at their own request).

When he makes a hiring decision, the executive should place more emphasis on what a man will bring to his job, as opposed to what he will be able to get out of it for himself. Whatever else, the technical salesman is not in business for himself—he is in business for his company.

In addition, the possession of a college degree, while not associated with high performance, *is* associated with low turnover; this suggests that technical selling provides more satisfaction to the educationally higher-qualified man than any other kind of selling. Therefore, the executive should:

□ Base hiring decisions more on an applicant's technical knowledge than on his desire to make money.

□ Seek out and hire college graduates in their late twenties and early thirties. (For this classification, employment agencies and advertisements are fair sources of applicants.)

For the technical sales force, training can play an important part in improving performance and reducing turnover. In addition, the data shown in *Exhibit III* indicate that the executive who faces major turnover problems might well consider the possibility of lengthening the period of initial training with a view to preparing the trainee more adequately before sending him out to face the company's customers. Therefore, the executive should:

□ Make sure trainees are adequately prepared to handle the selling and technical aspects of the job before assigning them to their territories.

□ Rely heavily on brief, but regular, retraining sessions to achieve the major training objectives.

Unlike the trade sales executive, who should be generous with salesman's

Turnover quintile	Average length of period (in days)	Average turnover rate
Very low	125	1.0%
Low	95	4.2
Average	97	7.5
High	62	11.7
Very high	65	24.3

pay, and the missionary sales executive, who can afford to be niggardly, the technical sales executive should ordinarily pay approximately the going industry rate. Because the competition for good technical salesmen is severe, the executive should recognize that he is likely to have to pay a premium for certain of his strategic deployment and selection decisions. Once again, a sensible pay scale appears to be the one suggested by the average of the companies in the highest-performance quintile, and the proportion of variable pay suggested by the average of the companies in the lowest-turnover quintile. Therefore, the executive should:

□ Make sure that, unless industry pay scales dictate otherwise, his lowest-paid salesman earns about $9,000, his average salesman between $12,000 and $13,000, and his highest-paid salesman earns between $20,000 and $26,000.

□ Adjust pay scales upward to compensate for either excessive cold-call activity or a college degree.

The incentive offered by commission and bonus payment may not be as important to the good technical salesman; the executive can follow the practice suggested by the high-performance sales forces here:

□ Pay about 80% of the average salesman's earnings in the form of fixed salary.

Close contact between salesman and supervisor supplements training and provides closer liaison between the home office and the marketplace. A good reporting system conduces to this close contact. The practice of companies in the highest-performance quintile suggests that the sales executive should:

□ Maintain a ratio of salesmen to field supervisors of about 7 to 1.

□ Place heavy emphasis on developing and improving the salesmen's reporting system, with special attention to the market information report.

Once again, a high rate of advancement opportunity, while not necessarily improving performance, contributes to excessive-turnover problems. On the other hand, this kind of environment may be necessary—within reasonable limits—to attract the younger salesmen necessary for achieving high levels of sales force performance. In keeping with practices associated with high-performance technical groups, then, the executive should:

□ Strive to keep the opportunity rate below 6%.

Implementing these recommendations demonstrates to the salesman that his *problem-solving skills are important*. He sees that his supervisor does not insist that he run around drumming up new business; that his job has been organized around the opportunity to provide important services to his customers; that he has been selected for his potential to become technically competent, and that he receives continuous training; that the company is investing above-average amounts in his fixed earnings; that it provides him with management assistance and guidance; and that he is given a fair chance of promotion.

The general thrust of these recommendations is that performance is maximized and turnover minimized when the executive makes the salesman perceive himself as performing an important consulting function for his customers on behalf of his company. Current practice is congruent with most of these recommendations. It emphasizes hiring college graduates, bringing in new salesmen through in-company transfers, training and continuously retraining them (especially in product knowledge), and paying a high proportion of compensation as fixed salary. It plays down cold-calling and calling at random. Other current practices are self-defeating —for example, building a force with a high average age and discounting the importance of the supervisor-salesman relationship.

It is interesting to note that technical sales forces as a whole exhibit a closer association between actual practice and desirable practice than the other three sales force classifications. This phenomenon is perhaps due to the wider recognition—among industrial marketers in particular—that selling has become a professional activity. In many instances, the new generation of products requires a professional to articulate their benefits. More important, new attitudes on the part of an increasingly sophisticated generation of purchasers demand a professional who can go beyond the articulation of product benefits and help the customer identify and solve a whole set of problems in which his product may play only a small part.

Using this concept of technical selling may pose problems for certain sales executives. A line may not need—or be able to support—this kind of salesman, especially if it is approaching the "commodity stage" because of customer familiarity and low margins. If it is important to a company that someone merely *calls on* users to keep them reordering, a shift to trade sales tactics may be in order.

Small organizations in which the cost of operating the sales force is a significant percentage of the sales dollar may find it difficult to invest the necessary money in training and supervision. Nevertheless, the increasing competition for both sales and salesmen makes it mandatory for even the small company to field a sales force well equipped to handle the challenges of the new technology.

New-Business Selling

This kind of selling has been variously called "canvassing," "bird-dogging," and "cold-calling." The primary responsibility of the new-business sales force is to obtain new accounts for its company, and the ability to convert a total stranger into a customer is the critical skill.

The great difficulty in this kind of selling is that the cold-calling it requires keeps the turnover rate high. The good new-business salesman is the rare bird dog who can balance the all-too-frequent exhilaration of "closing the tough one" and the equally frequent deflation that comes with the polite—or sometimes brutal—rejection.

The younger forces perform poorly and the older forces perform well, as the reader can clearly see from the percentages shown in *Exhibit I*. This bears out the conclusion that emotional maturity contributes to success in this area of selling. Younger men frequently find this activity impossibly difficult and burdensome, and tend to quit early in the game. Hence we find that the very young forces not only perform poorly, but are afflicted with excessive turnover.

The study data show that management practices are less important to successful sales operation than finding the right kind of man to begin with —the kind of man, as one executive phrased it, who has "the tough skin and the killer instinct of a shark."

The successful salesman also tends to be rather more independent of supervisory control than salesmen in the other classifications. To some extent, this must be adventitious: this classification showed much the highest rate of sales growth of the forces for the two-year period covered by the questionnaire—and the higher this growth rate, the less attention a company is likely to pay to providing training for its salesmen, presumably because the need for training is less obvious. Partly for this reason, therefore, there are no observable relationships between any training factors and the performance index.

GUIDELINES

The study makes it clear that applicant sources and selection methods are not correlated with performance levels, although they are correlated with turnover rate. This suggests that although executives have found ways to reduce failure (i.e., quick turnover) through their selection processes, they have not yet found ways to predict success (i.e., high performance). So far as the composition of the force is concerned, the balance turns in favor of the older man. Thus the executives should:

□ Seek out and hire salesmen in their forties and late thirties who enjoy cold-calling and have demonstrated their proficiency at it. (Company initiative is most important here.)

To some extent, the executive can regulate cold-calling where it is troublesome. One method is to restructure working patterns so that each man has enough regular business from established customers to take the sting out of the cold-call routine. The study data indicate that he should:

□ Schedule a salesman for no more than two cold calls a day unless the man is a proven "new-business specialist."

Younger sales forces really need adequate preparation for the cold-calling associated with new-business selling, and it appears worthwhile to spend considerable time and effort to improve initial and on-the-job phases of training. Therefore, the executive should:

□ Make sure that trainees are adequately prepared to cope with the vicissitudes of cold-calling before assigning them to their territories.

□ Rely heavily on on-the-job training for both new and experienced sales personnel.

The executive can be tempted toward generosity in making compensation decisions about the *average* for the new-business sales force, but be restrained in his attitude toward the *highest-paid* salesman. Also, a review of job content and fringe benefits appears worthwhile. The practices of companies in the lowest-turnover quintile suggest sensible guidelines here. The executive should:

□ Make sure that, unless industry pay scales dictate otherwise, his lowest-paid salesman earns about $8,000, his average salesman between $12,000 and $13,000, and his highest-paid salesman earns between $19,000 and $24,000. (*Exhibit* IV summarizes the optimal earnings levels for holding turnover down in the four sales classifications.)

□ Adjust pay scales upward to compensate for excessive cold-call activity.

□ After a thorough examination, consider adding new, or making increases in established, fringe benefits.

The optimal proportion of fixed salary to total earnings is just as surprising in this classification as it is in trade sales. The data indicate that it is much higher than I had expected—around 80% for the average new-business salesman.

Exhibit IV. Optimal levels of salesmen's earnings for controlling turnover

Sales force classification	Lowest-paid salesman	Average salesman	Highest-paid salesman
Trade	$8,000	$13,000	$20,000-26,000
Missionary	8,000	11,000-12,000	17,000-18,000
Technical	9,000	12,000-13,000	20,000-26,000
New-business	8,000	12,000-13,000	19,000-24,000

Many executives would reason that the new-business salesman exerts more direct influence on sales volume than any other kind of salesman, and therefore one ought to spur him on by increasing the proportion of commission and incentive in his total paycheck. But, here again, it is the salesman's point of view that is important. The cold-calling that the new-business salesman must do creates considerable tension for him in his job. Knowing that a large part of his earnings are fixed relieves him of a measure of financial uncertainty and allows him to concentrate better on the vital aspect of his work. Achieving victory in the cold call is difficult enough, it seems, without the salesman feeling that he is playing roulette with his take-home pay as well. Thus the executive should:

☐ Pay 80% of the average salesman's earnings in fixed form.

Since the data on new-business sales force supervision and control exhibit very little correlation with data on performance and turnover, the executive is well advised to follow the pattern of the companies in the highest-performance quintile. He should:

☐ Maintain a ratio of salesmen to field supervisors of around 10 to 1.

☐ Avoid the use of personal sales quotas for salesmen (these are particularly irritating to the older salesmen); improve the reporting system instead.

☐ Strive to keep the opportunity rate between 2% and 6%.

Implementing these recommendations would indicate to the salesman that he is a *valued and supported company employee*, not merely a bird dog. Salesmen are continually told this fact, but implementation convinces them: the salesman sees the company investing training time and money in him to ensure his success on the job; he sees the company compensating him in executive fashion; he sees himself protected insofar as possible from the tensions associated with cold-call activity; he feels responsible for his own performance, and is not pressed by an arbitrary quota; and he perceives his job as an important end in itself, not as a proving ground for a better one.

The broad concept here is that to achieve maximum performance and minimum turnover, the executive must hire men temperamentally compatible with cold-calling and then provide them with support and encouragement. In two ways, current practice reflects the trend of these recommendations: *one*, it emphasizes suitable methods of compensation; and *two*, it steers away from employee referrals as a source of applicants.

In a number of other ways, however, current practice is self-defeating. It encourages excessive cold-calling, use of advertisements to attract applicants, hiring on the basis of the applicant's drive to make money, and hiring young men. It also discourages significant training efforts, and plays down the importance of adequate levels of compensation. The executive should check his own practices against this list of trouble spots.

It is interesting to note that current practices in new-business selling diverge more from the study's recommendations than do those of any of the other three classifications. This may be because the new-business sales executive has usually been promoted from the ranks. He is likely to say, "I was a successful salesman, and the job was easy for *me*." But the job is not an easy one for the average salesman, as the high average turnover rate for this classification indicates.

Giving their salesmen more support may be difficult for some sales executives. Marketing strategy may dictate a great deal of cold-call activity, period. Unless he discovers better methods of selecting salesmen, the executive may have to resign himself to high turnover or pay very high salaries to attract and keep high-caliber people.

Conclusion

To some extent, every sales organization is a hybrid of the four main kinds of sales force, and the executive who wants to take practical advantage of the findings of this study may have to balance his practices to suit the mix of roles he must administrate. If, by chance, he is supervising a selling effort that uses both technical and new-business tactics, he will have to juggle the proportions of younger, better-educated, and highly talented men and older, aggressive, hard-shelled men on his force. As both the pretests of the survey and the survey itself show, however, it is usually easy to identify the main role of any given force easily.

It may be more difficult for the executive to identify the exact goals he wishes to pursue. As we have seen, maximizing performance and minimizing turnover are not always compatible goals; in the prescription for managing the missionary force, for example, the two goals come into direct collision. Each company, or each sales executive, must decide what turnover level is tolerable; once this has been established, the executive can concentrate on specific methods to improve performance.

The study yielded a good many results that could not be included here —for instance, data and conclusions relating to field superintendents, their development, their compensation, and so forth. Also, I could not document the methods of statistical manipulation and interpretation that were used to wash the effects of interacting variables out of the data. I could not even include full statistical evidence for any of the conclusions presented. Still, the working executive will perhaps find these conclusions challenging and thought-provoking, and they may help him make his practices more effective.

Appendix to Chapter 6

Study Sample

The survey population comprised companies and corporate divisions that employed 10 or more salesmen. It excluded companies that were primarily engaged in retail selling ("behind the counter") and delivery selling (route selling, for example). It also excluded companies whose businesses were primarily banking, insurance, and real estate. Retailing and delivery forces were excluded because companies engaged in these kinds of selling do not ordinarily compete for the kind of salesmen one ordinarily associates with "outside" selling. Banking, insurance, and real estate companies were excluded because their methods of measuring sales performance and turnover are not easily compared with those of the rest of industry.

Companies that employed fewer than 10 salesmen were not included, because pretests of the questionnaire indicated that such companies are likely to use only limited, *ad hoc* supervisory procedures in their sales force management.

7. Manage the Customer, Not Just the Sales Force

Benson P. Shapiro

The subject of sales management has many parts, each of them very important. One of the tasks of the sales manager is to see these parts in perspective and to understand their relationships. If, as so often happens, one activity or group of activities is magnified out of proportion, the overall goals of management are bound to suffer. This article discusses the four key areas of sales management: defining the role of personal selling, deploying the sales force, managing the accounts, and understanding the selling costs.

Recently I investigated the sales management problems of an apparel company that I will refer to by the fictitious name of Fitwell. At that time, the Fitwell Company had 50 salespeople and sales of $40 million in the medium to medium-high priced dress lines. The salespeople were paid on a variable commission rate, receiving 7% on dresses with a high gross margin for Fitwell and down to 5% on dresses with the lowest gross margin. The salespeople called on retail stores, paid their own out-of-pocket expenses, and averaged about $46,000 each in gross compensation per year.

A few years ago Fitwell introduced a higher priced dress line to keep pace with the market and to improve its margins. The line did not sell well despite its apparently fashion-right design, relatively heavy advertising, and extra high commissions (9%). The top executives who had developed the concept of the line were personally chagrined by the results.

The immediate reaction of Fitwell's sales managers was to push harder. The annual sales meeting included speeches by the chairman of the board, the president, the marketing vice president, and the national sales manager on the importance of the new line to the company and to the salespeople. The sales managers urged their regional managers to motivate their salespeople to "push the line." Contests were developed (e.g., a trip to Europe for the salesperson with the largest percentage of sales in the higher priced line and an automobile for the person with the largest total dollar volume). The more the sales managers "motivated," the more they frustrated them-

124

selves. Sales did not improve, and increasingly "powerful" speeches were met with frequent yawns.

The Fitwell Company's determination to motivate its salespeople to "push the line" is typical of the misplaced emphasis that occurs all through the business world. Too often top management thinks that motivation is the key to getting its people to follow a particular policy. However, man agement would be better off reevaluating its policy rather than focusing on motivating its employees, since often the problem is that top management has failed to develop an appropriate policy to begin with.

Let me hasten to say that the emphasis on managing the sales force is understandable. Since most sales managers—even national sales managers and sales vice presidents—were once active salespeople themselves, they naturally regard the sales force from the point of view of a salesperson. They ask, "How can we get more cooperation and more selling from the sales force?" But they do not ask, "How can we generate greater sales and profits?"

Sales managers sometimes forget that sales and profits are generated by the customer and that their objective is the management of the customer through the sales program, which is in turn implemented by the sales force. Their misplaced emphasis is serious because when they face problems like decreasing sales or market share, they change the means of managing the sales force but not its purpose.

Typically, sales managers change the compensation scheme, the most visible and talked about part of sales force management and the one which can be altered most rapidly. After monkeying around with compensation, sales managers usually focus on recruiting and selecting ("If we had more highly motivated salespeople to begin with, we wouldn't need such a clever compensation scheme"). So they have a brief romance with various testing and interviewing fads. Then they try training ("The salespeople don't know what we want or how to sell"). And finally they experiment with other motivational approaches like contests.

Although all of the foregoing are important, they should not be the only, or even the primary, consideration of sales managers. Sales management should be divided into two equally important parts: (1) formulating the sales policy and (2) implementing that policy. The first includes the detailed specification of the objectives, and the second, the accomplishment of the specified objectives.

Since the ultimate purpose of sales management is to generate loyal customers and high sales at reasonable costs, let us examine the four key questions that must be considered in formulating a customer-oriented sales program:

1. What is the general role that personal selling will play in the company's marketing strategy?

   2. How will the salespeople be assigned or deployed to various customers and prospects, products, territories, and selling tasks?
   3. How will each account and prospective account be managed?
   4. What will the program cost, and will that cost be justified?

Role of Personal Selling

From management's point of view, the customer is served not only by the company's personal representatives but also by its total marketing strategy, including product policy, pricing decisions, distribution channels, and communications methods. Personal selling and advertising are the two primary methods of communication.

One of the major marketing decisions facing all companies, and particularly those marketing consumer goods, is that of personal selling "push" versus advertising "pull." The choice largely depends on the way in which consumers make up their minds, the influence different communications approaches have on them, and the relative cost of the different approaches.

On the one hand, advertising is inexpensive in terms of cost per person reached, but its impact is relatively low. In addition, the message is standardized, at least for each advertisement, and the flow of communication is totally one way. On the other hand, personal selling is expensive, but its impact is high. In addition, the message can be tailored to the individual customer, and the flow of communication is in both directions.

Often, companies forget that there are two intermediate points on the scale between media advertising and personal selling: *direct mail advertising*, which can be more targeted than media advertising but is still a one-way communication flow, and *telephone selling*, which is more expensive than direct mail but has greater impact, more flexibility, and is a two-way flow. Telephone selling is cheaper than face-to-face selling but has less impact. With the increasing cost of the face-to-face sales call, telephone selling has received new impetus. It eliminates travel time and expense.

Because of its expense, personal selling should be used only in situations in which (a) the high impact, flexibility, and two-way communication flow are needed, and (b) the high cost is justified. Personal selling can be most effectively used when it is carefully coordinated with other communications tools and other parts of the marketing strategy.

For example, a company may choose to deemphasize its personal selling effort and pass on the savings to the customer as a price cut. At the retail level, this has been part of the strategy of the discount store. Cash-and-carry wholesalers have also chosen this route.

Then again, some companies may choose to take over the role of their distribution channels and in the process to emphasize personal selling.

Most consumer goods manufacturers have relatively small sales forces that call on wholesalers and retailers, who then sell the product to the consumer. Two major exceptions to this pattern are Avon Products and Fuller Brush, which employ large sales forces to sell their products directly to the consumer. To these companies, the personal selling effort is a basic part of their marketing strategy.

The customer is best served when the sales force is assigned only those tasks which it can perform more effectively and efficiently than other parts of the marketing strategy. Careful delineation of the role of personal selling in the marketing mix will help to prevent unfortunate situations in which sales managers attempt to motivate their salespeople to do things which are not in the interest of the company, the salesperson, or the customer.

Deploying the Sales Force

In assigning salespeople to territories, to accounts and prospective accounts, and to products, management should be aware that there are two parts to effective deployment: developing a policy and getting the salespeople to follow that policy. As we noted earlier, management sometimes emphasizes implementation of a particular policy without considering that it might have been incorrect to begin with. Let us return to the Fitwell Company as an example of such a management error. Fitwell's mistake was at the policy level, in the deployment of the selling effort across accounts and prospects:

When sales of Fitwell's higher priced dress line failed to increase in spite of the product's known appeal, the sales management team decided to step back and take a fresh look at the entire selling effort. It soon became clear that the problem was one of deployment, not motivation.

The individual salesperson knew he or she could make more money by selling the traditional lower priced lines to existing customers than by prospecting for new accounts for the new line. To prospect effectively, the salesperson would have had to learn about a new product line, a new type of customer, and a new sales approach. Also, to the better salespeople who made in excess of $60,000 per year, the contests were irrelevant. They also knew that they were impervious to management displeasure as long as they were selling in the vicinity of $1,000,000 worth of merchandise per year.

It soon became obvious that these salespeople should never have been assigned to the new line. And once the problem was identified as one of deployment, the sales managers could cope with it. No longer did they harangue the sales force. Instead, they went about developing an additional new sales force that was recruited, selected, and trained to call on the new type of outlet. Field sales managers were given the responsibility of opening accounts that could use a sizable volume of the line.

In the end, everyone at Fitwell was satisfied. But everyone would also have been better off had the problem been carefully analyzed in the first place. If management had approached the situation properly, it would have seen that the choice was between having a new line with new retailers served by a new sales force or having no new line.

Deployment of the sales force across products, geography, and tasks (e. g., opening new accounts, selling, serving existing accounts) can be approached in the same analytical way (a) by striking a balance between policy development and policy implementation, and (b) by focusing on the generation and maintenance of profitable accounts.

Managing the Account

The development and maintenance of account relationships are especially important in business selling (e.g., one company selling to another) because in almost all instances the selling process is continuous—a supplier sells the same type of merchandise to a buyer over and over again. Since the market for most products is finite, each seller must constantly face the same buyers. This is less true for the consumer market, where there are many more buying units and where the repeat buying process is infrequent for many products, such as houses, television sets, and so forth.

ORGANIZATIONAL INTERACTION

An account must be defined in terms of both the organization and the individuals within it. Selling to an organization is much more complex than selling to an individual for two reasons: an organization is made up of different individuals with different needs, and those individuals interact with one another in complex ways. Consider the different explicit needs of the various participants in a purchase decision.

When a company buys a large piece of equipment, the manufacturing managers want an efficient machine that will require little repair and is technically advanced, the treasurer's department is interested in the financing terms, and the purchasing department is primarily interested in the total cost of the manufacturing system (e.g., raw materials, depreciation, installation) and the outright cost of the machine.

Consider also that the selling company must take into account the various participants' needs as well as their importance and power in the company. Every participant has both organizational needs, based on his or her position and professional interests, and personal needs. Buying decisions, because they involve authority and responsibility, represent a primary focus for the satisfaction of personal needs in the organizational setting.

Thus the young treasurer, say, might be trying to consolidate his newly won power by showing how well he can do the job. Then again, the manufacturing people might be smarting over a recent rebuff by the engineering people and therefore seeking revenge.

The astute company, sales manager, and salesperson should of course work hard to find out any information such as that just mentioned. Knowing the buying company's dynamics is part of what selling and account management are all about.

THE SELLING PROCESS

The actual sale consists of five sequential steps: opening the relationship, qualifying the prospect, presenting the message, closing the sale, and servicing the account.

The *opening* has the dual purpose of determining the right person in the organization to approach initially and of generating enough interest so that it is possible to obtain the information necessary for the qualification. The end result of a good opening should be an appointment with an appropriate and enthusiastic person.

The *qualification* is the process by which a salesperson determines whether or not the prospect is worth the effort of a sales presentation. Although scholars tend to gloss over the qualifying process, salespeople and sales managers constantly discuss it.

The *presentation* is the core of the selling process and requires astute management by the salesperson. It is the "pitch" (i.e., the actual attempt at persuasion). The presentation sooner or later culminates in an attempt to close the sale.

The *closing* is obtaining the final agreement to purchase. This is the Achilles' heel of many a would-be-successful salesperson.

After the sale comes the *service* aspect. Often the salesperson will be reselling supplies, materials, parts, and so on. This service part of the sale is frequently the opening to new sales.

Multilevel selling: Traditionally, the salesperson has sold to a purchasing agent in the industrial area or to a store buyer in the consumer goods field. Since it was a one-on-one relationship, the sales manager could structure his policies and programs on that basis. But the situation is changing, and the policies used to manage the sales force must now reflect these changes.

One important change is the introduction of multilevel selling—the process by which several authority levels are called on. The salesperson calling on a retailer, say, may attempt to contact both the buyer and the merchandise manager so that when the buyer seeks approval of the sales proposal, the merchandise manager is presold or at least receptive. Thus multilevel selling is in a sense a product of system selling because the chief buying influence (a) is at a higher organizational level than are the traditional buyers and (b) is responsible for the total system instead of just the individual components.

For example, consider the case of a manufacturing company for which one person purchases the raw materials and another buys the machinery. If the selling company wants to sell a system involving both raw materials and machinery, it is almost required to move upward in the purchasing organization to reach the chief buying influence in charge of both.

Team selling: The one-on-one selling process is further broken down by the introduction of team selling, a process in which several people from the selling company call on the buying organization. Thus, in a team approach, each level of the selling company calls on his or her counterpart in the prospective buying organization.

One reason for team selling is business etiquette (e.g., it is more appropriate for the national sales manager to call on the general merchandise manager than to climb beyond his or her own level or to descend beneath it). It also demonstrates appropriate interest on the part of the selling company's management. Still another reason is that this method allows for an exchange of power. The two top managers can make arrangements (e.g., private branding, special products) that their subordinates cannot.

Team selling is not limited to different hierarchical levels in the buying and selling organizations. Often it involves people in different functional areas in both companies. Members of different functional areas in the buying organization have specific needs and viewpoints that can best be met and understood by their functional equivalents in the selling organization.

For example, if the treasurer of the buying organization is concerned about financing arrangements, then the treasurer of the selling company is probably better suited to deal with that executive than is the salesperson, whose primary job is to deal with manufacturing and purchasing personnel.

There are three important considerations to keep in mind about team selling:

1. It is not always appropriate. Sometimes the sale is simple, repetitive, or small. The team approach is most suitable for the selling of heavy capital equipment or long-term supply relationships, either formal contracts or informal commitments. These involve enough dollars and enough different functions in the buying organization to justify team selling's high expenditure of time.

2. It is complex and difficult to manage. Actually, it is possible for the sales team to spend more time getting coordinated than selling. Or worse, it can spend too little time getting coordinated and end up presenting contradictory impressions to the buying influences.

3. It is in a sense an extension of the marketing concept that stresses the

importance of having all parts of the selling company directed toward satisfying customer needs. Here, all relevant functional units become involved in the actual selling process.

Although team selling usually involves relatively high-level personnel and is used primarily to "open" an account, it can also involve lower level personnel and be used to provide continuing maintenance selling. A soft drink bottler, for example, may primarily use a route delivery person for selling but may supplement his efforts with an in-store display and merchandising expert. In other situations, inside sales liaison people, expediters, or shipping personnel may join the sales team in keeping accounts satisfied.

THE PYRRHIC SALE

The truly astute management is not interested in just making sales; it wants to build account relationships. These, of course, must result in sales sooner or later. The trade-off between immediate sales and long-term account relationships is part of the phenomenon that I call the Pyrrhic sale —one that immediately benefits the company but jeopardizes its future relationship with the account.

In business selling the customer is in the position of repeatedly being able to purchase the product. Thus this situation requires careful account management by the salesperson, who must be willing to forgo a sale that is not in the best long-term interest of the account and therefore of his relationship with it.

For example, the apparel salesperson who is willing to tell a customer that some items in his line do not sell well at retail in spite of their apparent appeal is helping his customer and himself over the long run. Or picture the response to the pump salesperson who says, "Yes, we offer the best pumps for your needs in applications a, b, and c, but unfortunately our pumps are not as good in application d as those offered by our competitors." The Pyrrhic sale, in contrast, occurs when the salesperson "forces" a marginal sale but risks losing the account.

THE SALESPERSON'S ROLE

Account relationships depend on more than just the salesperson's prudence in not pushing for orders. The salesperson can perform functions for the customer that make him or her valuable to the customer's organization. Two most important roles, merchandiser and ombudsman, are at the crux of the salesperson's account maintenance function.

As merchandiser, it is the salesperson's job to present those items in his product line which are most appropriate to the customer. In complex industrial situations, the salesperson is often responsible for designing the product to fit the customer's specific needs. In the apparel and furniture industries, the salesperson helps the buyer choose items which will sell best in his store.

As ombudsman, the salesperson is the customer's representative to the selling company in handling problems such as damaged merchandise, late or early shipments, credit arrangements, and the like. Obviously, the more effective the salesperson is in dealing with his own company, the more effective he can be in helping his customers.

THE COMPANY'S ROLE

The salesperson's function should not be the only important aspect of the company's account management procedures and policies. Many successful marketers develop special programs to help their customers. Some wholesalers, for example, offer site selection advice and store layout assistance to their retailers. Many companies provide their distributors with sales training assistance. Other companies help their dealers manage inventories.

Delivery and credit are two other important account management techniques. Fast delivery or emergency backup of spare parts inventories can cut down on the dealer's and user's inventory carrying costs. Special credit arrangements can help customers with their businesses. One important credit arrangement is "dating"—that is, extended credit provided in highly seasonal industries like toys that encourages the dealer to accept early delivery.

Some of these programs may be companywide, while others may be directed toward special categories of distributors or particular accounts. However, it is important to bear in mind that, according to the Robinson-Patman Act, all customers who compete with each other must be treated equitably.

As I indicated earlier, the nonselling parts of the company have an important role to play in account management. The rude receptionist and the truculent delivery man have probably lost as many accounts as the insensitive salesperson.

THE SALES MANAGER'S ROLE

All too often sales managers are more responsive to competitors than to customers in developing account management programs. Their attitude seems to be at best "we'll do it if they do it" but more often "it's a nice idea, but it costs money." They overlook the competitive benefits of being first with an innovative approach to customer satisfaction. They do not spend enough time thinking about the needs of the customer, because they are too busy motivating their salespeople.

Sales managers must make careful trade-offs between the costs of account management programs and the benefits to their customers. The ideal programs, of course, provide large benefits for small costs. Analytical, creative, and flexible sales managers can undoubtedly find a large number of approaches that meet this criterion.

The account management area is central to the difference between managing a sales program and a sales force. The real emphasis of the sales manager should be on customer management. The sales force should act as a conduit of communication, not as a barrier between the sales manager and the customer.

Understanding Selling Costs

In pursuing their ultimate objective of profitable account relationships, sales managers must look carefully at the cost of the sales force and the benefits received from it. Some of the concepts that we noted earlier in considering the role of personal selling in the marketing strategy are useful in deciding how much to spend on a sales force. The two primary determinants are the complexity of the selling task and the profit to be derived from the work done by one salesperson. The more complex the selling task, the more reason to have a talented sales force. The higher the profit created by a single salesperson, the greater the company's ability to pay for a "high-powered" sales force.

When the selling task is complex, the salesperson may actually be called on to "design the product" for the customer, as noted earlier. In tailoring the equipment to a particular customer's needs, the salesperson is developing a "product policy" for the smallest market segment—one buyer. To accomplish this difficult task, the salesperson operates in a customer-oriented, client-centered, problem-solving mode. He or she must transmit a great deal of complex intellectual information while providing reassurance in answer to psychological needs.

At the other extreme is the salesperson with the simple product whose function is to "go out and sell it." The mode is typically either persuasion or merely making the product available (e.g., the milkman). Little information needs to be transmitted. Often the task is merely to be "likeable," or at least not "unlikeable," and to actually deliver the products. Selling of this type demands only a low-powered sales force.

The high-powered sales force is expensive. The salesperson must be carefully selected. Often he or she has had substantial training prior to joining the company (e.g., the graduate engineer who sells complex equipment). Specialized training after joining the company is standard procedure. The only way to attract such an intelligent, trained, and trainable individual is to compensate well.

Exhibit I. The nature of the selling effort

		Intricacy of sales task			
		Simple	Moderately simple	Moderately complex	Complex
Aspects of the task	Mode	persuasion or delivery			problem solving
	Importance of information transmittal	low			high
	Needs served	personal and physical			intellectual and psychological
	Where prevalent	consumer and retail			industrial and commercial
Profit impact		low			high
Management of the sales force	Training	less			more
	Compensation	low			high
	Independence	low			high
	Number of customers	high			low
Typical examples	Consumer selling	milk	clothing	real estate insurance	stocks and bonds
	Industrial and commercial selling	simple industrial supplies		industrial equipment	high-volume OEM components
				fashion at wholesale	large private-label sales

Usually, such a salesperson thrives on independence. A "programmed pitch" does not work. Geographical territories are often large, but the number of customers per salesperson is small. Because each customer requires individualized service, the salesperson cannot cover many customers.

Other parts of the marketing mix also affect the nature of the selling effort. The more the company relies on sales service, the more it needs highly skilled salespeople. Conversely, if the company relies on its established reputation, innovative products, meticulous delivery, low price, or other attractions, the importance of the selling effort and the money available to pay for it are reduced. *Exhibit I* illustrates in diagrammatic fashion much of the preceding discussion on the nature of the selling task.

VARIABLE VS. FIXED COSTS

The total amount is only one important aspect of costs; often the relationship of cost to volume is equally important. Media advertising costs are fixed; they do not vary with the unit sales volume. But sales costs may be either fixed or variable.

Sales overhead costs, such as the salaries of sales managers, are usually fixed. Sometimes, however, they include a bonus portion that varies with unit or dollar sales volume. Order processing costs are usually semivariable with the costs going up in a partially stepwise manner.

The major costs of the sales force itself may be either fixed or variable. A commission sales force, whether independent representatives or company salespeople, is a variable cost except for fixed salary guarantees, fringe benefits, and expenses. A salaried sales force is primarily a fixed cost. Usually, however, as sales volume per salesperson increases, there is a tendency to increase salaries.

The cost for a particular company of a straight-salaried sales force is directly related to the number of calls made. Clearly, if the number of calls a salesperson can make in a given period of time is relatively fixed, the total number of calls which the sales force can make in a given period of time must depend on the number of salespeople. The number, in turn, is the key to the cost of the sales force.

Theoretically, expenses are a fixed cost. In practice, however, most companies are more liberal with expense money in times of high sales than in times of low sales. One could argue that this is contrary to the way it should be. When business is dismal, perhaps all possible action should be taken to increase expense money. Such reasoning is usually not followed, however, because the emphasis on cost control increases in poor times, especially among publicly held companies.

Sales promotion occupies an important point on the continuum between personal selling and media advertising. Some forms of promotion (like certain contests, presentation aids, and sales or distributor meetings) are fixed costs. However, price-off deals, special packages, certain other contests, and most types of promotions are purely variable costs.

Each type of cost has its own advantage. Variable costs are more conservative since they protect the company in times of poor sales (i.e., costs automatically decrease as volume does). Thus they lessen the effect of poor sales on profits. They also help those companies with a small share of the market.

On the one hand, whereas the largest competitor in a market can spread the fixed costs over the largest volume, yielding a low communication cost per unit sold, the smaller competitor does not have that advantage. If he spends as much per unit, his fixed costs of advertising or personal selling will be much smaller, but his program probably will not have as much impact. If the smaller competitor has as large a program, his costs per unit, and thus his percentage of sales spent on advertising or a salaried sales force, will be much higher, and his profits, all other things about equal, will be much lower.

On the other hand, competition on the basis of variable costs (like sales promotions) gives the smaller competitor a better chance. He can spend as much per unit as the larger competitor spends, yet enjoy equal impact.

Fixed costs have their advantages too. They offer great upside opportunity. As sales grow, costs increase more slowly and profits more rapidly. And as we just noted, fixed costs also provide the large competitor with an advantage over the smaller one.

Regardless of the situation, it is important for sales and marketing managers first to understand the relationship between costs and sales volume and then to build a program which provides the cost structure they desire.

Concluding Note

The customer ultimately determines the success (or failure) of a company's marketing approach. Every aspect of marketing, including the personal selling effort, must focus on the customer.

The sales force is important. It must be carefully managed. But in the final analysis, it is only a conduit to the customer. The object is customer satisfaction and sales. A disproportionate emphasis on the means must lead to a lack of attention to the objective. The prescription: manage the customer, not just the sales force.

8. Demarketing—Yes, Demarketing

Philip Kotler and Sidney J. Levy

The way marketers try to cope with excess demand or unwanted demand may affect the company's long-run objectives just as much as do marketing policies for normal times. What kinds of situations lead companies to cut back on their marketing efforts? How do methods of de-emphasis differ depending on the type of problem? This instructive and sometimes amusing analysis answers these and other questions that have never before been raised in HBR. It also suggests new directions for the study of marketing.

The popular conception of marketing is that it deals with the problem of furthering or expanding demand. Whether one takes the traditional view that marketing is finding customers for existing products, or the more recent view that it is developing new products for unmet consumer wants, it is seen as the technology of bringing about increases in company sales and profits. The marketer is a professional builder of sales volume who makes deft use of product, price, place, and promotion variables.

This is a narrow concept of marketing and the potential applications of marketing technology. It is a concept that arose in a period of goods over-supply. It also reflects a widespread tendency to define marketing in terms of what marketers ought to do rather than to analyze what they actually do under various circumstances. Much marketing literature approaches marketing with exhortations: define your objectives, know your market, meet consumer needs, and so on—all underlaid with the implied promise that then you will sell more. As a result, marketing has been too closely identified with the problem of buyer markets.

But suppose that an economy were suddenly plunged into a state of widespread product shortages. What would be the role of marketing management then? Would it evolve into a minor business function? Would it disappear altogether? Or would it continue to perform critical functions for the company?

Most production, financial, and marketing men who are asked this question opine that marketing's role would be greatly reduced in a scarcity economy. They see marketing as a "fair weather" profession, one that seems to be important chiefly in periods of excess supply. In this respect marketing differs from manufacturing, accounting, and other business functions that are critical in all stages of the economy.

But this is an untenable position. True, if marketers are narrowly seen as responsible primarily for finding customers or increasing demand, then they would seem superfluous when demand becomes unmanageably great. However, in practice *excess demand* is as much a marketing problem as excess supply. A company faces a host of difficult customer-mix and marketing-mix decisions in periods of excess demand. It has to find ways of reducing total demand or certain classes of demand to the level of supply without damaging long-run customer relations.

Our name for this kind of activity is "creative demarketing." More formally, we define demarketing as *that aspect of marketing that deals with discouraging customers in general or a certain class of customers in particular on either a temporary or permanent basis.* The tasks of coping with shrinking demand or deliberately discouraging segments of the market call for the use of all the major marketing tools. As such, marketing thinking is just as relevant to the problem of reducing demand as it is to the problem of increasing demand.

Once this view is appreciated, the true character of marketing's mission becomes clearer. Marketing is the business function concerned with controlling the level and composition of demand facing the company. Its short-run task is to adjust the demand to a level and composition that the company can, or wishes to, handle. Its long-run task is to adjust the demand to a level and composition that meets the company's long-run objectives.

In this article we will describe three different types of demarketing:

1. *General* demarketing, which is required when a company wants to shrink the level of total demand.

2. *Selective* demarketing, which is required when a company wants to discourage the demand coming from certain customer classes.

3. *Ostensible* demarketing, which involves the appearance of trying to discourage demand as a device for actually increasing it.

(A fourth type, *unintentional* demarketing, is also important but does not need to be considered here. So many abortive efforts to increase demand, resulting actually in driving customers away, have been reported in recent years that the dreary tale does not need to be told again.)

General Demarketing

At times excess demand can characterize a whole economy, and at other times, only a limited number of firms. Even in the absence of a general scarcity economy, there are always individual sellers who are facing excess demand for one or more of their products. While most other companies may be looking for customers, these sellers face the need to discourage customers, at least temporarily. Their marketing stance may become one of indifference or of arrogance. In a responsible organization, however, attempts are made to act in a framework that respects the marketing concept, i.e., the long-run aim of developing satisfied customers.

It is possible to distinguish at least three different situations that may give rise to general demarketing by a company. Let us consider each situation briefly.

TEMPORARY SHORTAGES

Many companies have the periodic fortune—or misfortune—of finding particular products in excess demand. Management underestimated demand, overestimated production, or did both. The following cases illustrate:

□ Eastman Kodak introduced its Instamatic camera in the early 1960's and found itself facing runaway demand. A few years passed before Kodak achieved enough capacity to handle demand.

□ Wilkinson Sword introduced its new stainless steel blade in the early 1960's and was besieged for supplies by regular and new dealers, not all of whom could be satisfied.

□ Anheuser-Busch underestimated the rate of growth in demand for its popular Budweiser beer and found itself in the late 1960's having to ration supplies to its better dealers and markets while it was making a crash effort to expand its plants.

□ Savings and loan associations in 1970-1971 faced an oversupply of savings relative to their ability to invest the funds and sought means to discourage the savings customers. They were willing to encourage small accounts, but refused large depositors.

These cases reflect temporary shortages of products that are corrected as the company manages to bring about sufficient plant expansion. In the interim, management must carry out two distinct tasks. The first is that of demand containment, i.e., curbing the growth of total demand. The second is that of product allocation, i.e., deciding which dealers and customers will receive the available product.

Steps to encourage deconsuming: Demand containment is the attempt to stabilize or reduce demand so that the product shortage is not further aggravated. This is largely accomplished by using the classic marketing instruments in reverse. To bring about deconsuming, management can:

□ Curtail advertising expenditures for the product, modifying the content of the messages.

□ Reduce sales promotion expenditures, investing less in trade exhibits, point-of-purchase displays, catalog space, and so on.

□ Cut back salesmen's selling time on the product and their entertainment budgets, asking them to concentrate on other products, spend more time in service and intelligence work, and learn to say *no* in a way that customers find acceptable.

□ Increase the price and other conditions of sale to the advantage of the marketing company. (This may include eliminating freight allowances, trade discounts, and so on.)

□ Add to the time and expense necessary for the buyer to procure the product or service—what might be called his "effort and psychological costs"—as a means of discouraging demand.

□ Reduce product quality or content, either to encourage deconsuming or to make more of the product available and thus demarket at a slower rate.

□ Curtail the number of distribution outlets, using the product shortage as an opportunity to eliminate undesirable dealers and/or customers.

Marketing management does not usually take these steps in isolation, but rather as part of a demarketing mix. It should make judicious estimates of the elasticity and cross-elasticities of the different instruments, i.e., their impact on demand when employed with varying intensity, both individually and in combination. Otherwise, the demarketing program may overinhibit demand, and the company may find itself facing a shortage of customers.

Alternatives in allocation: While these demarketing steps are being undertaken, marketing management should also develop a sound plan of product allocation. It must decide how, to whom, and in what quantities to allocate existing supply. There are four plausible solutions to this problem:

1. Management can allocate the product on a *first-come, first-serve* basis. This is a standard method regarded as fair by almost everyone except new customers. Dealers and customers get their stock in the order of their ordering.

2. Management can allocate the product on a *proportional demand* basis. This means determining that the company can satisfy x% of total demand and then supplying each customer with x% of its original order level. This is also held to be a fair solution.

3. A company can allocate supply on a *favored customer* basis. It determines its most valuable customers and satisfies their demand levels completely; the remaining customers may receive some fraction of their original order levels, with the rest being back-ordered. This is held to be a discriminatory solution, even if an understandable one.

4. A company can allocate products on a *highest bid* basis. The supply goes to those customers who offer the highest premium for early delivery. While many people consider this an exploitative strategy, economists typically argue that it makes the most sense since the product flows to those who presumably need it most.

Policies for allocating supply should be made by top management with marketing executives playing a central role in advising what impact the alternatives would have on long-run customer relations. If it assumes that the shortage is temporary, management should estimate customer feeling toward the company in the post-shortage period when the demand-supply balance is reestablished. Each general solution involves some amount and distribution of customer disappointment. If the company seeks to maximize its long-run, rather than short-run profits, it should choose solutions that minimize the total disappointment of customers during the period in question.

CHRONIC OVERPOPULARITY

There are some real, although perhaps rare, situations where an organization is faced with chronic overpopularity, and it wishes for one reason or another to bring demand down to a permanently lower level. Two situations can be distinguished:

In the first, the product's present popularity may be seen as posing a serious threat to the long-run "quality" of the product. For example, the island of Bali in the South Pacific has long been a tourist's dream. In recent years, it has attracted a larger number of tourists than can be handled comfortably with its facilities. The island is in danger of becoming over-crowded and spoiled. If tourism goes unchecked, Bali faces the same fate as Hawaii, which has lost its pristine appeal because of teeming crowds and soaring prices.

The authorities in Bali are aware of this danger and are considering measures to reduce demand. Their demarketing strategy is to reduce the island's attractiveness to middle-income tourists while maintaining or increasing its appeal to high-income tourists. They prefer fewer higher-spending tourists to a larger number of lower-spending tourists (in contrast to the savings and loan example cited earlier). To accomplish this, they will build luxury hotels and restaurants, place their advertising in media reaching the rich, and build a distinct image of catering to the affluent class.

Also because of fear that the area's natural beauty will be spoiled by congestion, officials in the state of Oregon are demarketing to prospective settlers. But the state does promote tourist trade; the governor encourages people to visit so long as they do not stay.

In the second situation, overpopularity is a problem because management does not want the strain of handling all of the demand. For example, there is an exceptionally fine restaurant in London that can seat only 30 persons. Word-of-mouth advertising has been so good that the restaurant is fully booked for months in advance. Nevertheless, tourists without reservations crowd around in the hope of cancellations. They add noise and detract from the intended atmosphere of leisurely dining.

The two men who run the restaurant enjoyed their role as managers of a small, intimate restaurant noted for its fine cuisine. For this reason, they decided on demarketing. They added a doorman who discouraged people from waiting for cancellations and from phoning about the availability of reservations. They also raised the prices. They were able to do all this without creating increased demand as a result of scarce resources—the reverse phenomenon to be described later in our discussion of ostensible demarketing.

PRODUCT ELIMINATION

Deft demarketing is called for when a company would like to elimate a product or service that some loyal customers still require or desire, e.g., a superseded model. Demand at any point in time can be considered as temporarily excessive in relation to the level at which the company prefers to see demand. So as not to create customer ill will, the company's task is not only to reduce production and inventory as soon as possible but also to reduce demand.

Among the demarketing strategies available are: informing the customer as to why the product is being dropped, offering partial or full compensation to important customers who are hurt by the disappearance of the product, and maintaining a minimal stock of the product to satisfy the hard-core customers. These strategies are warranted where the same customers purchase other items from the company and their goodwill must be maintained.

Selective Demarketing

Often an organization does not wish to contain or reduce the level of total demand but rather the demand coming from specific segments of the market. These segments or customer classes may be considered relatively unprofitable in themselves or undesirable in terms of their impact on other segments of demand. The company is not free to refuse sales outright, either as a matter of law or of public opinion. So it searches for other means to discourage demand from the unwanted customers. To illustrate:

□ A luxury hotel catering to middle-aged, conservative people has recently attracted rich hippies who come wearing long hair and odd clothes, and who sit on the lobby floor making a good deal of noise. This has turned off the hotel's main clientele, and the management must rapidly take steps to discourage further reservations by hippies.

□ An automobile manufacturer of a luxury car purchased mainly by affluent whites as a status symbol has discovered that an increasing number of sales are going to newly rich members of the black community. As a result, affluent whites are switching to another well-known luxury automobile. The automobile manufacturer has to decide whether to let the market take its natural course, attempt to market to both groups, or to demarket to the new customer class.

□ A small appliance manufacturer wants to keep one of its popular brands in selective distribution, but it receives continuous pressure from marginal channels that want to carry the product. Not wanting to put his product through these channels, the manufacturer faces the problem of depriving them without alienating them.

The common problem faced by management in such cases is that the main clientele is threatened by the emergence of a new clientele. The organization does not find it possible to maintain both clienteles simultaneously. Gresham's Law seems to operate: the "cheaper" segment appears to drive the "dearer" segment from circulation. For one reason or another, the organization expects a higher risk and/or lower return (whether financial or psychological) from the new clientele. The alternative is to demarket selectively to the new clientele.

METHODS AND IMPLICATIONS

How is this done? When a company markets to one segment of the public, it may discourage other prospects who are unresponsive to, or alienated by, the appeals employed. For instance, advertising which plays up the joys of conventional home life demarkets the product to singles. In this sense, demarketing is the negative of marketing.

Selective demarketing refers to (a) the deliberate choice of segments that are to be avoided and (b) the specific means chosen to ward off the undesired customers. Management decreases the benefit/cost ratio which the wanted segment receives from patronage.

In examples like those cited, the marketer is typically not free to charge a discriminatory price to the undesirable segment. The demarketing mix has to be built out of other elements. Activities like these may be pursued:

□ The company discourages hope for product availability. The hotel fears it will be out of rooms, or the automobile company indicates that the customer must wait a long time for delivery.

□ The salesmen do not make calls on small organizations.

□ The company provides poor service to the undesirable segment. The undesirable customers receive poorer hotel rooms, slower service, insolent treatment—all suggesting that their business is not welcome.

□ The company makes it harder for the undesirable segment to find product channels or information. Auto companies are careful to locate dealerships away from changing neighborhoods, and hotels are selective about where they advertise and who receives their information.

To describe these steps is not to approve them. They are cited as familiar examples of what companies may do to discourage demand from certain classes of customers. The steps may raise thorny issues in social ethics. On the one hand, it seems understandable that an organization should have the right to choose or protect its major clientele, especially if its long-run profits are at stake. On the other hand, it is unjust to discriminate against buyers who have long hair, black skin, lower status, or small orders. The injustice seems especially intolerable if the discriminated buyers are left without equivalent alternatives. In that case demarketing becomes entwined with the social, legal, and political problems relating to unacceptable forms of discriminatory demarketing.

Ostensible Demarketing

Sometimes an establishment goes through the motions of demarketing in the hope of achieving the opposite effect. By creating the appearance of not wanting more customers, it hopes to make the product even more desirable to people. The marketer works on the principle that people want what may be hard to get and may even masochistically "enjoy" being neglected by the seller. Consider the following possibilities:

□ An artist operates a small gallery in which hang some of his own and other artists' paintings. He works in the back room and seems to resent the intrusion of would-be buyers. A buyer has to wait for the artist to emerge from the back room, and even then is treated brusquely. But the sales are good; many persons enjoy being mistreated and buying on the artist's terms.

□ An antique dealer keeps his store in relative disarray with very good objets d'art buried in dust-laden clusters of junk. Patrons often comment that he would attract more customers by cleaning up his store, eliminating the junk, and thus achieving better presentation. But they may be mistaken. The owner feels he attracts more customers this way, reasoning that people love a bargain and dream of discovering a Rembrandt buried among the ancient cracking canvasses of third-rate painters.

□ A department store arranges very carefully a stock of new blouses on a counter to make sure all sizes are represented. Then, a few minutes before the first customers arrive, the sales personnel pull the blouses out of their boxes and mix them about in chaotic fashion, ostensibly making the goods less attractive. But the customers spot the blouses and are attracted in large crowds to the counter in search of a bargain.

□ The managers of a rock concert advertise it on the radio in a discouraging way, saying the crowds will be too large, and that seats are practically sold out. The hidden intention is to increase the number of attendees by attracting those who hate to feel left out.

Questions for Study

Marketers have dealt with the problem of increasing demand for so long that they have overlooked a host of situations where the problem is to reduce demand or cope with inability to meet it. Whether the task is to reduce the level of total demand without alienating loyal customers, to discourage the demand coming from certain segments of the market that are either unprofitable or possess the potential of injuring loyal buyers, or to appear to want less demand for the sake of actually increasing it, the need is for creative demarketing.

It is easy to assume that demarketing is only marketing in reverse—product, price, place, and promotion policies can also be used to *discourage* demand. Yet the optimal demarketing mix is not obvious. First, there is the danger of overreducing short-run demand, which can be more serious than increasing it too much. Second, there is the danger of doing irreparable harm to long-run demand through indelicate handling of current customers.

This means that there is a need for careful research into the phenomenon of demarketing. Some important issues are:

1. When do companies face demarketing situations? What are the major types of situations and how extensive are they?

2. What demarketing policies and instruments are commonly used by these companies? How do companies reduce total demand and selective demand? How do they allocate scarce products?

3. What are optimal marketing policies for different demarketing situations?

4. What role is played by marketing management in advising or deciding on appropriate demarketing policies? Does top management recognize that specialized marketing skill is as essential in demarketing situations as in marketing situations?

5. What are the public policy issues and needs with respect to company demarketing practices, especially discriminatory demarketing?

Research into these questions should help clarify the important and neglected phenomenon of demarketing. Of equal importance, it should help establish a more objective and realistic conception of marketing. Marketing's task is not blindly to engineer increases in demand; that view came about because marketing developed during a period of economic growth and surpluses, and it is too casually related to "hard sell" tactics and pervasive advertising. Rather, marketing functions to regulate the level and shape of demand so that it conforms to the organization's current supply situation and to its long-run objectives.

When this view is accepted, it is not necessary to contrast marketing and demarketing. We have used the term "demarketing" to dramatize semantically a neglected phenomenon, but this would not be necessary if all marketing situations were recognized. Marketing inevitably has a role to play in the face of excess demand: the challenge is to demarket thoughtfully and skillfully.

9. Grass Roots Market Research

Louis W. Stern and J. L. Heskett

Every sales territory in which a company operates is different. This is why the centralized marketing research organization operates at a disadvantage. It is not necessary that field sales forces usurp the traditional long-range planning role of centralized marketing research groups, only that the local sales people perform certain research tasks for themselves. Grass roots intelligence enables branch managers to acquire the flexibility needed to capitalize on sudden market shifts and to adjust rapidly to new challenges and trends in their territories.

The basic intent of this article is to demonstrate that market research tasks which are traditionally the responsibility of centralized marketing research departments can be performed better by the field sales force in certain cases. We have observed that a real need for a "grass roots" market research approach exists because:

□ Centralized research groups in corporations which operate in geographically dispersed areas are separated by space, time, and attitude from actual day-to-day operations of the field sales personnel.

□ Branch sales managers are at a serious disadvantage in trying to adjust to local competitive changes, which often occur at a faster rate than top-level corporate marketing intelligence would indicate or support.

□ Headquarters' insistence that branch managers rely on corporate policy directives, which originate from centralized research findings and top-management decisions, often encumbers the sales force in successfully meeting on-the-spot market changes.

□ In creating a centralized research group for planning long-range marketing efforts, top management neglects the possibilities for enlightened short-range sales action based on organized research carried out by qualified sales personnel in the field.

□ The intelligence made available to branch managers—as a by-product of their selling activities—can permit them to make on-the-spot decisions to stay abreast of sudden market shifts and to capitalize on or adjust to the changing competitive situation in their territories.

147

In this presentation we will look at some of the shortcomings in centralized marketing research, and discuss the various steps involved in initiating, implementing, and controlling a grass roots program. Our position will be supported by an authentic, but disguised, case example drawn from the dairy industry. Along the way, we will describe the strategic and tactical benefits to be derived from—as well as the potential problems in—such a system. Finally, we will point out the criteria for deciding whether to adopt a grass roots market research approach that, in turn, will enable corporations with far-flung operations to develop superior local marketing intelligence and managerial relationships with top-level decision-makers.

Centralized Shortcomings

Out of centralized corporate marketing research activities can arise one or more of these organizational shortcomings: (1) closed-circuit thinking; (2) proliferation of excessive, oftentimes unused data; (3) shortsighted directives.

Closed-circuit thinking on the part of central-staff marketing researchers is characterized by a distrust of all information inputs except the primary data that are collected by the researchers themselves. At the same time, the findings of the organization's research may have longer and longer range application and less and less meaning for day-to-day marketing efforts. As closed-circuit thinking develops, the rest of the company's organization becomes divorced from the input effort and, consequently, finds the output of decreasing practical value. Martineau has observed: "Too many research people have spun themselves a web of self-communication, a perfect system of mutual feedback whereby they have insulated themselves from the needs . . . of the business community."[1]

In addition, corporate marketing research departments have consistently prevailed on line marketing personnel for an excessive amount of data, often on a nonselective basis. Once fed into the system, much of this information may never be heard of again as it overwhelms its collectors with sheer volume.

Lastly, headquarters directives based on centralized research findings often suggest a sales strategy without any accompanying rationale for applying the strategy in future situations. Although the sales directives may be based on an effective field data collection effort involving sales personnel and first-rate analysis by a corporate staff, their rationale often becomes obscured as they move through lengthy channels from the bottom to the top and then back to the bottom of the organization.

1. See "Martineau Hits 'Sterility' in Market Research," *Advertising Age*, May 25, 1964, p. 64.

Program Characteristics

In contrast with centralized corporate *marketing* research, grass roots *market* research has these major characteristics: (1) collection of data accomplished by the lowest sales echelon or first-line sales management, (2) involvement of field marketing personnel not only in data collection but also in analysis and follow-up in the form of positive sales action, and (3) primary emphasis on market, rather than marketing, research. All of these must be present if a grass roots market research program is to be successfully implemented.

The fact that data are collected by field sales personnel does not necessarily distinguish grass roots market research from existing practice. The most common example of the use of field sales personnel for data collection is provided by the "sales force composite" method of preparing sales forecasts. However, when field sales effort is extended to the analysis and interpretation of data preliminary to taking action based on it, this constitutes a departure from current practice in all but a handful of companies. In those rare instances, top management and corporate market research groups supply only occasional policy guidance. In short, data collection for transmission to top management is a natural by-product, not an end objective, of true grass roots market research.

The primary emphasis of this type of research is on a continuing examination of local market situations as the basis for determining immediate sales strategy. This activity is centered on the identification of trade customers most likely to change sources of supply, and the design of both offensive and defensive strategies to improve company sales performance, based on an evaluation of local research and sales results. While data might be collected for top-level marketing research purposes as well, grass roots market research normally is not aimed at or concerned with the broader, longer-range questions of marketing policy.

SPLIT NEEDS

Rapidly changing market structures and vast differences among market areas are commonplace in certain industries and serve to emphasize critical factors which favor a split in research labor. Although these facts of marketing life offer evidence of the need for better on-the-spot local marketing decisions, the distance—in terms of time, space, and attitude—between the centralized corporate research staff and marketing line personnel represents a barrier to the flow of information on which those decisions can be based. The psychological distance between the branch manager and top-level corporate management may be so great as to restrict the flow of strategic communications between them except where company policy dictates.

In addition, corporate staff researchers traditionally become so deeply involved in marketing research efforts with long-term importance that investigations of individual short-term market situations have been neglected and perpetually orphaned. Clearly, some division of research labor is warranted.

MARKET CHANGES

Aggregate data often conceal the comparatively rapid competitive shifts which typify many local markets. Closer examinations of individual markets on a continuing basis are required to point out these shifts. For example, the analysis of a large metropolitan market undertaken for the producer and national distributor of a convenience food item disclosed that within the space of seven years the market situation would shift from one which was currently dominated by manufacturer-owned operations marketing their products by means of wholesale and retail stores and house-to-house distribution to one dominated by retail chains owning "captive" plants.

While the amount of time over which market shifts occur may be relatively lengthy from the point of view of local sales management, longer-term shifts typically are the result of a number of specific shorter-term decisions. Many of these decisions can be predicted in advance and affected by local sales action. Where such longer-term trends are identified by top management, the selling force can be an effective means not only of implementing policies to counteract or reinforce a trend, but also of maintaining up-to-date information about further shifts in structure, particularly those involving important current or potential customers.

TERRITORIAL DIFFERENCES

The days of the nationwide decision, if they ever existed, are gone for most marketing executives. Structural differences in seemingly related markets may alter the number and type of competing producers, the types of channels used for distribution and the popularity of each, and customer buying habits.

These factors are important in the distribution of home appliances, for which illustrative figures are shown in *Exhibit I*. In the home appliances industry problems of local distributor relationships also create distinctive market structures in different parts of the country. Together all of these forces, and perhaps others, explain why the importance of a given market for two nationally competing brands may vary widely.

For example, as shown in the exhibit, 31% of Brand A's sales were made

Exhibit I. *Proportion of selected brands of home appliances sold in major market areas*

Brands	Market region				
	Northeast	North Central	South	West	Total
A	32%	25%	31%	12%	100%
B	28	26	21	25	100
C	40	29	5	26	100
D	33	24	31	12	100
E	30	43	24	3	100
F	25	25	24	26	100
All other	27	29	26	18	100
Total	29%	29%	23%	19%	100%

SOURCE: "Myth of the National Market," based on data prepared by Audits & Surveys, Inc., *Dun's Review and Modern Industry*, May 1964, p. 40.

in the South in sharp contrast both to Brand C, which realized only 5% of its sales there, and the industry, which sold 23% of its goods in that region. This would suggest that, where nonstandard approaches to marketing problems are desirable, decisions ought to be based on research and follow-up action carried out by field managers most familiar with local problems.

DISTANCE DIMENSIONS

Three dimensions of distance—the temporal, spatial, and attitudinal—create a problem which exists between staff and line personnel, particularly in a decentralized organization with widespread markets. The importance of the distance problem is suggested by one sales training specialist who asserted, "Sales executives say that failure to communicate—upward and downward . . . is one of the ten greatest mistakes first-line sales managers make."

The time and space problems can be overcome with improved communications methods and a reporting routine. Attitudinal gaps are more difficult to bridge, as suggested by complaints voiced by one-half of a surveyed group of top company officers about their field sales managers. The managers were labeled as "often ineffective" in the vital areas of coordination, follow-through, problem diagnosis, and decision making. Attitudinal gaps can be lessened best by the development of a mutual respect on the part of communicants, coupled with a convenient method of organizing, analyzing, and reporting information.

A development which increases the need for improved two-way information flow in the marketing organization is the growing concentration of corporate sales efforts among a smaller number of important customers. Top management demonstrates a growing interest in these key accounts as the risks attendant on the loss of any one such account grow. To this extent, the company's local sales managers should be called on to develop a greater amount of information on a continuing basis about key-account activities. A grass roots market research program can assist in accomplishing the needed control for key-account management and a generally improved system of information feedback and marketing control.

PSYCHOLOGICAL BARRIERS

Within a regional or local sales organization, psychological barriers may exist between sales representatives and the branch manager, restricting the flow of vital information at its very source. This may be the case to a greater extent in the future if companies utilize the findings of recent research which indicate strongly that the determinants for success in sales management are greatly different from those for success in selling. Growing differences between the psychological makeup of branch managers and that of their sales representatives will require organized communications programs—the sort of programs which usually die a natural death when conducted on a voluntary basis—as a counteracting force.

Locally oriented market research has not been totally neglected. Where its importance is recognized, however, too often it is carried out by marketing research staff members from the headquarters organization. Typically, it requires a close observation of individual customer and competitor actions. Completely aside from the fact that specially assigned research personnel generally have greater difficulty and incur more expense obtaining accurate information than do permanently assigned sales personnel, the expenditure of effort on this type of research often precludes research work of longer-range significance at the headquarters level. Sales personnel have a comparative advantage in gathering local data.

Favoring Trends

Grass roots market research can be implemented relatively easily today, thanks to a number of trends observed in recent years. Among the trends are (1) involvement of the sales organization in various managerial activities; (2) decentralization of marketing decision making through the vehicles of brand and product management concepts; (3) improved qualifications of field sales personnel; (4) ready-made programs for the collection of sales control information.

SALES FORCE INVOLVEMENT

From time to time, companies have announced various programs designed to involve sales personnel and branch managers to a greater extent in various corporate activities. Information collection is perhaps the most common of these, ranging from product, price, and service comparisons with competitors to estimates of the amount of sales expected for a given period as part of the corporate sales forecasting process. A General Electric marketing consultant described one such extensive information collection process thus:

"Once we pulled together a complete picture of a competitor's distribution from reports turned in by 120 salesmen even up to and including its warehousing in the most strategic locations. It put us in a better position to plan and implement our own distribution needs. We have a planned program of sending questionnaires to our salesmen requesting information for a competitive analysis and we get a great deal of valuable information from them.

"We get research into how our competitors are marketing their products, how many salesmen they have, and how their products compare as to service, function, and quality. "

However, involvement extends beyond mere information collection. Many marketing organizations, including those of General Electric and Du Pont, have instituted product development systems which utilize salesmen in the first phases of the work. Sylvania Electric's Photolamp Division several years ago decided to go to its salesmen for more advice and participation in marketing strategy.

In many companies, regional sales management is being called on to assume some responsibility for such activities as packaging, test marketing, product planning, product evaluation, and individual promotions.

DECENTRALIZED DECISION MAKING

The emergence of brand and product management has been, in part, a result of the emphasis on the marketing concept. Typically, the tasks of the brand manager have been to assume both line and staff authority for a given product or group of products and coordinate production with advertising, research, and personal selling. This has resulted in some decentralization of responsibility and authority, and a shortening of communication channels from the field to a high-level managerial control center. Further, the decentralization of marketing decision making has provided the opportunity for a variety of research efforts geared to meet the particular needs of different markets.

Widespread developments in customer purchasing policies have influenced qualifications required for effective and intelligent sales representation and sales management. Such developments include not only the broadening of buying influences, many of which are hidden, but the relentless pressure on price, streamlining of procurement procedures, entrenchment of value analysis in purchasing programs, proliferation of purchasing committees, predetermined minimum inventories, computerized reorder systems, interminable demands for special services, centralized purchasing in large companies, and the systematizing of reciprocal buying procedures. As the analysts conducting one study concluded:

"These complex forces interact in the industrial marketplace and create new problems for the sales executive.

"He must re-evaluate the role of personal selling in his over-all marketing machine. He must continually weigh its contribution against that of advertising and promotion . . . decide whether to hire a new man or boost the ad budget.

"He may have to seek a different caliber of salesman, train him differently, pay him differently. Inevitably, he has got to send into the field a more knowledgeable and better equipped man."

Since field sales representatives already are prevailed on for a wide range of information by their organization managers, sales personnel of the type needed should prove to be made-to-order for the tasks facing them under a grass roots market research program.

Although grass roots market research consists of much more than just information collection, the vehicle necessary for this phase of the research —the sales control form—currently exists in many companies.

A Case Example

Despite the fact that this example has been disguised, the situation presented in the following pages is similar to that which actually existed.

A corporate staff group for a fluid milk processor was called on to design and implement a grass roots market research program.[2] We will trace the steps involved in the grass roots approach, which covered the program's initiation, implementation, and control.

PROGRAM INITIATION

Initiated by top management, the effort was delegated to the corporate staff, which had, through its previous work, obtained a broad overview of the structural operations of the marketplace and, therefore, had gained the background necessary to isolate key variables for intensive study at the grass roots level.

Step 1: Analysis. The initial task of the staff marketing research group

2. In accomplishing the adaptation of the example, the authors are grateful to Professors Daniel I. Padberg and Elmer F. Baumer, Department of Agricultural Economics, The Ohio State University; the following publication was particularly useful: *Structural Changes in the California Fluid Milk Industry* by Daniel I. Padberg and D. A. Clarke, Jr., Bulletin 802, California Agricultural Experimental Station, June 1964.

was to undertake an analysis of important industry trends and indicators. In the marketing of fluid milk, a major consideration was a study of demand-supply relations, with special reference to such factors as consumption patterns and excess production capacity. As a result of its analysis, the staff group found that the amount of fluid milk consumed per person was likely to remain quite stable and would not change quickly over the next ten years.

On the other hand, widespread adoption of high-temperature, short-time pasteurizing techniques had permitted shifts from batch processing to continuous flow operations, and therefore the production levels required for the profitable operation of fluid milk processing plants had increased significantly during recent years. These developments led to a further concentration of production in the hands of fewer processors and growing excess capacity.

The adoption of paper containers had brought about further technological changes. A monthly volume of about 250,000 gallons was normally sufficient to gain essentially all apparent scale economies for a glass operation, while such scale economies for a paper operation extended beyond 600,000 gallons per month. A paper container operation therefore created a considerable advantage for large-scale operations. Combining the information available on demand-supply relations, it was possible for the staff group to predict a situation of rather severe supply-demand disequilibrium in the industry.

The following factors were found to have important influence on the marketing programs of competitors in any given geographically defined market area: (1) concentration of wholesale selling and retail buying power, (2) private label movements, (3) acquisition or divestment of captive plants, (4) changes in market outreach, and (5) changes in distribution technology.

Among the findings the staff group uncovered in studying these factors were:

1. The concentration of grocery buying among relatively few centers of power strongly affected wholesale purchases. In eight selected urban areas in the Northeastern section of the United States, over 75% of total retail food sales were controlled by corporate and cooperative chain organizations. In addition, 40% of fluid milk sales were made by food stores, a fact which underlined the importance of keeping abreast of competitive activity in this sector.

2. Because of the desire of chains to enter into private label arrangements, large processors were virtually compelled to pursue private label sales in order to avoid production and distribution problems. In some instances, chains had given fluid milk processors the alternative of packing a private label brand or losing a large and important store account.

3. In some cases, chains actually became fluid milk processors, primarily

through the acquisition of plants of marginal companies. Conversely, other grocery chains owning fluid milk processing plants had divested themselves of the local plants for various reasons. Still others had been persuaded to forgo unprofitable milk processing operations when offered an attractive private label program from an independent processor.

4. Expansion of areas served by any one milk processor could be expected to increase at a fairly modest rate, particularly because of the development of major highways and better insulated transportation equipment. The likelihood of invasion from companies not serving any one particular area had increased. Actually, the growth of market outreach capabilities had facilitated dumping in some instances.

5. Because the adoption of self-service in retail food outlets had revolutionized distribution technology, shelf or case space had become an important determinant in the success or failure of specific brands. Many consumers showed indifference to brands of milk when the price was equated. Therefore, the processor had to strongly differentiate his brand from others or gain additional case space for his brand, or do both.

An analysis of these five factors enabled the marketing research group to appraise the relative growth of marketing and manufacturing institutions and activities in the fluid milk industry. However, because these factors were dynamic in nature and varied among geographically defined markets, the need for market research on a continuing basis was established.

Step 2: Assessment. At this point in designing the program, it was necessary to determine thresholds for changes in trade relationships. Once known or estimated, these thresholds could serve as guidelines for field sales managers (or plant managers) in deciding whether or not a shift in any one of the industry's local market structures was about to take place.

Specifically, it was essential that a field sales manager or plant manager have some prior knowledge of when and whether a retail food chain would add private brands. Through empirical evidence, developed by research analysis, it was determined that any grocery chain group that supplied as few as five large retail stores (stores with total sales approximately $15,000 per week or more) had a strong probability of being capable of managing a private label milk program. With such information, and with constant surveillance of his market area, the sales manager could present his private label program at the most opportune time.

Among a variety of estimated thresholds developed was one relating to the activities of small companies. It was known that a monthly volume of 600,000 gallons was necessary in order to utilize satisfactorily the equipment needed for a paper container operation. Therefore, it was established that when the sales of an organization selling milk in such containers fell below 500,000 gallons, its actions should be watched closely for signs of market withdrawal or "demoralizing" price or concessional activities. Desperation moves by a marginal company could positively or negatively affect the sales of all the plants in the market area.

In addition to, and in conjunction with, the determination of thresholds, it was necessary for the marketing research group, in cooperation with top-level executives, to develop rules of thumb on which field sales managers could base their decisions, if and when a threshold was reached. With regard to the two instances cited above, rules of thumb were established indicating the basic guidelines of private label programs to be offered, and the actions to be taken in exploiting the weakness of a marginal competitor.

It was known that several fluid milk processors had entered into unprofitable private label arrangements. In their zeal to make the sale, these companies had made concessions which had proved extremely costly, such as providing case service when the margin of profit would not pay for this service. On the other hand, large fluid milk processors had to be extremely cautious in their handling of competition vis-à-vis marginal companies. Their actions could be construed by the federal government as attempts to monopolize or restrain trade in a market area.

Step 3: Determination of Methods. After thresholds and rules of thumb were established by the corporate research group through top management, it was then appropriate to develop well-defined procedures to facilitate the collection of the right data at the grass roots level. For example, an essential piece of information to be obtained in each field sales manager's territory —defined as the area serviced by the home-delivery routes under his control —was an estimate of the market shares of retail grocery chains.

To obtain market shares of grocery chains, the sales manager was first advised to outline his territory on a map which distinguished counties within the territory. He could then arrive at an estimate of total food store sales by consulting *Sales Management's Annual Survey of Buying Power,* which provides county-by-county food store sales data.

Secondly, he was urged to obtain from newspapers, food brokers, or any similar source, estimates of the number of stores in each chain group— both corporate and cooperative—in his territory and the volume of sales for each group. In most instances these estimates were reliable enough for approximation purposes.

For the third step, the sales manager was asked to compare his territory with those outlined by the newspapers and brokers. If the territories differed, he was to adjust the estimates to reflect the differences by adding or subtracting the sales volume of stores falling within or outside his territory.

The sales manager was next counseled in using a set of estimating procedures, which not only provided information relating to a particular store's sales volume but could also be used as checks against each other. The following are illustrative of the types of guidelines generated by the corporate research staff:

☐ Multiply the square footage of store selling space by a factor of $2 to $12. The factor used varies with the aggressiveness of the store and can often be approximated by knowing the performance of the chain in the area, as shown by the newspaper's or brokers' data. The resulting figure gives an estimate of total store sales per week.

☐ Determine the number of full-time employees, and estimate the total number of man-hours per week for these employees. Multiply the number of man-hours by a factor of $12 to $25 to obtain an estimate of total sales per week.

☐ Obtain from suppliers estimates of weekly sales of certain staple items, and divide these by their percentage of total store sales to obtain an estimate of total sales per week for the store.

☐ Multiply the number of active checkout lanes (in use at least one day of the week) by $3,500 to $5,000. This will provide another estimate of weekly sales.

☐ Harvest the trade grapevine. Others may be attempting to make similar estimates.

When estimates of all chains' sales in the territory had been made, each was divided by the total food store sales figure obtained from *Sales Management* to arrive at an estimate of market share for each group. The residual—the difference between all chains' sales and total sales in food stores—served as a good approximation of the sales volume of unaffiliated independent food stores.

In addition to other well-defined procedures, the staff marketing research group also had the responsibility of isolating certain key regional estimators, such as the percent to be applied against store sales to determine the sales for any one product category. In the case example, fluid milk sales within grocery stores were estimated to be between 2% and 3% of total store sales. These estimates were sometimes achieved through a study of analyses made by trade publications. In other instances they were arrived at directly by asking the appropriate store buyers.

Step 4: Design of Data-Collection Form. The final step in the initiation of a grass roots market research program was the design of data-collection form which would facilitate analysis. The work sheets were relatively uncomplicated, which permitted speedy classification and tabulation of data. Field sales managers had little time to devote to additional paper work; their efforts were better spent in cultivating markets than in preparing long, complicated, and tedious forms for recording purposes.

Several work sheets were designed for use by field sales managers in determining the status of the fluid milk market in their territories. Primarily, these work sheets, shown in *Exhibit II*, concentrated on an analysis of sales to and by grocery chains, because these chains represented the key accounts for the company. The work sheets related, both directly and indirectly, to the analysis of industry trends and indicators mentioned previously.

PROGRAM IMPLEMENTATION

If it was to launch such a program in its field sales territories, top management had to take steps to provide a rationale, along with encouragement and incentives, in order to convince the field personnel that their efforts would be rewarded. One means for providing a rationale was through the use of a game technique. During a periodic meeting at corporate headquarters, sales managers were collectively introduced to the concept of grass roots market research. This was accomplished by an orientation session in which they completed a series of work sheets based upon hypothetical data given them. They were then asked to suggest courses of action which they might take when faced with the market conditions indicated in their reports. Not only did such a game provide a training experience, but it was useful in showing front-line managers the value of collecting data on a continuing basis.

Top management also provided an incentive system that furnished rewards relating to the fulfillment of research tasks. Copies of the data-collection work sheets or forms were required to be sent to corporate headquarters. This permitted headquarters to review field operations and to question the information appearing on the forms. It also provided top management with an over-all perspective, through a comparison of all field sales managers' reports. Rewards, in the form of bonuses, were paid if and when a manager capitalized on the information collected.

PROGRAM CONTROL

The work sheets designated in this situation also served as simple "feedback" mechanisms, because they facilitated the logging of essential data regarding the competitive elements in the company's sales territories. Through the program, it became possible for a branch manager to perceive basic changes in the market strategies and tactics of milk processors and grocery chains, provided he reviewed and revised his work sheets at least once every quarter. By maintaining the work sheets he was able to note, for example, the potential rewards of various private-label arrangements. As the market structures were altered, he was prepared to exploit the alternatives.

But what is most important is that information on which the branch

Exhibit II. Company X—forms used by branch managers to determine market status

Work Sheet A: Food store structure

Food stores	(1) Number of stores in Company X's market area	(2) Total dollar sales per week*	(3) Average dollar sales per store — (2) ÷ (1)†	(4) Market share — (2) ÷ grand total of sales†	PRIVATE LABEL ARRANGEMENTS‡ Supplier	Products supplied	Delivery arrangements	Wholesale prices and discount policies	Other information
Corporate chains with captive plants									
1. Chain A	6	$186,000	$31,000	10.2%					
2. Chain B	8	276,800	34,600	15.2					
3. Chain C	14	308,000	22,000	16.9					
Etc.									
Subtotal	35	$890,500		48.8%					
Corporate chains without captive plants									
1. Chain D	6	$144,000	$24,000	7.9%	Company R	gal.: ½ gal.	Store-Door	1-1000 gal.: 60¢/gal.: 35¢/½ gal.	
2. Chain E	2	79,000	39,500	4.3					
3. Chain F	2	37,000	18,500	2.0	Company S	½ gal.	Dock	1-1000 gal.: 34¢/½ gal.	
Etc.									
Subtotal	14	$302,400		16.6%					
Cooperative chains									
1. Chain G	10	$85,000	$8,500	4.6%	Company S	½ gal.	Dock	1-1000 gal.: 34¢/½ gal.	
2. Chain H	8	105,000	13,200	5.8	Company T	½ gal.: qts.	Dock	1-750 gal.: 35¢/½ gal.	
3. Chain I	8	88,000	11,000	4.8					
4. Chain J	2	54,800	27,400	3.0	Company X	½ gal.	Store-Door	1-750 gal.: 31¢/½ gal.	
Etc.									
Subtotal	34	$360,500		19.7%					
Independents §	137	273,400		14.9%					
Grand total		$1,826,800		100%					

*Based on estimates obtained from local sources.
†Obviously, this figure suffers from the weaknesses of any average.
‡Some of this information may have to be obtained through an intelligence system.
§Independents' sales = grand total minus sum of all chain sales.

Work Sheet B: Private label sales

Corporate and cooperative grocery chains without captive plants	PRIVATE LABEL MILK SUPPLIERS Company X (1) Estimated percentage of total fluid milk sales represented by label*	(2) Number of gallons sold per week†	Company R (1) Estimated percentage of total fluid milk sales represented by label*	(2) Number of gallons sold per week†	Company S (1) Estimated percentage of total fluid milk sales represented by label*	(2) Number of gallons sold per week†	Company T (1) Estimated percentage of total fluid milk sales represented by label*	(2) Number of gallons sold per week†	Total private label sales per week within chains (in gallons) — sum of (2) figures
1. Chain D	—	—	75%	3,240	—	—	—	—	3,240
2. Chain E	—	—	—	—	60%	1,422	—	—	1,422
3. Chain F	—	—	—	—	—	—	—	—	
4. Chain G	—	—	—	—	60%	1,530	—	—	1,530
5. Chain H	—	—	—	—	—	—	70%	2,218	2,218
6. Chain I	50%	1,320	—	—	—	—	—	—	1,320
7. Chain J	—	—	—	—	—	—	—	—	
Etc.									
Total		1,320		5,240		2,952		3,418	
Grand total									12,430

* By observing stores within a chain, an estimate of the percentage of shelf space allotted to private labels can be made.
† The total dollar sales column in Work Sheet A is relevant for this work sheet.

Exhibit II (continued)

Work Sheet C: Processors' food store sales

Captive plants*	(1) Total sales in Company X's territory per week	(2) Fluid milk sales — (1) × 3%	(3) Estimated percentage of captive plant sales out of total†	(4) Estimated captive plant milk sales in dollars — (2) × (3)	(5) Average retail price per gallon‡	(6) Total number of gallons sold per week — (4) ÷ (5)	Market share
1. Chain A	$186,000	5,580	80%	$4,464	$0.853	5,230	5.6%
2. Chain B	276,800	8,304	75	6,228	0.861	7,230	7.8
3. Chain C	308,000	9,240	85	7,854	0.848	9,270	9.9
Etc.							

Independent processors	(1) Grocery routes competitive with Company X in territory§	(2) Average fluid milk sales per route per week (in dollars)	(3) Average wholesale price per gallon‡	(4) Number of gallons sold per route per week	(5) Total number of gallons sold per week — (1) × (4)	
1. Company X	10	$770	$0.713	1,078	10,780	11.6%
2. Company R	8	1,825	0.695	2,627	21,020	22.5
3. Company S	9	800	0.702	1,141	10,270	11.0
4. Company T	13	1,090	0.695	1,564	20,340	21.8
Etc.						
Grand total					93,140	100%

* Fluid milk processing plants that are owned by food store chains.
† This estimate can be made either by observing shelf space allocations or asking store managers (or buyers) to estimate this percentage.
‡ Weighted average price for all sizes of containers.
§ In making this estimate, sales managers can draw on information secured by their salesmen in informal conversations with competitors' salesmen.

Work Sheet D: Processors' home delivery sales

Processors	(1) Home delivery routes competitive with Company X in territory*	(2) Average fluid milk sales per route per week (in dollars)	(3) Average retail price per gallon†	(4) Number of gallons sold per route per week — (2) ÷ (3)	(5) Total number of gallons sold per week — (1) × (4)	Market share of home delivery
1. Company X	42	550	$0.9425	580	24,360	21.9%
2. Company R	66	500	0.9425	530	34,980	31.4
3. Company S	30	590	0.9425	630	18,900	17.0
4. Company T	52	600	0.9425	635	33,020	29.7
Grand total	190				111,260	100%

* In making this estimate, sales managers can draw on information secured by their salesmen in informal conversations with competitors' salesmen.
† Weighted average price for all sizes of containers.

Work Sheet E: Combined food store and home delivery sales

Processors — independent and captive	(1) Total number of gallons sold per week — food stores*	(2) Total number of gallons sold per week — home delivery†	(3) Combined total — (1) + (2)‡	Market share combined total
1. Company X	10,780	24,360	35,140	17.1%
2. Company R	21,020	34,980	56,000	27.4
3. Company S	10,270	18,900	29,170	14.2
4. Company T	20,340	33,020	53,360	26.1
5. Chain A	5,230	—	5,230	2.6
6. Chain B	7,230	—	7,230	3.5
7. Chain C	9,270	—	9,270	4.5
Etc.				
Grand total	93,140	111,260	204,400	100%

* Data can be obtained from Work Sheet C.
† Data can be obtained from Work Sheet D.
‡ The combined total is useful in isolating marginal companies.

NOTE: Differences between individual items and total, if any, represent unspecified amounts for "Etc."

manager could base his day-to-day decisions became available at the local level through the work sheet system. Such a system provided an inexpensive means of collecting, tabulating, and analyzing essential data. After the first attempt at completing the work sheets, it was estimated that each field sales manager would need to spend no more time to keep them up-to-date than three man-days once every three months.

In order to be certain that the program was operating as originally conceived, top management authorized periodic checks by the corporate marketing research department to determine the accuracy of the grass roots information and also the extent of its usage by the local sales organizations. In addition, annual surveys were made by the corporate staff to define the extent of the program's cost.

Program Benefits

A grass roots market research program, if properly implemented and controlled, can be expected to facilitate two-way communications among field sales representatives, their branch managers, and centralized top management, and to establish a precedent for special field sales information collection efforts. Because the basic emphasis in such a program is on consultative management, it can also be expected to improve the morale of sales and first-line managerial personnel by giving them more important roles in determining local marketing tactics.

Other than these rather explicit benefits, such a program should: (1) grant management at several levels a "license" to act; (2) provide additional measurements of sales and managerial performance; (3) furnish aids for long-range planning; and (4) maintain "instant" information for use in emergency-decision situations.

License to act—Any research program that invests responsibility for information collection and analysis in the first-line sales manager must provide him with the authority to act within well-defined limits. While this is implicit in every grant of authority, too often the area of decision making is nebulous, and authority is left to be tested on a somewhat "cut-and-try" basis by the manager. Because of the magnitude of the decisions that can be based on market research conducted in a grass roots program, some definition of limits on authority and cues for managerial action should be instituted during the implementation of the program.

In the dairy industry example discussed previously, top management was able to reappraise the extent of the local manager's authority in making decisions based on experience gained through the program. It revised rules of thumb, established at the initiation of the program, in the light of market shifts. The program provided management with the information to determine when flexibility of action on the local level was necessary and when adherence to policies or operating plans should be relaxed or strengthened. Rather than being viewed in the negative sense of a limitation on authority, such rules of thumb were and should be regarded positively as licenses for action.

Additional measurements—Share-of-market trends along with key-account data generated by a grass roots market research program can provide measures of marketing performance in a given territory. In addition, managerial performance can be judged by a periodic top-management evaluation of information collection and analyses performed by field sales managers. Top management can determine whether or not a particular branch manager has a firm understanding of the competitive situation in his area by gauging the caliber of his analyses.

Under a program of this type, top management has an opportunity to judge actual front-line management decisions in the context of the available information on which the decisions are based. No longer is it necessary to carry out performance reviews in the vacuum of uncollected or disorganized information. Greater latitude in decision authority should accrue to the manager who effectively comprehends his role in the system and acts shrewdly in the light of market developments.

Long-range planning aids—If conducted on a continuing basis, a grass roots market research program provides periodic measures of the importance of various types of customers in a market area, the share of market being realized by the company conducting the program, and information regarding the economic stability of various types of competitors. By being able to trace past, and forecast future, market shifts of some significance, as outlined by the field sales managers, corporate planners can build more realistic long-range projections, or suggest ways of meeting competitive crises before they spread to other marketing territories.

Provision for crises—When a marketing crisis occurs, there is typically little time to collect information. A branch manager must act on past information, current incomplete impressions of the problem, and his own intuition. Even where necessary information on which to base an intelligent crisis decision exists somewhere in the company, first-line sales managers typically are unaware of its existence, unable to specify the type of information needed, or reluctant to involve others in the crisis. A grass roots market research program provides a continuing source of information immediately available to sales managers, and the availability of the information on a continuing basis may allow them to anticipate and alleviate crises before they occur.

As a case in point, the program in the dairy industry example was eventually extended to encourage the cross communication of information among local managers, especially among those in adjacent territories where there existed a similarity of competitive conditions prior to market invasion of one of the territories by a distant competitor. Where this happened, the sales manager in the invaded territory was encouraged to pass along information relative to the nature of the invasion to the sales manager in the territory not yet affected.

Potential Pitfalls

Although the benefits which can be realized from insights into competition and consultative management heavily favor the grass roots approach, this is not the whole story. There are some potential pitfalls inherent in such a market research program. Most important among these potential problems are (1) data availability, (2) individual bias, (3) union opposition, (4) time and cost, (5) morale, (6) local autonomy, and (7) duplication of research effort.

Data availability—The basic obstacle to the collection of data, in most cases, is the inability or the unwillingness of the source to provide the desired information. When the effectiveness of personal relations must be relied on in this phase of a research effort, success may hang by a thin thread. However, to the extent that most information-collection efforts under a grass roots program consist of direct observations and estimations by highly qualified sales representatives, this obstacle can be greatly minimized.

For example, head counts of store personnel, observations of store traffic, estimates of production rates and component material needs, counts of retail store checkout lanes, and the like, can generally be carried out with no personal contact or prearranged agreement. Measurement rules oi thumb provided by the corporate research staff should free information-collection procedures from total dependency on personal relations.

Individual bias—All research efforts are accompanied by bias. It is perhaps especially prevalent when the research is conducted by those whose skills lie elsewhere. In a local research program bias in information collection and analysis can be introduced by both the sales representative and his branch manager.

There is the danger, too, that managerial analyses, performed in the territorial or local sales office, might be flavored to justify a given decision already reached by the branch manager involved. In the short run it is possible that bias of this type might arise. However, control induced by a

Exhibit III. Cost of grass roots program for milk processor

Cost center	Amount
START-UP COSTS	
Corporate executives' time (10 man-days)	$1,500
Corporate researchers' time (25 man-days)	1,875
Local sales managers' time (3 man-days for each of 15 managers)	3,375
Travel	2,500
Total start-up costs	$9,250
CONTINUING PROGRAM COSTS PER YEAR	
Corporate executives' time (15 man-days)	$ 2,250
Corporate researchers' time (12 man-days)	900
Local sales managers' time (9 man-days for 15 managers)	10,125
Local sales representatives' time (5 man-days for each of 150 representatives)	15,750
Travel (for field control purposes)	3,000
Total continuing costs	$32,025

decision review process and periodic appraisal by corporate staff and line personnel should alleviate managerial bias over the long run.

Union opposition—In specialized selling situations a sales force may be unionized. This is particularly true for the company that employs driver-salesmen in the distribution of its goods. In these cases the assignment of information collection in addition to current tasks may be a subject for contract negotiation.

Time and cost—The time and cost required for a grass roots market research program depend largely on the nature of customer operations, competitive pressures, personnel capabilities, and a number of other factors. The approach designed for the fluid milk processor, discussed earlier, was estimated to cost the amounts shown in *Exhibit III.*

The estimated annual cost of about $32,000 for the program was somewhat inflated and, therefore, conservative. The milk processing company for which the estimates were generated had an extensive sales force. The information collection duties of the field men were handled, for the most part, during the performance of their regular duties, and could be accomplished during waiting periods at customers' places of business. Further, the importance of each of a number of key customers to this company was such that either gaining or forestalling the loss of one key account in one sales territory as a result of the program could have defrayed the total annual costs of the program for the entire company.

Loss of morale—A tendency for sales personnel to regard a grass roots program as either imposing additional paper work with little attendant value or allowing additional top management "spying" from above may be typical at the outset. Whether or not this attitude continues largely depends on the way the program is presented initially by top management to the field sales managers, and later by the managers to their sales personnel. Successful application of program-generated information and analyses is the best solvent for this type of problem.

Unbalancing "prerogatives"—Objection to implementing a grass roots market research program has centered around the sometimes unvoiced concern that, once given the opportunity to base certain decisions on research performed locally, a sales manager will assume additional decision-making freedoms not previously granted him. A company in which this is a prevalent practice is not likely to be in a position to implement a grass roots research program; the degree of centralization with which it operates would neither allow it nor make it advisable.

On the other hand, a major asset of decentralized management is the encouragement of lower- and middle-management personnel to take on greater responsibility and authority. To the extent this freedom is increased under the grass roots program, the opportunity for management development at lower organization levels is broadened.

Duplication of effort—Research efforts carried out by local sales staffs can overlap. This is especially probable where product-specialist sales representatives are employed, several of whom call on the same customers. It may involve little waste, however, where products sold by specialists have distinctly different market structures, with only occasional institutional duplication. At times, this duplication of effort can provide the basis for a top-management check on the relative quality of the research and analysis carried on by two or more sales representatives or territorial offices.

Program Criteria

So far in this article, we have discussed the potential profits and pitfalls inherent in employing grass roots market research. But how can top management decide whether to institute such a program? The following specific items should be examined: (1) market shifts, (2) existence of key accounts, (3) strong corporate staff, (4) decentralized control, (5) "bottoms-up" receptivity, and (6) capability of sales personnel in the field.

Market shifts—Consumer goods, particularly those bought on a convenience basis, are distributed through constantly shifting channels. Market patterns shift to a lesser extent for other consumer and industrial products.

A volatile market structure bears observation of the type which can be provided through a grass roots market research program.

Existence of key accounts—Corporations competing for business in an industry characterized by a limited number of large customers depend to a great extent on their success with those key accounts. A limited number of large customers can be observed closely enough through grass roots research to predict their economic health in the future. To the extent that drastic structural shifts in markets are the result of economic upheaval among important participants, this is a vital aspect of the program.

Strong corporate staff—Just as most successfully decentralized organizations have capable top-level managerial talent, so a grass roots market research program requires initiation and continuing guidance from a strong corporate marketing research organization. Responsibilities which encompass, for example, the recommendation and revision of guidelines for estimation to be followed by field sales managers, comparison and interpretation of system-wide research reports, and measurement of the profit performance of the grass roots program on a periodic basis, all require a corporate staff able not only to carry out its research mission effectively but to supervise and communicate with line marketing personnel who are also engaged in research activity.

Decentralized control—Organizations accustomed to a management philosophy which places emphasis on decentralization will have a head start in initiating a market research program of the type described in this article. Decentralization of other activities can set the precedent for the delegation necessary to accomplish research at the local or territorial level.

"Bottoms-up" receptivity—A grass roots market research effort doubly challenges management's receptivity to "bottoms-up" management. It is likely that both line-management personnel and corporate research staff members are not accustomed to the challenge. Whether the latter are capable of meeting the challenge will largely determine the success of the program.

Capability of sales personnel—This grass roots approach depends not only on individual abilities, but also on whether or not the local sales personnel are in a position to observe customer operations as a regular part of their sales efforts. The latter factor requires a type of call that is regularly made to the customer's place of business, whether it be a warehouse, wholesale, or retail facility. It goes without saying that a strategically positioned sales representative who is not otherwise capable of collecting the simple information needed under the program may not be of much value to the sales organization.

Conclusion

The prime value of the grass roots market research concept is its inherent recognition that each and every sales territory in which a company operates is different. This provides a mechanism whereby field personnel can capitalize on individual market shifts.

The processing and analysis of information by field sales personnel should enable both local and top management to develop strategies and tactics superior to those being used by competitors.

The program can furnish a formal means of facilitating communication among headquarters personnel, field managers, and salesmen. Feedback of important competitive information from salesmen to supervisors is assured. It can also provide both top and local management with licenses to act, particularly because current information is generated on a continuing basis for use in meeting rapid market changes. Once established, a grass roots program can furnish a lead-in, background, and/or precedent for special data-collection efforts, in addition to evidence on which to base long-range plans.

Aside from strategic and tactical benefits, the program can supply a means for evaluating, stimulating, and training management personnel. The decisions made or the strategies suggested by branch managers on the basis of an analysis of the data collected can be carefully scrutinized by those in a position to develop sales managers for positions of greater responsibility.

Although there are some potential pitfalls inherent in a grass roots research program, the benefits gained through competitive insights and consultative management far outweigh those problems. Although the program may require additional effort and forbearance on the part of line and staff personnel alike, this exercise in itself may bear fruit, even if no information outputs of great value are generated. For, when the chips are down in the commercial marketplace, the individual sales manager with the most local marketing intelligence *and* the most effective managerial relationships with corporate headquarters does have significant means to achieve his objectives.

Part III

Finance

Preface

"*The chief value of money lies in the fact that one lives in a world in which it is overestimated.*"—H. L. MENCKEN

To many others besides the irreverent Mencken, money is indeed overestimated. But to a corporate executive weighing the possibilities of financing his company's operations over the next two years, or substituting long-term debt for short-term debt, the value of money as power cannot be overestimated.

Like almost everything else in corporate life, finance has taken on great complexity in recent years. As everyone knows, there are two ways of obtaining capital for use in a business: from earnings it generates and by tapping outside sources. A table bearing the heading "Sources and Uses of Funds," which commonly details the disposition of dollars generated internally as well as any raised outside the company, is now a common sight in the corporate annual report. Retained earnings, once an internal source of funds every financial officer took for granted, have received much greater attention in the last two decades. Indeed, management of cash flows has become a high art, as corporate treasurers try to make every spare dollar work for the company—gathering interest, at least, if not being used directly to advance the business. Money markets have greatly expanded or have even been created (such as the bank certificate of deposit) as financial institutions rushed to meet the market need.

The question of how to tap the savings of others—corporate, governmental, or personal savings—is even more complicated. A host of considerations, both inside and outside the company, throw their weight into the decision. Obviously, a utility with a slow growth rate, a high dividend on its common stock, and an incessant need for money to underwrite construction will have a different financing problem from a fast-growing life insurance company with a steady cash inflow from premium payments and a record of low, if any, cash dividends. The former may well sell debentures to institutional investors, while the latter may prefer to shop for bank loans.

But a company cannot undertake financing in a vacuum; external considerations must be factored into the analysis. The most common consideration, of course, is the cost of money. Linked to it are its general availability in banks and other financial institutions and the health of the bond and equity markets.

171

As the issues and problems surrounding finance have grown in difficulty and complexity, the sophistication and resourcefulness of managers have grown to meet them. One important factor in that growth has been the ingenuity and research of practitioners and academics like those represented in this section. One of them, John G. McLean, was first an academic (professor at the Harvard Business School), then a corporate executive (chief executive officer of Continental Oil Company when he died in 1974).

His article outlines the use of the discounted cash flow technique—which places a time value on money—in weighing capital investment choices at Continental. Few companies employed the method as a matter of course when McLean and his associates introduced it in 1955; now it is used routinely everywhere.

Another, equally influential article was written by Gordon Donaldson as a result of his perception that standard rules of thumb for gauging debt capacity (such as industry norms) were grossly inadequate. For them he substituted a determination of the individual circumstances and needs of the company and analysis of its cash flows. Donaldson's work contributed to a more extensive and more imaginative use of long-term debt in financing. The third article in this section, by William Sihler, provides a helpful rationale for putting the financing questions into perspective.

10. Framework for Financial Decisions

William W. Sihler

This article is for the financial executive who would like to take advantage of the work of scholars and theorists but who has no time to absorb the literature himself. Distilling many leading contributions of financial theorists as he proceeds, the author begins with the question of how much debt a company should have. He examines two basic approaches to that question and their implications for policy makers. Then he takes up the matter of dividend policy, describing the relationships emphasized in theory, practical considerations that complicate the situation, and the significance of all these for deciding on a policy. Next he shows how the cost of capital is determined, following with a discussion of the minimum rate of return to use in evaluating proposed investment projects. Throughout the article, financial theory is seen as a very useful tool for businessmen if employed selectively and translated into terms that are pertinent and comprehensible.

The past few years have seen an extraordinary proliferation in ideas and theories about the two sides of the corporate financial management coin: capital structure and capital asset management. One can find at least one article on these subjects together with rebuttals and rejoinders to past articles in the current issue of any academically oriented financial management journal. Unfortunately, these essays, while making a contribution to theoretical frameworks, are frequently incomprehensible to the corporate financial executive. Even those articles that tend to confirm the assumptions under which he has operated all along are more comforting than they are practical; implementation of the insights is more difficult than explaining them to the general manager.

If we are to transform some of the leading ideas and theories into a usable form for management, we must first consider its needs and problems and look at what the scholars and theorists offer as answers.

The major financial issues confronting management are:
□ Which investments should be accepted?

Exhibit I. Asset-capital structure relationships

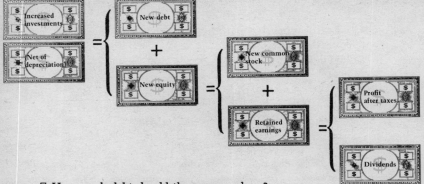

☐ How much debt should the company have?

☐ What portion of the equity should be financed by retention of earnings? What should be the dividend policy?

I believe it helps to consider these questions separately and sequentially: First, management should tentatively decide on the investment levels it wishes and prepare an estimate of cash flow and earnings over a planning period. Then the impact of debt/equity alternatives can be appraised, given the estimate of funds needed and available. At this point can come the question of whether to pay out dividends at a sufficiently high level so that new stock is required to provide the necessary equity base.

Finally, these three preliminary investment decisions should be reconsidered in order to look at their overall impact. Do they make sense together? Should the level of investment be altered? Does the debt/equity policy appear consistent with the dividend decision? Is it consistent with the investment plans?

This approach reflects the realities of life to the financial manager: *assets* must equal *liabilities* plus *equity*. Hence increases or decreases in net working capital and net fixed assets (investments) must be matched by increases or decreases in the capital structure—the debt, common stock, and retained earnings accounts. When the retained earnings account is traced to its source in profits less dividends, the entire arena for financial policy decisions can be shown as diagramed in *Exhibit I*.

Alternative decision patterns are available, such as relating dividends directly to investment requirements. In practice, however, these other combinations are generally inferior and substantially more confusing than the one I have sketched and will elaborate. Much of the ink spilled and tempers lost in arguments on financial policy appear to be the result of inconsistent or needlessly complex structuring of the trade-offs that must be made.

Having suggested a framework for analysis, I will review some of the more relevant thinking on these various points and bring together a number of the most useful ideas so that the manager can easily apply them to the financial policy of his company.

The Debt/Equity Decision

The debt/equity issue—that is, how much debt a company should carry in its capital structure—has been attacked in two ways. The more pragmatic approach[1] puts its emphasis on the following factors (sometimes known by the acronym FRICT): flexibility, risk, income, control, and timing.

In smaller companies, control may be more important, but, in any case, it is a straightforward problem to analyze and so I will not treat it here. Similarly, the timing problem is fairly straightforward, once the capitalization strategy has been settled. The other three items, more vital to the strategic decision, will be discussed in this section.

VITAL FACTORS

Let us begin with the question of *income*. It is easy to see that adding debt to the capital structure, in the vast majority of instances, increases earnings per share more than does raising the same amount of money from common stock. Once interest is paid, all additional income goes to the existing shareholders, and it does not have to be shared with newcomers. *Exhibit II* shows a typical example.

One exception occurs when the price/earnings ratio is in the "supergrowth" range. In this instance, the earnings yield (earnings per share divided by price) is less than the after-tax interest cost. Even in this case, however, as earnings rise, the additional shares will result in slower growth than would be the case if debt were added. Hence, assuming super-growth, after a short period debt wins out as the more attractive approach from an earnings standpoint. *Exhibit III* shows an example of this case comparable with the one illustrated in *Exhibit II*.

Given the favorable impact of leverage (as the effect of debt is called) on income for the common shareholder, there are obviously compensating factors that restrain companies in their use of borrowing. Two important ones are risk and flexibility:

□ *Risk* can be associated with events that have happened in the past

1. This analytical method is perhaps most fully developed by Pearson Hunt, Charles Williams, and Gordon Donaldson in their book, *Basic Business Finance*, 3rd edition (Homewood, Illinois, Richard D. Irwin, Inc., 1966).

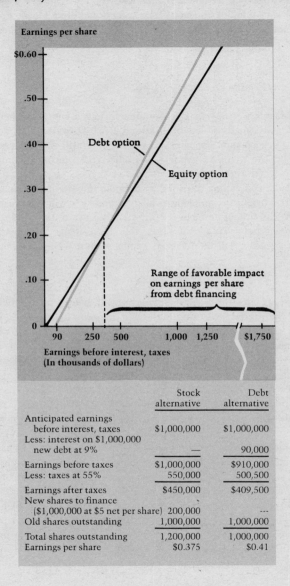

Exhibit II. Impact of new financing on earnings per share ($1,000,000 new financing required)

Earnings per share

Debt option

Equity option

Range of favorable impact on earnings per share from debt financing

Earnings before interest, taxes
(In thousands of dollars)

	Stock alternative	Debt alternative
Anticipated earnings before interest, taxes	$1,000,000	$1,000,000
Less: interest on $1,000,000 new debt at 9%	—	90,000
Earnings before taxes	$1,000,000	$910,000
Less: taxes at 55%	550,000	500,500
Earnings after taxes	$450,000	$409,500
New shares to finance ($1,000,000 at $5 net per share)	200,000	---
Old shares outstanding	1,000,000	1,000,000
Total shares outstanding	1,200,000	1,000,000
Earnings per share	$0.375	$0.41

Exhibit III. Impact of new financing on earnings per share in the high price/ earnings case ($1,000,000 new financing required)

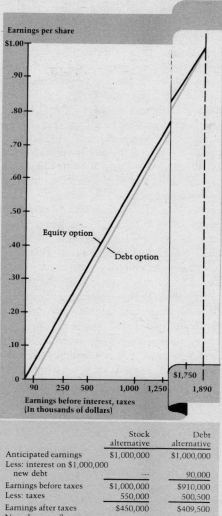

	Stock alternative	Debt alternative
Anticipated earnings	$1,000,000	$1,000,000
Less: interest on $1,000,000 new debt	---	90,000
Earnings before taxes	$1,000,000	$910,000
Less: taxes	550,000	500,500
Earnings after taxes	$450,000	$409,500
New shares to finance ($1,000,000 at post-dilution p/e ratio of 46.5)	50,000	---
Old shares outstanding	1,000,000	1,000,000
Total shares outstanding	1,050,000	1,000,000
Earnings per share	$0.43	$0.41

and that could happen again in the future. Because there are historic data, management can assess the probability and impact of these events. For example, it is not unreasonable for management to expect a recession from time to time. But the recession's timing and magnitude cannot be estimated precisely. Nor is it possible to be absolutely accurate in forecasting the impact of a specified recession on the company's cash flows. Nevertheless, because of historical knowledge and experience with recessions and cash-flow problems, both the recession and the company's cash-flow response do fall into foreseeable categories of risk.

Most companies limit their debt to a level that can be easily serviced in risky circumstances. For example, one automotive parts producer simulated its operations in order to test its probable cash-flow patterns under a variety of adverse business conditions. It found that it could safely manage these risky circumstances with a debt/capitalization ratio of 40% in all but the most severe, sustained depression.

□ *Flexibility* can be defined as the ability to borrow during periods of unexpected adversity—after "things that go bump in the night" have occurred. These are the "unexpected" unknowns, events whose likelihood or even magnitude are not easily assessible since they have not happened before. The automotive parts company mentioned in the last paragraph also explored how the company's finances would be affected if some of its plans were upset or failed. Such conditions as price cuts, product obsolescence, international difficulties, and loss of investment returns were investigated. It was found that several possible reverses would each require about $30 million, although others would be much less costly.

Management was thus faced with a question of how much borrowing capacity should be preserved to allow for these dangers. How much under the 40% debt/capitalization ratio should it go in order to protect itself against the unexpected?

DECISION RULES

Over the years a number of rules of thumb have been developed to assist management in making decisions about the capital structure. The rules are often stated in such forms as "Don't lose your bond rating," "Don't lose a double-A rating," "Borrow as much as you can get," or "Don't borrow more than the industry average." Gordon Donaldson, in his excellent study, *Corporate Debt Capacity*, enumerates and critically evaluates many of these traditional guidelines.[2] He doubts the usefulness of them all.

As a more operative alternative, he suggests that management should explore its firm's cash flows under various risky and adverse conditions, as did the management of the automotive parts company in the example

2. Boston, Division of Research, Harvard Business School, 1961; see also Donaldson's article, p. 326.

described earlier. The data thus generated suggest the maximum debt the company should have if it is to survive a period of business crisis without serious embarrassment. Of course the full extent of the potential crisis and its impact must be estimated by management on the basis of the specific nature of the company. Industry averages or other external points of reference should be used, but with care.

Management must also decide how severe a crisis it is willing to prepare for. This task is accomplished by weighing the likelihood of the situation against the impacts of the action which must be taken to allow for it. The cost of preparing for *all* eventualities is obviously prohibitively high— even an investment in government bonds is not without some risks. The cost of capital structure "insurance" for *many* possible disasters, however, is worthwhile. In the case of the automotive parts management, a 30% debt/capitalization ratio left the company with a minimum of $30 million for major adversities. Management decided that the company could afford to hold this amount as a debt reserve, but that it could not afford to hold $60 million or $90 million in the extremely unlikely event that several "bumps in the night" happened simultaneously.

IMPACT ON VALUE

A second approach to the debt/equity question identifies the impact of additional debt on the price/earnings ratio. As stated by Franco Modigliani and Merton H. Miller, in a taxless and economically "perfect" world the total market value of a company's debt plus equity should not change as debt is substituted for equity.[3] Although expected earnings per share will increase as debt is substituted for equity (or additional financing is done with debt rather than equity), this effect is exactly offset by a markdown in the company's price/earnings ratio. The markdown occurs because the additional debt exposes the common shareholders to an extra financial risk.

In the Modigliani and Miller position, the impact of these changes would be exactly offsetting. For example, if a company were to raise debt to repurchase shares, the value of the asset position of the shareholders before repurchase (stock only) and after (stock and cash) would be exactly the same. The total value of the company's securities would also be constant.

A less extreme point of view, often thought of as a more traditional approach, grants that debt levels can have an impact on the price/earnings ratio. For very low levels of debt, the added risk may be perceived as small relative to the risk that would be involved if the individual tried to lever

3. See "The Cost of Capital, Corporation Finance, and the Theory of Investment," *American Economic Review*, June 1958, p. 261.

his own portfolio in a similar way. Hence low levels of debt may be ignored by the market and have no negative impact on the price/earnings ratio. In fact, it has even been suggested that some companies do not have enough debt, that the assumption of debt would in these cases be a signal of more aggressive investment and financial policies, and that the result would be a favorable impact on the price/earnings ratio.

As more debt is added, however, it does become noticeable. The price/ earnings ratio may indeed begin to fall. But as long as the ratio does not fall as fast as extra earnings are added by leveraging the company, the ultimate market price will still be more favorable than if equity were used to raise additional sums. With increasing amounts of debt, the price/earnings ratio may at some point fall faster than the earnings rise, clearly indicating that an excessive amount of debt has been put on the books.

According to the traditional approach, the ideal capital structure is the one in which an additional dollar of debt adds no additional net value to the total market value of the company's securities. An additional dollar of debt would drive the price/earnings ratio down sufficiently so that the value of the equity would fall by a dollar despite the additional earnings generated from the debt funds.

But it is by no means easy to determine the precise response of the price/earnings ratio to the debt/equity ratio. It certainly varies by industry, and it no doubt varies within industries by company. In addition, the relationship probably varies over time, as is witnessed by the comment of a man who attended a conference of institutional investors shortly after Penn Central filed for protection from its creditors. "I have never seen," he remarked, "such a Victorian interest in the balance sheet or so many younger men paying attention to their elders." It is up to the corporate financial officers to determine this relationship and project its likely future. Their judgments are aided by keeping in touch with the company's professional advisers in the financial markets.

Among practicing financial executives, the traditional view has by far the widest support. It is not the purpose here to review the pros and cons and the many pages of evidence that have been adduced in support of the extreme or infinite number of intermediate positions.

DEFINING THE LIMITS

Although the FRICT factors approach and the valuation approach to capital structure are not formally related, they together form a pair of constraints which define a company's debt capacity. First, it is unlikely that a management would care to leverage the company's financial structure to such a point that it would be in frequent danger of financial failure, even if the price/earnings ratio were not depressed. But because the price/earnings ratio *would* be depressed, there is a second constraint. With great exposure to risk, the company's market value would begin to shrink. The high leverage from debt would create added potential earnings for the equity owners, but this advantage would be more than offset by a reduction in the price/earnings ratio.

Thus, management should decide on debt capacity only after appraising all aspects of the situation to ensure that the capital structure is not having an adverse impact on any of them. To illustrate:

The management of a major integrated foods company recently decided that entering potential markets would require large capital investments. These investments, totaling well over $100 million, far exceeded the internal funds which the company expected to generate during the period. Management was reluctant to dilute equity unnecessarily by issuing common stock to raise funds. Hence it studied the company's ability to service additional debt under a variety of conditions and concluded that it was extremely unlikely a cash-flow problem would arise.

At the same time, management was very uncertain about the impact of an additional $100 million of debt on the firm's price/earnings ratio. Debt of this magnitude would place the company's debt-to-capitalization ratio substantially in excess of the ratio common in its industry. To help secure an answer to the debt problem, company managers interviewed executives of financial institutions and investment bankers to determine their opinions and get their predictions of the public's reaction to the additional debt.

Management was pleased to find that there probably would be no diminution of the price/earnings ratio if it borrowed within the range contemplated. Concluding that the increase of debt would not exceed the bounds tolerated by the marketplace, it undertook an aggressive debt program to finance the capital expenditures.

Dividend Policy

Given decisions on the investment requirements and on the debt/equity structure of the company, the dividend question becomes simpler than is often suggested in financial literature. It has been common to mix the analysis of the dividend decision with either the debt or the investment question (or both). Such trade-offs are possible, but I do not recommend them because they blur the essential nature of the dividend problem.

For the sake of clarity, let's begin with an oversimplification. With the "givens" of investment and capital structure, management can choose either to (a) pay higher dividends at the expense of lower growth in earnings per share or (b) restrain its dividend policy in favor of higher earnings per share.

Exhibit IV. *Shareholder responses to company policies*

Company policy

Shareholder policy	a. Low dividends, no new stock	b. High dividends, new stock
1. Maintain position	No action needed	Purchase shares pro rata (as many as required to make the owner's position equivalent to that in 1a)
2. Reduce position	Sell shares (as many as required to make the owner's position equivalent to that in 2b)	Do not purchase new shares – ownership percentage falls

This proposition can be easily verified by referring to the relationships diagramed in *Exhibit I*. With investments fixed and with the appropriate debt/equity relationship established, the dividend question becomes one that involves *only* the equity account. If sufficient sums are paid out in the form of dividends so that *retained earnings* are smaller than *new equity required*, then these funds must be replaced by new equity raised from the capital market. Because the new shareholders will participate in the existing earnings as well as in the future earnings of the company, high dividends today serve to spread the total earnings, including growth, over a larger number of shares. Hence per-share growth is slowed. Therefore the choice is higher dividends today or higher earnings per share tomorrow.

COMPLICATING FACTORS

From a stockholder's point of view, the comparison just suggested may capture the essence of the problem. However, it is not actually a comparison of like alternatives because it makes different assumptions about the shareholder's actions. In the case of the low-dividend policy described, the shareholder is presumed to retain his proportionate equity position by virtue of the fact that no new shares are sold. In the high-dividend policy instance, however, the shareholder's position is presumably diluted because he fails to purchase additional shares. *Exhibit IV* shows the possible combinations of corporate and shareholder policies and consistent stockholder actions. The truly comparable alternatives are a and b opposite policies 1 and 2.

In early 1968, the General Public Utilities Corporation found occasion to make an explicit investigation of the impact on its shareholders of a high- versus a low-payout policy. A careful calculation of the differences showed that, *assuming a constant price/earnings ratio under either corporate policy*, the before-tax impact on the shareholder following consistent decision rules (the actions under a and b opposite 1 and 2 in *Exhibit IV*) would be the same under either corporate policy. That is, the shareholder's before-tax position, if he followed action 1a, was the same as for action

1b; and actions 2a and 2b also led to the same before-tax positions. However, the introduction of tax considerations did change this result. For example:

□ A shareholder who wished to reduce his position (shareholder policy 2 in *Exhibit IV*) had a greater after-tax benefit under a low-dividend policy than under a high-dividend policy. Under the low-dividend policy, his increase in wealth was subject primarily to capital gains taxes, whereas under the high-dividend policy it was subject to regular income taxation.

□ A similar differential was present for the shareholder who wished to maintain a position. In the high-dividend case, payments to the shareholder were subject to income taxes in the course of their round trip from the company to the owner and then back to the company again. A company policy of high retentions obviously reduced the tax impact by postponing taxes until the shares were sold and a capital gains tax was imposed.

The major critical assumption underlying this comparison, the big "if" of the analysis, is that the price/earnings ratio will remain constant under the high- and low-dividend options. The validity of this assumption is by no means certain. It is also far from certain that the stockholder can always make the responses (indicated in *Exhibit IV*) which are needed to maintain or reduce his position.

The realities creating these uncertainties will be described briefly.

Industry practices: Certain dividend patterns have become widely accepted in various industries. The utility industry, for instance, is characterized by the retention of a relatively small percentage of earnings. At the other extreme, the high-technology industries tend to pay little, if any, cash to their shareholders. A company which deviates greatly from the central tendency of its industry may get little credit and much harm from its deviation unless it has an unusual story to support its claim to special consideration.

Shareholder composition: An industry and a company may develop a special shareholder following partly because of industry dividend and growth practices. The "widows and orphans" in the utility stocks, the businessmen's risks on the fringes of the seasoned industrials, and the wild-eyed speculators investing in companies with potential but no established record of success are all security market stereotypes with a reasonable grounding in fact. Since one dividend policy may have attracted one group, a major change will perhaps require a substantial restructuring of the shareholders. For a time, at least, this may result in a disorderly market for a company's shares, as shown by depressed prices and price/earnings ratios.

Shareholder misconceptions: The analysis made in the General Public Utilities situation is neither straightforward to explain nor easy to follow. The shareholder must be convinced, for example, that the sale of some of his holdings is precisely the same in principle as a higher dividend policy. But this is not an easy point to make even to a sophisticated analyst, let alone to an average shareholder in whom the "do not touch capital" rule is deeply ingrained. One company of considerable size, for example, has paid stock dividends because members of the founding families liked to give the dividends away to charity, although they would not consider touching the shares which their grandfathers had left them.

Legal distinctions: The capital-income distinction is not merely a figment of the nonfinancial imagination. There is also a legal distinction between capital and income, and it becomes a critical factor for a trustee who must manage an estate for the present benefit of those with a life interest in the income and yet protect the capital or the ultimate beneficiaries. In some states, even stock dividends are troublesome because they count as principal rather than income. Selling off "capital" for the benefit of income beneficiaries is even more generally prohibited or hedged with legal complexities.

Institutional problems: The bookkeeping of receipt of cash dividends is relatively straightforward for income and tax accounting purposes. The complexities that occasional stock dividends create for individual tax returns are severe, but nothing compared to the problems they create for trustees who must prepare income tax returns for their clients. Furthermore, even for large shareholders, the problems of creating the equivalent of a cash dividend through a sale of stock would normally involve partial shares and rounding. For smaller shareholders, the equivalency would probably be virtually impossible to create. Thus, it is not easy to equate a liquidation of shares with the receipt of cash dividends, as indicated opposite shareholder policy 2 in *Exhibit IV*.

The General Public Utilities Corporation found that various factors like these weighed heavily against its proposed conversion from cash dividends to quarterly stock dividends. According to the case material, shareholder response was strongly opposed to the plan. The opposition was partly the "uninformed" variety, coming from shareholders who simply had not understood the nature of the plan. Perhaps more significant was the institutional response; institutional managers opposed the plan because of the paperwork the stock dividends would involve. General Public Utilities' management concluded that as much as 12% of the company's outstanding stock, representing two years of average trading, might change hands if the plan for low payouts and stock dividends were adopted.

Despite the conceptual inconsistency of the alternative, the basic decision management must make is one that its shareholders will interpret as a payout-growth choice. It must be made in light of the circumstances of the particular opportunities and environment. For instance, if the opportunities for growth are not attractive, if more cash is being generated than can be invested, or if the investor has a high propensity for "income today," then it is wise for management to pay liberal dividends even at the expense of raising additional equity. It can be argued, in terms of the U.S. financial scene at least, that many utilities display one or more of these characteristics. Their equity holders do not expect substantial growth; they are investing more for a current yield with some growth prospects rather than for major growth opportunities.

Companies with greater growth prospects, such as those in electronics and data processing, are quite justified, according to this concept, in retaining most or all of the funds generated internally. Their shareholders would perhaps interpret an increase in the payout as a sign of lack of internal investment opportunities and hence of possible declining growth rather than as an indication of a strong market position.

Cost of Capital

The remaining financial policy variable, which until this point has been assumed to have been fixed, is the capital investment program. It is now appropriate to review how the size of this budget is determined and to consider how the projects to be included in it are selected.

Basically the microeconomic approach to the investment decision is straightforward. It argues that the cost of a scarce resource rises as a greater quantity of that resource is demanded. Capital costs increase as the volume of financing rises in response to an increase in the investments undertaken. Also, as more investments are made, the return on the additional investment is presumed to fall. Thus investments are made and money raised until the point is reached at which the cost of the funds on the marginal financing equals the returns promised from the marginal investment. This is shown graphically in Part A of *Exhibit* V.

Wise decisions on the debt and dividend parameters, as indicated earlier, should put the company in the position of having a "minimum cost of capital" for each level of financing. Note that this position is reached without involvement in mechanical and mathematical manipulations (although these could be developed to supplement the strategy).

But how should management calculate capital costs? Many techniques

Exhibit V. Determination of optional financial policy

A. Microeconomic concept

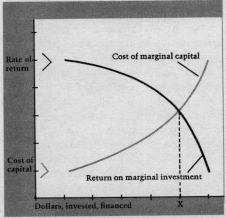

X = Amount of investment and financing to be undertaken

B. Managerial concept

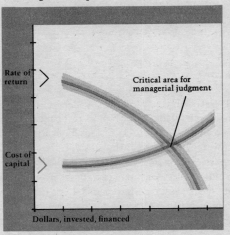

Key

Anticipated project returns, with uncertainty reflecting imperfect calculations of returns, questions of risk, and similar problems

Capital costs representing the best capital structure and dividend policies for each volume and best set of investment projects, with uncertainty due to problems in measuring capital costs, weights, and the interaction between investment and capital costs in current use obviously provide unreasonable answers, and a better method should be found. Authorities continue to debate how capital costs should be measured, although they generally agree that the process involves a weighting both by the shareholders and by the suppliers of fixed obligation funds of the returns expected. Hence an approach is required to determine both the costs to be assigned and the weights to be used. Let us examine these problems in turn.

ESTIMATING COSTS

The cost of *fixed obligations* is generally considered to be the coupon rate on debt and the dividend rate on straight preferred stock that would be demanded by the *current* market (temporary market aberrations aside).

Some companies may wish to use the embedded cost of existing obligations—that is, the cost of debt as it appears on the books. This should not result in major problems provided the proportion of debt in the capital structure is small. However, use of an embedded cost by a utility could result in serious erosion of the equity position as debt is rolled over into higher cost instruments. A debt-heavy nonutility that used this approach would be overinvesting in low-return projects.

Equity costs are more hotly debated; their dividend yield, the earnings yield, or one of these in some combination with an estimate of growth all have been advanced at various times. It is far easier (and no less appropriate) for the manager to estimate what total rate of return (in a combination of dividends and growth) the stockholder expects to receive on his investment that will justify holding on to his stock.

This estimate can be greatly simplified by categorizing companies in different "return groups" according to whether their equities have the characteristics of bonds, high-cash income with some risk, moderate risk, or high-risk situations. By thus reducing the "universe" to four, five, or perhaps a few more return categories, it is relatively easy to assign a company to its appropriate spot. The loss of accuracy—which is more often than not a spurious accuracy in many measuring methods—is more than compensated for by the fact that a sensible analysis, easily understood and utilized by management, can be quickly made and defended.

The cost of *convertible issues* is the most difficult cost to determine. (Also, to the best of my knowledge, no satisfactory treatment of this subject is available.) One possibility is to finance continually with convertibles so that as one issue is converted, another issue is put out. In this case, the coupon rate might be used. If, however, the company's use of convertibles is more of a one-shot transaction, designed to "issue common stock today at tomorrow's prices," then it is clear that a cost approximating the cost of common equity ought to be adopted for the security.

Whenever a cost of capital is being calculated, it is necessary to put the debt and equity on the same tax basis, computing both either before or after taxes.

USE OF WEIGHTS

A variety of weights have been suggested as appropriate for the cost-averaging calculation. These suggestions include book value of the capitalization, its market value, and the "target" capitalization (at either book or market) for which the company is aiming over the long run.

If the company has a target capital structure (as the preceding debt/equity discussion presumes that it will have), then the book value of the capital structure will eventually approach the target structure. Thus, the target structure is more appropriate to use than the book structure.

From another point of view, the microeconomist is concerned with the cost *on the margin* for new money—the cost of the funds raised today as opposed to the cost of those raised previously. Given a target capital structure, it is obvious that this marginal cost must be an average of some sort unless the company plans to use equity funds only. The presence of a planned proportion of debt means that some debt will be raised from time to time to match the retained earnings, but it would be blatantly inappropriate to specify the company's capital cost as the debt coupon in the year that debt is the primary financing vehicle. Thus the company's *marginal funds*, which are being raised at *current market value*, will be raised in proportion to the amounts called for in the target structure.

I suggest that the most defensible weights to use in averaging various costs are those of the company's long-run target capital structure.

ONE COMPANY'S CALCULATION

To illustrate the technique just described, let us use the hypothetical example of a chemical company which has decided to change its capital structure from 25% debt to 30% debt:

Management concludes that this change will neither harm the company's ability to borrow at the prevailing interest rate (say, 8%) nor increase the rate of return that the stockholders demand. Management believes that although the company has some high-risk (and high-return) operations, it should not be classified as truly speculative because it does have a sufficiently stable and profitable product base.

Yet earnings have fluctuated significantly in the past, and the dividends have been cut occasionally despite the directors' efforts never to establish a quarterly rate that cannot be maintained. In the bull market of 1965, the company traded at a price/earnings ratio of 30. Since then its ratio once

Exhibit VI. Capital cost calculation

	Debt (D)	Equity (E)	Weighted average target cost (D+E)
(A) Cost after 50% tax	4.0%	13.5%	—
(B) Proportion in target capital structure	30.0	70.0	—
(C) Weighting calculation (A × B)	1.2	9.4	10.6%

dropped to 10, when the market fell, although earnings remained strong at that time. Earnings have since suffered, but the price has held, so that the price/earnings ratio is back to 15.

After some thought, management concludes that the investor in the company is probably expecting the type of return he might get from a fairly mature organization, but one riskier than AT&T. It concludes that in the long run, and ignoring exceptionally high or low stock market levels, the investor is probably expecting a return of between 12% and 15%. A compromise of 13.5% is reached.

Management then calculates the new capital cost as shown in *Exhibit VI*. This cost may not be precisely the "true" cost in the platonic sense of the "true form." However, if prepared by an experienced management, it is probably as close to the mark as can reasonably be expected, given the inherent judgments made and the use of the figure as a rough screen for capital investments.

Capital Investments

The particular techniques for analyzing capital investments will not be treated in detail here. Over the years, these measures have developed from the simple payback (which remains an excellent measure in many circumstances) through more elaborate return-on-investment calculations and into the realm of discounted cash flows. One school of thought argues that the "net present value" method is the most correct conceptually and the least likely to result in confusing decisions.[4] Another approach admits the conceptual validity of the "net present value" calculation, but prefers an "internal rate of return" or "investors' yield" discounting technique because it is believed that management normally thinks in terms of rates of

4. Harold Bierman, Jr., and Seymour Smidt, *The Capital Budgeting Decision*, 2nd edition (New York, The Macmillan Company, 1966).

return, not net-present-value dollars.[5] Other refinements include discounting the depreciation flows at one rate and the remainder of the proceeds at another as a way of adjusting for risk.[6]

The remainder of this article will be concerned with the more philosophical question of whether the *minimum* demanded rate of return should be set equal to the company's cost of capital. A strict interpretation of microeconomics, supported by considerable literature, suggests that the capital cost should be the cutoff rate. I shall argue that it should *not* be.

MISPLACED EMPHASIS

Consider the supply of funds to the corporation. Investors, and particularly equity investors and others who do not have secured rights to income and assets, put their money into a diverse "basket of assets." The components of the basket have a variety of different earnings and different risk characteristics. The investor, in essence, buys a preselected portfolio, one structured for him by corporate management. In fact, the theoretical support for diversification and conglomeration is that such investment portfolios offer a higher return for a lower risk than do investments made by individuals in undiversified corporations.

It is likely that some of a corporation's investments have a lower risk and a lower return than the *average* risk and return characteristics of the entire portfolio. Other assets will have high-return and risk characteristics. The investor sets his overall or average return expectation on the basis of the combined performance of these various investments. His expectation is then used (with the expectations of other investors) as the basis for the company's cost of capital figure.

If management adopts the investors' average criterion as the company's minimum rate, it precludes investments in the lower risk, lower return projects. The company will tend to put all funds into higher risk, higher return opportunities. If this policy is followed over any length of time, its result will be ironic—a substantial shift in the nature of the company's assets and a change in its "portfolio" toward a higher risk and higher return character.

This action may induce investors, in turn, to compensate for the higher risk by demanding yet a higher average rate on their investment in the company's securities. If so, and if management then responds by further raising the hurdle rates set for acceptable investments, the company is again advanced to an even riskier state. The average cost of capital is thus

5. A. J. Merritt and Allen Sykes, *The Finance and Analysis of Capital Projects* (London, Longmans, 1963).

6. Pearson Hunt, *Financial Analysis in Capital Budgeting* (Boston, Division of Research, Harvard Business School, 1964).

ratcheted up, and value may be destroyed. Consider a situation like the following:

An integrated company in the energy business has operations ranging from wildcat petroleum exploration to refining of petroleum for its own use and for sale on the open market, to pipeline operation and retail market facilities. According to the company's calculations, its capital cost falls substantially above the returns offered by the less profitable but less risky portions of the venture, such as the retail units and the pipelines. On the other hand, it is clear that exclusion of additional investments in these areas would have the ultimate effect of liquidating such operations and of concentrating the company in areas such as wildcatting. Thus, slavish use of the cost of capital as a cutoff is clearly inappropriate for management.

REALISTIC APPROACH

Rather than regard the cost-return intersection as a point (a presumption of basic microeconomic thought illustrated in Part A of *Exhibit* V), it is more realistic and useful for management to think of it as an area or band of rather fuzzy boundaries (as Part B shows). There are several basic reasons for this imprecision:

1. The imperfections in the measurement of capital costs and of returns on projects blur the precision that is often presumed to be present in both types of calculations.

2. The interaction of investment decisions, financing decisions, and capital costs cannot be clearly defined except in unusual circumstances. Thus, for each level of investment, the capital structure and dividend policies appropriate for the company may change. These changes may frequently be imperceptible and recognizable only at major turning points. To allow for these uncertainties requires an *area* of choice.

3. The projects themselves differ with respect to risk. The effects of these differences are difficult to estimate. However, one way to explain the problem is to recognize that a project may return more or less on a risk-adjusted basis (that is, when the anticipated returns are weighted according to the amount of risk involved) than it will on the basis of the most likely outcome.

The intersection of these two broad bands of costs and returns roughly delineates the area where maximum managerial judgment is required—on both the financing policy and the investment policy sides of the equation. It is relatively easy to identify unquestionably good projects and unquestionably unattractive ones. Similarly, obviously good and poor capitalization policies do not require much talent to identify. Judgment is required when the decisions are no longer so obvious—that is, when the imprecision of the numbers, of the circumstances, or of both is present to confound the inflexible guidelines and thwart the rules of thumb.

The scheme suggested in Part B of *Exhibit* V does not provide any easy answer to problems falling in the critical area; rather, it is intended to warn the unwary of the area's existence and to suggest how its boundaries may be located. Then the best talents of the corporation can be focused on problems in the area, and management can be spared the routine task of settling the more obvious and less demanding questions.

SHARE REPURCHASE

Although the subject is tangential, it is appropriate at this point to comment briefly on the question of share repurchase. Many analysts have treated this common question as an investment decision, as though repurchase of a company's stock falls in the same category as buying another office machine or a lathe. This treatment confuses the investment decision with the capital structure decision; it is in the latter category that share repurchase most logically should be placed.

Adjustments to the capital structure are called for when funds are needed for attractive investment, when funds are generated in quantities larger than required for investment opportunities, or when the nature of the company's risk changes so that more or less debt should be undertaken. Thus the generation of excess funds indicates that excess capital is available to the company and that the organization can lower its capital costs (moving backward, or to the left, down the cost curve in Part A of *Exhibit* V) by decapitalizing. Whether this is done by reducing debt or equity, or some mixture of the two, depends on a determination of the appropriate capitalization for the company. The important thing is to keep the investment question separate and not mix it with the question of retiring equity by repurchasing stockholders' shares. The proper question now is only how best to lower capital costs—by retiring debt, buying back stock, increasing dividends, or using some combination of these steps.

It is not necessary to wait for fund needs or surpluses to arise before addressing the capital structure issue. In fact, capital structure should always be kept under evaluation. It is prefectly in order for management to consider continuously whether it should readjust the company's capital structure by borrowing and retiring stock or by issuing stock to retire debt.

Conclusion

It does not require an elaborate mathematical justification to show that the debt/equity and dividend polices affect the investment portfolio through their impact on the capital cost. Investment decisions, in turn, influence the capital cost and other areas of financial policy because of their impact on the return received from the company's assets and the risks taken in order to get that return.

Ideally, it would be desirable to settle simultaneously the problems raised in the three financial areas reviewed in this article. But the magnitude and complexity of the problems make this impossible in all but the simplest cases.

A more productive approach is the one outlined—that executives analyze the parts of the problem sequentially and then recheck their preliminary decisions in order to correct any early steps which may require adjustments as a result of later actions. I believe it is best to work on the decisions in the order discussed in this article. That means taking these steps:

1. Assume projected capital requirements of the company.
2. Tentatively settle the debt/equity question.
3. Make the dividend-growth analysis within the framework of the debt/equity choice.
4. Investigate the impact of steps 2 and 3 on capital costs and the impact of the capital costs on the investment volume.

The last step should determine whether the total result is reasonable in light of the company's situation and its posture in the financial market. If it is not, executives can change their original assumptions and go through the four steps again.

While this approach adds no new dimensions to the theory of financial management, it does enable management to profit from some of the excellent work done by theorists. This approach makes the issues clearer to executives. It enables them to decide more readily what they should do and to move in accordance with a sound, consistent plan of action.

11. How to Evaluate New Capital Investments

John G. McLean

Dissatisfied with the yardsticks it had been using to evaluate capital investment opportunities, Continental Oil Company determined to find a better way to measure one investment against another and extrapolate the potential returns which projects might earn on its investments. Continental settled on the method of discounting cash flows to present value. The author, who helped install this approach, describes how this major oil company employs it.

In evaluating new investment projects, why are return-on-investment figures preferable to years-to-pay-out figures? Of various possible methods for calculating return on investment, why is the discounted-cash-flow procedure likely to yield the best results? What techniques and assumptions will help executives who want to make practical use of the discounted-cash-flow method?

Obviously, I cannot answer these questions satisfactorily for all companies. I shall attempt only to describe some of the answers developed by the Continental Oil Company. Faced with a need for better methods of evaluating investment proposals, management decided in 1955 to adopt the discounted-cash-flow method. The procedures adopted, the reasons for choosing them, and the results obtained during the first three years may serve as a useful "case example" for other companies to study.

Of course, the techniques that I shall describe were not invented by Continental. They have been used for centuries in the field of finance and banking and have been fully described in many textbooks and articles in the field of industrial management and business economics.

Management Concern

Prior to 1955, we had relied heavily—as many oil companies do—on years-to-pay-out figures as the primary means of judging the desirability of investments and as a yardstick for measuring one investment opportunity against another. We had also' made use of return-on-investment figures computed in a variety of different ways, which I shall describe later.

In the latter part of 1954 our financial group, consisting of the controller, the financial vice president, and myself, undertook a comprehensive review of the techniques we were then using in making capital investment decisions. We were concerned about this matter because of the large amounts of new money we found it necessary to channel back into the oil business each year. Characteristically, oil companies have a very high rate of capital turnover because they operate assets which deplete at high rates, and large amounts of new funds must be reinvested each year if earnings are to be maintained and increased.

The capital expenditures of Continental Oil, for example, normally run in the neighborhood of $100 million per year, or about $385,000 each working day—roughly twice our net income, which is about $50 million per year. To the best of my knowledge, there are few, if any, other major industries with such a high ratio of capital expenditures to current net income.

In the oil business, therefore, the making of capital investment decisions assumes considerably more significance as a part of top management's job than is usually the case. In our own situation it was apparent that the management judgment exercised in directing the flow of new funds into our business had a very significant bearing upon current and future earnings per share and a profound influence on the long-term growth and development of our company. We decided, therefore, that we should make a maximum effort to develop the best possible yardstick for comparing one investment opportunity against another and for evaluating the returns that particular projects would earn on the stockholder's dollar.

New Techniques

As a background for outlining the new techniques which our financial group recommended as a result of its study and which were later implemented throughout the company, let me first outline the steps which are normally involved in the appraisal of new capital investments:

1. Estimate the volume of sales, prices, costs of materials, operating expenses, transportation costs, capital investment requirements, strength and nature of competition, rates of obsolescence or depletion, and other economic and business factors.

2. Summarize basic estimates of annual income, life of project, and capital investment in convenient form for appraisal purposes. (Commonly used yardsticks include years to pay out and return on investment.)

3. Exercise managerial judgment in determining whether or not:

(a) The anticipated return is large enough to warrant the business risks involved;

(b) The investment opportunity is attractive in view of the various alternative opportunities for capital spending;

(c) The timing of the investment is right relative to anticipated developments in the near future.

The discounted-cash-flow techniques which we introduced in 1955 had to do only with Step 2; that is, with the way we did our arithmetic in adding up the basic estimates of annual incomes, life of project, and capital investments to arrive at payout and return on investment.

It was clearly recognized that there was nothing in the discounted-cash-flow method which would make it any easier to estimate the items listed in Step 1 or which would improve the accuracy of those estimates. It was likewise recognized that there was nothing in the discounted-cash-flow techniques which would relieve management at any level of the responsibility for exercising judgment on the various matters listed under Step 3. We were concerned fundamentally, at this time, with improving the mechanics of our capital investment analyses in order that management might render better judgments on the three points under Step 3.

PAYOUT VS. RETURN

Our first recommendation was that we use the return-on-investment figures as the primary yardstick for evaluating new capital investments and pay much less attention to years-to-pay-out figures than had been our custom in the past.

Our reason for de-emphasizing payout figures was simply that they do not provide an adequate means of discriminating among new investment opportunities. They merely indicate how long it will take to recover the original capital outlay and do not tell us anything about the earning power of an investment. There is, of course, no point in making investments which just give us our money back. The true worth of an investment depends on how much income it will generate *after* the original outlay has been recovered, and there is no way that can be determined from a payout figure. Generally speaking, payout figures are reliable measures of the relative worth of alternative investments only when the income-producing life of all projects under consideration is about the same—which is far from the case in our particular situation.

To illustrate how misleading payout figures can be, I have prepared an example consisting of three different projects, each involving an investment of $125,000 (see *Exhibit I*:

The annual income generated by the investments begins at $25,000 and

Exhibit I. *Differences in rates of return when payout periods are equal*

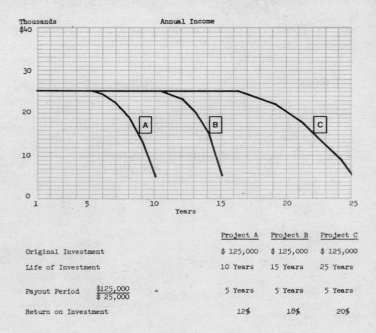

	Project A	Project B	Project C
Original Investment	$ 125,000	$ 125,000	$ 125,000
Life of Investment	10 Years	15 Years	25 Years
Payout Period $\frac{\$125,000}{\$ 25,000}$ =	5 Years	5 Years	5 Years
Return on Investment	12%	18%	20%

then declines in later years in each case as shown on the graph. Since the annual incomes are identical in the early years, each project has the same payout period; namely, five years. By this standard of measurement, therefore, the projects would be equal from an investment standpoint. But actually the returns on investment range from 12% per year for Project A, which has the shortest life, to 20% per year for Project B, which has the longest life.

At first glance, you might be inclined to say that this is all pretty simple —all you have to do is look at both the payout period and the total estimated life to reach a correct decision. And it *is* relatively easy if the payout periods are all the same, as they are in this example, or even if the payout periods are different but the total economic lives are the same.

Unfortunately, however, we are usually looking at projects where there is a difference in both the payout period and the project life. Under such circumstances, it becomes very difficult to appraise the relative worth of two or more projects on the basis of payout periods alone. For example, consider the three projects shown in *Exhibit II*:

The payout periods here range from 8 years in the case of Project A, which has a high initial income and a short life, to 11.5 years in the case of

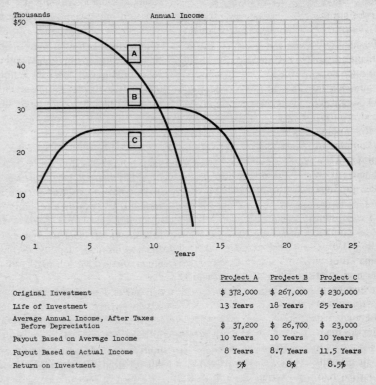

	Project A	Project B	Project C
Original Investment	$ 372,000	$ 267,000	$ 230,000
Life of Investment	13 Years	18 Years	25 Years
Average Annual Income, After Taxes Before Depreciation	$ 37,200	$ 26,700	$ 23,000
Payout Based on Average Income	10 Years	10 Years	10 Years
Payout Based on Actual Income	8 Years	8.7 Years	11.5 Years
Return on Investment	5%	8%	8.5%

Project C, which has a low initial income and a long life. On the basis of payout periods, therefore, Project A would appear to be the best of the three. Actually, however, the true rates of return on investment range from 5% for Project A to 8.5% for Project C. The order of desirability indicated by payout periods is thus exactly the reverse of that indicated by return-on-investment figures.

It was for these reasons that our financial group recommended that in the future we make use of return-on-investment figures as our primary guide in evaluating new projects rather than the payout figures which had customarily been our main guide in the past.

ALTERNATIVE CALCULATION

Our second recommendation had to do with the procedures used in calculating the return-on-investment figures. There are at least three general ways to make the calculation:

1. In the first method, the return is calculated on the *original investment*; that is, the average annual income from a project is divided by the total original capital outlay. This is the procedure we had been using in our producing, refining, petrochemical, and pipeline departments.

2. In the second method, the return is calculated on the *average investment*. In other words, the average annual income is divided by half the original investment or by whatever figure represents the mid-point between the original cost and the salvage or residual land value in the investment. This is the procedure which was used in our marketing department for calculating returns on new service station investments.

3. The third procedure—the *discounted-cash-flow* technique—bases the calculation on the investment actually outstanding from time to time over the life of the project. This was the procedure used in our financial department in computing the cost of funds obtained from various sources or in estimating the yields we might obtain by investing reserve working capital in various types of government or commercial securities.

These three methods will produce very different results, and the figures obtained by one method may be as much as twice as great as those obtained by another—i.e., a project that showed a return of 10% under the procedures used in our refining department could show as much as 20% under the procedures used by our marketing department, and might show 15% or 18% under those used by our financial department.

It was clear, therefore, that we must settle on one of these three methods and use it uniformly throughout all departments of the company. Otherwise, we would be measuring some investments with long yardsticks, others with short yardsticks, and we would never be sure exactly what we were doing.

RELATIVE ADVANTAGES

Our selection of discounted cash flow was based on three primary considerations:

□ It gives the true rate of return offered by a new project. Both of the other methods merely give an approximation of the return. The original-investment method usually understates the return, while the average-investment method usually overstates the return. By contrast, the discounted-cash-flow method is a compromise and usually gives figures lying in between those that would be obtained by the other two methods.

□ It gives figures which are meaningful in relation to those used throughout the financial world in quoting interest rates on borrowed funds, yields on bonds, and for various other purposes. It thus permits direct comparison of the projected returns on investments with the cost of borrowing money —which is not possible with the other procedures.

Exhibit III. Comparison of return-on-investment calculations

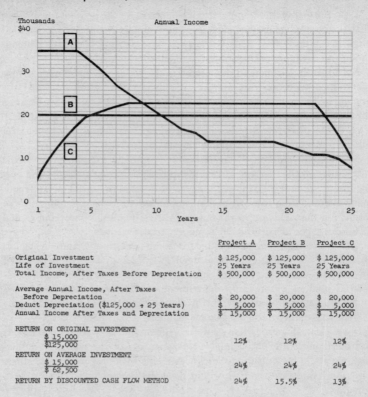

	Project A	Project B	Project C
Original Investment	$ 125,000	$ 125,000	$ 125,000
Life of Investment	25 Years	25 Years	25 Years
Total Income, After Taxes Before Depreciation	$ 500,000	$ 500,000	$ 500,000
Average Annual Income, After Taxes			
Before Depreciation	$ 20,000	$ 20,000	$ 20,000
Deduct Depreciation ($125,000 ÷ 25 Years)	$ 5,000	$ 5,000	$ 5,000
Annual Income After Taxes and Depreciation	$ 15,000	$ 15,000	$ 15,000
RETURN ON ORIGINAL INVESTMENT $\frac{\$\,15,000}{\$125,000}$	12%	12%	12%
RETURN ON AVERAGE INVESTMENT $\frac{\$\,15,000}{\$\,62,500}$	24%	24%	24%
RETURN BY DISCOUNTED CASH FLOW METHOD	24%	15.5%	13%

▢ It makes allowance for *differences in the time* at which investments generate their income. That is, it discriminates among investments that have (a) a low initial income which gradually increases, (b) a high initial income which gradually declines, and (c) a uniform income throughout their lives.

The last point was particularly important to us, because the investment projects which we normally have before us frequently have widely divergent income patterns. Refining projects usually have a relatively uniform annual income, because they must be operated at 75% to 100% of capacity from the time they go on stream in order to keep unit costs at reasonable levels. On the other hand, producing wells yield a high initial income, which declines as the oil reservoir is depleted; while new service station investments have a still different pattern in that they frequently increase their income as they gain market acceptance and build up their volume of business.

As an illustration of the usefulness of the discounted-cash-flow method in discriminating among investments with different income patterns, consider the three examples presented in *Exhibit III*:

These three projects all require the same original outlay, have the same economic life, and generate exactly the same total income after taxes and depreciation. The return on the original investment would be 12%, and the return on average investment 24% in each case. By these standards, therefore, the projects would appear to be of equal merit. Actually, however, Project A is by far the best of the three because it generates a larger share of its total income in the early years of its life. The investor thus has his money in hand sooner and available for investment in other income-producing projects. This highly important difference is clearly reflected in the discounted-cash-flow figures, which show 24% for Project A, 15.5% for Project B, and 13% for Project C.

Simple Application

To facilitate the adoption of the new system on a company-wide basis, we recommended a very simple application. Assumptions were made at many points in order to reduce the complexity of the calculations involved. In most instances, we found the range of possible error introduced by these simplifying assumptions to be negligible relative to that involved in the basic estimates of income, costs, and economic life of a project. As a further means of facilitating the computations, we prepared a number of special arrangements of the discount tables.

UNIFORM INCOME

The procedures that we developed for investments with a uniform annual income are illustrated in *Exhibit IV*.

The payout period is computed in the usual manner by dividing the cash flow after taxes into the original investment. Then, since the life of the project is estimated at 15 years, the payout period is carried into the 15-year line of a cumulative discount table, and the column in which a matching number is found indicates the discounted-cash-flow rate of return. The numbers in this table are simply sums of the discount factors for the time periods and rates indicated. Thus, $4.675 is the present worth of $1.00 received annually for 15 years, discounted at a 20% rate.

It is apparent, therefore, that the discounted-cash-flow procedure involves nothing more than finding the discount rate which will make the present worth of the anticipated stream of cash income from the project equal to the original outlay. In this case, the anticipated cash flow of $20,000 per annum for 15 years has a present worth equal to the original outlay—

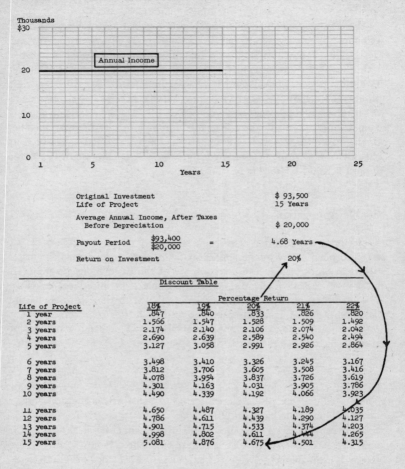

| Original Investment | $ 93,500 |
| Life of Project | 15 Years |

| Average Annual Income, After Taxes Before Depreciation | $ 20,000 |

| Payout Period | $\dfrac{\$93,400}{\$20,000}$ | = | 4.68 Years |

| Return on Investment | 20% |

Discount Table

Life of Project	Percentage Return				
	18%	19%	20%	21%	22%
1 year	.847	.840	.833	.826	.820
2 years	1.566	1.547	1.528	1.509	1.492
3 years	2.174	2.140	2.106	2.074	2.042
4 years	2.690	2.639	2.589	2.540	2.494
5 years	3.127	3.058	2.991	2.926	2.864
6 years	3.498	3.410	3.326	3.245	3.167
7 years	3.812	3.706	3.605	3.508	3.416
8 years	4.078	3.954	3.837	3.726	3.619
9 years	4.301	4.163	4.031	3.905	3.786
10 years	4.490	4.339	4.192	4.066	3.923
11 years	4.650	4.487	4.327	4.189	4.035
12 years	4.786	4.611	4.439	4.290	4.127
13 years	4.901	4.715	4.533	4.374	4.203
14 years	4.998	4.802	4.611	4.444	4.265
15 years	5.081	4.876	4.675	4.501	4.315

$93,400—when discounted at 20%. Alternatively, it can be said that the discounted-cash-flow procedure simply computes the rate of return on the balance of the investment actually outstanding from time to time over the life of the project, as illustrated in *Exhibit V*.

The cash flow of $20,000 per annum, continuing over 15 years, is shown in Column 1. Some part of this must be set aside to return the original outlay over the 15-year period, as shown in Column 2. The remainder, tabulated in Column 3, represents the true earnings.

On this basis, the balance of the original capital outlay outstanding (not yet returned to the investor) at the beginning of each year is shown in

Exhibit V. Return calculated by discounted-cash-flow method

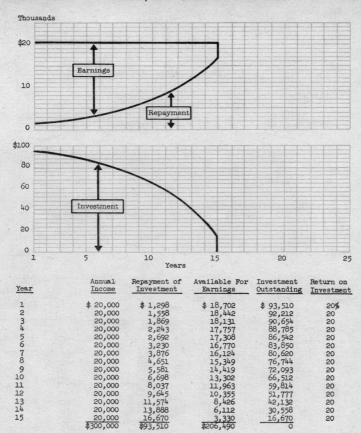

Year	Annual Income	Repayment of Investment	Available For Earnings	Investment Outstanding	Return on Investment
1	$ 20,000	$ 1,298	$ 18,702	$ 93,510	20%
2	20,000	1,558	18,442	92,212	20
3	20,000	1,869	18,131	90,654	20
4	20,000	2,243	17,757	88,785	20
5	20,000	2,692	17,308	86,542	20
6	20,000	3,230	16,770	83,850	20
7	20,000	3,876	16,124	80,620	20
8	20,000	4,651	15,349	76,744	20
9	20,000	5,581	14,419	72,093	20
10	20,000	6,698	13,302	66,512	20
11	20,000	8,037	11,963	59,814	20
12	20,000	9,645	10,355	51,777	20
13	20,000	11,574	8,426	42,132	20
14	20,000	13,888	6,112	30,558	20
15	20,000	16,670	3,330	16,670	20
	$300,000	$93,510	$206,490	0	

Column 4. The ratio of the earnings to this outstanding investment is 20% year by year throughout the life of the project, as shown in Column 5. The graph at the top of the form shows the declining balance of the investment and the division of the annual cash flow between repayment of principal and earnings.

It will immediately be recognized that the mechanism of the discounted-cash-flow procedure here is precisely the same as that involved in a household mortgage where one makes annual cash payments to the bank of a fixed amount to cover interest and payments on the principal. This is the reason for my earlier statement; i.e., that the discounted-cash-flow procedure gives rates of return directly comparable to the interest rates generally quoted for all financial purposes. It is worth noting that in this particular case the conventional procedure of computing a return on the original

203

Exhibit VI. Application of discounted-cash-flow method in a situation with increasing income

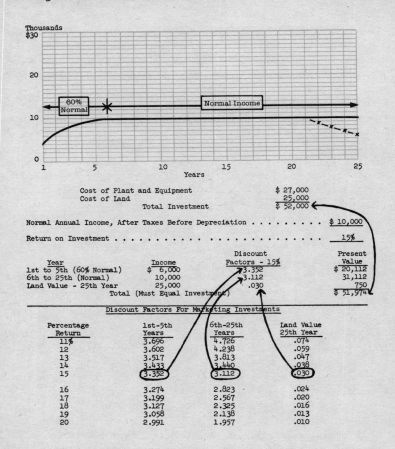

		Discount		Present
Year	Income	Factors - 15%		Value
1st to 5th (60% Normal)	$ 6,000	3.352		$ 20,112
6th to 25th (Normal)	10,000	3.112		31,112
Land Value - 25th Year	25,000	.030		750
Total (Must Equal Investment)				$ 51,974

Discount Factors For Marketing Investments

Percentage Return	1st-5th Years	6th-25th Years	Land Value 25th Year
11%	3.696	4.726	.074
12	3.602	4.238	.059
13	3.517	3.813	.047
14	3.433	3.440	.038
15	3.352	3.112	.030
16	3.274	2.823	.024
17	3.199	2.567	.020
18	3.127	2.325	.016
19	3.058	2.138	.013
20	2.991	1.957	.010

investment would have given a figure of 15%. Had the calculation been based on the average investment, a figure of 30% would have been obtained (assuming straight-line depreciation in both cases and zero salvage value).

INCREASING INCOME

Our application of the discounted-cash-flow procedure in a situation with increasing income—e.g., investment in new service stations—is illustrated in *Exhibit* VI. In this case, we assume a build-up of income during the first 5 years, a 20-year period of relatively stable income, and a 5-year period of declining income at the end of the station's life (assumptions now undergoing modification in the light of recent statistical studies of volume performance).

To simplify the calculations and to avoid discounting the income on a year-by-year basis, however, we break the calculations into three parts. We assume that the income in the first to the fifth years is roughly comparable to a uniform series of payments of 60% of the normal level. We also ignore the decline in income at the end of the life, since it would have little effect on the results, and assume that the normal level of income will continue for the sixth to twenty-fifth years. And, finally, we assume that the land would, or could, be sold at the end of the twenty-fifth year at its original cost.

We have thus been able to make use of a special, and much simplified, discount table like the one shown at the bottom of *Exhibit VI*. The first column contains the sum of the discount factors for the first five years, and the second column shows the sum of the factors for the sixth to twenty-fifth years. The last column shows the present worth of $1.00 received 25 years from now. These factors may then be applied directly to the three segments of the anticipated cash flow from the project in the manner shown. The calculation proceeds by trial and error until a series of factors, and a corresponding discount rate, are found which will make the present value of the future cash flow equal to the original outlay.

DECLINING INCOME

Our application of the discounted-cash-flow procedure in a situation of declining income is shown in *Exhibit VII*. In this case—e.g., an investment in producing wells with a gradually depleting oil reservoir—we have found, again, that the cash flow can usually be divided into three pieces, with a uniform annual income assumed for each. The first year must be treated separately, since the cash flow is usually high as a result of the tax credits for intangible drilling costs. We then select a middle and end period of varying lengths, depending on the characteristics of the particular well, and simply assume an average annual income throughout each period.

These assumptions make it possible to use a simplified arrangement of the discount tables. The first line contains the discount factors for the first year alone, while the remainder of the table consists of cumulative factors beginning in the second year.

The factors for the first year and the middle period may then be read directly from the table, and the factor for the end period is obtained by deduction, as shown. The calculation proceeds by trial and error until discount factors are found which will make the present value of the cash flow equal to the original outlay—in this case 22%.

Exhibit VII. Application of discounted-cash-flow method in a situation with declining income

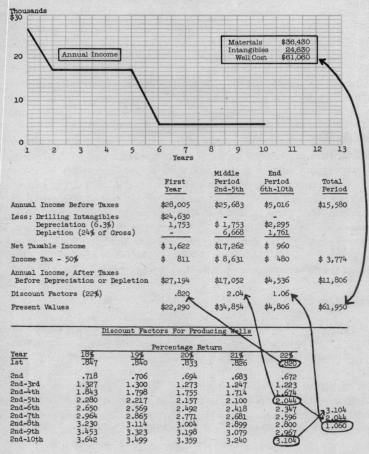

Annual Income, After Taxes, Before Depreciation and Depletion

	First Year	Middle Period 2nd-5th	End Period 6th-10th	Total Period
Annual Income Before Taxes	$28,005	$25,683	$5,016	$15,580
Less: Drilling Intangibles	$24,630	-	-	
Depreciation (6.3%)	1,753	$ 1,753	$2,295	
Depletion (24% of Gross)	-	6,668	1,761	
Net Taxable Income	$ 1,622	$17,262	$ 960	
Income Tax - 50%	$ 811	$ 8,631	$ 480	$ 3,774
Annual Income, After Taxes Before Depreciation or Depletion	$27,194	$17,052	$4,536	$11,806
Discount Factors (22%)	.820	2.04	1.06	
Present Values	$22,290	$34,854	$4,806	$61,950

Materials $36,430
Intangibles 24,630
Well Cost $61,060

Discount Factors For Producing Wells

Year	Percentage Return				
	18%	19%	20%	21%	22%
1st	.847	.840	.833	.826	.820
2nd	.718	.706	.694	.683	.672
2nd-3rd	1.327	1.300	1.273	1.247	1.223
2nd-4th	1.843	1.798	1.755	1.714	1.674
2nd-5th	2.280	2.217	2.157	2.100	2.044
2nd-6th	2.650	2.569	2.492	2.418	2.347
2nd-7th	2.964	2.865	2.771	2.681	2.596
2nd-8th	3.230	3.114	3.004	2.899	2.800
2nd-9th	3.453	3.323	3.198	3.079	2.967
2nd-10th	3.642	3.499	3.359	3.240	3.104

3.104
2.044
1.060
3.104

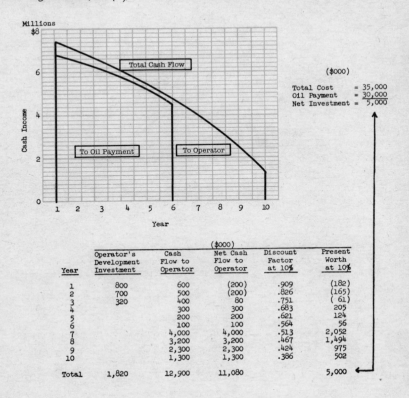

Year	Operator's Development Investment	Cash Flow to Operator	Net Cash Flow to Operator	Discount Factor at 10%	Present Worth at 10%
			($000)		
1	800	600	(200)	.909	(182)
2	700	500	(200)	.826	(165)
3	320	400	80	.751	(61)
4		300	300	.683	205
5		200	200	.621	124
6		100	100	.564	56
7		4,000	4,000	.513	2,052
8		3,200	3,200	.467	1,494
9		2,300	2,300	.424	975
10		1,300	1,300	.386	502
Total	1,820	12,900	11,080		5,000

($000)

Total Cost   = 35,000
Oil Payment   = 30,000
Net Investment = 5,000

IRREGULAR CASH FLOW

Somewhat more complicated applications of the discounted-cash-flow procedure occur whenever the cash flow is more irregular. To illustrate, here are two special situations:

A. *Oil Payment Deals.* Exhibit VIII shows the application when the problem is to analyze the profitability of acquiring a producing property under an oil payment arrangement.

The total cost of the property is $35 million, of which $30 million is supplied by an investor purchasing an oil payment. The terms of sale provide that he shall receive a specified percentage of the oil produced until he has recovered his principal and interest at 6%. The remaining $5 million is supplied by the new operator, who purchases the working and remaining interest and who agrees to do certain additional development drilling as shown in Column 1.

207

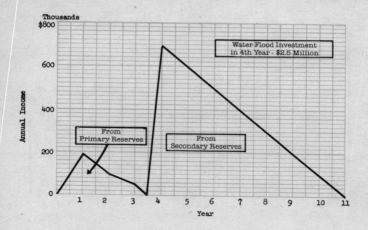

Year	Cash Flow	Present Worth of Cash Flow At:						
		10%	20%	28%	30%	40%	49%	50%
1	$ 200	$ 182	$167	$156	$154	$143	$134	$133
2	100	83	69	61	59	51	45	44
3	50	38	29	24	23	18	15	15
4	-1,800	-1,229	-868	-671	-630	-469	-365	-356
5	600	373	241	175	162	112	82	79
6	500	282	167	114	104	66	46	44
7	400	205	112	71	64	38	24	23
8	300	140	70	41	37	20	12	12
9	200	85	39	21	19	10	5	5
10	100	39	16	8	7	3	2	2
Total	+650	+198	+42	0	-2	-8	0	+1

The cash flow from the properties after expenses accruing to the operator is shown in Column 2. Column 3 shows the operator's net cash flow after deduction of the development expenses in Column 1. It is negative in the first two years, and remains small until the oil payment obligation is liquidated. Thereafter, it increases sharply and ultimately amounts to more than twice the original investment of $5 million. The discounted-cash-flow method recognizes that most of this income does not become available until late in the life of the project, and the resulting return on investment is 10% per annum. (If the same total income had been received in equal annual installments, the return would have been 15%.)

In situations of this kind, it is difficult to see how the analysis could be handled without resorting to the discounted-cash-flow approach. The conventional methods of calculating rates of return would give wholly misleading results.

B. *Water Flood Project. Exhibit IX* contains a second application of the discounted-cash-flow approach to situations in which the income generated by an investment is irregular. Normally, the free flow of oil from a reservoir (primary recovery) diminishes with the passage of time. In some cases, however, secondary recovery measures, such as injection of water into the reservoir, may result in a substantial increase in the total amount of oil produced.

The problem is to determine the profitability of acquiring a small producing property. The primary reserves have been nearly exhausted, and an investment of $2.5 million will be needed at the appropriate time for a water flood to accomplish recovery of the secondary reserves. No immediate payment will be made to the selling party, but he will receive a 12½% royalty on all oil produced from the property, whether from primary or secondary reserves.

The calculations in *Exhibit IX* are made under the assumption that the water flood investment will be made in the fourth year. During the first three years all the primary reserves will be recovered, and income in the fourth to the tenth years will be attributable solely to the water flood project.

As shown by the table, the discounted-cash-flow analysis gives *two solutions* to this problem. At both 28% and 49%, the net present worth of the cash flow is zero; i.e., the present worth of the cash income is equal to the present worth of the $2.5 million investment. The correct solution is 28%, because the net present worth is declining as we move from the lower to the higher discount rates. The reverse is true at the 49% level.

In general, two solutions may arise whenever the net cash flow switches from positive to negative at some stage in the life of the project, possibly as a result of additional capital outlays required at that time, as in the case of secondary recovery projects. It is important, therefore, to recognize the possibility of two solutions and not to settle for the first one found. A false solution can easily be identified by noting the direction of change in the present worths as higher discount rates are introduced in the trial-and-error calculations.

BENCH MARKS

As a final step in applying the discounted-cash-flow procedure to our business, it was necessary to develop some bench marks that could be used in appraising the figures resulting from the calculations.

As a starting point, we recommended that approximately 10% after taxes be regarded as the minimum amount we should seek to earn on investments involving a minimum of risk, such as those in new service stations and other marketing facilities. We further recommended that the minimum acceptable level of returns should be increased as the risks involved in the invest-ment projects increased. Accordingly, we set substantially higher standards for investments in manufacturing, petrochemical, and exploration and production ventures.

We arrived at these bench-mark figures by considering:

□   Our long-term borrowing costs.

□ The returns which Continental and other oil companies have cus-tomarily earned on their borrowed and invested capital (substantially more than 10%).

□ The returns which must be earned to make our business attractive to equity investors.

□ The returns which must be earned to satisfy our present shareholders that the earnings retained in the business each year are put to good use.

In this latter connection, it may be noted that whenever we retain earn-ings instead of paying them out as dividends, we in effect force our stock-holders to make a new investment in the Continental Oil Company. And clearly, we have little justification for doing that unless we can arrange to earn as much on the funds as the stockholders could earn by investing in comparable securities elsewhere.

Conclusion

The discounted-cash-flow method rests on the time-honored maxim that "money begets money." Funds on hand today can be invested in profitable projects and thereby yield additional funds to the investing company. Funds to be received at some future date cannot be profitably invested until that time, and so have no earning power in the interim. For this reason, a business concern must place a *time value* on its money—a dollar in hand today is much more valuable than one to be received in the distant future. The discounted-cash-flow method simply applies this general concept to the analysis of new capital investments.

The procedures which I have been describing in regard to the discounted-cash-flow method of analyzing new capital investments were adopted by Continental's top management in the fall of 1955 and were implemented throughout the company. Our subsequent experience in using the dis-counted-cash-flow approach may be summarized as follows:

□ We have found it to be a very powerful management tool. It is an extremely effective device for analyzing routine investments with fairly regular patterns of cash flow, and also for analyzing very complicated problems like those involved in mergers, acquisitions of producing properties under oil payment arrangements, and other ventures that require a series of capital outlays over a period of many years and generate highly irregular cash flows.

□ We have also found that the discounted-cash-flow techniques are far easier to introduce and apply than is commonly supposed. We had anticipated considerable difficulty in gaining acceptance of the new methods and in teaching people throughout the organization to use them; however, this turned out to be a very minor problem. Once the new methods were properly explained, they were quickly adopted throughout our operating and field organizations, and the mechanics of the calculations presented no problems of any importance.

□ There is one major theoretical and practical problem in using the discounted-cash-flow procedure for which we have not yet found a fully satisfactory solution. This problem is that of developing a return-on-investment figure for whole departments or groups of departments which may be computed year by year and compared with the returns calculated under the discounted-cash-flow procedures at the time individual investment projects were undertaken. Clearly, division of the cash income or the net income after taxes and depreciation by either the cost investment or the depreciated investment for the department as a whole will not produce statistics comparable to the discounted-cash-flow figures.

On the whole, our experience with the discounted-cash-flow techniques has been very satisfactory. To my mind, these techniques represent part of the oncoming improvements in the field of finance and accounting. Just as new technological discoveries continually bring us new opportunities in the fields of exploration, production, manufacturing, transportation, and marketing, so too there are occasionally new techniques in finance and accounting that offer opportunities to improve operations. The discounted-cash-flow method of investment analysis falls in that category.

12. New Framework for Corporate Debt Policy

Gordon Donaldson

How much debt is proper or prudent to take on? Conventional methods for evaluating debt capacity—such as analyzing what comparable companies are doing—can be misleading, claims an authority on the subject. In this landmark HBR article, he uses as his principal criterion the degree of risk which management thinks it can assume in deciding its investment priorities, risk being described as the chances of running short of cash. The question then becomes the extent to which the risks would be increased as the result of incurring a certain amount of debt, a question that is resolved by a test of cash adequacy.

□ Why are many common rules of thumb for evaluating a company's debt capacity misleading and even dangerous?

□ Why is outside experience and advice of limited value as a guide to top management's thinking about capacity?

□ What approach will enable management to make an independent and realistic appraisal of risk on the basis of data with which it is already familiar and in terms of judgments to which it has long been accustomed?

The problem of deciding whether it is wise and proper for a business corporation to finance long-term capital needs through debt, and, if so, how far it is safe to go, is one which most boards of directors have wrestled with at one time or another. For many companies the debt-capacity decision is of critical importance because of its potential impact on margins of profitability and on solvency. For *all* companies, however large and financially sound they may be, the decision is one to be approached with great care. Yet, in spite of its importance, the subject of corporate debt policy has received surprisingly little attention in the literature of business management. One might infer from this either that business has already developed a reliable means of resolving the question or that progress toward a more adequate solution has been slow.

In my opinion, the latter inference is closer to the truth. The debt-equity choice is still a relatively crude art as practiced by a great many corporate borrowers. It follows that there is a real opportunity for useful refinement in the decision-making process. However, there is little evidence, at present, of serious dissatisfaction with conventional decision rules on the part of those responsible for making this decision. In recent years I have been engaged in sampling executive opinions on debt policy, and I have found little indication of the same kind of ferment as is going on with regard to capital budgeting decisions.

The primary purpose of this article, therefore, is to stimulate dissatisfaction with present-day conventions regarding debt capacity and to suggest the direction in which the opportunity for improvement lies. I intend to show that the widely used rules of thumb which evaluate debt capacity in terms of some percentage of balance sheet values or in terms of income statement ratios can be seriously misleading and even dangerous to corporate solvency. I also intend to develop the argument that debt policy in general and debt capacity in particular cannot be prescribed for the individual company by outsiders or by generalized standards; rather, they can and should be determined by management in terms of individual corporate circumstances and objectives and on the basis of the observed behavior of patterns of cash flows.

The question of corporate debt capacity may be looked at from several points of view—e.g., the management of the business concerned, its shareholders or potential shareholders, and, of course, the lender of the debt capital. Because each of these groups may, quite properly, have a different concept of the wise and proper limit on debt, let me clarify the point of view taken in this article. I intend to discuss the subject from the standpoint of the management of the borrowing corporation, assuming that the board of directors which will make the final decision has the customary mandate from the stockholders to act on all matters concerning the safety and profitability of their investment. For the reader who ordinarily looks at this problem as a lender, potential stockholder, or investment adviser, the analysis described in this article may appear at first sight to have limited application. Hopefully, however, the underlying concepts will be recognized as valid regardless of how one looks at the problem, and they may suggest directions for improvement in the external as well as the internal analysis of the risk of debt.

Nature of the Risks

In order to set a background for discussing possible improvements, I will first describe briefly certain aspects of conventional practice concerning decision rules on long-term debt. These observations were recorded as a part of a research study which sampled practice and opinion in a group of relatively large and mature manufacturing corporations.[1] The nature

1. The complete findings have been published in book form; see Gordon Donaldson, *Corporate Debt Capacity* (Boston, Division of Research, Harvard Business School, 1961).

214   Finance

of this sample must be kept in mind when interpreting the practices
described.

HAZARDS OF TOO MUCH DEBT

The nature of the incentive to borrow as an alternative to financing
through a new issue of stock is common knowledge. Debt capital in the
amounts normally approved by established financial institutions is a comparatively cheap source of funds. Whether it is considered the cheapest
source depends on whether retained earnings are regarded as "cost free" or
not. In any case, for most companies it is easy to demonstrate that, assuming normal profitability, the combination of moderate interest rates and
high levels of corporate income tax enable debt capital to produce significantly better earnings per share than would a comparable amount of
capital provided by an issue of either common or preferred stock. In fact,
the advantage is so obvious that few companies bother to make the calculation when considering these alternatives.

Under these circumstances it is apparent that there must be a powerful
deterrent which keeps businesses from utilizing this source to the limits
of availability. The primary deterrent is, of course, the risks which are
inevitably associated with long-term debt servicing. While it is something
of an oversimplification to say that the debt decision is a balancing of
higher prospective income to the shareholders against greater chance of
loss, it is certainly true that this is the heart of the problem.

When the word "risk" is applied to debt, it may refer to a variety of
potential penalties; the precise meaning is not always clear when this subject is discussed. To most people, however, risk—so far as debt is concerned—is the chance of running out of cash. This risk is inevitably
increased by a legal contract requiring the business to pay fixed sums of
cash at predetermined dates in the future regardless of the financial
condition at that time. There are, of course, a great many needs for cash—
dividends, capital expenditures, research projects, and so on—with respect
to which cash balances may prove inadequate at some future point.

TOO LITTLE CASH

The ultimate hazard of running out of cash, however, and the one which
lurks in the background of every debt decision, is the situation where cash
is so reduced that legal contracts are defaulted, bankruptcy occurs, and
normal operations cease. Since no private enterprise has a guaranteed cash
inflow, there must always be *some* risk, however remote, that this event
could occur. Consequently, any addition to mandatory cash outflows resulting from new debt or any other act or event must increase that risk.

I have chosen to use the term "cash inadequacy" to refer to a whole family of problems involving the inability to make cash payments for any purpose important to the long-term financial health of the business; "cash insolvency" is the extreme case of cash inadequacy. It should be emphasized that although debt necessarily increases the chances of cash inadequacy, this risk exists whether the company has any debt or not, so that the debt-equity choice is not between some risk and no risk, but between more and less.

Conventional Approaches

Observation of present-day business practice suggests that businessmen commonly draw their concepts of debt capacity from one or more of several sources. Thus, they sometimes—

1. *Seek the counsel of institutional lenders or financial intermediaries (such as investment bankers)*—Most corporate borrowers negotiate long-term debt contracts at infrequent intervals, while the lender and the investment banker are constantly involved in loan decisions and so, presumably, have a great deal more experience and better judgment. Further, it is apparent that unless the lender is satisfied on the question of risk, there will be no loan. Finally, banks and insurance companies have a well-established reputation for being conservative, and conservative borrowers will take comfort from the fact that if the lender errs, it will likely be on the safe side.

2. *See what comparable companies are doing in this area of financial management*—Every business has an idea of those other companies in or out of the industry which are most like themselves so far as factors affecting risk are concerned. Since this is an aspect of corporate policy which is public information, it is natural that the debt-equity ratios of competitors will be carefully considered, and, lacking more objective guides, there will be a tendency to follow the mode and reject the extremes. This approach has an added practical appeal; group norms are important in the capital market's appraisal of a company's financial strength. If a company is out of line, it may be penalized—even though the deviation from the average may be perfectly appropriate for this company.

3. *Follow the practices of the past*—There is a very natural tendency to respect the corporation's financial traditions, and this is often apparent with regard to debt policy. Many businesses take considerable pride in "a clean balance sheet," an *Aa* rating, or a history of borrowing at the prime rate. It would border on sacrilege to propose a departure which would jeopardize these cherished symbols of financial achievement and respecta-

bility! The fact that these standards have apparently preserved corporate solvency in the past is a powerful argument for continuing them, particularly if the implications of a change cannot be precisely defined.

4. *Refer to that very elusive authority called "general practice," "industry practice," "common knowledge," or, less respectfully, "financial folklore"* —Remarkable as it seems in view of the great diversity among companies classified as industrials, there is widespread acceptance of the belief that an appropriate limit to the long-term borrowing of industrial companies is 30% of capitalization (or, alternatively, one third). The origin of, or rationale for, this particular decision rule has been obscured by the passage of time, but there is no doubt that it has become a widely honored rule of thumb in the decisions of both borrowers and lenders.

FALLACY OF DOUBLE STANDARD

Without denying the practical significance of some of the considerations which have led businessmen to follow these guides in formulating debt policy, it must be recognized that there are serious limitations inherent in using them (separately or as a group) as the *only* guides to appropriate debt capacity.

First, consider the practice of accepting advice from the lender. As the lender views the individual loan contract, it is one of a large number of investments which make up a constantly changing portfolio. When negotiated it is only one of a stream of loan proposals which must be acted on promptly and appraised in terms of the limited information to which generalized standards are applied. The nature of the risk to the lender is necessarily influenced by the fact that this loan is only a small fraction of the total sum invested and that intelligent diversification goes a long way to softening the impact of individual default. Further, even when default occurs, all may not be lost; in time the loan may be "worked out" through reorganization or liquidation.

All this is small comfort to the borrower. The individual loan which goes sour—if it happens to be *his* loan—is a catastrophe. There are few businessmen who can take a lighthearted attitude toward the prospect of default on a legal contract with the associated threat of bankruptcy. To most, this is viewed as the end of the road. Also, it is important to recognize that while the lender need only be concerned about servicing his own (high priority) claims, the borrower must also consider the needs which go unsatisfied during the period prior to the time of actual default when debt servicing drains off precious cash reserves.

This is not to imply that the lender is insensitive to individual losses and their effect on the business concerned; but it does mean that risk to the lender is not the same thing as risk to the borrower, and, consequently, the standards of one are not necessarily appropriate for the other. The lender's standards can at times be too liberal—as well as too conservative—from the borrower's point of view. Some will argue that, as a practical matter, the borrower must accept the debt-capacity standards of the lender, else there will be no contract. However, this implies that there is no bargaining over the upper limit of the amount that will be supplied, no differences among lenders, and/or no shopping around by borrowers. While all institutional lenders do have absolute limits on the risks they will take (even at a premium interest rate), there is often some room for negotiation if the borrower is so disposed. Under some circumstances there may be valid reasons for probing the upper limits of the lender's willingness to lend.

LESSONS OF EXPERIENCE

The second source of guidance mentioned is the observed practices of comparable businesses. This, too, has its obvious limitations. Even assuming strict comparability—which is hard to establish—there is no proof that the companies concerned have arrived at their current debt proportions in a deliberate and rational manner. In view of the wide variations in debt policy within any industry group, there can be little real meaning in an industry average. And what happens if every member of the group looks to the other for guidance? The most that can be said for this approach to debt policy is that the company concerned can avoid the appearance of being atypical in the investment market so far as its capital structure is concerned. But, as in most areas of business, there is a *range* of acceptable behavior, and the skill of management comes in identifying and taking advantage of the limits to which it can go without raising too many eyebrows.

Even a company's own direct experience with debt financing has its limitations as a guide to debt capacity. At best, the evidence that a particular debt policy has not been a cause of financial embarrassment in the past may only prove that the policy was on the conservative side. However, if assurance of adequate conservatism is the primary goal, the only really satisfactory policy is a no-debt policy.

For companies with some debt the experience of past periods of business recession is only partial evidence of the protection a particular policy affords. In most industries, the period of the past 20 years has produced a maximum of four or five periods of decline in sales and earnings. This limited recession experience with the behavior of cash flows—the critical consideration where debt servicing is involved—can be misleading since cash flows are affected by a variety of factors and the actual experience in any single recession is a somewhat unique combination of events which may not recur in the future. Thus, the so-called test of experience cannot be taken at face value.

In summing up a criticism of the sources from which management commonly derives its debt-capacity standard, there are two aspects which must be emphasized. Both of these relate to the practice of relying on the judgment of others in a situation where management alone is best able to appraise the full implications of the problem. The points I have in mind are as follows:

1. In assessing the risks of running out of cash because of excessive fixed cash obligations, the special circumstances of the individual firm are the primary data that the analyst has to work with. Management has obvious advantages over outsiders in using this data because it has free and full access to it, the time and incentive to examine it thoroughly, and a personal stake in making sensible judgments about what it observes. Even the judgments of predecessors in office are judgments made on information which is inadequate when compared to what management now has in its possession—if only because the predecessor's information is now 10 or 20 years old. (Subsequently, we will consider how management may approach an independent appraisal of risk for the individual business.)

2. The measurement of risk is only one dimension of the debt-capacity decision. In a free enterprise society, the assumption of risk is a voluntary activity, and no one can properly define the level of risk which another should be willing to bear. The decision to limit debt to 10%, 30% or any other percentage of the capital structure reflects (or should reflect) both the magnitude of the risk involved in servicing that amount of debt *and* the willingness of those who bear this risk—the owners or their duly authorized representatives—to accept the hazards involved.

In the last analysis, this is a subjective decision which management alone can make. Indeed, it may be said that a corporation has defined its debt policy long before a particular financing decision comes to a vote; it has done this in its choice of the men who are to make the decision. The ensuing decisions involving financial risk will reflect their basic attitudes— whether they see a situation as an opportunity to be exploited or a threat to be minimized.

A most interesting and fundamental question comes up here—one that underlies the whole relationship between management and the shareholder; namely, does management determine the attitude toward risk bearing which the stockholders must then adopt, or vice versa? This is part of the broader question of whether management should choose those financial policies which it prefers and attract a like-minded stockholder group (taking the "if they don't like it, they can sell out" approach) or by some means or other determine the attitudes and objectives of its present stockholder group and attempt to translate these into the appropriate action.

I do not propose to pass judgment on this difficult problem in the context of this article. The fact is, by taking one approach or the other—or some blend—management *does* make these decisions. With respect to risk bearing, however, one point is clear: responsible management should not be dealing with the problem in terms of purely personal risk preferences. I suspect that many top executives have not given this aspect the attention it deserves.

REASONS FOR CURRENT PRACTICE

Having considered the case for a debt policy which is internally rather than externally generated, we may well ask why so many companies, in deciding how far to go in using O.P.M. (other people's money), lean so heavily on O.P.A. (other people's advice). The answer appears to be threefold:

1. A misunderstanding of the nature of the problem and, in particular, a failure to separate the subjective from the objective elements.

2. The inherent complexity of the objective side—the measurement of risk.

3. The serious inadequacy of conventional debt-capacity decision rules as a framework for independent appraisal.

It is obvious that if a business does not have a useful way of assessing the general magnitude of the risks of too much debt in terms of its individual company and industry circumstances, then it will do one of two things. Either it will fall back on generalized (external) concepts of risk for "comparable" companies, or it will make the decision on purely subjective grounds—on how the management "feels" about debt. Thus, in practice, an internally generated debt-capacity decision is often based almost entirely on the management's general attitude toward this kind of problem without regard for how much risk is actually involved and what the potential rewards and penalties from risk bearing happen to be in the specific situation. The most obvious examples are to be found in companies at the extremes of debt policy that follow such rules as "no debt under any circumstances" or "borrow the maximum available." (We must be careful, however, not to assume that if a company has one or another of these policies, it is acting irrationally or emotionally.)

One of the subjects about which we know very little at present is how individual and group attitudes toward risk bearing are formed in practice. It is apparent, however, that there are important differences in this respect among members of any given management team and even for an individual executive with regard to different dimensions of risk within the business. The risk of excessive debt often appears to have a special significance; a man who is a "plunger" on sales policy or research might also be an arch-conservative with regard to debt. The risk of default on debt is more directly associated with financial ruin, regardless of the fundamental cause of failure, simply because it is generally the last act in a chain of events which follows from a deteriorating cash position.

There are other bits of evidence which are possible explanations for a Jekyll-and-Hyde behavior on risk bearing in business:

◻ Debt policy is always decided at the very top of the executive structure whereas other policies on sales or production involving other dimensions of risk are shaped to some degree at all executive levels. The seniority of the typical board of directors doubtless has some bearing on the comparative conservatism of financial policy, including debt policy.

◻ There is also some truth in the generalization that financial officers tend to be more conservative than other executives at the same level in other phases of the business, and to the extent that they influence debt policy they may tend to prefer to minimize risk per se, regardless of the potential rewards from risk bearing.

WHAT IS A SENSIBLE APPROACH?

The foregoing is, however, only speculation in an area where real research is necessary. The point of importance here is that, whatever the reason may be, it is illogical to base an internal decision on debt policy on attitudes toward risk *alone*, just as it is illogical to believe that corporate debt policy can be properly formulated without taking these individual attitudes into account.

For the purposes of a sensible approach to corporate debt policy we need not expect management to have a logical explanation for its feelings toward debt, even though this might be theoretically desirable. It is sufficient that managers know how they feel and are able to react to specific risk alternatives. The problem has been that in many cases they have not known in any objective sense what it was that they were reacting to; they have not had a meaningful measure of the specific risk of running out of cash (with or without any given amount of long-term debt).

It is therefore in the formulation of an approach to the measurement of risk in the individual corporation that the hope for an independent appraisal of debt capacity lies.

Inadequacy of Current Rules

Unfortunately, the conventional form for expressing debt-capacity rules is of little or no help in providing the kind of formulation I am urging. Debt capacity is most commonly expressed in terms of the balance sheet relationship between long-term debt and the total of all long-term sources, viz., as some per cent of capitalization. A variation of this ratio is often found in debt contracts which limit new long-term borrowing to some percentage of net tangible assets.

The alternative form in which to express the limits of long-term borrowing is in terms of income statement data. This is the *earnings coverage* ratio—the ratio of net income available for debt servicing to the total amount of annual interest plus sinking fund charges. Under such a rule, no new long-term debt would be contemplated unless the net income available for debt servicing is equal to or in excess of some multiple of the debt servicing charges—say, three to one—so that the company can survive a period of decline in sales and earnings and still have enough earnings to cover the fixed charges of debt. As we will see shortly, this ratio is more meaningful for internal formation of policy but also has its limitations.

Now, let us go on to examine each type of expression more closely.

CAPITALIZATION STANDARD

Consider a company which wishes to formulate its own debt standard as a per cent of capitalization. It is apparent that in order to do so the standard must be expressed in terms of data which can be related to the magnitude of the risk in such a way that changes in the ratio can be translated into changes in the risk of cash inadequacy, and vice versa. But how many executives concerned with this problem today have any real idea of how much the risk of cash inadequacy is increased when the long-term debt of their company is increased from 10% to 20% or from 20% to 30% of capitalization? Not very many, if my sample of management information in this area has any validity. This is not surprising, however, since the balance sheet data on which the standard is based provide little direct evidence on the question of cash adequacy and may, in fact, be highly unreliable and misleading.

While we do not need to go into a full discussion here of the inadequacies of relating the principal amount of long-term debt to historical asset values as a way of looking at the chances of running out of cash, we should keep in mind the more obvious weaknesses:

1. There is a wide variation in the relation between the principal of the debt and the annual obligation for cash payments under the debt contract. In industrial companies the principal of the debt may be repaid serially over the life of the debt contract, which may vary from 10 years or less to 30 years or more. Thus, the annual cash outflow associated with $10 million on the balance sheet may, for example, vary from $500,000 (interest only at 5%) to $833,000 (interest plus principal repayable over 30 years) to $1,500,000 (interest plus principal repayable over 10 years).

2. As loans are repaid by partial annual payments, as is customary under industrial term loans, the principal amount declines and the per-cent-of-capitalization ratio improves, but the annual cash drain for repayment *remains the same* until maturity is reached.

3. There may be substantial changes in asset values, particularly in connection with inventory valuation and depreciation policies, and as a consequence, changes in the per-cent-of-capitalization ratio which have no bearing on the capacity to meet fixed cash drains.

4. Certain off-the-balance-sheet factors have an important bearing on cash flows which the conventional ratio takes no cognizance of. One factor of this sort which has been receiving publicity in recent years is the payments under leasing arrangements. (While various authorities have been urging that lease payments be given formal recognition as a liability on balance sheets and in debt-capacity calculations, there is no general agreement as to how this should be done. For one thing, there is no obvious answer as to what the capitalization rate should be in order to translate lease payments into balance sheet values. In my opinion this debate is bound to be an artificial and frustrating experience—and unnecessary for the internal analyst—since, as will be discussed later, it is much more meaningful to deal with leases, as with debt, in terms of the dollars of annual cash outflow rather than in terms of principal amounts. Thus, a footnoting of the annual payments under the lease is entirely adequate.)

EARNINGS-COVERAGE STANDARD

The earnings-coverage standard affords, on the surface at least, a better prospect of measuring risk in the individual company in terms of the factors which bear directly on cash adequacy. By relating the total annual cash outflow under all long-term debt contracts to the net earnings available for servicing the debt, it is intended to assure that earnings will be adequate to meet charges at all times. This approach implies that the greater the prospective fluctuation in earnings, the higher is the required ratio (or the larger the "cushion" between normal earnings and debt-servicing charges).

This standard also has limitations as a basis for internal determination of debt capacity:

1. The net earnings figure found in the income statement and derived under normal accounting procedures is *not* the same thing as net cash inflow—an assumption which is implicit in the earnings-coverage standard. Even when adjustments are made for the noncash items on the income statement (depreciation charges), as is commonly done in the more sophisticated applications, this equivalence cannot safely be assumed. The

time when it may be roughly true is the time when we are least concerned about the hazards of debt, i.e., when sales are approximately the same from period to period. It is in times of rapid change (including recessions) that we are most concerned about debt burden, and then there *are* likely to be sharp differences between net income and net cash flow.

2. The question of what the *proper* ratio is between earnings and debt servicing is problematical. In a given case should the ratio be two to one or twenty to one? If we exclude externally derived standards or rules of thumb and insist that a company generate its own ratio in terms of its own circumstances, how does it go about doing it? Perhaps the best that could be done would be to work backward from the data of past recessions, which would indicate the low points of net earnings, toward a ratio between this experience and some measure of "normal" earnings with the intention of assuring a one-to-one relationship between net earnings and debt servicing at all times. However, if this is the way it is to be done, the estimate of minimum net earnings would itself provide the measure of debt capacity, and it would be unnecessary to translate it into a ratio. Further, as already noted, there are hazards in a literal translation of past history as a guide for the future. And what of the case where the company has experienced net losses in the past? Does this mean that it has no long-term debt capacity? If a net loss is possible, *no* ratio between normal net earnings and debt servicing, however large, will assure the desired equality in future recessions.

The earnings-coverage standard does not appear to be widely used by industrial corporate borrowers as a basis for formulating debt policy. Where it is used, it appears either to derive from the advice of institutional lenders or investment bankers or merely to reflect the borrower's attitude toward risk bearing. Its use does not seem to indicate an attempt to measure individual risk by some objective means.

A More Useful Approach

Granted the apparent inadequacies of conventional debt-capacity decision rules for purposes of internal debt policy, is there a practical alternative? I believe there is, but it must be recognized immediately that it rests on data which are substantially more complex than what the conventional rules require, and involve a considerably larger expenditure of time and effort to obtain and interpret. However, in view of the unquestioned importance of the debt-equity decision to the future of individual businesses, and in view of the fact that, as will be shown later, the data have a usefulness which goes well beyond the debt-capacity decision, there is reason to give this alternative serious consideration.

The basic questions in the appraisal of the magnitude of risk associated with long-term debt can be stated with deceptive simplicity: What are the chances of the business running out of cash in the foreseeable future? How are these chances changed by the addition of X thousands of dollars of annual interest and sinking fund payments? First, it is necessary to specify whether our concern is with "running out of cash" in an absolute sense (cash insolvency) or merely with the risk of cash inadequacy, i.e., running out of cash for certain purposes considered essential to management (for example, a minimum dividend on common stock). We can consider both of these possibilities, but let us focus for the moment on the ultimate hazard, the one commonly associated with excessive debt—the chance of complete depletion of cash reserves resulting in default on the bond contract and bankruptcy.

There are, of course, a variety of possible circumstances under which a company might have its cash reserves drained off. However, considering the problem from the point of view of mature, normally profitable, and reasonably well-managed companies, it is fair to say that the primary concern with debt is with what might happen during a general or industry recession when sales and profits are depressed by factors beyond the immediate control of management. Thus, when the experienced business executive wishes to instill the proper respect for the hazards of too much debt in the minds of aggressive young men eager for leverage, he will recount harrowing tales of disaster and near-disaster in the early 1930's.

REFOCUSING ON PROBLEM

The data we seek are information on the behavior of cash flows during the recession periods. An internal analysis of risk must therefore concern itself not with balance sheet or income statement ratios but directly with the factors which make for changes in cash inflow and outflow. Further, since we are dealing with the common denominator of all transactions, analysis must inevitably take into account *all* major influences on cash flow behavior. In short, the problem is a company-wide problem. All decisions involving cash should be included, and where cash solvency is at stake, there can be no meaningful boundaries on risk except those imposed by the corporate entity itself.

Therefore, it is somewhat artificial to think in terms of "the cash available for debt servicing," as the earnings-coverage standard does, as if it were an identifiable hoard when a number of needs equally as urgent are competing for a limited cash reserve. Consequently, the problem to which this article was originally addressed—determining the capacity to bear the incremental fixed charges of long-term debt—is in reality a much more general one: viz., the problem of *determining the capacity to bear incremental fixed cash outflows for any purpose whatever.*

ASSESSING KEY FACTORS

The analysis which is proposed in this article as a way of resolving this problem can only be briefly summarized here. It includes:

1. *Identification*—At the outset, it is important to identify the primary factors which produce major changes in cash flow with particular reference to contractions in cash flow. The most significant factor will be sales volume; many of the other factors will be related in greater or lesser degree to sales. However, to cite the example of another major factor, cash expenditures for raw materials, the relationship to sales volume in a downswing is not at all an automatic one since it also depends on:

□ The volume of finished-goods inventory on hand at the onset of the recession.

□ The working relationship between finished goods on hand, work scheduled into production, and raw-materials ordering.

□ The level of raw-materials inventory.

□ The responses of management at all levels to the observed change in sales.

For most factors affecting cash flow there will be a degree of interdependence and also a range of independent variation, both of which must be identified for the purpose of the analysis.

2. *Extent of refinement desired*—Obviously the list of factors affecting cash flow which are to be given separate consideration could be lengthy depending on the degree of refinement desired; and the longer the list, the greater the complexity of the analysis. It is therefore essential to form a judgment in advance as to how far refinement in the analysis can or should be carried in view of the objectives of the analysis. It is possible for this cash flow analysis to range all the way from simple and relatively crude approximations to the other extreme of involved mathematical and statistical formulas and even to the programming of recession cash flows on a computer.

In their simplest form, cash flows can be considered in terms of accounting approximations derived from balance sheet and income statement data. Thus, for example, sales revenues might be adjusted for changes in accounts receivable to derive current cash inflow, and cost of goods sold could be converted into expenditures for goods actually produced by adjusting for changes in inventory levels. However, the hazard of simplification is that important changes may be obscured by combining factors that at one time may "net each other out" and at some other time may reinforce each other. For instance, changes in dollar sales are produced by changes in product mix, physical volume, and price.

Here is where the internal analyst has a major advantage. Experience tells him what factors should be given separate treatment, and he has access to the data behind the financial statements so he can carry refinement as far as he wishes. Ideally, the analysis should be in terms of cash and not accrual accounting information; that is, it should be in terms of cash receipts (not dollar sales) and cash expenditures for raw materials received (not an accounting allocation for raw materials according to the number of units sold).

3. *Analysis of behavior*—Given a list of all major factors affecting cash flow, the next step is to observe their *individual* behavior over time and in particular during recessions. The objection raised earlier to using historical evidence as a guide to debt capacity was that, as usually employed, it is an observation of the *net* effect of change in all these factors on particular occasions—an effect which can be seriously misleading. But if management takes the individual behavior of these factors into account, the problem is minimized to a point where it can be disregarded.

Past experience in a company with an established position in its industry commonly leads its management to the sensible conclusion that, while it is theoretically possible for the physical volume of sales, for example, to contract to zero in a recession period, in practice there are reasons why this is highly unlikely to occur. These reasons relate to fundamental and enduring forces in the economy, the industry, the competitive position of the firm, consumer buying habits, and so on. Thus, past experience will suggest a range of recession behavior which describes the outside limits of what recession can be expected to do in the future. These limits I wish to refer to as the *maximum favorable limit* and the *maximum adverse limit* (referring to the effect on cash flows and the cash position). By combining the evidence contained in historical records and the judgment of management directly involved in the making of this history, we can describe these limits of expected behavior for all factors affecting cash flow. It will be part of our analysis to do so, taking careful account of interdependent variation for reasons given earlier.

4. *Expected range of recession behavior*—On the basis of such informed observation it may be concluded, for example, that the recession contraction in physical volume of sales is not expected to be less than 5% nor more than 25% of the sales of the period immediately preceding the recession. These are the maximum favorable and maximum adverse limits of sales for the company in question. It may also be concluded that the recession is not expected to last less than one year nor more than three years and that no more than 40% of the contraction will be concentrated in the first year of the recession. Naturally, our interest focuses on the maximum *adverse* limit, since we are attempting to assess the chances of running out of cash. By setting such boundaries on the adverse recession behavior of a major factor influencing cash flows we are beginning to set similar boundaries on the recession behavior of the cash flows themselves.

At this point a question presents itself which has major implications for the subsequent character of the analysis: Is it possible to say anything meaningful about the behavior of sales volume or any other factor *within* the limits that have just been described?

Probability Analysis

It is possible that there may be some historical evidence in the company on the comparative chances or probabilities of occurrence of sales contractions of, say 5%-11%, 12%-18%, 19%-25% (or any other breakdown of the range), but the statistical data are likely to be sketchy. It is perhaps more likely that management might, on the basis of experience, make some judgments such as, for example, that the contraction is most likely— say, five chances out of ten—to fall in the 12%-18% range; that the chances of its falling in the 5%-11% range are three chances out of ten; and that the chances of falling in the 19%-25% range are two chances out of ten.

If this kind of information can be generated for all factors affecting cash flow, then it is possible to come up with a range of estimates of the cash flow in future recession periods based on all possible combinations of the several factors, and for each estimate a numerical measure of its probability of occurrence. The whole set collectively will describe all anticipated possibilities. By totaling the separate probabilities of those combinations of events exhausting the initial cash balance, we can describe in quantitative terms the over-all chances of cash insolvency. Ideally we want to know that the chances of cash insolvency, as described by this process of analysis of cash flows are, say, one in twenty or one in fifty.

PROBLEMS TO SURMOUNT

However, in order to get such a precise measure of the risk of cash insolvency, we need estimates of probability that are within the expected range of behavior and not just the limits of behavior. There are important practical problems that stand in the way of obtaining this type of information and conducting this type of analysis:

□ Although the analysis suggested above appears relatively simple, in practice it could be quite complex, requiring the guidance of someone experienced in probability theory as well as in financial analysis to steer the study of cash flows around potential pitfalls. The problems center mainly on (1) accurately describing the patterns of adjustment over time, and (2) assessing the varying degrees of interdependence among the variables. These difficulties are not insurmountable, however, since statisticians have resolved similar ones in the case of other types of business problems.

□ Past recession periods may not have provided enough experience with respect to the behavior of sales, collections, inventory levels, and so forth, on which to base firm estimates of probabilities over the entire range of possible behavior. Some companies have had only two or three recessions in the past 20 years, and even then sometimes statistics are lacking (although presumably management will have some impressions about the events). But *some* experience with varying recession circumstances is essential even to make a guess. Speaking generally, this limitation on a comprehensive appraisal of the risk magnitude is far more serious than the one of technical competence mentioned first.

☐ Top management will not base critical decisions, such as debt policy, on data which it does not understand and/or in which it does not have confidence. This, I believe, is the primary obstacle which stands in the way of widespread use of a comprehensive cash flow analysis as a basis for risk measurement and the determination of debt capacity at the present time. Because the method is complex (particularly in contrast to the customary rules of thumb) and because the judgments on probabilities and other aspects of the analysis may appear—and may in fact be—tenuous, management may well be unwilling to use the results, particularly when corporate solvency is at stake.

However, when all this is said, the fact remains that much of present-day practice is seriously inadequate, and there is an urgent need for a more meaningful approach to the problem, particularly so far as the borrower is concerned. Thus, there is a strong incentive to explore the opportunities for partial or approximate measures of the risk of cash insolvency within the general framework suggested by the comprehensive analysis. One such approach is that to be described. Its aim is to produce an indicator of risk magnitude which can be derived from more conventional and less complex data in which management has confidence.

ANALYSIS OF ADVERSE LIMITS

The new approach focuses on the expected *limits* of recession behavior and in particular on the maximum adverse limit. It is based on the assumption that while management may be unable to assess with confidence the probabilities within the range, it usually has strong opinions as to the expected limits and would be prepared to base decisions upon such expectations. Thus, to return to the example of the sales contraction, management may be unwilling to assign the "betting odds" to the three intervals between a 5% and a 25% contraction, but it probably does have strong feelings that 25% is the "absolute" limit of adversity within the foreseeable future. This feeling is based not merely on past statistics but on an expert appraisal of all the facts surrounding the customer's buying habits and circumstances, the competitive situation, and so on.

Following this procedure leads to a set of estimates of the maximum adverse limit of recession behavior covering each factor affecting cash flow, and it is a comparatively simple matter then to come up with an estimate of the maximum adverse behavior in any future recession of net cash flow itself—in terms of the minimum dollars of net inflow (or maximum dollars of net outflow), period by period. Making similar judgments as to the maximum adverse conditions immediately preceding the recession —including prerecession cash balances—it is next possible to determine whether, under such maximum assumptions, the company would become insolvent and, if so, how soon and by how much.

This calculation in itself will give management some "feel" for the nearness or remoteness of the event of cash insolvency. It may demonstrate, as I have done in the case of certain companies, that even under these maximum adverse assumptions the company still has a positive cash balance. If this is so, the amount of this minimum balance is an objective judgment of the total amount of incremental fixed cash charges which the company could assume without *any* threat of insolvency. Making some assumptions about the nature and the terms of the debt contract, this figure could be converted into the principal amount of additional debt which could be assumed with the expectation of complete safety.

Suppose, on the other hand, that the maximum adverse assumptions produce a negative cash balance, indicating the possibility of insolvency under certain adverse conditions. This does not mean that the long-term debt is excluded (except for those managements for whom any action which creates or increases the risk of insolvency, no matter how small it may be, is intolerable). The more likely response will be that, provided the chances are "sufficiently remote," the company is fully prepared to run the risk.

Thus, we are back to the problem of assessing the magnitude of the risk and the extent to which it would be increased by any given amount of debt. As a means of gaining a more precise impression of the chances of insolvency at the adverse end of the range of recession behavior, without going through the formal process of assigning probability values, I suggest that a second adverse limit be defined for each of the factors affecting cash flow. This will be called the *most probable adverse limit*. It reflects management's judgment as to the limit of *normal* recession behavior, as opposed to the maximum adverse limit, which includes all possibilities, however remote.

MODES AND RANGES

A visual representation of these two adverse limits of behavior is shown in *Exhibit I.* Assuming experience and expected behavior are somewhat

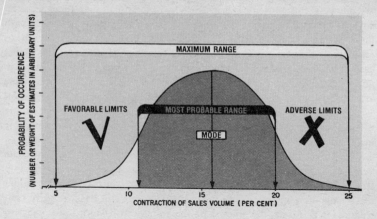

normally distributed about a mode (i.e., the value of most frequent occurrence), there will be:

1. A range of values clustered around this point, where most of past experience has been concentrated and where "bets" as to what the future is likely to bring will also be concentrated.

2. Extremes at either end of the range representing events that have a relatively small chance of happening.

It will be seen that the most probable limit cuts off the extreme "tail" of the frequency distribution in a somewhat imprecise and yet meaningful way. In setting the limits of expected sales contractions, for example, management would be saying that while sales *could*, in its judgment, contract as much as 25%, a contraction is *not likely* to exceed, say, 20%. This 20% is then the most probable adverse limit. While my terms may be new to businessmen, the distinction described is one which is commonly made and one on which judgments as to risk are often based.

From the data on the most probable adverse limits of the various factors affecting cash flow, the most probable adverse limit of recession *net* cash flows would be calculated and, from this, the most probable minimum recession cash *balance*. This last figure reflects management's best judgment as to the adverse limit of what is "likely to happen" as opposed to what "could happen" to net cash flows.

GUIDELINES FOR POLICY

At this point it should be noted that, when considering cash flows from the point of view of solvency, the list of possible expenditures would be stripped down to those which are absolutely essential for continuity of corporate existence and for the generation of current income. (We will presently bring into consideration other less mandatory expenditures such as dividends and capital expenditures.) Thinking in these terms, suppose the recession cash flow analysis indicates that under the maximum adverse assumptions the minimum cash balance would be negative, say, a deficit of $1,500,000. Suppose further that under the most probable adverse assumptions the minimum recession cash balance is a surplus of $3,000,000. How are these estimates to be interpreted as a guide to corporate debt capacity?

First, it is obvious in this example that management's expectations about the factors governing cash flow include the possibility that the company could become insolvent without any additional debt. However, this possibility is considered to have a relatively remote chance of occurrence since when the analysis is restricted to the most probable limit of recession behavior, the company is left with a positive minimum cash balance. The amount of this balance is a rough measure of the *total amount of additional fixed cash outflows (e.g., debt charges) which could be incurred without creating the threat of insolvency* in the event of normal recession conditions. Thus:

If the likely limit of the recession is expected to be two years, the company could stand additional debt servicing of $1,500,000 per year of recession. This sum can be readily converted into an equivalent principal amount. Assuming a 20-year term loan repayable in equal annual installments and bearing 5% interest, an additional debt of approximately $15,000,000 could be considered safe under ordinary recession conditions.

Let me emphasize that the cash balance would not be taken as a guide to debt capacity unless management were prepared to live with some chance of insolvency—a chance which would obviously be increased by the new debt. If management were not so inclined, it would reject debt or alternatively adopt a debt limit somewhere between zero and $15,000,000. In any case, management would not increase debt *beyond* $15,000,000 unless it were prepared to accept the chance of insolvency within the most probable range of recession experience. Because of the way the most probable limit has been defined, the chances of insolvency would be expected to increase rapidly and substantially if debt were to exceed $15,000,000 by any significant amount.

There is, of course, nothing sacred about the $15,000,000 limit set by management's judgment on the limits of normal recession experience. There is no reason why some managements would not increase debt capital substantially above this figure, assuming the funds were available. Such a step depends entirely on the willingness to bear the financial risks and on the potential rewards for such risk bearing. The foregoing type of analysis does, however, perform the essential function of alerting management to the range of debt beyond which risks may be expected to increase substantially.

It is now apparent that the analytical approach proposed here produces a criterion stated in terms of *the number of dollars of debt servicing* that are acceptable within management's concepts of risk bearing at a given point in time. The criterion is derived entirely from within and is completely independent of external judgments or rules of thumb. While it is admittedly crude and approximate when compared with the theoretical ideal of risk management, I believe it to be meaningful and useful in practice and, in this as in other respects, superior to the conventional forms for expressing debt limits.

It must be added, however, that because the recommended analysis is partial and approximate, those who adopt it must use it as they use current decision rules. That is, they must use it as a general guide and not as a precision instrument. For most managements this will be entirely adequate.

Better Decision Making

One of the real advantages of this approach to debt capacity is that it raises—and answers—a much broader question. As previously indicated, the analysis is actually concerned with the capacity to assume additional fixed cash outflows of any kind, and whatever capacity is demonstrated is not confined to debt servicing. Thus, if it is concluded from the example just given that the company in question can stand an additional outflow in recessions totaling $3,000,000, the first decision to be made by management is *how to use this capacity*.

There are a variety of ways in which the capacity may be used: to cover payments under a lease contract, to maintain a continuous research program, to stabilize employment, to pay a regular dividend in good times and bad, and so on. These are all competing uses for whatever capacity exists. With the information that the cash flow analysis provides, management now can begin to assign priorities and have some idea of how far it can hope to go in realizing its objectives. If debt servicing is given top priority, then the data have been a means of defining debt capacity.

It is because the proposed analysis has much broader significance than the question of debt (important as that question may be) that I believe the expenditure of time, effort, and money required to generate the data needed is well justified for the individual corporation. The analysis provides information which lies at the base of a whole range of financial and other decisions and has continuing significance. Moreover, most corporate treasurers have the staff and the basic data to undertake a careful and de-tailed study of the behavior of factors affecting cash flow.

TESTING FOR CASH ADEQUACY

Up to this point the analysis of cash flows has been discussed in terms of cash solvency. As indicated earlier, this means that attention is confined to outflows which are vital to survival. It was also indicated, however, that the risk of insolvency was part of a broader family of risks, described as the risk of cash inadequacy. In discussing the question of solvency with man-agement we often find that while there are certain expenditures which *could* be slashed to zero in an emergency, there is a reluctance to take action which would put management in a position of having to do so. These are expenditures which must be treated as mandatory for policy reasons, be-cause management believes that to interrupt them would be detrimental to the long-term interest of the corporation. Among the best examples of such expenditures are certain minimum payments for research, for capital assets, and for preferred and common dividends.

This situation can readily be incorporated into the type of analysis out-lined earlier. I refer to the method for doing this as the *test for cash ade-quacy* as opposed to the test for cash solvency. As soon as management has defined the "irreducible minimum" for these expenditures under recession conditions, they are merely added to the outflows of the previous analysis; then the figure generated for the maximum adverse or most probable adverse recession cash balance is the balance which remains over and above such payments. To return to the example previously used:

The effect would be to wipe out all or some portion of the most probable minimum balance ($3,000,000) or to add to the maximum adverse deficit ($1,500,000). Thus, if the irreducible minimum is considered to be two years of common dividends at $500,000 a year plus $1,000,000 of minimum capital expenditures, the result would be to cut the most probable balance back to $1,000,000. The capacity to assume additional fixed cash outflows is thereby substantially reduced. Obviously management in this case is giving priority to the dividend and capital expenditures over debt leverage —or over any other use for the funds on hand.

One of the benefits of such an analysis is to make management's priorities explicit, to recognize their competing character, and to make pos-sible a re-evaluation of their relative importance to the company.

Making separate tests for cash solvency and cash adequacy serves another important purpose. Most discussions of the hazards of debt imply that the danger is the risk of insolvency, and this danger is usually treated with proper respect. However, our analysis may demonstrate that within the range of management's expectations there is little or no risk of insolvency but a substantial risk of cash inadequacy, particularly if large amounts of long-term debt are added. If, in the past, management has been setting limits on debt in terms of an assumed risk of insolvency and now finds that the only significant risk is that of inability to meet certain minimum dividend payments and the like, it may well be disposed to assume a greater magnitude of risk and take on more debt. A management which would reject the risk of insolvency if it exceeded a chance of one in fifty might be prepared to accept a risk of abandoning cash dividends for a year or two if the chance did not exceed, say, one in twenty.

In short, once management knows the *kind* of risk it is taking, it may begin to draw distinctions between one form of contingency and another and not operate on the general assumption that the only concern is that of possible insolvency. Better information is thus a prerequisite for better decisions.

REAPPRAISING PRESENT RULES

Assuming management can, by the means described, come up with an independent appraisal of its long-term debt capacity, what does this imply for existing decision rules obtained from external sources or inherited from the past? Does it mean that they will be ignored completely? The answer is likely to be no. Debt policy cannot be made in a vacuum. It must take account of the lenders' willingness to lend and also of the reactions of equity investors who make judgments on the risks inherent in the corporation.

One of the first results of the analysis, therefore, is to reappraise existing debt-capacity decision rules. To illustrate:

Suppose a company has been assuming, as many do, that it can safely incur long-term debt up to a maximum of 30% of capitalization. This rule can be translated into its equivalent of dollars of annual debt-servicing charges and directly compared with the results of the recession cash flow analysis. In view of the fact that the rule probably has been derived from external sources, it is likely that the annual debt servicing which it permits either exceeds or falls short of the amount of cash flow indicated by the internal analysis.

In view of the approximate nature of the analysis, however, this is not likely to cause a change in debt policy unless the amount of the variation is substantial. It is also possible, of course, that the existing decision rule and the cash flow analysis will produce the same result—in which case the existing rule will appear verified. But this cannot be known in advance of the analysis, and in any case the data have been converted into a form which is much more meaningful for the purposes involved.

Such a comparison gives a measure of management's attitude toward the risk that is implicit in the existing decision rule (although management probably had no clear idea of what the risk magnitude was at the time the rule was established).

The results of the cash flow analysis can also be compared with the lender's concept of debt capacity—if different from that of the corporation. While lenders are often reluctant to make statements on the outside limits of what they will lend, they will, from time to time, give indications of what they consider an appropriate capital structure for a given industry and company. If the borrower's appraisal of his capacity exceeds that of the lender, he may well decide to push the latter to the limit of his willingness to lend. Without good cash flow data, many borrowers appear reluctant to argue their case aggressively, probably because of uncertainty as to where the safe limit lies.

The results can also be related to other aspects of the debt-capacity question, such as the requirements for an A bond rating or the risk expectations of equity investors which appear to be implicit in some price-earnings ratio (assuming this can be determined). Once again, the comparison is between whatever unused debt capacity is indicated by the internal analysis and the standards imposed by external considerations with the aim of probing the acceptable and useful upper limits of long-term debt.

I have carried out this type of analysis for a sample of companies in different industries and made comparisons with existing debt-capacity standards of both the corporations themselves and their lending institutions. The data strongly indicate that there are, in fact, major inconsistencies between managements' explicit expectations regarding recession cash flows and the expectations which are implicit in accepted ratios of debt capacity. The evidence is by no means adequate to make any safe or meaningful generalization about the over-all character of industrial debt policy. Nevertheless, among the large and mature corporations which are the basis of the study the evidence seems to suggest:

◻ Either the risks of debt have been significantly overrated by a substantial number of firms;

◻ Or some managements tend to be unusually conservative toward this aspect of corporate risk.

Future Trends

The trend of economic events in the past few decades suggests that there is both a need and an opportunity for a more refined approach to the debt-equity choice in corporate structures. As the specter of the depression of the 1930's has faded into the past and confidence in our capacity to avoid a repetition of extreme economic stagnation has grown, a new generation of corporate executives has shown increasing willingness to use long-term debt financing as a source of funds for consolidation and expansion.

So long as long-term debt is avoided or kept to minor proportions, crude decision rules providing wide margins of safety are quite adequate. As the proportions of debt increase, however, the need for a sharper pencil and a more careful analysis grows. This need is further reinforced by the increase in other kinds of fixed cash commitments such as lease payments and the noncontractual but none-the-less-vital steady flows required for research, dividends, and the like. Greater stability in the economy over an extended period is likely to encourage a variety of rigidities in cash outflows, and simple rules of thumb are inadequate to cope with the problems these present.

Along with the increasing need for improved analysis has come a greater capacity to carry out this analysis. This improvement derives both from better data and from improved techniques of processing and analyzing data. Financial executives today have access to far more data on cash flows and the factors behind cash flows than they did 20 years ago—far more, in fact, than many are actually putting to use. They also have access to more sophisticated approaches to the analysis of complex data and to machines which can reduce it to manageable proportions. As time goes on and financial management becomes increasingly familiar with these tools of analysis and more aware of the opportunities they afford, the current reluctance to adopt a more complex analytical framework is bound to diminish.

But there is one hitch. However sophisticated the financial officer may be in the newer techniques, there is little merit in serving up a diet of financial data to the board of directors, as a basis for the financial decision, which is too rich for their current digestive capacity. It is for this reason that I have not attempted in this article to convert the reader to a full-scale internal analysis of risk and its components. Rather, I have taken on the more modest objective of alerting top management to four key points bearing on the debt-capacity decision:

1. While external sources of advice can and should be consulted as an aid to decision making, the question of debt capacity is essentially an internal one to be settled by management with reference to its individual circumstances and individual preferences.

2. Current rules of thumb regarding debt capacity are seriously inadequate as a framework for this decision.

3. The answer lies in a knowledge of the behavior of cash flows and in having a useful measure of the capacity to assume incremental fixed cash outflows.

4. Management needs approaches that will enable it to approximate its

debt capacity within the context of data with which it is already familiar and in terms of judgments to which it has long been accustomed. The approach described in this article meets these criteria.

By accepting and acting on these points, management would take an important step forward toward debt-equity decisions in which borrowers and lenders alike could have greater confidence.

Part IV

Control

Preface

In every economy and every age since economic activity began, control has been a preoccupation of alert executives. It influences organizational success and may also have a decisive bearing on a manager's style of operating. In any book on general management, therefore, management control systems need to be discussed. But advances in technology and methodology have brought other important issues under the rubric of control. One of these issues is management information systems, which in company after company have captured the attention of top executives and been a continuing topic of discussion and debate. Information systems affect both the substance and forms of management control. The second issue is forecasting, which sometimes is classified with marketing but is treated here as an aspect of control because of its vital implications for management's cost and income expectations.

The article on "What Kind of Management Control Do You Need?" deals with the importance of considering the strategy and structure of a company before designing measures of financial responsibility. "Managing the Four Stages of EDP Growth" concerns the phases of growth typically experienced by computer departments—the "life crises" they go through as well as the varying techniques needed to manage computer facilities. "How to Choose the Right Forecasting Technique" describes the strengths and limitations of various qualitative and quantitative approaches, from the Delphi method to exponential smoothing, diffusion indexes, and input-output models.

13. What Kind of Management Control Do You Need?

Richard F. Vancil

A good method of measuring a manager's financial contribution to a company must meet two criteria. It must seem fair to the manager, and it must reward him for working for the benefit of the whole company, not just his department or division. Although simple in theory, these criteria become difficult to meet in practice. The characteristics of the business may lead managers to work at cross-purposes; moreover, the strategy of a business should have a profound effect on the kinds of decisions made. In this article the requirements of designing effective management control systems are examined in both simple and complex organizations. Pointing to realities with which businessmen are familiar, the author seeks to guide executives in weighing the advantages and disadvantages of functional forms of organization, product division forms, and the so-called matrix concept of organization. He points out that profit centers are by no means a universal answer, however appealing they may be in principle to business leaders.

Profit centers are a major tool for management control in large industrial corporations. They possess important advantages:

1. Profitability is a simple way to analyze and monitor the effectiveness of a segment of a complex business. For example, a product division competes in the marketplace against several other companies in its industry, and also competes among other divisions in its company for an allocation of corporate resources for its future growth. Relative profitability in both types of competition is a useful decision criterion for top management.

2. Profit responsibility is a powerful motivator of men. Managers understand what profit is all about, and aggressive managers welcome the opportunity to have their abilities measured by the only real entrepreneurial yardstick.

Simple and powerful, profit centers sounds like a panacea, the answer to a top manager's prayer. No wonder the concept has been so widely adopted. However, as with many a miracle drug, all too often the side effects of the medicine may be worse than the illness it was intended to cure.

There is an excellent body of literature on the problems that arise in implementing the profit center concept. The question I shall discuss is a more basic one: *When* should profit centers be used? More precisely, what executives below the president of a corporation (who clearly is responsible for profits) should be held responsible for the profits from segments of the business?

Parts of this discussion will come as no surprise to corporate presidents or to their controllers. I shall stress the relevance of corporate strategy and organization structure to profit center systems—an approach that may seem obvious to such executives. But I cannot find a discussion of these considerations in the literature, and thus I am led to believe that a concise statement of the conventional wisdom may be worthwhile.

Types of Financial Responsibility

The principal types of financial responsibility can be classified as follows:

Standard cost centers are exemplified by a production department in a factory. The standard quantities of direct labor and materials required for each unit of output are specified. The foreman's objective is to minimize the variance between actual costs and standard costs. He also is usually responsible for a flexible overhead expense budget, and his objective, again, is to minimize the variance between budgeted and actual costs.

Revenue centers are best illustrated by a sales department where the manager does not have authority to lower prices in order to increase volume. The resources at his disposal are reflected in his expense budget. The sales manager's objective is to spend no more than the budgeted amounts and to produce the maximum amount of sales revenue.

Discretionary expense centers include most administrative departments. There is no practical way to establish the relationship between inputs and outputs. Management can only use its best judgment to set the budget, and the department manager's objective is to spend the budgeted amount to produce the best (though still unmeasurable) quality of service that he possibly can.

Profit centers, the focus of this article, are units, such as a product division, where the manager is responsible for the best combination of costs and revenues. His objective is to maximize the bottom line, the profit that results from his decisions. A great many variations on this theme can be achieved by defining "profit" as including only those elements of cost and revenue for which the manager is responsible. Thus a sales manager who is allowed to set prices may be responsible for gross profit (actual revenue less standard direct manufacturing costs). Profit for a product-line marketing manager, on the other hand, might reflect deductions for budgeted factory overhead and actual sales promotion expenses.

Investment centers are units where the manager is responsible also for the magnitude of assets employed. He makes trade-offs between current profits and investments to increase future profits. Stating the manager's objective as maximizing his return on investment or his residual income (profit after a charge for the use of capital) helps him to appraise the desirability of new investments.

Choice of Financial Goals

The cornerstone of every management control system is the concept of responsibility accounting. The basic idea is simple: each manager in a company has responsibility for a part of the total activity. The accounting system should be designed so that it yields a measurement of the financial effects of the activities that a manager is responsible for. This measurement can be stated in the form of a financial objective for each manager. Specifying that objective helps in delegating authority; a manager knows that the "right" decision is the course of action that moves him down the path toward his financial objective.

But this system does not go far enough. No single measurement, no matter how carefully constructed, can accurately reflect how well a manager has done his job. Part of the failure is simply due to the fact that corporations—and their managers—have multiple objectives. For instance, there is the matter of corporate social responsibility. Good performance toward that goal, even if measurable, cannot be added to the profit equation. Another major inadequacy of a single financial measurement is that it reflects performance during a particular time period, ignoring the effects that current actions may have on future performance. Every manager must make trade-offs between conflicting short-term and long-term needs; examples range all the way from the shop foreman who defers preventive maintenance in order to increase this month's output, but at the expense of a major breakdown next month, to the division manager who cuts his R&D budget in order to improve the year's profits but loses or delays the opportunity to introduce a profitable new product three years from now.

Despite these flaws, oversimplified financial measurements are almost universally used. The reason is not their value in evaluating a manager's performance—the faults noted are too obvious and important to ignore— but their effect on future performance. Specifying a financial objective can help a manager to think realistically about the tough decisions he must make, even if the objective does not always point the way to the right decision.

The selection of the right financial objective for each manager, therefore, can have an important effect on how he does his job. Although the range of *possible* objectives is very great, the financially measurable results of any manager's activities can usually be classified into one of the five categories of responsibility centers described above. As indicated, financial responsibility is simplest in the case of standard cost centers, most complex in the case of investment centers.

How should management measure the financial results achieved? It is not enough simply to say that a particular product division is a profit center; decisions are also required that specify how the profit is to be calculated, focusing in particular on how transfer prices shall be set and how the costs of services received from other organization units shall be charged against the division. Similarly, while the basic concept of an investment center is simple, it is difficult to decide which assets to include in the investment base and how they shall be valued. Therefore, although there may be only five types of financial responsibility centers, there are *many* methods of financial measurement that can be used for specific organizations.

CRITERIA FOR SELECTION

Figuring out the best way to define and measure the financial performance for each manager is the corporate controller's most challenging—and analytically demanding—task. Two types of considerations affect each choice. The first is the strategy of the company: its broad objectives, the nature of the industries in which it operates, and the niche it seeks to carve for itself in each industry on the basis of its distinctive competence. The second is the organization structure of the company—the way the total task is divided among the managers to permit delegation of authority and specialization of effort.

The controller must have a thorough knowledge of his company's strategy and organization structure. He draws on this knowledge to apply two criteria for deciding which measure of financial responsibility to use for each organization unit and how it should be calculated:

1. *Fairness*—Each manager must believe that the summary financial measurement used to report on his performance is appropriate. This means he must see all of the signals he receives about his job as consistent with each other. Moreover, he must believe that the measurement encompasses all the factors he can control and excludes those over which he has no control. And he must be convinced the measurement is calculated in such a way that a "good" decision on his part will be reflected as such by the financial measurement. The "fairness" of a financial measurement is not a fact; it is a perception through the eyes of the manager to whom it applies.

2. *Goal congruence*—The most difficult compromises that must be made in designing a management control system have to do with varying goals.

When a manager is assigned a financial objective for his activities and a fair measurement of performance is determined, ideally he should be able to pursue his objective without concern for whether or not his actions are in the best interests of the corporation. But in reality, as we know, that ideal is not easy to attain. The controller, designing a management control system with a corporatewide perspective, must ensure that managers are not working at cross-purposes. He must select objectives and measurements in such a way that a good decision by any manager is also a good decision for the corporation as a whole.

For the controller, applying these two criteria simultaneously means that he must combine the points of view of both the individual manager and the corporation. That becomes progressively more difficult as the complexity of the organization structure and the business increases. In the balance of this article I shall discuss the use of the two criteria, dealing first with relatively simple organization structures and then with more complex ones.

Use in Simple Structures

Discussing the design of a management control system for "simple" organizations is not a theoretical or academic exercise. Some small businesses have simple organization structures, and even the largest corporations progressively subdivide the management tasks to the point where an individual manager is responsible for a single functional activity. Functional units are the organizational building blocks in the most complex corporations.

What varieties of control system are possible and feasible in simple organizations? When are the criteria of fairness and goal-congruence satisfied? How does a company's strategy affect the choice of a system?

PRACTICAL ALTERNATIVES

The simplified organization chart shown in *Exhibit I* is typical of a great many companies or parts of companies. The structure of the organization is simple in two respects:

1. There are only two levels of line managers in the hierarchy (the "general manager" might be thought of as the president of a small company).

2. The subordinate managers each have responsibility for a functional activity, which implies a rather natural distribution of tasks and authority between them.

Exhibit I. Functionally organized business

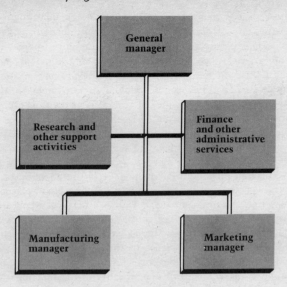

The business also requires some administrative and support activities, but the choice of financial measurements for these organizational units is less complex and will not be discussed here.

Selecting an appropriate financial measurement for this president's performance is not really a problem. He is responsible for the entire business, its profits, and the investment required. The financial responsibility of his two principal subordinates, however, is not so easily determined. The manufacturing manager, responsible for all production operations in the plant, could be charged with the responsibility of running either a standard cost center or a profit center. And the marketing manager, responsible for all sales and promotion activities, could be treated as the head either of a revenue center or of a profit center. With just two functional units, and two alternatives available for each, there are still four alternatives for the design of a management control system for this business:

Alternative	Manufacturing	Marketing
1.	Standard cost center	Revenue center
2.	Standard cost center	Profit center
3.	Profit center	Revenue center
4.	Profit center	Profit center

These four alternatives are not simply theoretical possibilities; each may be appropriate under different circumstances. The critical circumstances concern the nature of the key decisions to be made and the way decision-making authority is delegated in the organization.

As for the decisions, most of them involve choices in allocating resources. There are questions of *purpose* (e.g., whether incremental marketing expenditures should be used for advertising or for hiring more salesmen) and of *timing* (e.g., when a piece of production equipment should be replaced). In an ideal world, an all-wise and all-knowing president could make every decision, and his decision would always be "right" in the sense that it is the best course of action for the company at the time even though it may turn out to be wrong as future events unfold. The problem is that no president can make all the decisions and that, as he delegates power to subordinates, he runs the risk they will make decisions that are different from those he would make.

Effective decision making in a functionally organized business is hampered by the fact that no subordinate has the same broad perspective of the business that the president or general manager has. Many decisions, and almost all the important ones, affect more than one function in the business. They are seen differently by managers according to the functions they manage. One possible response to this problem is not to delegate authority for important decisions below the level of general manager. Another approach is to broaden the perspective of the functional manager by delegating such authority to him and then holding him responsible for the profitability of his decisions.

The implications of the second approach can best be seen by examining a series of examples. I shall describe a company situation for each of the four design alternatives mentioned.

1. *No profit centers:* Company A manufactures and distributes fertilizer. It buys chemicals, minerals, and other components from large suppliers and mixes them in various combinations to produce a limited variety of standard fertilizers with specified chemical properties. These are sold to farmers in bulk. Because the quality is specified and subject to verification by chemical analysis, all producers sell at the same price and offer identical volume discounts. Transportation costs are a major factor, and Company A thus enjoys a relative advantage in its local market. Its salesmen call on purchasing agents for large corporate farms and on distributors that sell to smaller farmers. Most orders are placed well in advance of the growing season, so the mixing plant is busy several months of the year, but there is still a large seasonal peak in both marketing and manufacturing.

Prices tend to fluctuate with the cost of the primary chemical components. The result is that an efficient fertilizer producer tends to earn about the same profit, as a percentage of the sales dollar, on each of the products in his line.

In this company the mission of the marketing manager is to sell as much fertilizer as he can. He has no control over product design or pricing, and promotional activities other than direct selling efforts are ineffective. His primary concern is with the effective use of his salesmen's time and with the development and maintenance of good customer relations. His stated objective is to produce as much revenue as he can with the number of salesmen currently authorized. In technical terms he is a "revenue center." He is also responsible for the expense budget for his activities.

The mission of the manufacturing manager, on the other hand, is to produce fertilizer in the required quantities as efficiently as possible. The work force is only semiskilled, and his primary concern is to ensure that they are properly trained and well supervised and that material wastage is held to a minimum. He is a "standard cost center," financially responsible for meeting the standard direct cost of each unit produced and for controlling overhead expenses against a variable budget reflecting the volume of throughput.

The president of Company A is the only man financially responsible for the profit of the company. There are a limited number of key, cross-functional decisions to be made, and he makes them. One concerns the size of the sales force; another concerns the acquisition of equipment to increase the capacity or reduce the labor costs in the mixing plant. Both of these are what are called "capacity decisions." While the evaluation of alternatives for either decision is not easy, it can be handled as well or better by the president than by either of his two subordinates.

2. *Marketing profit centers:* Company B produces a line of branded consumer toiletries. The products are heavily advertised and made available to consumers in drugstores, supermarkets, and other retail outlets throughout the country. The marketplace is in continual turmoil as competitors jockey for consumer attention through price promotions, premium offers, and "new" formulas and "secret" ingredients announced through both media advertising and point-of-purchase promotion. The company's field sales force is small; salesmen call on distributors and purchasing agents for large retail chains. The product itself is simple to manufacture, but consistently reliable quality is considered important to maintain customer goodwill.

Marketing is where the action is in Company B. The marketing manager is responsible for profitability, which is defined as sales revenue less standard direct manufacturing costs and all marketing costs. The president of the company is very interested in the marketing function and devotes much of his time to it. At the same time, he realizes that there are a myriad of marketing decisions to be made, many of them requiring specialized knowledge of local markets and detailed current information on competitors' actions. Therefore, he needs to delegate considerable authority to the marketing manager.

The manufacturing manager, like his counterpart in Company A, is a standard cost center, responsible for standard direct costs and a variable overhead budget.

3. *Production profit centers:* Company C produces a line of specialty metal products sold as semifinished components, primarily to manufacturers of high-style lighting fixtures. The company has only a few dozen customers, four of which account for over 50% of the sales volume. The business is price-competitive; Company C's equipment is not unique, and other manufacturers are frequently asked to bid against Company C on prospective contracts. Company C is renowned, however, for its technical skills in solving difficult manufacturing problems. Even on relatively routine contracts, the company is sometimes able to charge a slightly higher price because of its consistently high quality and its responsiveness in meeting its customers' "emergency" delivery requirements.

Price quotations on each contract are prepared by an estimator in the plant. The field sales force calls on old customers and prospective new ones, maintaining and developing relationships and soliciting opportunities to bid for their business.

Manufacturing is the name of the game at Company C. The manufacturing manager is responsible for profit, defined as the contribution to overhead after subtracting all direct manufacturing costs. He keeps himself informed of the backlog of orders against each type of equipment in his shop and personally reviews all bids over a nominal amount, estimating the price to quote in view of his desire for the business and his assessment of the customer's loyalty. He is also responsible for meeting his variable overhead budget.

As for the marketing manager, he is a revenue center, like his counterpart in Company A. He endeavors to use his sales force as effectively as possible to turn up attractive bidding opportunities on which the company can compete successfully.

4. *Multiple profit centers:* Company D is a partly integrated oil refining and marketing organization. The company's refinery purchases crude oil and refines it into gasoline, kerosene, and other products. The company also operates a regional chain of service stations, advertising its brand of gasoline to consumers. The company's strategy is to be less than self-sufficient in producing enough gasoline to meet its retail requirements. Thus the refinery is usually able to operate at capacity, and gasoline is purchased from other refiners as required.

Both the manufacturing (refinery) manager and the marketing manager are responsible for *part* of the profits earned by Company D. The refinery manager sells his gasoline to the marketing department at the same price charged by other refiners; the profit on the refinery is an important measure of the efficiency of his operations. The marketing manager, much like his counterpart in Company B, is also a profit center; he attempts to find the optimum balance and mix of marketing expenditures that will be most profitable for the company.

In this kind of situation, therefore, the president needs to delegate considerable decision-making power to not one but two subordinates. With respect to each he acts in the way described for Companies B and C.

The foregoing examples, simple as they are, show how difficult it is to generalize on the question of whether or not a functional manager should be held responsible for profit. The first, most obvious, statement is that the decision turns on the nature of the business. The tangible differences between businesses and the unique tasks they imply for management must be reflected in the management control system. The challenge for the controller is to synthesize the characteristics of the business and select a financial objective for each manager that (1) motivates him to achieve the company's objectives, and (2) minimizes unnecessary conflict between managers.

However, the characteristics of a business are not the sole determinants of financial responsibility. In fact, they are not the most important ones. This brings us to the next point: the implications of corporate strategy.

CRUCIAL ROLE OF STRATEGY

As an illustration, let us consider the situation of a franchised automobile dealership called Connelly Autos, Inc. The company sells new and used cars and auto repair services. Connelly's organization structure is simple; under the president there are two marketing managers, one for new cars and one for used cars, and a service department manager.

In this case, and in retail distribution businesses generally, it is easy to see the advantages of holding a sales manager responsible for the profits of his department. Moreover, suppose a customer with a certain amount of money to spend is undecided about buying a stripped-down new car or a more expensive model that is a year or two old. If Connelly's two sales managers compete for this customer's business, the result is probably that the customer is better served, in the sense that he has more information about the relative advantages of his two major alternatives and can ultimately make a choice that satisfies him better.

Also, the dealership is probably better off as a result of the competiton. There are many other new car and used car dealers, so if the company itself offers both choices in a manner that is as competitive as the two departments would be if they were in separate dealerships, it stands a better chance of getting a customer's business no matter which car he chooses to drive.

The difficult problem is designing a management control system for Connelly's service department manager. What is his financial responsibility? How should Connelly measure his performance in financial terms? The service department is not simply another sales department, delivering retail repair services to customers. It is also a "manufacturing" department producing services for the two automobile sales departments; it prepares new cars for delivery and services them during the warranty period, and it repairs and reconditions used cars to be sold at retail.

The real question becomes: What does Connelly want his service department manager to do? Here are several possible answers:

□ Run the service department as though it were an independent auto repair shop. With this mission, the service department manager would be responsible for profits and should probably sell his services to the new and used car departments at the regular retail price, or perhaps with a slight "dealer" discount.

□ Employ the capacity of the shop to the fullest, using renovation work on used cars as a way of absorbing slack capacity. With this mission, repair services should probably be sold to the used car department at standard direct costs. The used car manager would buy cars needing repair work, at wholesale auctions if necessary, thus providing all the volume the service department could handle. The service department would be essentially a standard cost center, and the profit on retail repairs would be de-emphasized.

□ Run the shop in such a way as to maximize customer goodwill, attempting to build a reputation that will yield regular, repeat customers for new cars. Under these circumstances, it would be very difficult to calculate a financial measurement that would appropriately reflect the performance of the service department manager. He should not be held responsible for profits, nor should he be expected to run close to capacity if he is to be responsive to customer emergencies. The shop should probably be treated as a standard cost center, but without emphasis being placed on financial performance.

Finding an answer: Thus the answer to the question of what the service department manager should do turns on Connelly's strategy for his dealership. The three alternatives outlined really characterize three different strategies. The first envisions a "balanced" dealership, the second has a strong used-car focus, and the third emphasizes new car sales.

Not all automobile dealers pursue the same strategy, nor should they. Local competitive conditions are a major factor in selecting a strategy, and the quality and type of resources available to Connelly are also critical factors in his choice. (Resources include the location of the dealership, the capital available for investment in new and used car inventories, and the competence and aggressiveness of Connelly's three subordinates.) Finally, the strategy Connelly selects will affect his image in the community as a businessman and a citizen, and his personal aspirations concerning the size and reputation of the business also have a bearing on the problem.[1]

There are thousands of automobile dealers in the United States, and they appear to be identical in terms of the characteristics of their business. Managers adopt different strategies, however, in order to differentiate their business from that of their competitors. The controller, designing a management control system, must understand both the nature of the business and the strategy being pursued if he is to create a set of financial measurements that will motivate functional managers to contribute to the achievement of company objectives. This task is not easy even in simple, functional organizations; it is more difficult still in complex organizations.

Use in Complex Structures

As a business grows and the magnitude of the management task increases, its organization structure tends to become more complex. Products come to be manufactured in more than one location and sold in more than one market; new models and lines may be added. Such multiplant, multimarket, multiproduct corporations typically have a multitier organization structure consisting of three or more layers of managers. Naturally, the management control system becomes more complex, too.

Part A of *Exhibit II* is an organization chart for a complex, functionally organized business (it may have started as the company shown in *Exhibit I*). As long as the business continues to be functionally organized, much of the discussion in the preceding section about the design of a management control system is applicable.

But an important difference should be noted. In the simple organization shown in *Exhibit I*, top management has very little choice about how to divide the functional tasks among subordinates. In many situations of the type shown in Part A of *Exhibit II*, however, reorganization along the lines shown in Part B of the same exhibit may be feasible and appropriate. In such cases, what pros and cons should be considered in deciding whether to adopt the product division approach? Except in cases where that approach seems a "natural" (for example, a conglomerate that has grown

1. For a more complete discussion of all the factors influencing the formulation of strategy, see Kenneth R. Andrews, *The Concept of Corporate Strategy* (Homewood, Illinois, Dow Jones–Irwin, Inc., 1971).

Exhibit II. Complex organizations

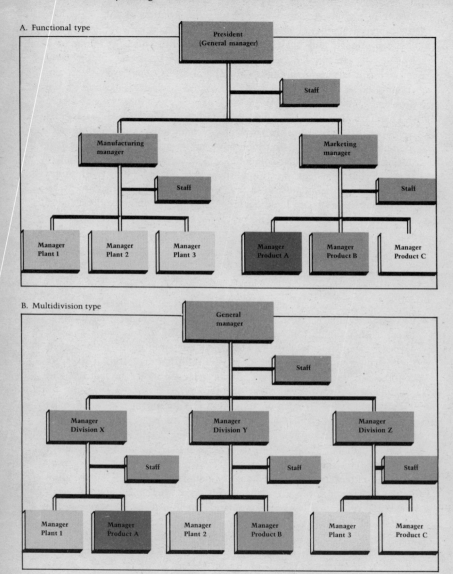

A. Functional type

President
(General manager)

Staff

Manufacturing
manager

Staff

Marketing
manager

Staff

Manager
Plant 1

Manager
Plant 2

Manager
Plant 3

Manager
Product A

Manager
Product B

Manager
Product C

B. Multidivision type

General
manager

Staff

Manager
Division X

Staff

Manager
Division Y

Staff

Manager
Division Z

Staff

Manager
Plant 1

Manager
Product A

Manager
Plant 2

Manager
Product B

Manager
Plant 3

Manager
Product C

through the acquisition of independent businesses), the answer depends largely on how much management wants to maximize efficiency and on how much it wants to maximize responsiveness to markets. Let us consider this trade-off in some detail.

TURN TO PRODUCT DIVISIONS?

Product divisions are almost always treated as profit or investment centers. The responsibility of the division manager is usually broad enough so that he can conceive of his division as though it were an independent company. In addition, the scope and substance of his task and the objective he is to strive for may be delineated clearly. In such circumstances, the task of designing a management control system for the functional subordinates of the division manager is precisely the same as that discussed earlier; the division manager is really the general manager shown in *Exhibit I*.

Now, what can functional organizations do that product divisions cannot? Functional organizations have the potential of great efficiency. The efficiency of an activity can frequently be measured in terms of the quantity of inputs required to yield one unit of output. For a great many activities, efficiency increases as the size of the activity grows—at least, up to some point where there are no further "economies of scale" to be realized. The reason that efficiency increases is that large-scale operations permit the utilization of increasingly specialized inputs. For instance, a general-purpose machine tool and a skilled operator may be able to produce 100 parts per hour; but a specially designed piece of equipment might produce 1,000 parts per hour and require no operator at all. Also, specialization of workers can yield economies of scale, as the learning curve of production workers demonstrates.

The arguments, then, in favor of retaining the organization structure shown in Part A of *Exhibit II* might run as follows. While it is technically feasible to equip each plant so that it turns out one of the three products of the company, it would be a great waste to do so. Manufacturing costs would be much lower if each plant specialized in certain aspects of the manufacturing process, doing only a limited number of functions on all three products. Further, the quality of manufacturing supervision and technical services, such as engineering and quality control, is better when those activities are centralized under one manufacturing manager. Scattering such activities across three product divisions would both lower the quality of the personnel that could be afforded and reduce the efficiency of their services. Similar arguments might be made about the efficiency of the marketing organization.

What advantages are unique to product divisions? They hold out the promise of more *effective* management than is the case with functional organizations. (One way of contrasting effectiveness with efficiency is to say that efficiency means doing something right and effectiveness means doing the right something.) The benefits are harder to document or quantify, but the potential for improvement exists both in strategy formulation and in tactical decision making.

In a strategic sense, it is easier for a product division than a functional organization to focus on the needs of its customers, rather than on simply manufacturing or selling the current line of products. The division manager can develop a strategy for his particular business, finding a competitive niche for it that may be different from the strategy being pursued by other division managers with different product lines. Tactically, a product division can also be more responsive to current customer needs. The division manager has the authority to change the production schedule in response to the request of an important customer; in a functional organization, by contrast, such a request must "go through channels," which may be ponderous and time-consuming.

Finally, it can be argued that product divisions are an excellent training ground for young managers, fostering entrepreneurship and increasing the number of centers of initiative in a corporation.

A business organization must be both efficient and effective if it is to survive, be profitable, and grow. The fundamental choice in organizational design is not an either-or question, but one of achieving the best possible balance between the benefits from economies of scale and those from strategic and tactical responsiveness.[2] One approach that is being used increasingly in a variety of settings is the matrix form of organization.

ADOPT THE MATRIX FORM?

This relatively new form of organization apparently was developed first in the aerospace industry nearly three decades ago. Companies in that industry had massive capacity, both human and physical, for the design and manufacturing of weapons systems, and they were organized according to functional specialties. At any one moment, such a company might have had several large contracts in its shop, each at various stages of completion and each drawing on the various functional departments to a greater or lesser extent.

In these cases, management's focus was on the efficient use of each department's capacity; this meant that inadequate attention was devoted to cost and schedule performance on each contract. The solution was to

---

2. For an excellent treatise on the complex factors that must be considered in making a basic change in organization structure, see Alfred D. Chandler, Jr., *Strategy and Structure: Chapters in the History of the American Industrial Enterprise* (Cambridge, The M.I.T. Press, 1962).

Exhibit III. Concept of a matrix organization

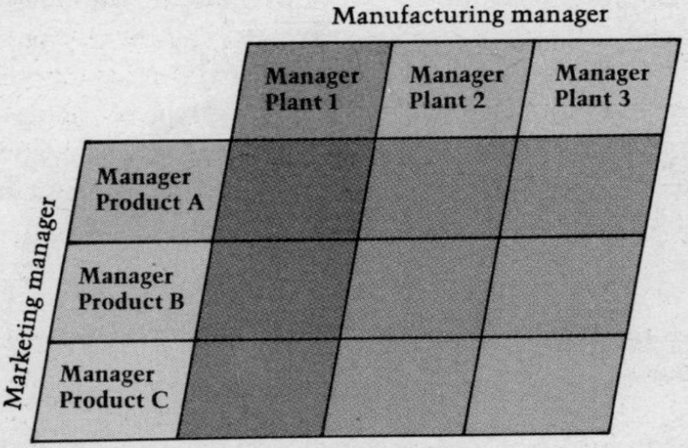

Manufacturing manager

	Manager Plant 1	Manager Plant 2	Manager Plant 3
Manager Product A			
Manager Product B			
Manager Product C			

Marketing manager

establish a new set of project managers, one for each contract, and to superimpose them across the existing functional hierarchy. A project manager's responsibility was to coordinate the inputs from each department in such a way that contractual performance requirements would be fulfilled.

Although matrix organizations, in a formal sense, are not widely used in industry, the concept has several attractive features. It holds the promise of both efficiency *and* effectiveness. Functional specialization is retained, thus permitting the efficiencies of economies of scale. But at the same time that program or product managers are viewed as the users of functional skills, they are also charged with producing a result that is competitively attractive to the customer and profitable for the company.

A matrix organization is essentially a functional organization. The six third-level managers in Part A of *Exhibit II* appear in *Exhibit III* and could still report to their respective functional superiors. However, there is an important difference: the relationships between the six managers are much more explicit in *Exhibit III*.

The matrix form of organization may be appropriate when much interaction between the functions is necessary or desirable. It can be particularly useful when one function (such as marketing) is concerned with planning for the effective combination of resources, while another function (such as manufacturing) is concerned with acquiring resources and using them efficiently. These two tasks obviously must be integrated and coordinated continuously. The matrix organization is intended to describe the interrelationships between the manufacturing and marketing functions and, without dismantling the old hierarchy, to legitimatize and encourage direct contact between the two parties concerned with any interlocking tasks or "cell" in the matrix. The matrix design does not really represent a structural change; it is simply a more realistic, comprehensive description of organizational relationships.

From the point of view of the designer of a management control system, a matrix organization poses no special problems and may offer an opportunity for a unique type of control system. Selecting the appropriate financial measurement for each functional manager may require nothing more, in some circumstances, than an application of the type of analysis described earlier. But management may need to go a step further if the nature of the business and its strategy are more complex than in those examples previously cited.

Problems in responsibility: In some businesses, both the marketing and the manufacturing functions may be highly interdependent and responsible for activities which have major effects on profits. How can the managers of the two functions be held jointly responsible?

One way is to hold each man responsible for a portion of the profits of the company, using a transfer price to permit a calculation of that profit. The determination of transfer prices in highly interdependent situations may be difficult, but it may be worth the trouble in order to motivate each manager properly.

Another approach is to use the matrix form of organization as an acknowledgment of the interdependence, and to hold each functional manager responsible for the entire profit of the business. This approach requires "double counting" of each profit dollar. In terms of *Exhibit III*, the manufacturing manager would be responsible for profit, defined as sales revenues less all manufacturing costs and all direct marketing expenses, for all products manufactured in the three plants. Each plant manager might have a similar responsibility for his plant. The sum of the defined profits for the three plants would be the total contribution to corporate overhead and net profit. Each product manager would also be responsible for profits, defined in the same way, for the products in his line. The sum of the profits for the three product managers would be the same as the total profit of the three plants.

Such a management control system may seem confusing at first, but it can be effective. The intent of double counting the profit is to make clear to all managers involved that they must work together in order to achieve their own individual objective. A profitable action which requires cooperation does not reflect to the credit of only one party, nor does it require a fictitious division of the profit between them. Both men benefit. Thus Plant Manager 1 would work with all three product managers, trying to find ways to use the facilities at his disposal in order to yield the highest profit for his plant. And Product Manager A would work with all three plant managers, attempting to utilize their resources in such a way as to maximize the profitability of his product line.

An intended effect of such a system is a certain amount of tension in the organization—an atmosphere of constructive conflict in which the managers in one function know they are working toward the same goal and must compete among themselves to cooperate with managers from the other functional area. Such conflict, if handled sensitively by a sophisticated top manager, can break down some of the parochialism of a purely functional organization without splintering it into less efficient product divisions.

Because of these potential advantages, we may see increasing use of the matrix concept in companies where functional interdependence is high and the rewards from functional specialization are too great to ignore.

Conclusion

Responsibility for the design of a management control system rests inescapably on top management. For one thing, it is top management that decides on the strategy and organization structure of a business. For another, the control system is a major tool for implementing those decisions effectively. The controller, as a member of the top management team, has an important role to play because the design of a control system is too complex a task for the chief executive to undertake without the benefit of staff support.

The president and his controller, joint designers of the management control system, face a great many choices as they try to decide (a) the type of financial objective to be specified for each organizational unit, and (b) how to calculate that measurement. There is a natural bias among corporate executives in favor of responsibility for profit. Profit is a powerful measurement; it provides a clear objective, is easily understood, and is a good motivator of such men. But not all managers are responsible for profits in any meaningful sense of that term. Creating a set of profit centers may cause more problems than it is worth.

Profit should be used as a measure of financial responsibility only when it is possible to calculate it in such a way that a manager's "profit" increases as the result of actions for which he is responsible and which he has taken in the best interests of the company.

14. Managing the Four Stages of EDP Growth

Cyrus F. Gibson and Richard L. Nolan

In all that has been said about the computer in business, there are few clues as to how the EDP department ought to grow or what management ought to be doing about the department at each stage of its growth. Here is a convenient categorization for placing the life crises of the EDP department in perspective, for developing the management techniques necessary or useful at various points, and for managing the human issues involved. These human issues, as a matter of fact, complicate the problems of growth at least as much as the hardware and software questions, which have been so well massaged in the literature; the authors show how these issues change shape as a company moves through the four stages of development. This article will be particularly helpful to the new business that is about to buy its first computer. For the company in the throes of later-stage development, it offers a framework useful for identifying issues and evaluating and controlling the growth of EDP.

From the viewpoint of the executive vice president, "The EDP manager always waffles around when he has to explain his budget." From the viewpoint of the EDP manager, "The executive vice president never seems to understand why this department needs a lot of money."

The reason for this kind of impasse is clear enough: EDP, as corporations use it today, is so complex that controlling it, or even understanding it, is almost too difficult for words. However, through our work with a number of companies, we have reached certain conclusions about how EDP departments grow and how they should fit into the company's organization. These conclusions offer a framework for communication for both the EDP manager and the senior managers to whom he reports.

There are four distinct stages in the growth of all EDP facilities, each with its distinctive applications, its rewards and its traumata, and its managerial problems. By breaking the evolution of the EDP department into four easy stages, it is possible to sort out the affairs of the department, if not into four neat, sequential packages, at least into four relatively small, sequential cans of worms.

The basis for this framework of stages is the discovery that the EDP budget for a number of companies, when plotted over time from initial investment to mature operation, forms an S-shaped curve. This is the curve that appears in the exhibits accompanying this article. The turnings of this curve correspond to the main events—often crises—in the life of the EDP function that signal important shifts in the way the computer resource is used and managed. There are three such turnings, and, consequently, four stages.

In the companies we know, there are remarkable similarities in the problems which arise and the management techniques applied to solve them at a given stage, despite variations among industries and companies, and despite ways in which EDP installations are used. Moreover, associated with each stage is a distinctive, informal organizational process. Each of these seems to play an important role in giving rise to the issues which need to be resolved if the stage is to be passed without a crisis and if the growth of the resource is to be managed to yield maximum benefit to the company.

Our purpose here is to describe the four stages in turn, listing the key characteristics of each and explaining the underlying organizational forces at work in each.

In the space of an article we can touch only on the main problems of EDP management at the different stages. Hence the view we present is bound to be somewhat simplified. Caution is advisable in another respect, too: history has not yet come to an end, and we are sure that the S-curve we describe and the stages it seems to follow do not represent the whole story. At the end of the S-curve of contemporary experience there will doubtless be more S-curves, as new EDP technologies emerge, and as companies become more ambitious in their use of EDP techniques and more sophisticated in systems analysis. However, we hope that the dynamics of later cost escalations will be clearer after the reader has finished with our description—clearer, and perhaps even predictable and controllable.

Four Stages of Growth

Three types of growth must be dealt with as an EDP department matures:

☐ A growth in computer applications—see *Exhibit I*.
☐ A growth in the specialization of EDP personnel—see *Exhibit II*.
☐ A growth in formal management techniques and organization—see *Exhibit III*.

The S-curve that overlies these three kinds of growth breaks conveniently into four segments, which represent the four stages of EDP growth:

Exhibit I. Growth of applications

Stage 1 Cost-reduction accounting applications	Stage 2 Proliferation of applications in all functional areas	Stage 3 Moratorium on new applications; emphasis on control	Stage 4 Data-base applications
Payroll	Cash flow	Purchasing control	Simulation models
Accounts receivable	General ledger	Scheduling	Financial planning models
Accounts payable	Budgeting		On-line personnel query system
Billing	Capital budgeting		On-line customer query system
	Forecasting		On-line source data entry (e.g., cost collection, order entry)
	Personnel inventory		
	Order processing		
	Sales		
	Inventory control		

initiation, expansion, formalization, and maturity. Most notable are the proliferation of applications in Stage 2 (as reflected in *Exhibit I*) that causes the budget to increase exponentially, and the proliferation of controls in Stage 3 designed to curb this increase (as reflected in *Exhibit III*).

This sequence of stages is a useful framework for placing a company's current problems vis-à-vis EDP in perspective and helping its management understand the problems it will face as it moves forward. It is especially helpful for discussing ways to smooth out the chaotic conditions of change that have caused so many derailments in Stages 2 and 3. Even in our work with small companies, we have found the framework helpful—in obviating crises before they arise and in suggesting the kinds of planning that will induce smooth growth.

Thus one virtue of this framework is that it lays out for the company as a whole the nature of its task at each stage—whether it is a new company planning to buy its first computer, or a company in the throes of developing advanced applications, or a company with a steady, mature EDP facility.

Stage 1: Initiation

When the first computer is implanted in the organization, the move is normally justified in terms of cost savings. Rarely, at this point, does senior management assess the long-term impact of the computer on personnel,

262

Exhibit II. Growth of personnel specialization

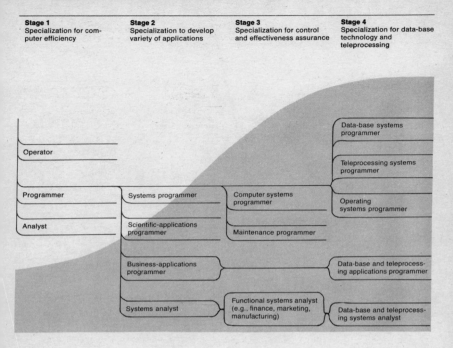

Stage 1	Stage 2	Stage 3	Stage 4
Specialization for computer efficiency	Specialization to develop variety of applications	Specialization for control and effectiveness assurance	Specialization for data-base technology and teleprocessing

or on the organization, or on its strategy. Thus management can easily ignore a couple of crucial issues.

THE LOCATION QUESTION

In Stage 1, the priority management issue is to fix departmental responsibility for the computer:

□ Initially it makes economic sense to locate the computer in the department where it is first applied—very frequently, in accounting—and to hold that department responsible for a smooth introduction and a sound control of costs and benefits. The costs and benefits can be clearly stated and rigidly controlled under this approach—and they usually are.

□ However, the department where the computer will first be used—accounting, say—may not be the best location for the EDP facility later on. The later and more complex applications, such as inventory control and simulation modeling, should ideally be located in an autonomous department of computer services or management information systems which reports through a high-level manager.

But granted this longer perspective, management may decide on a less

Stage 1 Lax management	Stage 2 Sales-oriented management	Stage 3 Control-oriented management	Stage 4 Resource-oriented planning and control
Organization			
EDP is organized under the department of first-applications justification; it is generally a small department.	The EDP manager is moved up in the organization; systems analysts and programmers are assigned to work in the various functional areas.	EDP moves out of the functional area of first applications; a steering committee is set up; control is exerted through centralization; maintenance programming and systems programming become dominant activities.	EDP is set up as a separate functional area, the EDP manager taking on a higher-level position; some systems analysts and sometimes programmers are decentralized to user areas; high specialization appears in computer configuration and operation; systems design and programming take on a consulting role.
Control			
Controls notably lacking; priorities assigned by FIFO; no chargeout.	Lax controls, intended to engender applications development; few standards, informal project control.	Proliferation of controls to contain a runaway budget; formal priority setting; budget justification. Programming controls: documentation, standards. Project management initiated; management reporting system introduced: project plan, project performance, customer service, personnel resources, equipment resources, budget performance. Chargeout introduced; postsystem audits. Quality control policies for computer system, systems design, programming, operations.	Refinement of management control system—elimination of ineffective control techniques and further development of others; introduction of data-base policies and standards; focus on pricing of computer services for engendering effective use of the computer.
Planning			
Loose budget	Loose budget	Strong budgetary planning for hardware facilities and new applications.	Multiple 3–5 year plans for hardware, facilities, personnel, and new applications.

rigorous application of payback criteria for judging the performance of the initial application. Costs for "future development" may not be scrutinized too closely at this stage, and budgets may expand very early under this arrangement.

Many companies resolve this issue in obvious fashion. Management simply locates the facility within the department of first application for an initial period; then, when its viability has been proved and other applications develop, management creates the autonomous EDP unit.

In practice, however, this seemingly simple resolution conceals a serious trap. The department that controls the resource becomes strongly protective of it, often because a manager or a group within it wants to build up power and influence. When the time comes for computing to assume a broader role, real conflict arises—conflict that can be costly in terms of management turnover and in terms of lingering hostilities that inhibit the provision of computer services and applications across functional areas.

FEAR OF THE COMPUTER

Another priority issue is to minimize the disruption that results when high technology is injected into an organization. Job-displacement anxieties appear; some people become concerned over doing old jobs in new ways; and others fear a loss of personal identity with their work. These fears may lead to open employee resistance. While reactions of this kind may occur at any of the stages, they can be particularly destructive in Stage 1, where the very survival of the EDP concept is at stake.

In plain fact some of these fears are probably justified. For example, some employees (although usually relatively few) may indeed lose their jobs when the computer is first installed.

On the other hand, the concerns that develop from rumor or false information are usually overblown, and they are readily transformed and generalized into negative sentiments and attitudes toward management, as well as the computer itself. The wise course for management is to spike rumors with the most honest information it has, however the chips may fall. Such openness will at worst localize fears and resistances that must be dealt with sooner or later anyway.

Unless management is willing to recognize the seriousness of this anxiety, it risks a more generalized reaction in the form of unresponsive and uncreative work behavior, a broader and higher level of uncertainty and anxiety, and even sabotage, as a surprising number of cases have demonstrated.

Management can make no bigger mistake than to falsely reassure all concerned that the computer will not change their work or that it will mean no less work for everyone. Such comfort blankets lead to credibility gaps that are notoriously hard to close.

Thus the key to managing this process of initiation to the computer is to accept the fact that people's perceptions of reality and their views of the situation are what have to be understood and dealt with, rather than some "objective" reality. These perceptions will be diverse; management cannot assume that all organizational members are equally enthusiastic about introducing efficiency and reducing costs. Where you stand depends on where you sit and on who you are. In communicating its intention to introduce EDP, management should remember this and tailor its communications accordingly.

There will be variations from one situation and company to another in the manner and detail in which management releases information about future location and about the impact of the computer. Depending on circumstance, management directives may best be communicated downward by an outsider, by a department head, or by the new EDP manager. In settings where employees are rarely informed of management planning, it may even be wise to explain to the echelons why they are being given the explanation; again, in settings where the echelons have participated in planning, a formal presentation may be less effective than open group discussion.

Stage 2: Expansion

The excess computing capacity usually acquired when a company first initiates an EDP facility, combined with the lure of broader and more advanced applications, triggers a period of rapid expansion. The EDP area "takes off" into new projects that, when listed, often seem to have been selected at random. As *Exhibits I–III* show, Stage 2 represents a steady and steep rise in expenditures for hardware, software, and personnel. It is a period of contagious, unplanned growth, characterized by growing responsibilities for the EDP director, loose (usually decentralized) organization of the EDP facility, and few explicit means of setting project priorities or crystallizing plans.

It is a period, further, in which the chaotic effects of rapid development are moderated (if they are moderated at all) only by the quality and judgment of the personnel directly involved in the process. While top management may be sensitive to some of the ill effects of the computer, it tends to be attracted to and carried along with the mystique of EDP as well.

This stage often ends in crisis when top management becomes aware of the explosive growth of the activity, and its budget, and decides to rationalize and coordinate the entire organization's EDP effort. The dynamic force of expansion makes this a fairly difficult thing to do, however.

DYNAMICS OF EARLY SUCCESS

Once Stage 1 has passed, and the management and personnel of the computer area have justified and assured their permanent place in the organization, a new psychological atmosphere appears as the users from other departments (the customers) grow in number and begin to interact with the technical EDP staff. Although some users stick to economic value in judging the utility of computer applications to their particular problems and functions, other users develop a fascination with the computer and its applications as a symbol of progressive management techniques or as a status symbol for a department or individual. This fascination breeds an enthusiasm not moderated by judgment.

For their part, the technically oriented systems analysts tend to over-generalize from the successes they have achieved with transaction-oriented computer-based systems (e.g., order processing, payroll, accounts receivable) in Stage 2. They often feel that "now we can do anything"—in other words, that they have mastered problems of communication with users, that their expertise is solid, and that they are ready to select and deal with projects primarily on the basis of their technical and professional interest. In this heady atmosphere, criteria of economic justification and effective project implementation take a back seat.

When the users' exploding demands meet the technicians' euphoric urge to supply, in the absence of management constraint, exponential budget growth results. Overoptimism and overconfidence lead to cost overruns. And once this sharp growth has begun, rationales created in the mood of reinforced enthusiasm are used to justify the installation of additional capacity; this in turn provides the need for larger numbers of personnel and for more rationales for applying the now expanded resource to whatever new projects seem attractive to the crowd. So the spiral begins.

The spiral is fed by the fact that as the resource increases in size and ambition, it must have more specialists. Indeed, even without this capacity expansion, the continuing pace of technological development in the computer industry creates a constant need for new specialist talent, especially in Stage 2 and beyond. This "technological imperative" is a driving force that has caused the growth of numerous and quite diverse professional groups of computer personnel in the industrial environment. (The reader might find it helpful to review *Exhibit II* at this point.)

Many of these personnel come into the company with a primarily professional orientation, rather than an understanding of or sympathy for the long-term needs of an organization. Like the EDP specialists already employed by the company, these people will be far more interested in tackling technically challenging problems than in worrying about computer payback. If they are allowed to pursue their interests at will, the projects potentially most valuable from the company's viewpoint may never be worked on. Moreover, the chores of program maintenance and data-base development may be neglected, sowing the seeds of costly future problems.

All these factors together lead to the evolution of an informal structure among computer personnel and between computer personnel and users. The lack of clear management guidelines for project priorities, for example, often results in sympathetic wheeling and dealing between EDP systems analysts and the user groups with a preference for those projects which offer the greatest professional challenge. Without specific directives for project developments or new hardware acquisition, too, computer personnel develop expectations of a loose work environment. Some of the users, at the other end of the string, are easily enmeshed in impractical, pie-in-the-sky projects.

For short periods such an environment may be highly motivating for some, but, as we need hardly point out again, the other side of the coin is a rapidly growing budget—and a number of vocal and dissatisfied users.

In view of these informal dynamics and structures, what can management do to make this period one of controlled growth? How can control be introduced that will head off the impending crisis and dramatic cutbacks characteristic of such situations but at the same time not choke off experimentation with the resource and not turn off the motivation of specialists?

Here it is useful to compare the lists of management techniques shown for Stages 2 and 3 in *Exhibit III*. For the most part, the problems that arise toward the end of Stage 2 can be greatly alleviated by introducing right at the start of Stage 2 the techniques that companies ordinarily use in Stage 3. Before carrying out this step, however, attention should be given to two other important strategies: acquiring necessary middle-management skills and improving the company's procedures for hiring computer personnel.

ACQUIRING MANAGERS

The main key to successful management in this stage is acquiring or developing middle managers for EDP who recognize the need for priorities and criteria in project selection and who have strong administrative skills: the ability to prepare plans and stick to budgets, the ability to seek out significant projects from users who may not be demanding attention, and, generally, the ability to manage projects.

Finding such managers more often than not means going outside the company, especially since most potential middle managers among systems analysts are usually caught up in the computer growth spiral. However, where it is possible, selection from within, particularly from the ranks of systems analysts, can serve the important function of indicating that career paths exist to management ranks. This can show computer technicians and technical experts that there are career rewards for those who balance organizational needs with professional interests.

Once those at the general-management level have determined that the time has come to institute such "human controls," the EDP manager must be brought to recognize the need for them (if, indeed, he does not recognize that need already) and the fact that he has the countenance and support of top management.

For his part, the EDP manager himself must resist the tempting pressures to see his resource grow faster than is reasonable. He has a delicate and important selling job to do in communicating this to other department managers who want his services. Once he is shored up with competent subordinate managers he will be free to carry out this role.

Finally, in addition to applying administrative controls, management needs to assess continually the climate of the informal forces at work and plan growth with that assessment in mind. The formal organization of middle managers in the EDP department makes such planning, and its implementation, viable.

ACQUIRING DIVERSE PERSONNEL

Senior management must also recognize the increasing specialization of personnel within the computer department:

□ At one extreme are the highly skilled and creative professionals, such as computer systems programmers. Their motivation and interest are oriented to the technology with which they work; they have relatively little interest in organizational rewards. Their satisfaction and best performance may be assured by isolating them organizationally, to some degree.

□ At the other extreme are the analysts who work closely with functional departments of the company. These people may be expert in particular fields relevant to only a few industries or companies, performing tasks that require close interaction with both users and programmers. Their interests and value to the company can coincide when they preceive that career-path opportunities into general management are open to them.

□ There are also the operators with important but relatively low-level skills and training, with some capabilities for organizational advancement, and with relatively little direct interdependence with others.

To organize and control these diverse specialists requires decisions based on one basic trade-off: *balancing professional advancement of specialists against the need for organizational performance.*

To cater to specialist professionals, for example, a company might isolate them in a separate department, imposing few organizational checks and gearing quality control to individual judgment or peer review. Such an arrangement might motivate a systems analyst to become the world's best systems analyst.

Emphasis on organizational values, in contrast, suggests that the company locate and control the specialists in such a way as to increase the chances that short-run goals will actually be achieved on schedule. This strategy risks obsolescence or turnover among specialists, but it successfully conveys the important message that some specialists' skills can advance a management career.

However, in the early stages management is well advised to avoid the issue entirely: the highly sophisticated professional should not be hired until his expertise is clearly required. Moreover, at the time of hiring, the specialist's expectations for freedom and professional development should be explicitly discussed in the context of organizational structure and controls (these controls include those administered by the middle level of EDP management), as part of the "psychological contract."

Such discussion can go a long way toward avoiding misunderstanding during the period of rapid growth of computer applications. In effect, making clear the terms of the psychological contract is an example of the management of expectations. In this instance, it is one of the means that can be employed to introduce the organization, controls, and planning procedures that are needed to head off the crisis atmosphere of Stage 3.

Stage 3: Formalization

Let us assume that Stages 1 and 2 have run their bumpy courses without too much direct attenion from top management. More likely than not, top management becomes aware of the runaway computer budget suddenly, and it begins a crash effort to find out what is going on. Its typical question at this point is, "How can we be sure that we can afford this EDP effort?"

Top management frequently concludes that the only way to get control of the resource is through drastic measures, even if this means replacing many systems analysts and other valuable technical personnel who will choose to leave rather than work under the stringent controls that are imposed during the stage. Firing the old EDP manager is by no means an unusual step.[1]

From the perspective of computer personnel who have lived through the periods of initial acceptance and growth, but who have not developed a sense of the fit of the computer resource within company functions and objectives, the changes top management introduces at this time may seem radical indeed. Often what was a decentralized function and facility is rather suddenly centralized for better control. Often informal planning suddenly gives way to formal planning, perhaps arbitrarily. This stage frequently includes the first formalization of management reporting systems for computer operation, a new chargeout system, and the establishment of elaborate and cumbrous quality-control measures (again, see Exhibit III).

In short, action taken to deal with the crisis often goes beyond what is needed, and the pendulum may swing too far. In response, some computer personnel may leave. What may be worse, most will "hunker down" —withdrawing from innovative applications work, attending to short-

1. See Richard L. Nolan, "Plight of the EDP Manager," HBR May-June 1973, p. 143.

term goals, and following the new control systems and plans to the letter. All of this can occur at the expense of full resource utilization in the long run.

In addition, there is a parallel development that dovetails with the budget crisis to reinforce the overcontrol syndrome. Studies of computer usage show that the machines are first applied to projects that reduce general and administrative expenses—typically, replacement of clerical personnel in such tasks as accounting. Next come projects that reduce cost of goods, such as inventory control systems. The crisis atmosphere of Stage 3 roughly coincides with completion of these first two types of applications.

At this juncture the applications that have real potential for increasing revenues and profits and facilitating managerial decision making are still untouched. Financial-planning models and on-line customer service systems are two examples of such applications.

As senior management ponders the problems of Stage 3, it tends to associate the applications of the earlier stages with preexisting manual systems and straightforward cost-justification and control. In contrast, it finds projected applications for revenue-producing and decision-making projects hard to envision and define. The natural tendency is to assume that these projects will call for a faster, higher spiral of risk and cost. Thus senior management tends to introduce inappropriately strong controls that are designed, consciously or unconsciously, to put a stop to growth. This clearly may be too strong a reaction for the company's good.

THREE SOUND STEPS

In general, three control steps that are appropriate and not unduly restrictive are available for most large EDP facilities in Stage 3. First, certain of the more established and less complex operations and hardware can be centralized. Second, the increasing impacts of computer applications can be flagged and defined for the top by introducing overseer and resource-allocation mechanisms at the general-management level. Third, some parts of the systems analysis function can be decentralized and other parts centralized, depending on where the systems work can best be done (we shall say more about this shortly). Of course, this final step requires that the decentralized systems work be coordinated through a formal integrative mechanism.

But the real problem in Stage 3 is not what steps to take; it is how to take them. Management here is introducing change into a web of informal relationships and expectations. *How* the changes are managed is as important as *what* the changes should be, but more difficult to define.

That is, although there are few formal controls in the first two stages, the *informal* social structures and norms that have grown up by Stage 3 are very much a reality to the personnel involved. While it may appear that systems are replacing no systems, this will not be true:

☐ Lacking guidelines for project selection, systems analysts will have projected their own sets of priorities, either individually, as a group within the company, or as members of their profession.

☐ They will have created criteria and standards, although these will not ordinarily have been written down or otherwise articulated for higher levels of management.

☐ Without project management guidelines, systems analysts and users will have developed their own rules and procedures for dealing with each other.

On the whole, the stronger these informal controls and structures are (and the weaker the formal controls and structures are, the stronger they will be), the more resistant the personnel will be to change and the more chaotic and traumatic the introduction of formal systems will be.

In managing changes as pervasive as these there is probably nothing worse than doing the job halfway. Doing nothing at all is disaster, of course; but management action that is undertaken on a crash basis—without enough attention to execution and second- and third-order consequences—will sharpen, not resolve, the crisis.

For example, management cannot afford to be either squeamish or precipitous in making personnel changes. Trying to introduce needed formalization of controls with the same personnel and the same organizational structure more often than not encourages conflict and the reinforcement of resistance rather than a resolution of the crisis; by refusing to fire or to enforce layoffs, senior management may simply prolong the crisis, create further dissension, and further demoralize personnel. On the other hand, management must be sure that it retains the experienced personnel who have the potential to function well in the mature stages of the operation—it may not always be obvious who these people are or what their future roles will be.

Thus, although the crisis of Stage 3 calls for action, it first calls for analysis and planning—planning that sets forth clear and explicit objectives for exploitation of the computer resource vis-à-vis the user departments. Such a plan, once it is developed and understood, can turn anarchy back into evolution, while at the same time avoiding the kind of overkill control that results in underutilization and underrealization of the potential of the resource. Here are our suggestions for general plan direction.

1. Reposition the established components of the resource.

Whether or not EDP has been carefully managed in the past, most companies need to centralize some parts and decentralize other parts of the computer resource at about this point.

The issue arises here because the company reaches a turning point in the way it uses the resource. As the EDP function evolves from the early cost-reduction applications of initiation and early growth toward projects aimed at improving operations, revenues, and the quality of unprogrammed and strategic decisions, the influence of the computer will begin to move up and spread out through the organization. The function may truly be called "MIS" instead of "EDP" from this stage forward.

We have already discussed the need for middle managers' involvement in this stage or an earlier stage. The internal structure they represent reinforces the desirability of making the MIS department autonomous and having it report to a senior level of management. At this point, also, it becomes imperative to reexamine and make explicit the rationales for existing applications that have proved beneficial and to routinize them, so that expensive specialist skills can be turned to new applications.

The pressures of new applications ventures, maturing management, specialist personnel, and increasing routine make centralization of the company's core hardware resources just about mandatory at this stage. Too, the centralization eases the tasks of maintenance of data and programs, data-base development, and some of the applications that will be coming up in Stage 4.

The very creation of a central "MIS division," however, creates additional problems.

2. Provide for top-management direction.

While centralization goes a long way toward placing the longer lead times, the greater complexity, and the higher development costs of new applications in perspective, it does not automatically help senior management to control the direction the resource takes.

Effective control derives from understanding, and some device is needed to educate senior management so that it can track and evaluate the department's progress sensibly. The device must also let the resource know what senior management's policies are and what is expected of it operationally and strategically.

This communications device becomes vital in Stage 3 because the resource has grown to a size and a power whereby its applications can affect the strategy and structure of the company as a whole. In a company where a working data base can be used to back up the corporate planning process, for example, corporate planning assumes a somewhat different shape from what it does in a company that has no such data base available. This is clearly a point at which a person at the vice-presidential level (or even the presidential level) must accept responsibility for directing the evolution of the resource.

An active, high-level steering committee is one such device. It provides a means for setting project priorities. It not only brings together those who should be concerned with overall management and planning for the company; it also provides a vehicle for confronting and resolving the political problems that inevitably arise with the computer's more direct impact on managers' roles, organizational structure, and resource allocation in Stage 3.

For, from a behavioral perspective, political issues dominate at this time as never before. Managers throughout the company now see that the applications coming through the pipeline may affect their own roles directly. In the past it was their subordinates who were most affected, and it was largely their own decision to approve or not approve a project; but now a given application may be supported from above and may impinge on their established patterns of work, their decision making, and even their ideas about what it is they do for a living.

Moreover, the prospect of applications that hint at long-term changes in organizational structures and formal departmental roles raises concern within both formal and informal groups of managers—concern about the impacts these changes will have on the strengths of their positions relative to other groups.

Such political issues can only be debated fruitfully before top management, and an expert, informed steering committee provides a convenient forum for this debate.

For his part, as a member of this committee as well as the head of his own department, the MIS manager should expect to assume a stronger role in general management councils. He should not, of course, expect to be exclusively responsible for setting priorities among projects that would benefit different groups, or for implementing significant changes completely under his own initiative.

3. Reorganize the systems analysis function.

Centralization, and tight guidelines and arbitration from a steering committee, however, can create a distance between the resource and its customers throughout the company. As Stage 3 draws to a close, the company will be planning its most important, most ambitious MIS applications to date. This is hardly a point at which to divorce the users from the resource by erecting an impenetrable divisional barrier. Complete centralization of the systems analysis function would constitute such a barrier.

In fact, gearing up for this new era of applications and controlling their impacts requires that the company revise the Stage 3 concept, staffing, and organization of the systems analysis function. The concept should change from systems analysts as developers of *products for* users to systems analysts as developers of *processes affecting* users. The distinction between product and process means, among other things, that the new applications should rarely be considered bounded projects; they will require continual modification as they are integrated into user decision making.

Therefore, systems analysts themselves will necessarily become more and more a constant element in the functioning of the users' areas. As a corollary, they will act as communications conduits between the users, on the one hand, and the computer resource and its programmers, on the other.

Organizationally, this suggests that some systems analysts should be decentralized to user locations while others are retained at the core to build a research and testing facility for the company and its planners. Thus the problem boils down to a trade-off between centralization and decentralization of systems analysts.

These, then, are our best suggestions for minimizing the strains of Stage 3: centralize certain components of the resource, install a steering committee or some equivalent thereof, and spread enough of the systems analysts through the company to ensure that users' needs are met adequately. For the company wise enough to employ these suggestions at the outset of Stage 2, the trauma of Stage 3 may be almost entirely avoidable.

Stage 4: Maturity

When the dust has settled over the changes of Stage 3, the computer resource will have reached maturity in the organization, and it will have the potential to return continuing economic benefits. The applications listed for Stage 4 in *Exhibit I* suggest how very significant the contributions of the resource can be, if only they can be achieved.

THE MANAGER'S DILEMMA

At this point the MIS manager has broken into the ranks of senior management, having risen to the level of vice president or equivalent thereof. In some instances he may even enjoy more than proportional support from the president for his view of his own function within the company. He faces this integrative dilemma:

□ On the one hand, he is under pressure to maintain a steady work environment within his own unit. His line managers and specialists are now familiar with relatively formal structure and procedures; they are presumably satisfied with their career prospects, either within their professions or within the company. Thus they may well constitute a force resisting dramatic change, reorganization, or innovation. Similarly, at this point, senior management and the users probably have a general grasp of the existing technology and existing applications of the resource, and they are reluctant to see major changes.

□ On the other hand, the MIS manager, if he is doing his job well, will be heavily involved in planning for the future. He will be aware that computer technology and modes of application and organization are continuing to change.

Thus, if he chooses to maintain stability, he knowingly runs the risk that his resource will become outdated and inefficient. If he chooses to keep up with technology, he knowingly runs the risk that he will lose the integrative fabric that makes his function applicable to the user groups and the company as a whole.

The MIS manager must strike a balance between protecting an organizational entity and keeping that entity up to date in its technical environment. He has power and credibility, but he sees that these can be threatened either by too little change or by too much change.

There are no hard and fast rules for resolving this trade-off. The key, however, lies in the quality of communications between the MIS manager and top management, and between the MIS department and users.

COMMUNICATIONS WITH THE BOSS

By definition, the mature Stage 4 function is one which is being applied to the key tasks of the organization. This may well mean that most of the funding for MIS development is devoted to applications touching directly on critical business operations. This is the case of a large petrochemical firm with which we are familiar, where new applications focus on synthetic-fiber production activities.

But whether applications are for line operations or for management decision making, the computer manager in Stage 4 is, perhaps for the first time, in a position to communicate with top management in terms of meaningful, detailed plans.

Because of the nature of his dilemma, he is bound to come under fire from the users—either for allowing parts of his department to obsolesce, in the name of stability, or for introducing change, in the name of progress and the state of the art. His relationship and communications with the top must be sound enough to allow him to weather the inevitable storms —given, of course, that the balance he strikes between stability and change is indeed reasonable in broad outline.

The experience of many suggests that the MIS manager and senior management think in terms of a three-year contract for the position, with explicit recognition that there will be organizational pressures to push out the MIS manager.

With long-term support from the top founded in such a basis, the MIS manager is in a position to legislate policies internally that will exploit the computer as fully as possible.

For his part, the senior line manager to whom a mature EDP department reports can little afford not to know the language of the computer personnel—at least to the extent necessary to evaluate project proposals.

RELATIONS WITH USERS

In Stage 4, the MIS manager must also move to strengthen the bridges that have developed between the users and computer personnel. Assuming that it is well managed internally, the computer resource still has a continuing extensive interdependence with departments it serves.

The first difficulty here is that the users are many and the MIS manager only one. He cannot hope for identical relationships with all departments.

Secondly, users naturally tend to co-opt computer personnel into their organizational spheres. If this occurs to any significant extent, user parochialisms will erode the potential for the computer unit to act as an agent for innovation and change.

However, the bridges can be strengthened and the innovative capability of the unit can be increased simultaneously through a policy of "buffering" the different subunits from user influence. Specifically, performance standards and short-term control devices should be formalized for the more routine tasks (such as all machine operations and some programming) and the MIS personnel involved with these should be removed from frequent interaction with the users. A system of project management, too, serves much the same function.

Finally, the systems analysis function at the core should by this time have taken on the character of an influential research unit, controlled primarily through checks on the progress of its projects. These projects will probably not be within the direct purview of the user groups; in a mature department, they are usually focused on long-term applications not likely to be demanded spontaneously by user groups or by the systems analysts decentralized into those groups (e.g., corporate inventory control). The weight of this core group of analysts can be used to counterbalance undue user influence.

For example, when a user needs a new application, the core group might rough it out and approve the final, detailed design; but the final, detailed design itself should be the work of the systems analysts located in the user department. The decentralized analysts will be most familiar with the user's needs and best able to produce a working system for him; for their part, the systems analysts at the core can ensure that the system that is finally designed will mesh efficiently with the company's MIS efforts as a whole, to whatever extent this is possible.

The picture of EDP-user relationships that emerges here is one of considerable complexity and subtlety. Correspondingly, integrating this more specialized and internally differentiated EDP resource into the company as a whole becomes more difficult. This integration requires that the MIS manager take steps to achieve common understanding of his objectives, not only with senior management but with all other functional managers at the vice-presidential level as well. The steering committee will be important as never before, not only as a committee for determining project priorities, but also as a sounding board for new techniques, policies, and changes within the MIS department itself.

Beyond Stage 4

Some large companies have reached the tail end of the S-shaped EDP budget curve: their departments are mature, in the sense defined by the exhibits. But has EDP evolution really come to an end for these companies? What can they expect in the future?

In retrospect, the curve seems to have been primarily driven by developments in hardware technology in the second- and third-generation computer systems. One thing certain is that computer technology advancements are continuing at an unrelenting pace. More S-shaped curves are inevitable.

Now, however, the advancements seem to be taking place more in software than in hardware; and at present the breakthrough most likely to start off another S-shaped EDP budget curve is the development of data-base technology. This development is providing a way to make the data collected and retained by the organization a companywide resource; and scores of middle management applications, such as computer modeling, appear to be on the way.

In the blush of enthusiasm for this advancement in computer technology, however, it is important to remember the painful lessons of the past. To efficiently exploit the newest technology, it must be managed. It must be reconciled with the capacity of the organization to assimilate new ways of doing business better. It is our belief that the forces underlying the crises and problems of the four stages we have described will also underlie future S-curves, such as one created by the emerging data-base technology. Consequently, management may be able to anticipate the problems and resolve them before they begin. A sign of success would be a dampening of the S-curve, with budgets rising more smoothly as future needs demand continuing investments and increasing budgets.

How to Choose the Right
Forecasting Technique

*John C. Chambers, Satinder K. Mullick,
and Donald D. Smith*

*In virtually every decision he makes, the executive today considers some kind
of forecast. Sound predictions of demands and trends are no longer luxury items,
but a necessity, if the manager is to cope with seasonality, sudden changes in
demand levels, price-cutting maneuvers of the competition, strikes, and large
swings of the economy. Forecasting can help him deal with these troubles; but
it can help him more, the more he knows about the general principles of forecasting, what it can and cannot do for him currently, and which techniques are
suited to his needs of the moment. Here the authors try to explain the potential
of forecasting to the manager, focusing special attention on sales forecasting
for products of Corning Glass Works as these have matured through the product
life cycle. The authors also include a rundown of the whole range of forecasting
techniques.*

To handle the increasing variety and complexity of managerial forecasting
problems, many forecasting techniques have been developed in recent years.
Each has its special use, and care must be taken to select the correct
technique for a particular application. The manager as well as the forecaster
has a role to play in technique selection; and the better he understands
the range of forecasting possibilities, the more likely it is that a company's
forecasting efforts will bear fruit.

The selection of a method depends on many factors—the context of the
forecast, the relevance and availability of historical data, the degree of
accuracy desirable, the time period to be forecast, the cost/benefit (or
value) of the forecast to the company, and the time available for making
the analysis.

These factors must be weighed constantly, and on a variety of levels.
In general, for example, the forecaster should choose a technique that
makes the best use of available data. If he can readily apply one technique
of acceptable accuracy, he should not try to "gold plate" by using a more
advanced technique that offers potentially greater accuracy but that requires nonexistent information or information that is costly to obtain. This

kind of trade-off is relatively easy to make, but others, as we shall see, require considerably more thought.

Furthermore, where a company wishes to forecast with reference to a particular product, it must consider *the stage of the product's life cycle for which it is making the forecast.* The availability of data and the possibility of establishing relationships between the factors depend directly on the maturity of a product, and hence the life-cycle stage is a prime determinant of the forecasting method to be used.

Our purpose here is to present an overview of this field by discussing the way a company ought to approach a forecasting problem, describing the methods available, and explaining how to match method to problem. We shall illustrate the use of the various techniques from our experience with them at Corning, and then close with our own forecast for the future of forecasting.

Although we believe forecasting is still an art, we think that some of the principles which we have learned through experience may be helpful to others.

Manager, Forecaster and Choice of Methods

A manager generally assumes that when he asks a forecaster to prepare a specific projection, the request itself provides sufficient information for the forecaster to go to work and do his job. This is almost never true.

Successful forecasting begins with a collaboration between the manager and the forecaster, in which they work out answers to the following questions.

1. *What is the purpose of the forecast—how is it to be used?*
This determines the accuracy and power required of the techniques, and hence governs selection. Deciding whether to enter a business may require only a rather gross estimate of the size of the market, whereas a forecast made for budgeting purposes should be quite accurate. The appropriate techniques differ accordingly.

Again, if the forecast is to set a "standard" against which to evaluate performance, the forecasting method should not take into account special actions, such as promotions and other marketing devices, since these are meant to change historical patterns and relationships and hence form part of the "performance" to be evaluated.

Forecasts that simply sketch what the future will be like if a company makes no significant changes in tactics and strategy are usually not good enough for planning purposes. On the other hand, if management wants a

(*Text continues on page 281*)

BASIC FORECASTING TECHNIQUES

	A. Qualitative methods	
Technique	1. Delphi method	2. Market research
Description	A panel of experts is interrogated by a sequence of questionnaires in which the responses to one questionnaire are used to produce the next questionnaire. Any set of information available to some experts and not others is thus passed on to the others, enabling all the experts to have access to all the information for forecasting. This technique eliminates the bandwagon effect of majority opinion.	The systematic, formal, and conscious procedure for evolving and testing hypotheses about real markets.
Accuracy		
Short term (0-3 months)	Fair to very good	Excellent
Medium term (3 months-2 years)	Fair to very good	Good
Long term (2 years & up)	Fair to very good	Fair to good
Identification of turning points	Fair to good	Fair to very good
Typical applications	Forecasts of long-range and new-product sales, forecasts of margins.	Forecasts of long-range and new-product sales, forecasts of margins.
Data required	A coordinator issues the sequence of questionnaires, editing and consolidating the responses.	As a minimum, two set of reports over time. One needs a considerable collection of market data from questionnaires, surveys, and time series analyses of market variables.
Cost of forecasting*		
With a computer	$2,000+	$5,000+
Is calculation possible without a computer?	Yes	Yes
Time required to develop an application & make a forecast	2 months+	3 months+
References	North & Pyke, " 'Probes' of the Technological Future," HBR May-June 1969, p. 68.	Bass, King & Pessemeier, *Applications of the Sciences in Marketing Management* (New York, John Wiley & Sons, Inc., 1968).

*These estimates are based on our own experience, using this machine configuration: an IBM 360-40, 256 K system and a Univac 1108 Time-Sharing System, together with such smaller equipment as G.E. Time-sharing and IBM 360-30's and 1130's.

3. Panel consensus	4. Visionary forecast	5. Historical analogy
This technique is based on the assumption that several experts can arrive at a better forecast than one person. There is no secrecy, and communication is encouraged. The forecasts are sometimes influenced by social factors, and may not reflect a true consensus.	A prophecy that uses personal insights, judgment, and, when possible, facts about different scenarios of the future. It is characterized by subjective guesswork and imagination; in general, the methods used are non-scientific.	This is a comparative analysis of the introduction and growth of similar new products, that bases the forecast on similarity patterns.
Poor to fair Poor to fair Poor	Poor Poor Poor	Poor Good to fair Good to fair
Poor to fair	Poor	Poor to fair
Forecasts of long-range and new-product sales, forecasts of margins.	Forecasts of long-range and new-product sales, forecasts of margins.	Forecasts of long-range and new-product sales, forecasts of margins.
Information from a panel of experts is presented openly in group meetings to arrive at a consensus forecast. Again, a minimum is two sets of reports over time.	A set of possible scenarios about the future prepared by a few experts in light of past events.	Several years' history of one or more products.
$1,000+ Yes	$100+ Yes	$1,000+ Yes
2 weeks+	1 week+	1 month+
————	————	Spencer, Clark & Hoguet, *Business & Economic Forecasting* (Homewood, Illinois, Richard D. Irwin, Inc., 1961).

B. Time series analysis & projection

1. Moving average	2. Exponential smoothing	3. Box-Jenkins
Each point of a moving average of a time series is the arithmetic or weighted average of a number of consecutive points of the series, where the number of data points is chosen so that the effects of seasonals or irregularity or both are eliminated.	This technique is similar to the moving average, except that more recent data points are given more weight. Descriptively, the new forecast is equal to the old one plus some proportion of the past forecasting error. Adaptive forecasting is somewhat the same except that seasonals are also computed. There are many variations of exponential smoothing: some are more versatile than others, some are computationally more complex, some require more computer time.	Exponential smoothing is a special case of the Box-Jenkins technique. The time series is fitted with a mathematical model that is optimal in the sense that it assigns smaller errors to history than any other model. The type of model must be identified and the parameters then estimated. This is apparently the most accurate statistical routine presently available but also one of the most costly and time-consuming ones.
Poor to good Poor Very poor	Fair to very good Poor to good Very poor	Very good to excellent Poor to good Very poor
Poor	Poor	Fair
Inventory control for low-volume items.	Production and inventory control, forecasts of margins and other financial data.	Production and inventory control for large-volume items, forecasts of cash balances.
A minimum of two years of sales history, if seasonals are present. Otherwise, less data. (Of course, the more history the better.) The moving average must be specified.	The same as for a moving average.	The same as for a moving average. However, in this case more history is very advantageous in model identification.
$.005 Yes	$.005 Yes	$10.00 Yes
1 day—	1 day—	1-2 days
Hadley, *Introduction to Business Statistics* (San Francisco, Holden-Day, Inc., 1968).	Brown, "Less Risk in Inventory Estimates," HBR July-August 1959, p. 104.	Box-Jenkins, *Time Series Analysis, Forecasting & Control* (San Francisco, Holden-Day, Inc., 1970).

4. X-11	5. Trend projections
Developed by Julius Shiskin of the Census Bureau, this technique decomposes a time series into seasonals, trend cycles, and irregular elements. Primarily used for detailed time series analysis (including estimating seasonals); but we have extended its uses to forecasting and tracking and warning by incorporating other analytical methods. Used with special knowledge, it is perhaps the most effective technique for medium-range forecasting – three months to one year – allowing one to predict turning points and to time special events.	This technique fits a trend line to a mathematical equation and then projects it into the future by means of this equation. There are several variations: the slope-characteristic method, polynomials, logarithms, and so on.
Very good to excellent Good Very poor	Very good Good Good
Very good	Poor
Tracking and warning, forecasts of company, division, or department sales.	New-product forecasts (particularly intermediate- and long-term).
A minimum of three years' history to start. Thereafter, the complete history.	Varies with the technique used. However, a good rule of thumb is to use a minimum of five years' annual data to start. Thereafter, the complete history.
$10.00 No	Varies with application Yes
1 day	1 day—
McLaughlin & Boyle, "Time Series Forecasting," American Marketing Association Booklet, 1962, Marketing Research Technique Series No. 6.	Hadley, *Introduction to Business Statistics* (San Francisco, Holden-Day, Inc., 1968); Oliver & Boyd, "Techniques of Production Control," Imperial Chemical Industries, 1964.

C. Casual methods

1. Regression model	2. Econometric model	3. Intention-to-buy & anticipations surveys
This functionally relates sales to other economic, competitive, or internal variables and estimates an equation using the least-squares technique. Relationships are primarily analyzed statistically, although any relationship should be selected for testing on a rational ground.	An econometric model is a system of interdependent regression equations that describes some sector of economic sales or profit activity. The parameters of the regression equations are usually estimated simultaneously. As a rule, these models are relatively expensive to develop and can easily cost between $5,000 and $10,000, depending on detail. However, due to the system of equations inherent in such models, they will better express the causalities involved than an ordinary regression equation and hence will predict turning points more accurately.	These surveys of the general public (a) determine intentions to buy certain products or (b) derive an index that measures general feeling about the present and the future and estimates how this feeling will affect buying habits. These approaches to forecasting are more useful for tracking and warning than forecasting. The basic problem in using them is that a turning point may be signaled incorrectly (and hence never occur).
Good to very good Good to very good Poor	Good to very good Very good to excellent Good	Poor to good Poor to good Very poor
Very good	Excellent	Good
Forecasts of sales by product classes. forecasts of margins.	Forecasts of sales by product classes, forecasts of margins.	Forecasts of sales by product class.
Several years' quarterly history to obtain good, meaningful relationships. Mathematically necessary to have two more observations than there are independent variables.	The same as for regression.	Several years' data are usually required to relate such indexes to company sales.
$100 Yes	$5,000+ Yes	$5,000 Yes
Depends on ability to identify relationships.	2 months+	Several weeks
Clelland, de Cani, Brown, Bush & Murray, *Basic Statistics with Business Applications* (New York, John Wiley & Sons, Inc., 1966).	Evans, *Macro-economic Activity: Theory, Forecasting & Control* (New York, Harper & Row Publishers, Inc., 1969).	Publications of Survey Research Center, Institute for Social Research, University of Michigan; and of Bureau of the Census.

4. Input-output model	5. Economic input-output model	6. Diffusion index
A method of analysis concerned with the interindustry or interdepartmental flow of goods or services in the economy or a company and its markets. It shows what flows of inputs must occur to obtain certain outputs. Considerable effort must be expended to use these models properly, and additional detail, not normally available, must be obtained if they are to be applied to specific businesses. Corporations using input-output models have expended as much as $100,000 and more annually to develop useful applications.	Econometric models and input-output models are sometimes combined for forecasting. The input-output model is used to provide long-term trends for the econometric model; it also stabilizes the econometric model.	The percentage of a group of economic indicators that are going up or down, this percentage then becoming the index.
Not applicable Good to very good Good to very good	Not applicable Good to very good Good to excellent	Poor to good Poor to good Very poor
Fair	Good	Good
Forecasts of company sales and division sales for industrial sectors and subsectors.	Company sales for industrial sectors and subsectors.	Forecasts of sales by product class.
Ten or fifteen years' history. Considerable amounts of information on product and service flows within a corporation (or economy) for each year for which an input-output analysis is desired.	The same as for a moving average and X-11.	The same as an intention-to-buy survey.
$50,000+ No	$100,000 No	$1,000 Yes
6 months+	6 months+	1 month+
Leontief, *Input-Output Economics* (New York, Oxford University Press, 1966).	Evans & Preston, "Discussion Paper #138," Wharton School of Finance & Commerce, The University of Pennsylvania.	Evans, *Macro-economic Activity: Theory, Forecasting & Control* (New York, Harper & Row Publishers, Inc., 1969).

7. Leading indicator	8. Life-cycle analysis	
A time series of an economic activity whose movement in a given direction precedes the movement of some other time series in the same direction is a leading indicator.	This is an analysis and forecasting of new-product growth rates based on S-curves. The phases of product acceptance by the various groups such as innovators, early adapters, early majority, late majority, and laggards are central to the analysis.	
Poor to good Poor to good Very poor	Poor Poor to good Poor to good	Accuracy
Good	Poor to good	Turning point identification
Forecasts of sales by product class.	Forecasts of new-product sales.	Applications
The same as an intention-to-buy survey + 5 to 10 years' history.	As a minimum, the annual sales of the product being considered or of a similar product. It is often necessary to do market surveys.	Data required
$1,000 Yes	$1,500 Yes	Cost
1 month+	1 month+	Time required to develop forecast
Evans, *Macro-economic Activity: Theory, Forecasting & Control* (New York, Harper & Row Publishers, Inc., 1969).	Bass, "A New Product Growth Model for Consumer Durables," *Management Science*, January 1969.	References

Some additional techniques for finer tuning

Not directly related to product life-cycle forecasting, but still important to its success, are certain applications which we briefly mention here for those who are particularly interested.

Inventory control

While the X-11 method and econometric or causal models are good for forecasting aggregated sales for a number of items, it is not economically feasible to use these techniques for controlling inventories of individual items.

Some of the requirements that a forecasting technique for production and inventory control purposes must meet are these:

○ It should not require maintenance of large histories of each item in the data bank, if this can be avoided.

○ Computations should take as little computer time as possible.

○ The technique should identify seasonal variations and take these into account when forecasting; also, preferably, it will compute the statistical significance of the seasonals, deleting them if they are not significant.

○ It should be able to fit a curve to the most recent data adequately and adapt to changes in trends and seasonals quickly.

○ It should be applicable to data with a variety of characteristics.

○ It also should be versatile enough so that when several hundred items or more are considered, it will do the best overall job, even though it may not do as good a job as other techniques for a particular item.

One of the first techniques developed to meet these criteria is called *exponential smoothing*, where the most recent data points are given greater weight than previous data points, and where very little data storage is required. This technique is a considerable improvement over the moving average technique, which does not adapt quickly to changes in trends and which requires significantly more data storage.

Adaptive forecasting also meets these criteria. An extension of exponential smoothing, it computes seasonals and thereby provides a more accurate forecast than can be obtained by exponential smoothing if there is a significant seasonal.

There are a number of variations in the exponential smoothing and adaptive forecasting methods; however, all have the common characteristic (at least in a descriptive sense) that the new forecast equals the old forecast plus some fraction of the latest forecast error.

Virtually all the statistical techniques described in our discussion of the steady-state phase except the X-11 should be categorized as special cases of the recently developed Box-Jenkins technique. This technique requires considerably more computer time for each item and, at the present time, human attention as well. Until computational shortcuts can be developed, it will have limited use in the production and inventory control area.

However, the Box-Jenkins has one very important feature not existing in the other statistical techniques: the ability to incorporate special information (for example, price changes and economic data) into the forecast.

The reason the Box-Jenkins and the X-11 are more costly than other statistical techniques is that the user must select a particular version of the technique, or he must estimate optimal values for the various parameters in the models, or both. For example, the type and length of moving average used is determined by the variability and other characteristics of the data at hand.

We expect that better computer methods will be developed in the near future to significantly reduce these costs.

Group-item forecasts

In some instances where statistical methods do not provide acceptable accuracy for individual items, one can obtain the desired accuracy by grouping items together, where this reduces the relative amount of randomness in the data.

Forecasters commonly use this approach to get acceptable accuracy in situations where it is virtually impossible to obtain accurate forecasts for individual items.

Long-term demands

Also, it is sometimes possible to accurately forecast long-term demands, even though the short-term swings may be so chaotic that they cannot be accurately forecasted. We found this to be the case in forecasting individual items in the line of color TV bulbs, where demands on CGW fluctuate widely with customer schedules. In this case, there is considerable difficulty in achieving desired profit levels if short-term scheduling does not take long-term objectives into consideration.

Hence, two types of forecasts are needed:

O One that does a reasonably good job of forecasting demand for the next three to six periods for individual items.

O One that forecasts total bulb demand more accurately for three to thirteen periods into the future.

For this reason, and because the low-cost forecasting techniques such as exponential smoothing and adaptive forecasting do not permit the incorporation of special information, it is advantageous to also use a more sophisticated technique such as the X-11 for groups of items.

This technique is applied to analyze and forecast rates for total businesses, and also to identify any peculiarities and sudden changes in trends or patterns. This information is then incorporated into the item forecasts, with adjustments to the smoothing mechanisms, seasonals, and the like as necessary. Frequently one must develop a manual-override feature, which allows adjustments based on human judgment, in circumstances as fluid as these.

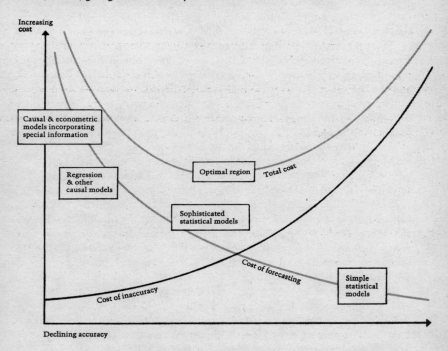

forecast of the effect that a certain marketing strategy under debate will have on sales growth, then the technique must be sophisticated enough to take explicit account of the special actions and events the strategy entails.

Techniques vary in their costs, as well as in scope and accuracy. The manager must fix the level of inaccuracy he can tolerate—in other words, decide how his decision will vary, depending on the range of accuracy of the forecast. This allows the forecaster to trade off cost against the value of accuracy in choosing a technique.

For example, in production and inventory control, increased accuracy is likely to lead to lower safety stocks. Here the manager and forecaster must weigh the cost of a more sophisticated and more expensive technique against potential savings in inventory costs.

Exhibit I shows how cost and accuracy increase with sophistication and charts this against the corresponding cost of forecasting errors, given some general assumptions. The most sophisticated technique that can be economically justified is one that falls in the region where the sum of the two costs is minimal.

Once the manager has defined the purpose of the forecast, the forecaster can advise him on how often it could usefully be produced. From a strategic point of view, they should discuss whether the decision to be made on the basis of the forecast can be changed later, if they find the forecast was inaccurate. If it *can* be changed, they should then discuss the usefulness of installing a system to track the accuracy of the forecast and the kind of tracking system that is appropriate.

2. What are the dynamics and components of the system for which the forecast will be made?

This clarifies the relationships of interacting variables. Generally, the manager and the forecaster must review a flow chart that shows the relative positions of the different elements of the distribution system, sales system, production system, or whatever is being studied.

Exhibit II displays these elements for the system through which CGW's major component for color TV sets—the bulb—flows to the consumer. Note the points where inventories are required or maintained in this manufacturing and distribution system—these are the *pipeline elements*, which exert important effects throughout the flow system and hence are of critical interest to the forecaster.

All the elements in gray directly affect forecasting procedure to some extent, and the color key suggests the nature of CGW's data at each point, again a prime determinant of technique selection since different techniques require different kinds of inputs. Where data are unavailable or costly to obtain, the range of forecasting choices is limited.

The flow chart should also show which parts of the system are under the control of the company doing the forecasting. In *Exhibit II*, this is merely the volume of glass panels and funnels supplied by Corning to the tube manufacturers.

In the part of the system where the company has total control, management tends to be tuned in to the various cause-and-effect relationships, and hence can frequently use forecasting techniques that take causal factors explicitly into account.

The flow chart has special value for the forecaster where causal prediction methods are called for because it enables him to conjecture about the possible variations in sales levels caused by inventories and the like, and to determine which factors must be considered by the technique to provide the executive with a forecast of acceptable accuracy.

Once these factors and their relationships have been clarified, the forecaster can build a causal model of the system which captures both the facts and the logic of the situation—which is, after all, the basis of sophisticated forecasting.

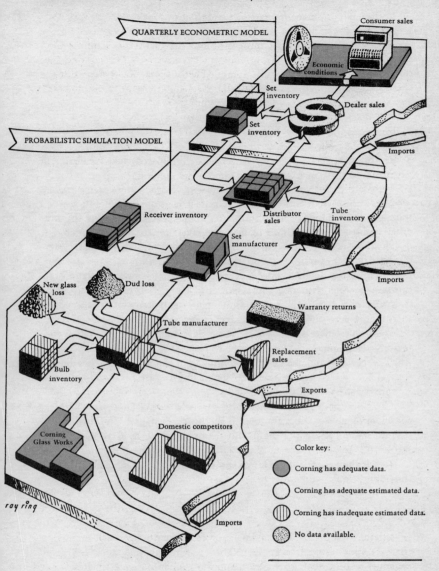

Exhibit II. Flow chart of TV distribution system

QUARTERLY ECONOMETRIC MODEL

Consumer sales

Economic conditions

Set inventory

Dealer sales

PROBABILISTIC SIMULATION MODEL

Set inventory

Imports

Receiver inventory

Distributor sales

Tube inventory

Set manufacturer

New glass loss

Dud loss

Tube manufacturer

Imports

Warranty returns

Bulb inventory

Replacement sales

Exports

Corning Glass Works

Domestic competitors

Color key:

Corning has adequate data.

Corning has adequate estimated data.

Corning has inadequate estimated data.

No data available.

ray ring

Imports

283

3. *How important is the past in estimating the future?*

Significant changes in the system—new products, new competitive strategies, and so forth—diminish the similarity of past and future. Over the short term, recent changes are unlikely to cause overall patterns to alter, but over the long term their effects are likely to increase. The executive and the forecaster must discuss these fully.

Three General Types

Once the manager and the forecaster have formulated their problem, the forecaster will be in a position to choose his method.

There are three basic types—*qualitative techniques, time series analysis and projection,* and *causal models.* The first uses qualitative data (expert opinion, for example) and information about special events of the kind already mentioned, and may or may not take the past into consideration.

The second, on the other hand, focuses entirely on patterns and pattern changes, and thus relies entirely on historical data.

The third uses highly refined and specific information about relationships between system elements, and is powerful enough to take special events formally into account. As with time series analysis and projection techniques, the past is important to causal models.

These differences imply (quite correctly) that the same type of forecasting technique is not appropriate to forecast sales, say, at all stages of the life cycle of a product—for example, a technique that relies on historical data would not be useful in forecasting the future of a totally new product that has no history.

The major part of the balance of this article will be concerned with the problem of suiting the technique to the life-cycle stages. We hope to give the executive insight into the potential of forecasting by showing how this problem is to be approached. But before we discuss the life cycle, we need to sketch the general functions of the three basic types of techniques in a bit more detail.

QUALITATIVE TECHNIQUES

Primarily, these are used when data are scarce—for example, when a product is first introduced into a market. They use human judgment and rating schemes to turn qualitative information into quantitative estimates.

The objective here is to bring together in a logical, unbiased, and systematic way all information and judgments which relate to the factors being estimated. Such techniques are frequently used in new-technology areas, where development of a product idea may require several "inventions," so that R&D demands are difficult to estimate, and where market acceptance and penetration rates are highly uncertain.

The gatefold chart facing page 280 presents several examples of this type (see the first section), including market research and the now-familiar Delphi technique. In this chart we have tried to provide a body of basic information about the main kinds of forecasting techniques. Some of the techniques listed are not in reality a single method or model, but a whole family. Thus our statements may not accurately describe all the variations of a technique and should rather be interpreted as descriptive of the basic concept of each.

A disclaimer about estimates in the chart is also in order. Estimates of costs are approximate, as are computation times, accuracy ratings, and ratings for turning-point identification. The costs of some procedures depend on whether they are being used routinely or are set up for a single forecast; also, if weightings or seasonals have to be determined anew each time a forecast is made, costs increase significantly. Still, the figures we present may serve as general guidelines.

The reader may find frequent reference to this gatefold helpful for the remainder of the article.

TIME SERIES ANALYSIS

These are statistical techniques used when several years' data for a product or product line are available and when relationships and trends are both clear and relatively stable.

One of the basic principles of statistical forecasting—indeed, of all forecasting when historical data are available—is that the forecaster should use the data on past performance to get a "speedometer reading" of the current rate (of sales, say) and of how fast this rate is increasing or decreasing. The current rate and changes in the rate—"acceleration" and "deceleration"—constitute the basis of forecasting. Once they are known, various mathematical techniques can develop projections from them.

The matter is not so simple as it sounds, however. It is usually difficult to make projections from raw data since the rates and trends are not immediately obvious; they are mixed up with seasonal variations, for example, and perhaps distorted by such factors as the effects of a large sales promotion campaign. The raw data must be massaged before they are usable, and this is frequently done by time series analysis.

Now, a *time series* is a set of chronologically ordered points of raw data —for example, a division's sales of a given product, by month, for several years. Time series *analysis* helps to identify and explain:

☐ Any regularity or systematic variation in the series of data which is due to seasonality—the "seasonals."

☐ Cyclical patterns that repeat any two or three years or more.

☐ Trends in the data.

☐ Growth rates of these trends.

(Unfortunately, most existing methods identify only the seasonals, the combined effect of trends and cycles, and the irregular, or chance, component. That is, they do not separate *trends* from *cycles*. We shall return to this point when we discuss time series analysis in the final stages of product maturity.)

Once the analysis is complete, the work of projecting future sales (or whatever) can begin.

We should note that while we have separated analysis from projection here for purposes of explanation, most statistical forecasting techniques actually combine both functions in a single operation.

A *future like the past:* It is obvious from this description that all statistical techniques are based on the assumption that existing patterns will continue into the future. This assumption is more likely to be correct over the short term than it is over the long term, and for this reason these techniques provide us with reasonably accurate forecasts for the immediate future but do quite poorly further into the future (unless the data patterns are extraordinarily stable).

For this same reason, these techniques ordinarily *cannot* predict when the rate of growth in a trend will change significantly—for example, when a period of slow growth in sales will suddenly change to a period of rapid decay.

Such points are called *turning points.* They are naturally of the greatest consequence to the manager, and, as we shall see, the forecaster must use different tools from pure statistical techniques to predict when they will occur.

CAUSAL MODELS

When historical data are available and enough analysis has been performed to spell out explicitly the relationships between the factor to be forecast and other factors (such as related businesses, economic forces, and socio-economic factors), the forecaster often constructs a *causal model.*

A causal model is the most sophisticated kind of forecasting tool. It expresses mathematically the relevant causal relationships, and may include pipeline considerations (i.e., inventories) and market survey information. It may also directly incorporate the results of a time series analysis.

The causal model takes into account everything known of the dynamics of the flow system and utilizes predictions of related events such as competitive actions, strikes, and promotions. If the data are available, the model generally includes factors for each location in the flow chart (as illustrated in *Exhibit II*) and connects these by equations to describe overall product flow.

If certain kinds of data are lacking, initially it may be necessary to make assumptions about some of the relationships and then track what is happening to determine if the assumptions are true. Typically, a causal model is continually revised as more knowledge about the system becomes available.

Again, see the gatefold for a rundown on the most common types of causal techniques. As the chart shows, causal models are by far the best for predicting turning points and preparing long-range forecasts.

Methods, Products and the Life Cycle

At each stage of the life of a product, from conception to steady-state sales, the decisions that management must make are characteristically quite different, and they require different kinds of information as a base. The forecasting techniques that provide these sets of information differ analogously. *Exhibit III* summarizes the life stages of a product, the typical decisions made at each, and the main forecasting techniques suitable at each.

Equally, different products may require different kinds of forecasting. Two CGW products that have been handled quite differently are the major glass components for color TV tubes, of which Corning is a prime supplier, and CORNING WARE® cookware, a proprietary consumer product line. We shall trace the forecasting methods used at each of the four different stages of maturity of these products to give some firsthand insight into the choice and application of some of the major techniques available today.

Before we begin, let us note how the situations differ for the two kinds of products:

□ For a consumer product like the cookware, the manufacturer's control of the distribution pipeline extends at least through the distributor level. Thus he can affect or control consumer sales quite directly, as well as directly control some of the pipeline elements.

Many of the changes in shipment rates and in overall profitability are therefore due to actions taken by the manufacturer himself. Tactical decisions on promotions, specials, and pricing are usually at his discretion as well. The technique selected by the forecaster for projecting sales therefore

Exhibit III. *Types of decisions made over a product's life cycle, with related forecasting techniques*

Stage of life cycle	Product development	Market testing & early introduction	Rapid growth	Steady state
Typical decisions	Amount of development effort Product design Business strategies	Optimum facility size Marketing strategies, including distribution & pricing	Facilities expansion Marketing strategies Production planning *Sales*	Promotions, specials Pricing Production planning Inventories
Forecasting techniques	Delphi method Historical analysis of comparable products Priority pattern analysis Input-output analysis Panel consensus	Consumer surveys Tracking & warning systems Market tests Experimental designs	Statistical techniques for identifying turning points Tracking & warning systems Market surveys Intention-to-buy surveys	Time series analysis & projection Causal & econometric models Market surveys for tracking & warning Life-cycle analysis

should permit incorporation of such "special information." One may have to start with simple techniques and work up to more sophisticated ones that embrace such possibilities, but the final goal is there.

□ Where the manager's company supplies a component to an OEM, as Corning does for tube manufacturers, the company does not have such direct influence or control over either the pipeline elements or final consumer sales. It may be impossible for the company to obtain good information about what is taking place at points further along the flow system (as in the upper segment of *Exhibit II*), and, in consequence, the forecaster will necessarily be using a different genre of forecasting from that he uses for a consumer product.

Between these two examples, our discussion will embrace nearly the whole range of forecasting techniques. As necessary, however, we shall touch on other products and other forecasting methods.

1. PRODUCT DEVELOPMENT

In the early stages of product development, the manager wants answers to questions such as these:

□ What are the alternative growth opportunities to pursuing product X?
□ How have established products similar to X fared?
□ Should *we* enter this business; and if so, in what segments?
□ How should we allocate R&D efforts and funds?
□ How successful will different product concepts be?
□ How will product X fit into the markets five or ten years from now?

Forecasts that help to answer these long-range questions must necessarily have long horizons themselves.

A common objection to much long-range forecasting is that it is virtually impossible to predict with accuracy what will happen several years into the future. We agree that uncertainty increases when a forecast is made for a period more than two years out. However, at the very least, the forecast and a measure of its accuracy enable the manager to know his risks in pursuing a selected strategy and in this knowledge to choose an appropriate strategy from those available.

Systematic market research is, of course, a mainstay in this area. For example, priority pattern analysis can describe the consumer's preferences and the likelihood he will buy a product, and thus is of great value in forecasting (and updating) penetration levels and rates. But there are other tools as well, depending on the state of the market and the product concept.

For a defined market: While there can be no direct data about a product that is still a gleam in the eye, information about its likely performance can be gathered in a number of ways, provided the market in which it is to be sold is a known entity.

First, one can compare a proposed product with competitors' present and planned products, ranking it on quantitative scales for different factors. We call this *product differences measurement.*

If this approach is to be successful, it is essential that the (in-house) experts who provide the basic data come from different disciplines—marketing, R&D, manufacturing, legal, and so on—and that their opinions be unbiased.

Second, and more formalistically, one can construct *disaggregate market models* by separating off different segments of a complex market for indivdual study and consideration. Specifically, it is often useful to project the S-shaped growth curves for the levels of income of different geographical regions.

When color TV bulbs were proposed as a product, CGW was able to identify the factors that would influence sales growth. Then, by disaggregating consumer demand and making certain assumptions about these factors, it was possible to develop an S-curve for rate of penetration of the household market that proved most useful to us.

Third, one can compare a projected product with an "ancestor" that has similar characteristics. In 1965, we disaggregated the market for color television by income levels and geographical regions and compared these submarkets with the historical pattern of black-and-white TV market growth. We justified this procedure by arguing that color TV represented an advance over black-and-white analogous to (although less intense than) the advance that black-and-white TV represented over radio. The analyses of black-and-white TV market growth also enabled us to estimate the variability to be expected—that is, the degree to which our projections would differ from actual as the result of economic and other factors.

The prices of black-and-white TV and other major household appliances in 1949, consumer disposable income in 1949, the prices of color TV and other appliances in 1965, and consumer disposable income for 1965 were all profitably considered in developing our long-range forecast for color-TV penetration on a national basis. The success patterns of black-and-white TV, then, provided insight into the likelihood of success and sales potential of color TV.

Our predictions of consumer acceptance of CORNING WARE® cookware, on the other hand, were derived primarily from one expert source, a manager who thoroughly understood consumer preferences and the housewares market. These predictions have been well borne out. This reinforces our belief that sales forecasts for a new product that will compete in an existing market are bound to be incomplete and uncertain unless one culls the best judgments of fully experienced personnel.

For an undefined market: Frequently, however, the market for a new product is weakly defined or few data are available, the product concept is still fluid, and history seems irrelevant. This is the case for gas turbines, electric and steam automobiles, modular housing, pollution measurement devices, and time-shared computer terminals.

Many organizations have applied the Delphi method of soliciting and consolidating experts' opinions under these circumstances. At CGW, in several instances, we have used it to estimate demand for such new products, with success.

Input-output analysis, combined with other techniques, can be extremely useful in projecting the future course of broad technologies and broad changes in the economy. The basic tools here are the input-output tables of U.S. industry for 1947, 1958, and 1963, and various updatings of the 1963 tables prepared by a number of groups who wished to extrapolate the 1963 figures or to make forecasts for later years.

Since a business or product line may represent only a small sector of an industry, it may be difficult to use the tables directly. However, a number of companies are disaggregating industries to evaluate their sales potential and to forecast changes in product mixes—the phasing out of old lines and introduction of others. For example, Quantum-Science Corporation (MAPTEK) has developed techniques that make input-output analyses more directly useful to today's electronics businessmen. (Other techniques, such as panel consensus and visionary forecasting, seem less effective to us, and we cannot evaluate them from our own experience.)

2. TESTING AND INTRODUCTION

Before a product can enter its (hopefully) rapid penetration stage, the market potential must be tested out and the product must be introduced —and then more market testing may be advisable. At this stage, management needs answers to these questions:

 □ What shall our marketing plan be—which markets should we enter and with what production quantities?

 □ How much manufacturing capacity will the early production stages require?

 □ As demand grows, where should we build this capacity?

 □ How shall we allocate our R&D resources over time?

Significant profits depend on finding the right answers, and it is therefore economically feasible to expend relatively large amounts of effort and money on obtaining good forecasts, short-, medium-, and long-range.

A sales forecast at this stage should provide three points of information: the date when rapid sales will begin, the rate of market penetration during the rapid-sales stage, and the ultimate level of penetration, or sales rate, during the steady-state stage.

Using early data: The date when a product will enter the rapid-growth stage is hard to predict three or four years in advance (the usual horizon). A company's only recourse is to use statistical tracking methods to check on how successfully the product is being introduced, along with routine market studies to determine when there has been a significant increase in the sales rate.

Furthermore, the greatest care should be taken in analyzing the early sales data that start to accumulate once the product has been introduced into the market. For example, it is important to distinguish between sales to *innovators,* who will try anything new, and sales to *imitators,* who will buy a product only after it has been accepted by innovators, for it is the latter group that provides demand stability. Many new products have initially appeared successful because of purchases by innovators, only to fail later in the stretch.

Tracking the two groups means market research, possibly via opinion panels. A panel ought to contain both innovators and imitators, since innovators can teach one a lot about how to improve a product while imitators provide insight into the desires and expectations of the whole market.

The color TV set, for example, was introduced in 1954, but did not gain acceptance from the majority of consumers until late 1964. To be sure, the

Exhibit IV. *Expenditures on appliances versus all consumer goods*
[In billions of dollars]

[In billions of dollars]

Year (1)	All consumer goods* (2)	Household appliances† (3)	Radio, TV & other† (4)	Totals of columns 3 & 4 (5)	Column 5 ÷ Column 2 (6)	Column 4 ÷ Column 2 (7)
1947	110.9	3.18	1.43	4.61	4.16%	1.29%
1948	118.9	3.47	1.48	4.95	4.16	1.23
1949	119.1	3.13	1.70	4.83	4.06	1.43
1950	128.6	3.94	2.46	6.40	4.98	1.91
1951	138.4	3.87	2.26	6.13	4.43	1.63
1952	143.3	3.82	2.37	6.19	4.32	1.65
1953	150.0	3.99	2.61	6.60	4.40	1.74
1954	151.1	4.02	2.74	6.77	4.48	1.81
1955	162.9	4.69	2.79	7.48	4.59	1.71
1956	168.2	4.89	2.87	7.76	4.61	1.71
1957	176.4	4.63	3.00	7.63	4.33	1.70
1958	178.1	4.44	3.07	7.51	4.22	1.72
1959	190.9	4.86	3.42	8.28	4.34	1.79
1960	196.6	4.74	3.62	8.36	4.25	1.84
1961	200.1	4.77	3.76	8.53	4.26	1.88
1962	212.1	5.01	3.94	8.95	4.22	1.86
1963	222.5	5.24	4.54	9.78	4.40	2.04
1964	237.9	5.74	5.41	11.15	4.69	2.27
1965	257.4	6.03	6.01	12.04	4.68	2.33
1966	277.7	6.77	6.91	13.68	4.93	2.49
1967	288.1	7.09	7.41	14.50	5.03	2.57
1968	313.9	7.80	7.85	15.65	4.99	2.50

*Data obtained from *Survey of Current Business*, Personal Consumption Expenditure Tables (U.S. Department of Commerce, July issues).   † Data obtained from the *Survey of Current Business Statistics* (U.S. Department of Commerce, 1969 Biennial Edition).

color TV set could not leave the introduction stage and enter the rapid-growth stage until the networks had substantially increased their color programming. However, special flag signals like "substantially increased network color programming" are likely to come after the fact, from the planning viewpoint; and in general, we find, scientifically designed consumer surveys conducted on a regular basis provide the earliest means of detecting turning points in the demand for a product.

Similar-product technique: Although statistical tracking is a useful tool during the early introduction stages, there are rarely sufficient data for statistical forecasting. Market research studies can naturally be useful, as we have indicated. But, more commonly, the forecaster tries to identify a similar, older product whose penetration pattern should be similar to that of the new product, since overall markets can and do exhibit consistent patterns.

Again, let's consider color television and the forecasts we prepared in 1965.

For the years 1947-1968, *Exhibit IV* shows total consumer expenditures, appliance expenditures, expenditures for radios and TVs, and relevant percentages. Column 4 shows that total expenditures for appliances are relatively stable over periods of several years; hence, new appliances must compete with existing ones, especially during recessions (note the figures for 1948-1949, 1953-1954, 1957-1958, and 1960-1961).

Exhibit V. Long-term household penetration curves for color and black-and-white TV

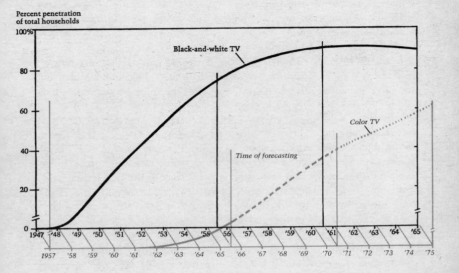

Certain specific fluctuations in these figures are of special significance here. When black-and-white TV was introduced as a new product in 1948-1951, the ratio of expenditures on radio and TV sets to total expenditures for consumer goods (see column 7) increased about 33% (from 1.23% to 1.63%), as against a modest increase of only 13% (from 1.63% to 1.88%) in the ratio for the next decade. (A similar increase of 33% occurred in 1962-1966 as color TV made its major penetration.)

Probably, the acceptance of black-and-white TV as a major appliance in 1950 caused the ratio of all major household appliances to total consumer goods (see column 5) to rise to 4.98%; in other words, the innovation of TV caused the consumer to start spending more money on major appliances around 1950.

Our expectation in mid-1965 was that the introduction of color TV would induce a similar increase. Thus, although this product comparison did not provide us with an accurate or detailed forecast, it did place an upper bound on the future total sales we could expect.

The next step was to look at the cumulative penetration curve for black-and-white TVs in U.S. households, shown in *Exhibit V*. We assumed color-TV penetration would have a similar S-curve, but that it would take longer for color sets to penetrate the whole market (that is, reach steady-state sales). Whereas it took black-and-white TV 10 years to reach steady state, qualitative expert-opinion studies indicated that it would take color twice that long—hence the more gradual slope of the color-TV curve.

At the same time, studies conducted in 1964 and 1965 showed significantly different penetration sales for color TV in various income groups, rates that were helpful to us in projecting the color-TV curve and tracking the accuracy of our projection.

With these data and assumptions, we forecast retail sales for the remainder of 1965 through mid-1970 (see the dotted section of the lower curve in *Exhibit* V). The forecasts were accurate through 1966 but too high in the following three years, primarily because of declining general economic conditions and changing pricing policies.

We should note that when we developed these forecasts and techniques, we recognized that additional techniques would be necessary at later times to maintain the accuracy that would be needed in subsequent periods. These forecasts provided acceptable accuracy for the time they were made, however, since the major goal then was only to estimate the penetration rate and the ultimate, steady-state level of sales. Making refined estimates of how the manufacturing-distribution pipelines will behave is an activity that properly belongs to the next life-cycle stage.

Other approaches: When it is not possible to identify a similar product, as was the case with CGW's self-cleaning oven and flat-top cooking range (COUNTERANGE™), another approach must be used.

For the purposes of initial introduction into the markets, it may only be necessary to determine the minimum sales rate required for a product venture to meet corporate objectives. Analyses like input-output, historical trend, and technological forecasting can be used to estimate this minimum. Also, the feasibility of not entering the market at all, or of continuing R&D right up to the rapid-growth stage, can best be determined by sensitivity analysis.

Predicting rapid growth: To estimate the date by which a product will enter the rapid-growth stage is another matter. As we have seen, this date is a function of many factors: the existence of a distribution system, customer acceptance of or familiarity with the product concept, the need met by the product, significant events (such as color network programming), and so on.

As well as by reviewing the behavior of similar products, the date may be estimated through Delphi exercises or through rating and ranking schemes, whereby the factors important to customer acceptance are estimated, each competitor product is rated on each factor, and an overall score is tallied for the competitor against a score for the new product.

As we have said, it is usually difficult to forecast precisely when the turning point will occur; and, in our experience, the best accuracy that can be expected is within three months to two years of the actual time.

It is occasionally true, of course, that one can be certain a new product will be enthusiastically accepted. Market tests and initial customer reaction made it clear there would be a large market for CORNING WARE® cookware. Since the distribution system was already in existence, the time required for the line to reach rapid growth depended primarily on our ability to manufacture it. Sometimes forecasting is merely a matter of calculating the company's capacity—but not ordinarily.

3. RAPID GROWTH

When a product enters this stage, the most important decisions relate to facilities expansion. These decisions generally involve the largest expenditures in the cycle (excepting major R&D decisions), and commensurate forecasting and tracking efforts are justified.

Forecasting and tracking must provide the executive with three kinds of data at this juncture:

   □ Firm verification of the *rapid-growth rate forecast* made previously.

   □ A hard date when sales will level to "normal," *steady-state growth*.

   □ For component products, the deviation in the growth curve that may be caused by characteristic *conditions along the pipeline*—for example, inventory blockages.

Forecasting the growth rate: Medium- and long-range forecasting of the market growth rate and of the attainment of steady-state sales requires the same measures as does the product introduction stage—detailed marketing studies (especially intention-to-buy surveys) and product comparisons.

When a product has entered rapid growth, on the other hand, there are generally sufficient data available to construct *statistical* and possibly even *causal* growth models (although the latter will necessarily contain assumptions that must be verified later).

We estimated the growth rate and steady-state rate of color TV by a crude econometric-marketing model from data available at the beginning of this stage. We conducted frequent marketing studies as well.

The growth rate for CORNING WARE® cookware, as we explained, was limited primarily by our production capabilities; and hence the basic information to be predicted in that case was the date of leveling growth. Because substantial inventories buffered information on consumer sales all along the line, good field data were lacking, which made this date difficult to estimate. Eventually we found it necessary to establish a better (more direct) field information system.

As well as merely buffering information, in the case of a component product, the pipeline exerts certain distorting effects on the manufacturer's demand; these effects, although highly important, are often illogically neglected in production or capacity planning.

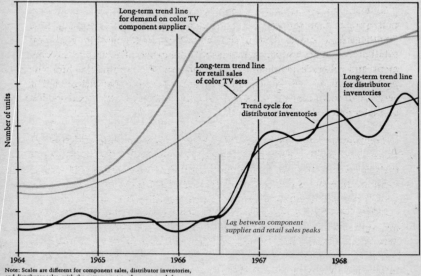

Long-term trend line for demand on color TV component supplier

Long-term trend line for retail sales of color TV sets

Long-term trend line for distributor inventories

Trend cycle for distributor inventories

Lag between component supplier and retail sales peaks

Number of units

1964   1965   1966   1967   1968

Note: Scales are different for component sales, distributor inventories, and distributor sales, with the patterns put on the same graph for illustrative purposes.

Simulating the pipeline: While the ware-in-process demand in the pipeline has an S-curve like that of retail sales, it may lag or lead sales by several months, distorting the shape of the demand on the component supplier.

Exhibit VI shows the long-term trend of demand on a component supplier other than Corning as a function of distributor sales and distributor inventories. As one can see from this curve, supplier sales may grow relatively sharply for several months and peak before retail sales have leveled off. The implications of these curves for facilities planning and allocation are obvious.

Here we have used components for color TV sets for our illustration because we know from our own experience the importance of the long flow time for color TVs that results from the many sequential steps in manufacturing and distribution (recall *Exhibit II*). There are more spectacular examples; for instance, it is not uncommon for the flow time from component supplier to consumer to stretch out to two years in the case of truck engines.

To estimate total demand on CGW production, we used a retail demand model and a pipeline simulation. The model incorporated penetration rates, mortality curves, and the like. We combined the data generated by the model with market-share data, data on glass losses, and other information to make up the corpus of inputs for the pipeline simulation. The simulation output allowed us to apply projected curves like the ones shown in *Exhibit* VI to our own component-manufacturing planning.

Simulation is an excellent tool for these circumstances because it is essentially simpler than the alternative—namely, building a more formal, more "mathematical" model. That is, simulation bypasses the need for analytical solution techniques and for mathematical duplication of a complex environment and allows experimentation. Simulation also informs us how the pipeline elements will behave and interact over time—knowledge that is very useful in forecasting, especially in constructing formal causal models at a later date.

Tracking and warning: This knowledge is not absolutely "hard," of course, and pipeline dynamics must be carefully tracked to determine if the various estimates and assumptions made were indeed correct. Statistical methods provide a good short-term basis for estimating and checking the growth rate and signaling when turning points will occur.

In late 1965 it appeared to us that the ware-in-process demand was increasing, since there was a consistent positive difference between actual TV bulb sales and forecasted bulb sales. Conversations with product managers and other personnel indicated there might have been a significant change in pipeline activity; it appeared that rapid increases in retail demand were boosting glass requirements for ware-in-process, which could create a hump in the S-curve like the one illustrated in *Exhibit* VI. This humping provided additional profit for CGW in 1966 but had an adverse effect in 1967. We were able to predict this hump, but unfortunately we were unable to reduce or avoid it because the pipeline was not sufficiently under our control.

The inventories all along the pipeline also follow an S-curve (as shown in *Exhibit* VI), a fact that creates and compounds two characteristic conditions in the pipeline as a whole: initial overfilling and subsequent shifts between too much and too little inventory at various points—a sequence of feast-and-famine conditions.

For example, the simpler distribution system for CORNING WARE® cookware had an S-curve like the ones we have examined. When the retail sales slowed from rapid to normal growth, however, there were no early indications from shipment data that this crucial turning point had been reached. Data on distributor inventories gave us some warning that the pipeline was overfilling, but the turning point at the retail level was still not identified quickly enough, as we have mentioned before, because of lack of good data at that level. We now monitor field information regularly to identify significant changes, and adjust our shipment forecasts accordingly.

Main concerns: One main activity during the rapid-growth stage, then, is to check earlier estimates and, if they appear incorrect, to compute as accurately as possible the error in the forecast and obtain a revised estimate.

In some instances, models developed earlier will include only "macroterms"; in such cases, market research can provide information needed to break these down into their components. For example, the color-TV forecasting model initially considered only total set penetrations at different income levels, without considering the way in which the sets were being used. Therefore, we conducted market survey to determine set use more precisely.

Equally, during the rapid-growth stage, submodels of pipeline segments should be expanded to incorporate more detailed information as it is received. In the case of color TV, we found we were able to estimate the overall pipeline requirements for glass bulbs, the CGW market share factors, and glass losses, and to postulate a probability distribution around the most likely estimates. Over time, it was easy to check these forecasts against actual volume of sales, and hence to check on the procedures by which we were generating them.

We also found we had to increase the number of factors in the simulation model—for instance, we had to expand the model to consider different sizes of bulbs—and this improved our overall accuracy and usefulness.

The preceding is only one approach that can be used in forecasting sales of new products that are in a rapid growth.

4. STEADY STATE

The decisions the manager makes at this stage are quite different from those he has made earlier. Most of the facilities planning has been squared away, and trends and growth rates have become reasonably stable. It is possible that swings in demand and profit will occur because of changing economic conditions, new and competitive products, pipeline dynamics, and so on, and the manager will have to maintain his tracking activities and even introduce new ones. However, by and large, he will concentrate his forecasting attention on these areas:

◻ Long- and short-term production planning.
◻ Setting standards to check the effectiveness of marketing strategies.
◻ Projections designed to aid profit planning.

He will also need a good tracking and warning system to identify significantly declining demand for the product (but hopefully that is a long way off).

To be sure, the manager will want margin and profit projection and long-range forecasts to assist planning at the corporate level. However, short- and medium-term sales forecasts are basic to these more elaborate undertakings, and we shall concentrate on sales forecasts.

Adequate tools at hand: In planning production and establishing marketing strategy for the short and medium term, the manager's first considerations are usually an accurate estimate of the present sales level and an accurate estimate of the rate at which this level is changing.

The forecaster thus is called on for two related contributions at this stage:

□ He should provide estimates of *trends* and *seasonals,* which obviously affect the sales level. Seasonals are particularly important for both overall production planning and inventory control. To do this, he needs to apply time series analysis and projection techniques—that is, *statistical* techniques.

□ He should relate the future sales level to factors that are more easily predictable, or have a "lead" relationship with sales, or both. To do this, he needs to build *causal models.*

The type of product under scrutiny is very important in selecting the techniques to be used.

For CORNING WARE® cookware, where the levels of the distribution system are organized in a relatively straightforward way, we use statistical methods to forecast shipments and field information to forecast changes in shipment rates. We are now in the process of incorporating special information— marketing strategies, economic forecasts, and so on—directly into the shipment forecasts. This is leading us in the direction of a causal forecasting model.

On the other hand, a component supplier may be able to forecast total sales with sufficient accuracy for broad-load production planning, but the pipeline environment may be so complex that his best recourse for short-term projections is to rely primarily on salesmen's estimates. We find this true, for example, in estimating the demand for TV glass by size and customer. In such cases, the best role for statistical methods is providing guides and checks for salemen's forecasts.

In general, however, at this point in the life cycle, sufficient time series data are available and enough causal relationships are known from direct experience and market studies so that the forecaster can indeed apply these two powerful sets of tools. Historical data for at least the last several years should be available, and he will use all of it, one way or another.

We might mention a common criticism at this point. People frequently object to using more than a few of the most recent data points (such as sales figures in the immediate past) for building projections, since, they say, the current situation is always so dynamic and conditions are changing so radically and quickly that historical data from further back in time have little or no value.

We think this point of view has little validity. A graph of several years' sales data, such as the one shown in *Part A* of *Exhibit VII,* gives an impression of a sales trend one could not possibly get if one were to look only at two or three of the latest data points.

In practice, we find, overall patterns tend to continue for a minimum of one or two quarters into the future, even when special conditions cause sales to fluctuate for one or two (monthly) periods in the immediate future.

For short-term forecasting for one to three months ahead, the effects of such factors as general economic conditions are minimal, and do *not* cause radical shifts in demand patterns. And because trends tend to change gradually rather than suddenly, statistical and other quantitative methods are excellent for short-term forecasting. Using one or only a few of the most recent data points will result in giving insufficient consideration of the nature of trends, cycles, and seasonal fluctuations in sales.

Granting the applicability of the techniques, we must go on to explain how the forecaster identifies precisely what is happening when sales fluctuate from one period to the next and how he forecasts such fluctuations.

A trend and a seasonal are obviously two quite different things, and they must be handled separately in forecasting.

Consider what would happen, for example, if a forecaster were merely to take an average of the most recent data points along a curve, combine this with other, similar average points stretching backward into the immediate past, and use these as the basis for a projection. He might easily overreact to random changes, mistaking them for evidence of a prevailing trend; he might mistake a change in the growth rate for a seasonal; and so on.

To avoid precisely this sort of error, the moving average technique, which is similar to the hypothetical one just described, uses data points in such a way that the effects of seasonals (and irregularities) are eliminated.

Furthermore, the executive needs accurate estimates of trends *and* accurate estimates of seasonality to plan broad-load production, to determine marketing efforts and allocations, and to maintain proper inventories—that is, inventories that are adequate to customer demand but are not excessively costly.

Before going any further, it might be well to illustrate what such sorting-out looks like. *Parts A, B,* and *C* of *Exhibit VII* show the initial decomposition of raw data for factory sales of color TV sets between 1965 and mid-1970. *Part A* presents the raw data curve. *Part B* shows the seasonal factors that are implicit in the raw data—quite a consistent pattern, although there is some variation from year to year. (In the next section we shall explain where this graph of the seasonals comes from.)

Part C shows the result of discounting the raw data curve by the seasonals of *Part B;* this is the so-called deseasonalized data curve. Next, in *Part D,* we have drawn the smoothest or "best" curve possible through the deseasonalized curve, thereby obtaining the *trend cycle.* (We might further note that

Exhibit VII. Data plots of factory sales of color TV sets

Part A. Raw data for factory sales of color TV sets
Sets (thousands)

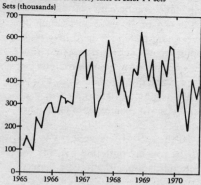

Part B. Seasonals for factory sales of color TV sets
Seasonal (Percent of average
monthly sales rate)

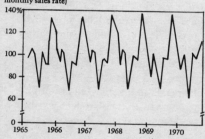

Part C. Factory sales of color TV sets (deseasonalized)
Sets (thousands)

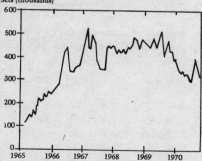

Part D. Final trend cycle of factory sales of color TV sets
Sets (thousands)

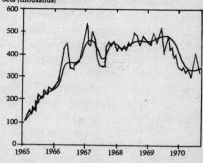

Part E. Changes in final trend cycle (growth rate)
of factory sales of color TV sets
Sets (thousands)

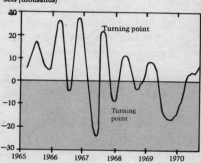

the differences between this trend-cycle line and the deseasonalized data curve represent the irregular or nonsystematic component that the forecaster must always tolerate and attempt to explain by other methods.)

In sum, then, the objective of the forecasting technique used here is to do the best possible job of sorting out trends and seasonalities. Unfortunately, most forecasting methods project by a smoothing process analogous to that of the moving average technique, or like that of the hypothetical technique we described at the beginning of this section, and separating trends and seasonals more precisely will require extra effort and cost.

Still, sorting-out approaches have proved themselves in practice. We can best explain the reasons for their success by roughly outlining the way we construct a sales forecast on the basis of trends, seasonals, and data derived from them. This is the method:

□ Graph the rate at which the trend is changing. For the illustration given in *Exhibit VII*, this graph is shown in *Part E*. This graph describes the successive ups and downs of the trend cycle shown in *Part D*.

□ Project this growth rate forward over the interval to be forecasted. Assuming we were forecasting back in mid-1970, we should be projecting into the summer months and possibly into the early fall.

□ Add this growth rate (whether positive or negative) to the present sales rate. This might be called the unseasonalized sales rate.

□ Project the seasonals of *Part B* for the period in question, and multiply the unseasonalized forecasted rate by these seasonals. The product will be the forecasted sales rate, which is what we desired.

In special cases where there are no seasonals to be considered, of course, this process is much simplified, and fewer data and simpler techniques may be adequate.

We have found that an analysis of the patterns of change in the growth rate gives us more accuracy in predicting turning points (and therefore changes from positive to negative growth, and vice versa) than when we use only the trend cycle.

The main advantage of considering growth change, in fact, is that it is frequently possible to predict earlier when a no-growth situation will occur. The graph of change in growth thus provides an excellent visual base for forecasting and for identifying the turning point as well.

X-11 technique: The reader will be curious to know how one breaks the seasonals out of raw sales data and exactly how one derives the change-in-growth curve from the trend line.

One of the best techniques we know for analyzing historical data in depth to determine seasonals, present sales rate, and growth is the X-11 Census Bureau Technique, which simultaneously removes seasonals from raw information and fits a trend-cycle line to the data. It is very comprehensive: at a cost of about $10, it provides detailed information on seasonals, trends, the accuracy of the seasonals and the trend cycle fit, and a number of other measures. The output includes plots of the trend cycle and the growth rate, which can concurrently be received on graphic displays on a time-shared terminal.

Although the X-11 was not originally developed as a forecasting method, it does establish a base from which good forecasts can be made. One should note, however, that there is some instability in the trend line for the most recent data points, since the X-11, like virtually all statistical techniques, uses some form of moving average. It has therefore proved of value to study the changes in growth pattern as each new growth point is obtained.

In particular, when recent data seem to reflect sharp growth or decline in sales or any other market anomaly, the forecaster should determine whether any special events occurred during the period under consideration —promotion, strikes, changes in the economy, and so on. The X-11 provides the basic instrumentation needed to evaluate the effects of such events.

Generally, even when growth patterns can be associated with specific events, the X-11 technique and other statistical methods do not give good results when forecasting beyond six months, because of the uncertainty or unpredictable nature of the events. For short-term forecasts of one to three months, the X-11 technique has proved reasonably accurate.

We have used it to provide sales estimates for each division for three periods into the future, as well as to determine changes in sales rates. We have compared our X-11 forecasts with forecasts developed by each of several divisions, where the divisions have used a variety of methods, some of which take into account salesmen's estimates and other special knowledge. The forecasts using the X-11 technique were based on statistical methods alone, and did not consider any special information.

The division forecasts had slightly *less* error than those provided by the X-11 method; however, the division forecasts have been found to be slightly biased on the optimistic side, whereas those provided by the X-11 method are unbiased. This suggested to us that a better job of forecasting could be done by combining special knowledge, the techniques of the division, and the X-11 method. This is actually being done now by some of the divisions, and their forecasting accuracy has improved in consequence.

The X-11 method has also been used to make sales projections for the immediate future to serve as a standard for evaluating various marketing strategies. This has been found to be especially effective for estimating the effects of price changes and promotions.

As we have indicated earlier, trend analysis is frequently used to project annual data for several years to determine what sales will be if the current trend continues. Regression analysis and statistical forecasts are sometimes used in this way—that is, to estimate what will happen if no significant changes are made. Then, if the result is not acceptable with respect to corporate objectives, the company can change its strategy.

Econometric models: Over a long period of time, changes in general economic conditions will account for a significant part of the change in a product's growth rate. Because economic forecasts are becoming more accurate and also because there are certain general "leading" economic forces that change before there are subsequent changes in specific industries, it is possible to improve the forecasts of businesses by including economic factors in the forecasting model.

However, the development of such a model, usually called an econometric model, requires sufficient data so that the correct relationships can be established.

During the rapid-growth state of color TV, we recognized that economic conditions would probably affect the sales rate significantly. However, the macroanalyses of black-and-white TV data we made in 1965 for the recessions in the late 1940's and early 1950's did not show any substantial economic effects at all; hence we did not have sufficient data to establish good econometric relationships for a color TV model. (A later investigation did establish definite losses in color TV sales in 1967 due to economic conditions.)

In 1969 Corning decided that a better method than the X-11 was definitely needed to predict turning points in retail sales for color TV six months to two years into the future. Statistical methods and salesmen's estimates cannot spot these turning points far enough in advance to assist decision making; for example, a production manager should have three to six months' warning of such changes if he is to maintain a stable work force.

Adequate data seemed to be available to build an econometric model, and analyses were therefore begun to develop such a model for both black-and-white and color TV sales. Our knowledge of seasonals, trends, and growth for these products formed a natural base for constructing the equations of the models.

The economic inputs for the model are primarily obtained from information generated by the Wharton Econometric Model, but other sources are also utilized.

Using data extending through 1968, the model did reasonably well in predicting the downturn in the fourth quarter of 1969 and, when 1969 data were also incorporated into the model, accurately estimated the magnitude of the drop in the first two quarters of 1970. Because of lead-lag relationships and the ready availability of economic forecasts for the factors in the model, the effects of the economy on sales can be estimated for as far as two years into the future.

In the steady-state phase, production and inventory control, group-item forecasts, and long-term demand estimates are particularly important. The interested reader will find a discussion of these topics on the reverse of the gatefold.

Finally, through the steady-state phase, it is useful to set up quarterly reviews where statistical tracking and warning charts and new information are brought forward. At these meetings, the decision to revise or update a model or forecast is weighed against various costs and the amount of forecasting error. In a highly volatile area, the review should occur as frequently as every month or period.

Forecasting in the Future

In concluding an article on forecasting, it is appropriate that we make a prediction about the techniques that will be used in the short- and long-term future.

As we have already said, it is not too difficult to forecast the immediate future, since long-term trends do not change overnight. Many of the techniques described are only in the early stages of application, but still we expect most of the techniques that will be used in the next five years to be the ones discussed here, perhaps in extended form.

The costs of using these techniques will be reduced significantly; this will enhance their implementation. We expect that computer time-sharing companies will offer access, at nominal cost, to input-output data banks, broken down into more business segments than are available today. The continuing declining trend in computer cost per computation, along with computational simplifications, will make techniques such as the Box-Jenkins method economically feasible, even for some inventory-control applications. Computer software packages for the statistical techniques and some general models will also become available at a nominal cost.

At the present time, most short-term forecasting uses only statistical methods, with little qualitative information. Where qualitative information is used, it is only used in an external way and is not directly incorporated into the computational routine. We predict a change to total forecasting systems, where several techniques are tied together, along with a systematic handling of qualitative information.

Econometric models will be utilized more extensively in the next five years, with most large companies developing and refining econometric models of their major businesses. Marketing simulation models for new products will also be developed for the larger-volume products, with tracking systems for updating the models and their parameters. Heuristic programming will provide a means of refining forecasting models.

While some companies have already developed their own input-output models in tandem with the government input-output data and statistical projections, it will be another five to ten years before input-output models are effectively used by most major corporations.

Within five years, however, we shall see extensive use of man-machine systems, where statistical, causal, and econometric models are programmed on computers, with man interacting frequently. As we gain confidence in such systems, so that there is less exception reporting, human intervention will decrease. Basically, computerized models will do the sophisticated computations, and man will serve more as a generator of ideas and a developer of systems. For example, man will study market dynamics and establish more complex relationships between the factor being forecast and those of the forecasting system.

Further out, consumer simulation models will become commonplace. The models will predict the behavior of the consumer and forecast his reactions to various marketing strategies such as pricing, promotions, new product introductions, and competitive actions. Probabilistic models will be used frequently in the forecasting process.

Finally, most computerized forecasting will relate to the analytical techniques described in this article. Computer applications will be mostly in established and stable product businesses. Although the forecasting techniques have thus far been used primarily for sales forecasting, they will be applied increasingly to forecasting margins, capital expenditures, and other important factors. This will free the forecaster to spend most of his time forecasting sales and profits of new products. Doubtless, new analytical techniques will be developed for new-product forecasting, but there will be a continuing problem, for at least 10 to 20 years and probably much longer, in accurately forecasting various new-product factors, such as sales, profitability, and length of life cycle.

Final Word

The decision maker can help the forecaster formulate the forecasting problem properly, and he will have more confidence in the forecasts provided to him and use them more effectively, if he understands the basic features and limitations of the techniques. The forecaster, for his part, must blend the techniques he uses with the knowledge and experience of the managers.

The need today, we believe, is not for better forecasting methods, but for better application of the techniques at hand.

Part V

Production and Operations

One way to think of management is as the art of measuring. A successful manager is one who knows, among other things, which yardsticks to use in his or her job, and how to use them appropriately.

There are four "yardsticks" in the five articles in this section that the manager may find useful in evaluating certain elements of his organization's production and operations functions. For the operating manager, the articles can serve as measures with which he can better determine which new methods and ideas can be profitably applied in his own situation and how he can go about implementing them. The articles can also help provide the general manager with insights into what key tasks confront those within these functions today, and how to integrate these tasks with the rest of the organization's strategy.

In the first article, "Manufacturing—Missing Link in Corporate Strategy," the yardstick presented attempts to measure manufacturing's potential to strengthen or weaken a company's competitive ability. In focusing on such imprecise measures of success as "efficiency," "low cost," or "productivity," top management too often overlooks that potential, the author asserts. He discusses the fundamental trade-offs inherent to the function that the manager must weigh in order to avoid such oversight.

The next two articles, "Production Planning and Control Integrated" and "Requirements Planning for Inventory Control," together present a yardstick by which the manager can take the measure of his organization's adaptation to modern technological practices. The first details how computer-based approaches can aid managers in solving such problems as unbalanced capacity, unrealistic sales forecasting, poor master and short-term scheduling, and inadequate inventory control. The second one takes a closer look at specific situations in which one such approach—requirements planning—provides for better parts management than do statistical methods such as "safety stocks," "reorder points," and "economic order quantities."

"Sweeping Changes in Distribution" covers new thinking and new ventures to provide a yardstick that marks an era in the redevelopment and restructuring of business logistics industries and services. The author predicts that further improvements in logistics will come about as a result of institutional changes *rather than as a result of technological changes as they have in the past.*

Finally, "Production-Line Approach to Service" illustrates how the yardstick used for products "in the factory" applies equally well for services "in the field." The author suggests that a production-type systemic orientation toward the efficient production of results must replace the antequated conception that service is simply something performed by individuals directly for other individuals. Only by measuring by this yardstick, he maintains, can meaningful improvements in quality and productivity be forthcoming for service industries.

16. Manufacturing—Missing Link in Corporate Strategy

Wickham Skinner

The thesis of this article is that manufacturing has too long been dominated by experts and specialists. For many years these were the industrial engineers; now they are the computer experts. As a result, top executives tend to avoid involvement in manufacturing policy making, manufacturing managers are ignorant of corporate strategy, and a function that could be a valuable asset and tool of corporate strategy becomes a liability instead. The author shows how top management can correct this situation by systematically linking up manufacturing with corporate strategy.

A company's manufacturing function typically is either a competitive weapon or a corporate millstone. It is seldom neutral. The connection between manufacturing and corporate success is rarely seen as more than the achievement of high efficiency and low costs. In fact, the connection is much more critical and much more sensitive. Few top managers are aware that what appear to be routine manufacturing decisions frequently come to limit the corporation's strategic options, binding it with facilities, equipment, personnel, and basic controls and policies to a noncompetitive posture which may take years to turn around.

Research I have conducted during the past few years reveals that top management unknowingly delegates a surprisingly large portion of basic policy decisions to lower levels in the manufacturing area. Generally, this abdication of responsibility comes about more through a lack of concern than by intention. And it is partly the reason that many manufacturing policies and procedures developed at lower levels reflect assumptions about corporate strategy which are incorrect or misconstrued.

Millstone Effect

When companies fail to recognize the relationship between manufacturing decisions and corporate strategy, they may become saddled with seriously noncompetitive production systems which are expensive and time-consuming to change. Here are several examples:

□ Company A entered the combination washer-dryer field after several competitors had failed to achieve successful entries into the field. Company A's executives believed their model would overcome the technical drawbacks which had hurt their competitors and held back the development of any substantial market. The manufacturing managers tooled the new unit on the usual conveyorized assembly line and giant stamping presses used for all company products.

When the washer-dryer failed in the market, the losses amounted to millions. The plant had been "efficient" in the sense that costs were low. But the tooling and production processes did not meet the demands of the marketplace.

□ Company B produced five kinds of electronic gear for five different groups of customers; the gear ranged from satellite controls to industrial controls and electronic components. In each market a different task was required of the production function. For instance, in the first market, extremely high reliability was demanded; in the second market, rapid introduction of a stream of new products was demanded; in the third market, low costs were of critical importance for competitive survival.

In spite of these highly diverse and contrasting tasks, production management elected to centralize manufacturing facilities in one plant in order to achieve "economies of scale." The result was a failure to achieve high reliability, economies of scale, or an ability to introduce new products quickly. What happened, in short, was that the demands placed on manufacturing by a competitive strategy were ignored by the production group in order to achieve economies of scale. This production group was obsessed with developing "a total system, fully computerized." The manufacturing program satisfied no single division, and the serious marketing problems which resulted choked company progress.

□ Company C produced plastic molding resins. A new plant under construction was to come on-stream in eight months, doubling production. In the meantine, the company had a much higher volume of orders than it could meet.

In a strategic sense, manufacturing's task was to maximize output to satisfy large, key customers. Yet the plant's production control system was set up—as it had been for years—to minimize costs. As a result, long runs were emphasized. While costs were low, many customers had to wait, and many key buyers were lost. Consequently, when the new plant came on-stream, it was forced to operate at a low volume.

The mistake of considering low costs and high efficiencies as the key manufacturing objective in each of these examples is typical of the over-simplified concept of "a good manufacturing operation." Such criteria frequently get companies into trouble, or at least do not aid in development of manufacturing into a competitive weapon. Manufacturing affects corporate strategy, and corporate strategy affects manufacturing. Even in an apparently routine operating area such as a production scheduling system, strategic considerations should outweigh technical and conventional industrial engineering factors invoked in the name of "productivity."

SHORTSIGHTED VIEWS

The fact is that manufacturing is seen by most top managers as requiring involved technical skills and a morass of petty daily decisions and details. It is seen by many young managers as the gateway to grubby routine, where days are filled with high pressure, packed with details, and limited to low-level decision making—all of which is out of the sight and minds of top-level executives. It is generally taught in graduate schools of business administration as a combination of industrial engineering (time study, plant layout, inventory theory, and so on) and quantitative analysis (linear programming, simulation, queuing theory, and the rest). In total, a manufacturing career is generally perceived as an all-consuming, technically oriented, hectic life that minimizes one's chances of ever reaching the top and maximizes the chances of being buried in minutiae.

In fact, these perceptions are not wholly inaccurate. It is the thesis of this article that the technically oriented concept of manufacturing is all too prevalent; and that it is largely responsible for the typically limited contribution manufacturing makes to a corporation's arsenal of competitive weapons, for manufacturing's failure to attract the top talent it needs and *should* have, and for its failure to attract more young managers with general management interests and broad abilities. In my opinion, manufacturing is generally perceived in the wrong way at the top, managed in the wrong way at the plant level, and taught in the wrong way in the business schools.

These are strong words, but change is needed, and I believe that only a more relevant concept of manufacturing can bring change. I see no sign whatsoever that we have found the means of solving the problems mentioned. The mathematically based "total systems" approaches to production management offer the promise of new and valuable concepts and techniques, but I doubt that these approaches will overcome the tendency of top management to remove itself from manufacturing. The years of development of quantitative techniques have left us each year with the promise of a "great new age" in production management that lies "just ahead." The promise never seems to be realized. Stories of computer and "total systems" fiascoes are available by the dozen; these failures are always expensive, and in almost every case management has delegated the work to experts.

I do not want to demean the promise—and, indeed, some present contributions—of the systems/computer approach. A few years ago I felt more sanguine about it. But, since then, close observation of the problems in U.S. industry has convinced me that the "answer" promised is inadequate. The approach cannot overcome the problems described until it does a far better job of linking manufacturing and corporate strategy. What is needed is some kind of integrative mechanism.

Pattern of Failure

An examination of top management perceptions of manufacturing has led me to some notions about basic causes of many production problems. In each of six industries I have studied, I have found top executives delegating excessive amounts of manufacturing policy to subordinates, avoiding involvement in most production matters, and failing to ask the right questions until their companies are in obvious trouble. This pattern seems to be due to a combination of two factors:

1. A sense of personal inadequacy, on the part of top executives, in managing production. (Often the feeling evolves from a tendency to regard the area as a technical or engineering specialty, or a mundane "nuts and bolts" segment of management.)

2. A lack of awareness among top executives that a production system inevitably involves trade-offs and compromises and so must be designed to perform a limited task well, with that task defined by corporate strategic objectives.

The first factor is, of course, dependent in part on the second, for the sense of inadequacy would not be felt if the strategic role of production were clearer. The second factor is the one we shall concentrate on in the remainder of this article.

Like a building, a vehicle, or a boat, a production system can be designed to do some things well, but always at the expense of other abilities. It appears to be the lack of recognition of these trade-offs and their effects on a corporation's ability to compete that leads top management to delegate often-critical decisions to lower, technically oriented staff levels, and to allow policy to be made through apparently unimportant operating decisions.

In the balance of this article I would like to . . .

—sketch out the relationships between production operations and corporate strategy;

—call attention to the existence of specific trade-offs in production system design;

—comment on the inadequacy of computer specialists to deal with these trade-offs;

—suggest a new way of looking at manufacturing which might enable the nontechnical manager to understand and manage the manufacturing area.

Strategic Implications

Frequently the interrelationship between production operations and corporate strategy is not easily grasped. The notion is simple enough—namely, that a company's competitive strategy at a given time places particular demands on its manufacturing function, and, conversely, that the company's manufacturing posture and operations should be specifically designed to fulfill the task demanded by strategic plans. What is more elusive is the set of cause-and-effect factors which determine the linkage between strategy and production operations.

Strategy is a set of plans and policies by which a company aims to gain advantages over its competitors. Generally a strategy includes plans for products and the marketing of these products to a particular set of customers. The marketing plans usually include specific approaches and steps to be followed in identifying potential customers, determining why, where, and when they buy, and learning how they can best be reached and convinced to purchase. The company must have an advantage, a particular appeal, a special push or pull created by its products, channels of distribution, advertising, price, packaging, availability, warranties, or other factors.

CONTRASTING DEMANDS

What is not always realized is that different marketing strategies and approaches to gaining a competitive advantage place different demands on the manufacturing arm of the company. For example, a furniture manufacturer's strategy for broad distribution of a limited, low-price line with wide consumer advertising might generally require:

☐ Decentralized finished-goods storage.
☐ Readily available merchandise.
☐ Rock-bottom costs.

The foregoing demands might in turn require:

☐ Relatively large lot sizes.
☐ Specialized facilities for woodworking and finishing.
☐ A large proportion of low- and medium-skilled workers in the work force.
☐ Concentration of manufacturing in a limited number of large-scale plants.

In contrast, a manufacturer of high-price, high-style furniture with more exclusive distribution would require an entirely different set of manufacturing policies. While higher prices and longer lead times would allow more leeway in the plant, this company would have to contend with the problems implicit in delivering high-quality furniture made of wood (which is a soft, dimensionally unstable material whose surface is expensive to finish and easy to damage), a high setup cost relative to running times in most wood-machining operations, and the need to make a large number of nonstandardized parts. While the first company must work with these problems too, they are more serious to the second company because its marketing strategy forces it to confront the problems head on. The latter's manufacturing policies will probably require:

☐ Many model and style changes.
☐ Production to order.
☐ Extremely reliable high quality.

These demands may in turn require:

☐ An organization that can get new models into production quickly.
☐ A production control group that can coordinate all activities so as to reduce lead times.
☐ Technically trained supervisors and technicians.

Consequently, the second company ought to have a strong manufacturing-methods engineering staff; simple, flexible tooling; and a well-trained, experienced work force.

In summary, the two manufacturers would need to develop very different policies, personnel, and operations if they were to be equally successful in carrying out their strategies.

IMPORTANT CHOICES

In the example described, there are marked contrasts in the two companies. Actually, even small and subtle differences in corporate strategies should be reflected in manufacturing policies. However, my research shows that few companies do in fact carefully and explicitly tailor their production systems to perform the tasks which are vital to corporate success.

Instead of focusing first on strategy, then moving to define the manufacturing task, and next turning to systems design in manufacturing policy, managements tend to employ a concept of production which is much less effective. Most top executives and production managers look at their production systems with the notion of "total productivity" or the equivalent, "efficiency." They seek a kind of blending of low costs, high quality, and acceptable customer service. The view prevails that a plant with reasonably modern equipment, up-to-date methods and procedures, a cooperative work force, a computerized information system, and an enlightened management will be a good plant and will perform efficiently.

But what is a "good plant"? What is "efficient performance"? And what should the computer be programmed to do? Should it minimize lead times or minimize inventories? A company cannot do both. Should the computer minimize direct labor or indirect labor? Again, the company cannot do both. Should investment in equipment be minimized—or should outside purchasing be held to a minimum? One could go on with such choices.

The reader may reply: "What management wants is a combination of both ingredients that results in the lowest *total* cost." But that answer, too, is insufficient. The "lowest total cost" answer leaves out the dimensions of time and customer satisfaction, which must usually be considered too. Because cost *and* time *and* customers are all involved, we have to conclude that what is a "good" plant for Company A may be a poor or mediocre plant for its competitor, Company B, which is in the same industry but pursues a different strategy.

The purpose of manufacturing is to serve the company—to meet its needs for survival, profit, and growth. Manufacturing is part of the strategic concept that relates a company's strengths and resources to opportunities in the market. Each strategy creates a unique manufacturing task. Manufacturing management's ability to meet that task is the key measure of its success.

Trade-offs in Design

It is curious that most top managements and production people do not state their yardsticks of success more precisely, and instead fall back on such measures as "efficiency," "low cost," and "productivity." My studies suggest that a key reason for this phenomenon is that very few executives realize the existence of trade-offs in designing and operating a production system.

Yet most managers will readily admit that there are compromises or trade-offs to be made in designing an airplane or a truck. In the case of an airplane, trade-offs would involve such matters as cruising speed, takeoff and landing distances, initial cost, maintenance, fuel consumption, passenger comfort, and cargo or passenger capacity. A given stage of technology defines limits as to what can be accomplished in these respects. For instance, no one today can design a 500-passenger plane that can land on a carrier and also break the sonic barrier.

Much the same thing is true of manufacturing. The variables of cost, time, quality, technological constraints, and customer satisfaction place limits on what management can do, force compromises, and demand an explicit recognition of a multitude of trade-offs and choices. Yet every-where I find plants which have inadvertently emphasized one yardstick at the expense of another, more important one. For example:

☐ An electronics manufacturer with dissatisfied customers hired a computer expert and placed manufacturing under a successful engineering design chief to make it a "total system." A year later its computer was spewing out an inch-thick volume of daily information. "We know the location of every part in the plant on any given day," boasted the produc-tion manager and his computer systems chief.

Nevertheless, customers were more dissatisfied than ever. Product managers hotly complained that delivery promises were regularly missed—and in almost every case they first heard about failures from their cus-tomers. The problem centered on the fact that computer information runs were organized by part numbers and operations. They were designed to facilitate machine scheduling and to aid shop foremen; they were not organized around end products, which would have facilitated customer service.

How had this come about? Largely, it seemed clear, because the manu-facturing managers had become absorbed in their own "systems approach"; the fascination of mechanized data handling had become an end in itself. As for top management, it had more or less abdicated responsibility. Because the company's growth and success had been based on engineering and because top management was R&D-oriented, policy-making executives saw production as a routine requiring a lower level of complexity and brainpower. Top management argued further that the company had production experts who were well paid and who should be able to do their jobs without bothering top-level people.

RECOGNIZING ALTERNATIVES

To develop the notion of important trade-off decisions in manufacturing, let us consider *Exhibit I*, which shows some examples.

In each decision area—plant and equipment, production planning and control, and so forth—top management needs to recognize the alternatives and become involved in the design of the production system. It needs to become involved to the extent that the alternative selected is appropriate to the manufacturing task determined by the corporate strategy.

Making such choices is, of course, an on-going rather than a once-a-year or once-a-decade task; decisions have to be made constantly in these trade-off areas. Indeed, the real crux of the problem seems to be how to ensure that the continuing process of decision making is not isolated from com-petitive and strategic facts, when many of the trade-off decisions do not at first appear to bear on company strategy. As long as a technical point

Decision area	Decision	Alternatives
PLANT AND EQUIPMENT	Span of process	Make or buy
	Plant size	One big plant or several smaller ones
	Plant location	Locate near markets or locate near materials
	Investment decisions	Invest mainly in buildings or equipment or inventories or research
	Choice of equipment	General-purpose or special-purpose equipment
	Kind of tooling	Temporary, minimum tooling or "production tooling"
PRODUCTION PLANNING AND CONTROL	Frequency of inventory taking	Few or many breaks in production for buffer stocks
	Inventory size	High inventory or a lower inventory
	Degree of inventory control	Control in great detail or in lesser detail
	What to control	Controls designed to minimize machine downtime or labor cost or time in process, or to maximize output of particular products or material usage
	Quality control	High reliability and quality or low costs
	Use of standards	Formal or informal or none at all
LABOR AND STAFFING	Job specialization	Highly specialized or not highly specialized
	Supervision	Technically trained first-line supervisors or nontechnically trained supervisors
	Wage system	Many job grades or few job grades; incentive wages or hourly wages
	Supervision	Close supervision or loose supervision
	Industrial engineers	Many or few such men
PRODUCT DESIGN/ ENGINEERING	Size of product line	Many customer specials or few specials or none at all
	Design stability	Frozen design or many engineering change orders
	Technological risk	Use of new processes unproved by competitors or follow-the-leader policy
	Engineering	Complete packaged design or design-as-you-go approach
	Use of manufacturing engineering	Few or many manufacturing engineers
ORGANIZATION AND MANAGEMENT	Kind of organization	Functional or product focus or geographical or other
	Executive use of time	High involvement in investment or production planning or cost control or quality control or other activities
	Degree of risk assumed	Decisions based on much or little information
	Use of staff	Large or small staff group
	Executive style	Much or little involvement in detail; authoritarian or nondirective style; much or little contact with organization

of view dominates manufacturing decisions, a degree of isolation from the realities of competition is inevitable. Unfortunately, as we shall see, the technical viewpoint is all too likely to prevail.

Technical Dominance

The similarity between today's emphasis on the technical experts—the computer specialist and the engineering-oriented production technician— and yesterday's emphasis on the efficiency expert—time-study man and industrial engineer—is impossible to escape. For 50 years, U.S. management relied on efficiency experts trained in the techniques of Frederick W. Taylor. Industrial engineers were kings of the factory. Their early approaches and attitudes were often conducive to industrial warfare, strikes, sabotage, and militant unions, but that was not realized then. Also not realized was that their technical emphasis often produced an inward orientation toward cost that ignored the customer, and an engineering point of view that gloried in tools, equipment, and gadgets rather than in markets and service. Most important, the cult of industrial engineering tended to make top executives technically disqualified from involvement in manufacturing decisions.

Since the turn of the century, this efficiency-centered orientation has dogged U.S. manufacturing. It has created that image of "nuts and bolts," of greasy, dirty, detail jobs in manufacturing. It has dominated "production" courses in most graduate schools of business administration. It has alienated young people with broad management educations from manufacturing careers. It has "buffaloed" top managers.

Several months ago I was asked by a group of industrial engineers to offer an opinion as to why so few industrial engineers were moving up to the top of their companies. My answer was that perhaps a technical point of view cut them off from top management, just as the jargon and hocus-pocus of manufacturing often kept top management from understanding the factory. In their isolation, they could gain only a severely limited sense of market needs and of corporate competitive strategy.

ENTER THE COMPUTER EXPERT

Today the industrial engineer is declining in importance in many companies. But a new technical expert, the computer specialist, is taking his place. I use the term "computer specialist" to refer to individuals who specialize in computer systems design and programming.

I do not deny, of course, that computer specialists have a very important job to do. I do object, however, to any notion that computer specialists have more of a top management view than was held by their predecessors, the industrial engineers. In my experience, the typical computer expert has been forced to master a complex and all-consuming technology, a fact which frequently makes him parochial rather than catholic in his views. Because he is so preoccupied with the detail of a total system, it is necessary for someone in top management to give him objectives and policy guidance. In his choice of trade-offs and compromises for his computer system, he needs to be instructed and not left to his own devices. Or, stated differently, he needs to see the entire corporation as a system, not just one corner of it—i.e., the manufacturing plant.

Too often this is not happening. The computer is a nightmare to many top managers because they have let it and its devotees get out of hand. They have let technical experts continue to dominate; the failure of top management truly to manage production goes on.

How *can* top management begin to manage manufacturing instead of turning it over to technicians who, through no fault of their own, are absorbed in their own arts and crafts? How can U.S. production management be helped to cope with the rising pressures of new markets, more rapid product changes, new technologies, larger and riskier equipment decisions, and the swarm of problems we face in industry today? Let us look at some answers.

Better Decision Making

The answers I would like to suggest are not panaceas, nor are they intended to be comprehensive. Indeed, no one can answer all the questions and problems described with one nice formula or point of view. But surely we can improve on the notion that production systems need only be "productive and efficient." Top management can manage manufacturing if it will engage in the making of manufacturing policy, rather than considering it a kind of fifth, independent estate beyond the pale of control.

The place to start, I believe, is with the acceptance of a theory of manufacturing which begins with the concept that in any system design there are significant trade-offs (as shown in *Exhibit I*) which must be explicitly decided on.

DETERMINING POLICY

Executives will also find it helpful to think of manufacturing policy determination as an orderly process or sequence of steps. *Exhibit II* is a schematic portrayal of such a process. It shows that manufacturing policy must stem from corporate strategy, and that the process of determining

Exhibit II. The process of manufacturing policy determination

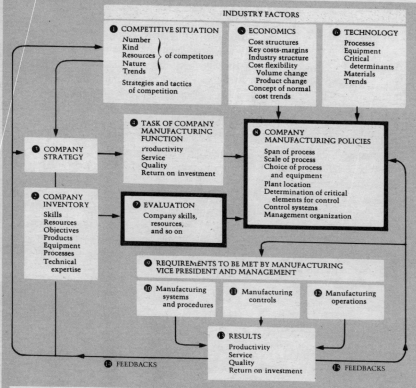

INDUSTRY FACTORS

① COMPETITIVE SITUATION
Number
Kind
Resources } of competitors
Nature
Trends

Strategies and tactics
of competition

② ECONOMICS
Cost structures
Key costs-margins
Industry structure
Cost flexibility
Volume change
Product change
Concept of normal
cost trends

③ TECHNOLOGY
Processes
Equipment
Critical
determinants
Materials
Trends

**④ TASK OF COMPANY
MANUFACTURING
FUNCTION**
Productivity
Service
Quality
Return on investment

**③ COMPANY
STRATEGY**

**② COMPANY
INVENTORY**
Skills
Resources
Objectives
Products
Equipment
Processes
Technical
expertise

⑦ EVALUATION
Company skills,
resources,
and so on

**⑧ COMPANY
MANUFACTURING POLICIES**
Span of process
Scale of process
Choice of process
and equipment
Plant location
Determination of critical
elements for control
Control systems
Management organization

**⑨ REQUIREMENTS TO BE MET BY MANUFACTURING
VICE PRESIDENT AND MANAGEMENT**

**⑩ Manufacturing
systems
and procedures**

**⑪ Manufacturing
controls**

**⑫ Manufacturing
operations**

⑬ RESULTS
Productivity
Service
Quality
Return on investment

⑭ FEEDBACKS

⑮ FEEDBACKS

Key

1. What the others are doing

2. What we have got or can get to compete with

3. How we can compete

4. What we must accomplish in manufacturing in order
to compete

5. Economic constraints and opportunities common to
the industry

6. Constraints and opportunities common to the technology

7. Our resources evaluated

8. How we should set ourselves up to match resources,
economics, and technology to meet the tasks required
by our competitive strategy

9. The implementation requirements of our
manufacturing policies

10. Basic systems in manufacturing (e.g., production
planning, use of inventories, use of standards, and
wage systems)

11. Controls of cost, quality, flows, inventory, and time

12. Selection of operations or ingredients critical to success
(e.g., labor skills, equipment utilization, and yields)

13. How we are performing

14. Changes in what we have got, effects on competitive
situation, and review of strategy

15. Analysis and review of manufacturing operations and
policies

322

A. Economics of the industry

Labor, burden, material, depreciation costs
Flexibility of production to meet changes in volume
Return on investment, prices, margins
Number and location of plants
Critical control variables
Critical functions (e.g., maintenance, production control, personnel)
Typical financial structures
Typical costs and cost relationships
Typical operating problems
Barriers to entry
Pricing practices
"Maturity" of industry products, markets, production practices, and so on
Importance of economies of scale
Importance of integrated capacities of corporations
Importance of having a certain balance of different types of equipment
Ideal balances of equipment capacities
Nature and type of production control
Government influences

B. Technology of the industry

Rate of technological change
Scale of processes
Span of processes
Degree of mechanization
Technological sophistication
Time requirements for making changes

---

this policy is the means by which top management can actually manage production. Use of this process can end manufacturing isolation and tie top management and manufacturing together. The sequence is simple but vital:

□ It begins with an analysis of the competitive situation, of how rival companies are competing in terms of product, markets, policies, and channels of distribution. Management examines the number and kind of competitors and the opportunities open to its company.

□ Next comes a critical appraisal of the company's skills and resources and of its present facilities and approaches.

□ The third step is the formulation of company strategy: How is the company to compete successfully, combine its strengths with market opportunities, and define niches in the markets where it can gain advantages?

□ The fourth step is the point where many top executives cut off their thinking. It is important for them to define the implications or "so-what" effects of company strategy in terms of specific manufacturing tasks. For example, they should ask: "If we are to compete with an X product of Y price for Z customers using certain distribution channels and forms of advertising, what will be demanded of manufacturing in terms of costs, deliveries, lead times, quality levels, and reliability?" These demands should be precisely defined.

□ The fifth and sixth steps are to study the constraints or limitations imposed by the economics and the technology of the industry. These factors are generally common to all competitors. An explicit recognition of them is a prerequisite to a genuine understanding of the manufacturing problems and opportunities. These are facts that a nontechnical manager can develop, study, understand, and put to work. *Exhibit III* contains sample lists of topics for the manager to use in doing his homework.

□ The seventh and eighth steps are the key ones for integrating and synthesizing all the prior ones into a broad manufacturing policy. The question for management is: "Given the facts of the economics and the technology of the industry, how do we set ourselves up to meet the specific manufacturing tasks posed by our particular competitive strategy?" Management must decide what it is going to make and what it will buy; how many plants to have, how big they should be, and where to place them; what processes and equipment to buy; what the key elements are which need to be controlled and how they can be controlled; and what kind of management organization would be most appropriate.

□ Next come the steps of working out programs of implementation, controls, performance measures, and review procedures (see Steps 9-15 in *Exhibit II*).

Conclusion

The process just described is, in my observation, quite different from the usual process of manufacturing management. Conventionally, manufacturing has been managed from the bottom up. The classical process of the age of mass production is to select an operation, break it down into its elements, analyze and improve each element, and put it back together. This approach was contributed years ago by Frederick W. Taylor and other industrial engineers who followed in his footsteps.

What I am suggesting is an entirely different approach, one adapted far better to the current era of more products, shorter runs, vastly accelerated product changes, and increased marketing competition. I am suggesting a kind of "top-down" manufacturing. This approach starts with the company and its competitive strategy; its goal is to define manufacturing policy. Its presumption is that only when basic manufacturing policies are defined can the technical experts, industrial and manufacturing engineers, labor relations specialists, and computer experts have the necessary guidance to do their work.

With its focus on corporate strategy and the manufacturing task, the top-down approach can give top management both its entrée to manufacturing and the concepts it needs to take the initiative and truly manage this function. When this is done, executives previously unfamiliar with manufacturing are likely to find it an exciting activity. The company will have an important addition to its arsenal of competitive weapons.

17. Production Planning and Control Integrated

William K. Holstein

Although much has been written about the individual segments of production planning and control systems, little has appeared in the literature to help practitioners develop an integrated view of the whole process. Many complaints about department overloads or poor delivery performances—particularly in fabrication and assembly operations—focus on scheduling or control. Actually, the basic cause may be unbalanced capacity or an unrealistic sales commitment made months previously. Thus managers must not only look at decision making at all levels, but must also recognize that good short-term performances result from an integrated set of decisions made over a long time span.

□ Where did that huge pile of work in the turret lathe department come from?

□ Why can't we get the Ajax Bearing job done before next week?

□ Should we accept such a large order for delivery in eight weeks?

□ We're up to our armpits in castings on the shop floor. What can be done to reduce this congestion?

□ Why in the devil are we still working overtime in the assembly area?

These questions are representative of real and pressing questions that many production managers face. They are also symptomatic of basic management problems in running numerous production operations.

In this article I shall discuss the contributions that modern, computer-based production planning and control systems can make to aid in the solution of these kinds of problems. I am particularly interested in identifying and tying together the various parts of a production planning and control system, and in so doing I shall focus on tasks to be fulfilled rather than on detailed methods. The systems I shall discuss are applicable to a broad range of industries, but apply most directly to fabrication and assembly operations that make a large number of parts in relatively small lots either for assembly into finished products or for sale to outside customers.

326

Much has been written about individual segments of production planning and control systems and the specific analytical tools and techniques for handling these separate parts. However, little has been done to help the practitioner use the many tools and techniques that are applicable to his situation in such a way that they relate to one another. Managers are frequently heard to complain about department overloads or poor delivery performances and to blame these on "poor scheduling" or "poor control." The real cause, however, may be unbalanced capacity or an unrealistic sales commitment that was made months ago.

This article is designed, therefore, to help the manager relate the various parts of production planning and control, and to develop an integrated view of the whole process. I shall present the parts in a sequence that begins with long-term planning and ends with day-to-day control of shop floor activity, using exhibits to clarify the individual parts and the way they relate to one another. I shall also cite examples of companies that have made excellent progress on one specific part of a production planning and control system and those that have been successful in tying together two or more of the parts. All of the examples are based on actual situations.

Toward Better Control

Webster's dictionary definition of a system includes "a regularly interacting or interdependent group of items forming a unified whole." The items or parts in a production planning and control system fit together in a time dimension and interact in a certain way. Long-term strategic plans that commit the company to a configuration of manpower, skills, plant, and equipment are based on very crude information and analysis. Moreover, these plans constrain the development of more complete, detailed plans closer to actual production dates. Long-term plans are made by high-level management, and, as the time span shortens and the time of actual production approaches, decision making is passed down to lower-level managers. Within the guide-lines formed by long-term plans, tactical control must be exercised over the "uncontrollable" variation in product mix and productivity in the short term.

In the very short term this control involves putting men in the right places, working on the right jobs, and regulating inventory levels. The criteria against which management's production planning and control performance is measured include inventory investment, labor cost, manufacturing cycle time (time to get work through the shop), equipment utilization, and meeting delivery deadlines.

In my view, the most important task in designing any production planning and control system which will measure up well against these criteria is to ensure that the plans and guidelines from higher levels guide, but do not unduly restrict, decision making at lower levels. Flexibility to react to new information and significant deviations from higher-level plans must be built into the system at all levels. Also, feedback information on actual conditions and performance must flow upward through the system to ensure that long-term plans are based on a realistic assessment of the production organization's ability to produce.

Production managers usually do not see their job roles in these clear, general terms. Since the "moment of truth"—that is, when poor performance becomes obvious—occurs at the time of actual production, there is a tendency to find fault in the shortest time dimension and thus focus largely on problems at the lowest level. Many production managers spend their time in a continuous, and at times frantic, search for information. In the face of a stream of demanding problems calling for immediate attention and decisions, and because of the sometimes chaotic nature of work flow and clerical decision making on the shop floor, production managers often find themselves chained to an endless sequence of routine decision making.

The consequence is little time to think about next week's or next month's possible problems and to lay plans for solving those problems. Nor is there time to evaluate recent performance and to seek ways of improving it. Despite the fact that managers often spend a great deal of time in the short term, because of the tremendous number of jobs in process, they still must delegate many seemingly small, detailed decisions to their first-line supervisors, clerical assistants, or even to the workers themselves. Management thus loses control over decisions which, taken together, may have a great impact on how efficiently the plant is run.

But things can be much better. Recently, many production managers have changed the way they manage, utilizing new systems for production planning and control. New systems do not eliminate all the crises, but they do point the way toward better control with less management involvement at the detail level. Thus they are making it possible for management to plan, redesign, and execute in a more rational manner.

Long-Term Capacity Planning

Plant facilities, equipment, skilled labor, and working capital to support inventory investments usually cannot be made available to production managers on short notice. Consequently, most organizations must be concerned with laying long-term plans for future capacities. In a sense, long-term planning is the starting point for production planning and control; thus it is the logical starting point for our consideration of production planning and control systems.

FORECASTS OF FUTURE DEMAND

The production organization competes with engineering and marketing for the company's limited resources, so production plans must be developed, refined, and defended. The long lead times on new construction and equipment acquisition require that some major expansion plans be developed years in advance of actual installation. Analyses of future market conditions and forecasts of future demands thus become important inputs in long-term planning. Even in make-to-order shops where no formal forecasts of future demands are developed, top management's collective hunch about the state of the economy and its impact on the company's future business is a vital ingredient in plans for the future. In some cases the forecasted demand will exceed existing production capacity. When this occurs, sales forecasts must be predicated on capacity plans.

Generation of long-term forecasts of demand, sales, and economic activity is often the responsibility of marketing. The approach utilized by one major U.S. appliance manufacturing company provides a case illustration:

□ The marketing research manager spends two or three days a month reviewing the economic indicators that might aid him in projecting cyclical turning points, predicting the economic climate likely to prevail during the forecast period, and factoring in industry information on inventories, product innovations, and so on, to yield a forecast of industry sales. His forecast is then compared and reconciled with the forecast developed by a senior marketing manager who generates company sales forecasts from detailed company information on consumer surveys; product, marketing, and pricing plans; and estimates of competitors' activities.

As another example of such forecasting, a large food products company is obtaining excellent results with a computer model which generates forecasts for grocery product sales:

□ Forecasts are developed that show expected sales by regions for existing products and new products not yet on the market. As the time period covered by the forecasts approaches, more and more detail is added.

For instance, the program used to generate quarterly forecasts contains information about planned advertising promotions and seasonal consumer habits. The computer-generated forecasts are carefully scrutinized by marketing managers and production planners, who may revise them to reflect such things as expected price trends, or perhaps a conviction that a given product will have a particularly strong regional appeal.

Subsequent computer runs reorganize the revised forecasts to provide a breakdown of sales by warehouse territories. These warehouse territory forecasts form the basis of comprehensive production planning for the company's manufacturing plants, pointing up situations where additional capacity will be needed in the future.

While forecasts come in many varieties (e.g., some cover different time periods, others contain different levels of detail), they are used by manufacturing mainly in setting future capacities. Examples of long-term capacity decisions based on forecasts are plant expansion, equipment acquisition, large work force additions, and major changes in inventory investment. (Inventory is included here, since it can be viewed as comprising stored capacity. A part on the shelf represents so many hours of capacity from a past period and eliminates the need for holding the same number of hours ready to serve a future demand.)

CONTINUAL ADJUSTMENT

Given forecasts of future demand, planning of capacity is not a one-shot problem that calls for one decision per year, but, rather, a problem that calls for constant review, fiddling, and adjusting. A well-designed system will provide many buffers to soften the impact of variations in demand, but even the best buffered systems will require basic adjustment from time to time through the purchase of plant and equipment, changes in the size of the work force, and major changes in inventory investment.

For a given company, a review of its recent history and current forecasts can often provide the guidelines for future action. A shop that has been choked with work for several months, which is having increasing difficulties meeting delivery deadlines, but nevertheless still has good labor efficiencies and control procedures, probably needs a boost in capacity. Well-organized information from a production planning and control system can provide a clue as to where the capacity is most needed, and the data can even aid in analyzing the effectiveness of alternative courses of action for providing capacity.

A large Connecticut company keeps details on its purchasing requirements and shop loads as far as three years ahead. This information enables management to consider carefully the long-range planning of inventory investment as well as production capacity. The use of shop load forecasts for inventory planning is an excellent example of what I referred to

Exhibit I. *Information flows for long-term capacity planning*

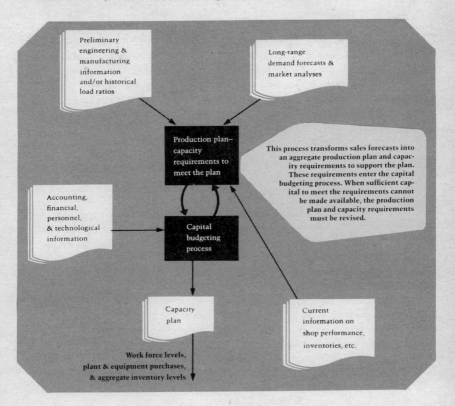

earlier as fitting together the parts of a production planning and control system.

Inventory control, when considered as a separate function, deals largely with individual item levels, order quantities, safety stocks, reorder points, and so forth. Yet one of the most important aspects of inventory management concerns the control of aggregate investment in all finished goods, subassemblies, work in process, and raw materials. The manager who understands the relationship of aggregate inventory investment to capacity, and who also has access to meaningful information on forecasted capacity requirements, can do a more effective capacity planning job than the manager who views the task as unrelated to other parts of the system.

The information flows in the capacity planning process are shown in *Exhibit I.* Capacity planning is a high-level, long-term planning activity which involves not only production managers, but also marketing, financial, and engineering managers. The element labeled "Production plan—

capacity requirements to meet the plan" is the heart of this process of (a) developing long-term production plans on the basis of demand forecasts, and (b) determining the capacity required to support the plans.

At present, this task is normally not performed by a computer, but the computer can provide some of the input information. The general problem of capacity planning has attracted researchers working at the theoretical level, and it seems likely that within a few years computer-oriented approaches will be available for many practical situations.

The next section concerns the development of rough production plans from sales forecasts and capacity plans.

Master Scheduling

This is the activity that determines the overall production plan for the next several months. After forecasts of future sales have been given and capacity and aggregate inventory levels have been pretty well fixed, master scheduling assigns productive capacity to individual end products or customer orders. Space terminology provides an analogy. A space rocket, if it is to hit the moon, must be launched within a "window" of a few hours and miles per hour. The limits on the window at launching are much rougher than they are at the other end, when the rocket nears the moon; if the launch falls outside the window, the target will be missed.

Similarly, master scheduling is done within coarse limits, but the objective is to ensure that the actual load in the shop two or three months hence will fall within rather narrow limits. Shop load is usually expressed in hours per time period, but the limits I am referring to have an added dimension. An example should help to clarify this concept.

In a two-machine shop that works a regular 40-hour week, the optimum load scheduled for a given week should be 80 machine-hours of work. If more than 80 machine-hours of work are scheduled, overtime can be used, or some of the current week's work can be pushed ahead into the following week. If less than 80 machine-hours of work are scheduled, some work can be pulled back from the next week's schedule to fill up the currently available capacity. Importantly, since master scheduling is done considerably ahead of the time of production, the actual load in the shop will not fit the shop's capacity exactly, and some "push-ahead" or "pull-back" will inevitably exist.

If, on the one hand, considerable push-ahead is required because the master schedule calls for more production in a given time period than the shop is able to produce, work in process will build up, most jobs will fall behind schedule, and almost all work in the shop will become "rush" or high priority. On the other hand, if the shop is not scheduled to capacity, pull-back will result in some jobs being completed ahead of schedule and may result in subsequent unused capacity.

Thus the lower limit on a master schedule should be a load which in hours of work and delivery date requirements will keep the shop's capacity efficiently utilized on current jobs that are neither far ahead nor behind schedule. The upper limit should be the highest load in hours and the tightest load in delivery requirements that can be handled by the shop and still allow for the inevitable rush job from a highly regarded customer, the last minute engineering change or rerun because of scrap losses, and the other occurrences which cannot be predicted in advance.

ESTIMATING SHOP LOADS

The key to successful master scheduling lies in the ability to forecast the lead times that will translate existing or prospective orders into an approximate shop load and delivery schedule. Often this is done by management intuition based, for example, on the knowledge that the shop cannot produce more than 20 model A machines per month, or that the shop load generated by a model B machine is approximately equal to the load created by 2 model A's. Intuitive planning is adequate for many situations, but the computer is making possible more sophisticated approaches.

Existing shop loads, or the forecasted load for orders already on the books, can often be a helpful input for determining the lead times required for master scheduling. The computer's ability to store a tremendous amount of detailed information in many instances means that approximate measures of aggregate shop load can be replaced with more detailed estimates of department, work center, or even machine load. To illustrate:

□ A Midwestern manufacturer of metalworking presses has a program which compiles—from the master schedule for finished presses—weekly estimates of the total load in each work center that will be contributed by the individual component parts. This load information gives management a "20-week peek into the future, an ample length of time for problem solving." With such an advance notice, not only can future master schedules be planned on the basis of recent actual performance, but potential capacity bottlenecks can be spotted and avoided through subcontracting or other capacity adjustments.

□ To assist in developing master schedules, a manufacturer of complex electronic and mechanical measuring equipment has a computer program that converts sales information on new or proposed orders into shop load long before detailed manufacturing information is available. The program is the result of a careful statistical analysis of the shop load contributed per sales dollar by various product classes. While not 100% reliable in predicting the load consequences of a given order, this program is of great

Exhibit II. Information flows for master scheduling

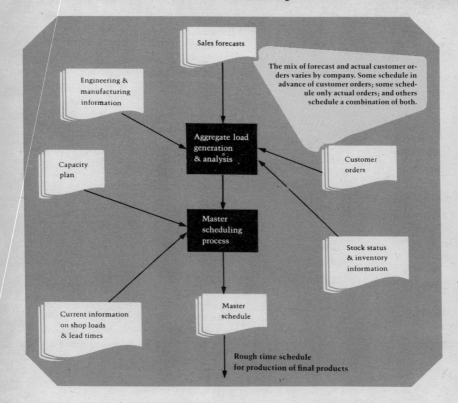

value in narrowing the limits on master scheduling and in making better estimates of the actual load hours and tightness in delivery times that the shop will encounter.

Master scheduling is graphically portrayed in *Exhibit II* as a two-step process. Sales forecasts and orders already on hand are first broken down into approximate shop loads, and then compared with the capacity plan and current shop information. The feedback information shown coming up from lower levels is a vital input to master scheduling.

One illustration of the importance of this information is its application in modifying the standard lead times used to convert orders into shop load. Lead times vary directly with shop loads. Thus, on the one hand, a master scheduling system that overlooks actual shop loads and simply uses standard lead times may make commitments which exceed the shop's capacity to produce. On the other hand, the increasing of lead times when shop loads go up and no capacity adjustments are made may cause total manufacturing cycle times to rise beyond the point where the company can compete effectively. Here, again, we see a relationship between two elements of a system that calls for careful managment consideration.

Inventory Control

Thus far inventories have been mentioned several times, and this is as it should be. Inventory control is not a separate entity but, rather, a pervasive factor that runs throughout any production planning and control system. A common system for the control of item inventories involves ordering replenishments in economic lots calculated according to one of a number of well-known "square root" formulas.[1] The lot is ordered when the stock on hand reaches a previously determined reorder point based both on estimates of the lead time required to fill the replenishment order and on the expected variability in demand during the lead time.

EOQ-REORDER POINT SYSTEM . . .

Not long ago, I had a conversation with a machine tool company manager who said, "If we are in error on the economic order quantity [EOQ] figure, we are in no great trouble; but, if we are in error on our reorder point, we can be in serious difficulty. We'll run out of parts needed to meet our assembly schedule, or, equally bad, we will be carrying an unnecessary inventory of parts."

Unfortunately, because the reorder point is directly related to what is going on in the shop, it is difficult to get straight. A typical development occurs at a time of sharply rising sales, when stock items hit their reorder points sooner than normal, resulting in an increased load on the shop. As shop load rises, lead times go up. Longer lead times, in turn, yield higher reorder points that trigger replenishment orders still faster. If all such orders are allowed to get onto the shop floor, a spiraling situation can develop where nothing gets through the shop on time. When sales drop, the reverse spiral is just as bad, or even worse, to deal with.

. . . VS. TIME-PHASED REQUIREMENTS

An alternative to the EOQ-reorder point system is time-phased requirements planning; this ties the control of piece parts and subassemblies to the assembly schedule of final products. With this system, parts can be manufactured in economic lots; but the timing of parts orders is based on

1. See, for example, John F. Magee, "Guides to Inventory Policy: I. Functions and Lot Sizes," HBR January-February 1956, p. 49.

Exhibit III. Example of time-phased requirements planning

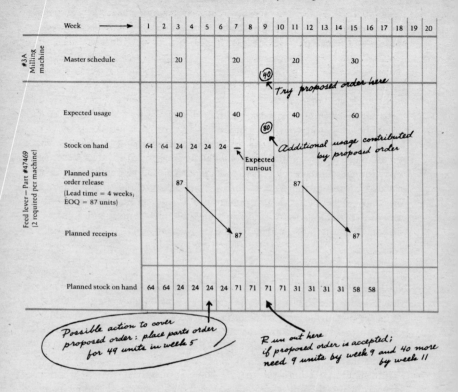

a date that is exploded back from the date of the final product assembly, rather than on a reorder point.

In the simplest version of time-phased requirements planning, a parts order is placed a standard lead time ahead of the time when assembly is expected to deplete the stock on hand. As shown in *Exhibit III*, the current supply of part #47469 is expected to run out during week 7 if no new replenishment orders are placed for the part. To prevent this stock-out and still allow the standard 4-week lead time for parts manufacturing, an order must be placed during week 3. This replenishment order for an economic lot of 87 units, along with a similar order during week 11, is shown in the exhibit.

Exhibit III also illustrates what can be accomplished when systems that support requirements planning, such as a bill-of-material processor and an inventory record system, are automated. The circled figures show how the system could handle the question: "What action is necessary if we accept an order for 40 #3A milling machines to be delivered in week 9?" Working through the bill of material for these milling machines, the system could identify all the parts required, check on-hand and on-order inventory status, and determine what action would be necessary to have the parts ready in time.

The action to handle the addition of the proposed order is triggered by an expected shortage of part #47469 in week 9. To cover this shortage, a parts order would have to be placed in week 5. More sophisticated logic could explore other alternatives, such as increasing the parts order placed in week 3, or moving the assembly lot in week 11 to a later week.

The automated bill-of-material handling also makes possible time-phased requirements planning by assembly level. Here, the due date for each component part of the final assembly is not the same, but reflects the actual time during the assembly and subassembly process when the part will be required. Thus a component part for a low-level (early in the assembly sequence) subassembly would be noted as being required several weeks ahead of an attachment to be installed late in the assembly process.

REPLENISHMENT PROBLEM

A major difficulty with any inventory system is the variability of the load placed on the production facility. Replenishment orders—whether determined by assembly schedules, reorder points, or other rules—tend to arrive without regard to the shop's capacity to handle them. Because these orders represent shop load, the inventory system is linked directly to master scheduling and lower-level systems. Although most companies attempt to provide some protection against variable demand by providing buffer inventories and safety factors in lead time estimates, a more direct approach which ties inventory control to master scheduling and short-term scheduling can greatly assist in smoothing out the load caused by inventory replenishment orders.

An example of such an approach, which squarely faces the problem of tying together the control of item inventories and shop loads, is that developed by a Wisconsin industrial goods manufacturer:

□ Working from forecasts, shop load reports, and other information, company managers develop a monthly manpower plan that extends six months into the future. The manpower plan sets the basic capacity, while detailed machine load reports provide information for short-term capacity adjustments through personnel shifts and overtime. When the inventory system does not generate enough orders to maintain production at the planned rate, the company's computer can identify jobs which will bring the plant's load up to desired levels and still maintain a well-balanced inventory.

This is a good example of how the computer has helped with shop load planning for the intermediate time range between long-term capacity planning and short-term scheduling. Later we will see how the computer, by focusing attention on critical jobs on the shop floor, can also provide help during actual production.

Short-term Scheduling

As we have seen, master scheduling entails an aggregate plan which ensures that the demands on the shop's capacity will be reasonable. I use the phrase "short-term scheduling" to describe the activity which develops the detailed plans necessary to meet the delivery commitments represented by the master schedule.

The result of short-term scheduling is a set start and completion time for every component part for final products. If, for example, a particular lot of 20 milling machines is to be assembled during week 15, 40 feed levers may be scheduled to start in the shop at the beginning of week 11 and to be completed by the end of week 14. Parts for stock would be scheduled for completion by the time the current supply is expected to be depleted.

One other important output of short-term scheduling is an estimate of the load for the next few weeks or months for each machine or work center in the shop. Indeed, *machine loading* is a term often used for the activity I call short-term scheduling. Machine load estimates can be used to assist management in (a) assigning men to machines to balance the capacities of various work centers, (b) spotting and reducing bottlenecks in work flow, and (c) planning activities on the shop floor.

Short-term scheduling is an activity that is very much like master scheduling, but it has a shorter time horizon and involves considerably more detail. The distinction between master and short-term scheduling is academic in some companies, especially those specializing in made-to-order items or products with short manufacturing cycle times. Also, the computer's ability to make large quantities of detailed information easily available tends to encourage the use of detailed information at higher levels and thus blur the distinction even more.

The foregoing discussion brings us to a level in the production planning process where the information required is often extensive and detailed. The data generally include such things as a bill of materials, showing all component parts and assembly sequences; routings or operations sheets for all parts to be manufactured; lists of raw materials, tools, and fixtures required, as well as information on their availability and their condition; estimates of existing loads already scheduled against machines or work centers in the shop, or estimates of expected lead times or delays to be encountered as work moves through the shop; and estimates of the machining and setup time for each operation on each part.

The concern here is with developing a schedule for each component part and subassembly so that (a) all raw materials arrive on time, and (b) all parts and subassemblies arrive at the appropriate assembly or stock area in time to ensure that the final product will be ready for shipment on schedule. Short-term scheduling is usually accomplished by one of two basic approaches—capacity loading and loading to infinite capacity. I will discuss each of these approaches in turn.

CAPACITY LOADING . . .

This fundamental approach begins with the specification of capacity for the scheduling period. Usually, capacity loading involves stating the number of machines to be manned in each department or work center and the number of shifts to be worked. (At a later date, individual decisions on overtime and so on may change these capacities slightly, but a reasonable estimate is good enough to start.) In the process of capacity loading, component parts requirements are exploded from a bill of materials, and the due date for each part is determined by backdating from the master schedule's due date for the final product.

After a due date has been assigned for each part, standard times for the individual manufacturing operations on the components are scheduled (loaded) in the appropriate work centers, starting with the last operation and allowing for normal material movement and delays. As each job's machining and setup time is added to a particular work center's load, a check is made to ensure that the addition of that job does not cause the total load to exceed the capacity of the work center. If the capacity is exceeded, the job is moved to another time period. If no available capacity can be found within the time required to get the job done on time, either the due date must be changed or capacity adjustments must be made through subcontracting or overtime.

While this capacity loading approach is simple to describe, it is in fact quite difficult to implement. What about the important job that cannot find room because other less important jobs have been loaded ahead of it? How do you shift the loads around when capacity is exceeded? A point to keep in mind is that it is not necessarily the last job (the cause of the overload) which should be shifted to another week.

Several companies have developed imaginative approaches to capacity loading that deal with problems of this kind. One of the best programs reported is used by a large electronics company. Its computer program loads to actual work-center capacity by scheduling backward, but the person using the program can exert considerable control over how the schedules are developed. Rush jobs can be specially coded, and instructions can be varied from "use full move and wait times" to "use no move and wait times," or even to "use more than one machine where possible." The program develops a provisional timetable according to the rules given by the scheduler, and prints a brief report that shows the scheduler whether the job can be handled within the time period he originally specified.

However, if the job cannot be accommodated as desired, the scheduler has several alternative courses of action available. He can:

☐ Try another priority.

☐ Cut the lot size (i.e., break the job into two lots).

☐ Try an earlier start time (if tools, material, and so on are available).

☐ Negotiate a later delivery date.

☐ Allow the program to overload one or more work centers after agreeing with the manufacturing superintendent and the foreman on an overtime plan or other capacity adjustment to handle the overload.

. . . VS. INFINITE CAPACITY

The second common approach to short-term scheduling is a method whereby jobs are scheduled forward, beginning with the first operation at the earliest start date. Using standard move and delay times, load is accumulated as in capacity loading. The load is allowed to fall where it may, and no consideration is given to overloads that may develop. Such overloads are called to the attention of production planners, who attempt to adjust shop capacity to handle the work as scheduled or to rework the schedule to eliminate the overloads.

Loading to infinite capacity is definitely easier to program and implement than capacity loading schemes. There are other advantages, too. Infinite capacity loading focuses attention on bottlenecks and forces action when problems develop. Furthermore, scheduled manufacturing cycle times normally have less variance because the lead times used in developing the schedules never change. If actual manufacturing cycle times are to have low variance as well, however, the shop must have good procedures for adjusting capacity to handle overloads.

Capacity loading, on the other hand, usually presents the shop with a more level load and cuts down on the need for continual capacity adjustments. The price, however, is variance in the manufacturing cycle time or poorer delivery performance that will occasionally result from smoothing the peaks and valleys in demand. The feedback from capacity loading is better than that from infinite capacity schedules because the actual lead times accurately reflect what is likely to develop in the shop. This information on expected lead times can be passed upward to revise master schedules and other higher-level plans.

One problem with any loading approach is that unloading is a difficult task when plans are changed. When a customer cancels an order for a large machine, for example, all the individual loads contributed by the hundreds of piece parts already scheduled must be erased. This may leave idle capacity in several work centers, and questions then arise as to what to do with that capacity. A similar problem crops up when a customer changes the desired delivery date on a large order. These kinds of problems can be overcome only with great difficulty with manual systems, but the versatility of the computer makes possible the rapid readjustment of shop loads when changes are required.

A STATISTICAL VIEW

It is one thing to develop schedules, but quite another to run the shop so work will be accomplished according to schedule. I shall say more about this in the next section, dispatching and shop floor control, but for the time being let me state that the schedules resulting from the kinds of loading programs just described are usually not sufficient to determine how work will be done in the shop. This is so because of machine breakdowns, engineering changes, delivery promise changes, personnel absences, missing tooling, missing raw materials, and other roadblocks to following the schedule exactly as planned.

Thus the short-term schedule is at best a close approximation of what will transpire in the shop itself. This leads one to think about the level of detail required in short-term scheduling and to wonder whether rough, approximate procedures might be used to generate schedules, especially if production is carefully controlled on the shop floor.

Stanley Reiter, a former Purdue University economics professor now at Northwestern University, and I have developed a short-term scheduling program which takes a statistical view of the shop and attempts to ensure that promised delivery dates on new orders take into account the congestion the job is going to encounter as it works its way through the shop. The program was developed as part of a larger production planning and control system for a gear company whose scheduling problem differs somewhat from other problems I have described here in that virtually all work in the shop is for a specific customer order. Master scheduling to forecasts is not done. Instead, a promise date must be generated for each order accepted.

The program works from two basic data files: (1) estimated load by work center (about 200) and by week (six months ahead), and (2) estimated delay (waiting time) that a job will encounter in each work center for each week. The delays are calculated from both the load estimates and manpower (capacity) plans by mathematical formula. When a new order is received, the promise date is determined by (a) estimating the start

Exhibit IV. Information flows for short-term scheduling

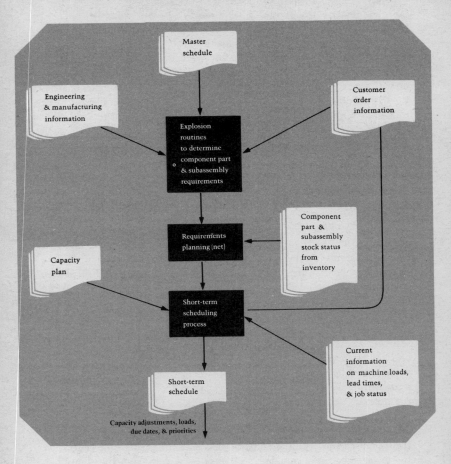

date for the job, and (b) adding the setup, machining, and delay times for each operation in the job. The delay estimates are taken from the computer file for the appropriate work center and week, and—as the job is scheduled —the setup and machine hours are added to the existing load already in the file.

Every week new delay estimates are calculated on the basis of updated load estimates. If an order is loaded and then subsequently canceled, no unloading is done. While this introduces known error into the system, there are probably other, unknown errors that are at least as important. This does not mean that accuracy is unimportant. Rather, my point is that a quick, approximate approach to setting promise dates is useful if

342

the basic sentiments of the approach are in the right direction. To me, "in the right direction" means that a scheduling program lengthens delivery times when shop loads increase, and the output of the program gives management information for making capacity adjustments when necessary.

The delays generated by the program just described can provide management with a picture of where overloads are likely to develop. Thus management can take corrective action before the overload occurs. In fact, management can test the effect of adding capacity through overtime or extra shifts by recalculating the delays on the basis of proposed capacity additions in bottleneck work centers. Again—just so this point is not overlooked—general approximating methods may be adequate in some situations if the methods are properly designed and controlled, and if the shop is not constrained so tightly that it cannot respond to occasional errors in scheduling.

The general process of short-term scheduling is shown in *Exhibit IV*. While the information flows may appear to be similar to those shown in *Exhibit II*, the short-term scheduling process is based on considerably more detail than the master scheduling process and requires the handling of more supporting data. For example, the combining of master schedule information and customer order detail with engineering, manufacturing, and inventory information to yield data on net component parts requirements for short-term scheduling requires the processing of vast amounts of information. Although this supporting data processing task is large and complex, it should not draw management's eyes away from the main management task that is being supported—namely, the generation of a time schedule for the processing of orders in the shop to make efficient use of the company's capacity and to meet customer demands.

Dispatching and Shop Control

The scheduling and control of work actually on the shop floor is a complex and demanding task. In most large shops there are thousands, or even tens of thousands, of job orders in process at any given time. Thus there is not only the problem of limited capacity, but also the problem of what individual operation can be done next, due to sequence constraints and material, tool, and machine availability. Even though every job order in the shop may have a scheduled start and finish time, the particular sequence for the individual machine operations remains to be determined.

Many management problems are caused by a lack of up-to-date information on the status of jobs in the shop. Often even the location of a job is not known, let alone whether it is ahead of or behind schedule and what work remains to be done. In this section we shall see how a well-designed dispatching and shop floor control system can help to organize and rationalize the flow of work through the shop, and to ensure that the right jobs are being worked on at all times. We shall also see how timely reports can greatly assist management in the continuous decision-making process that is required to keep a shop going—that is, in controlling the level of in-process inventory, tracking down troublesome jobs, and spotting difficult situations before they develop.

Dispatching is the shortest-term scheduling activity performed, because the scheduling takes place right in the shop where the decision has to be made on what job to do next. Some companies with good short-term scheduling or loading systems develop start dates for each individual operation to be performed on the job, and then dispatch on the basis of these scheduled start dates. In other words, when a machine becomes available, then, out of all the jobs waiting for it, the one with the earliest scheduled start time is chosen to be worked on next.

This approach works well if (a) the shop is able to follow the schedule with reasonable accuracy—that is, the jobs move through the shop without holdups for such things as missing material, tools, documents, or machine breakdowns; or if (b) the delay, move, processing, and setup times used to generate the schedule accurately reflect what is happening in the shop. Usually this is difficult, however, and the shop "drifts" off the short-term schedule between the time the schedule was generated and the time the job is actually run. This drift is caused by changes in the specification or timing of the job that may not have been rerun in the short-term schedule, the addition of last-minute rush work not included in the original schedule, and the previously cited random occurrences in the shop that prevent jobs from being run exactly according to the schedule.

To state it simply, time is the all-important ingredient in a production schedule. When timing of a schedule reflects the up-to-the-minute condition of the shop, materials flow smoothly through the shop, in-process work is completed and leaves the shipping dock at the right time, and machines are utilized efficiently.

Because of the vital importance of proper timing in the execution of work in the shop, dispatching has received considerable attention, and several companies have automated this function. All dispatching programs schedule work from a preplanned priority scheme that allows each job in queue for an available machine to be given a priority ranking relative to all other jobs competing for the same capacity.

The particular method for determining priority can vary from a simple

```
                              ORDER STATUS REPORT
                             MACHINE GROUP 62-01
                             MANUFACTURING DAY 212
     PRIORITY        PART      PREVIOUS   ARRIVAL    ORDER PROCESSING OPERATIONS PROCESSING
                    NUMBER     LOCATION     TIME      QTY     TIME        LEFT    TIME LEFT
        (ORDERS IN STATION)

     HOT  -3.8       324409     61-03      INSTA      212     2.3         03        8.6
     HOT   1.9       448305     60-06      INSTA      172     3.4         02       12.3
          -5.5       104961     72-08      INSTA       53     1.3         13      147.2
          -2.3       665128     61-11      INSTA       87     2.4         06       38.9
           1.2       401759     72-08      INSTA      200    12.1         00         .0

        (INCOMING ORDERS)

     HOT  -9.2       489618     61-03      8-30       137     2.9         02       12.6
     HOT  -1.6       393474     72-07      9-00        52     0.8         01        5.5
     HOT   0.3       506632     60-03      8-30       217    13.1         00         .0
          -2.1       170300     72-08     10-30        62     3.2         06       24.2
           .5        463218     60-03     10-30        72     .7          09      126.
```

ranking by due date to complex rankings that consider not only the scheduled completion date, but also the calendar and processing time remaining, the time required for the next operation, future congestion likely to be encountered, priority codes imposed by management, and even the current inventory status of the part (see page 354 for examples of dispatching rules).

The use of any dynamic dispatching rule—that is, one in which priorities change with the passage of time or the completion of work—requires that up-to-date information be maintained to keep priorities current. This inevitably means that data on each job must be maintained in computer files. With current information on job status and priority available in machine-readable form, dispatchers or foremen can be provided with lists showing the current location and priority of all jobs in the shop. If these lists are sorted by work center, the man on the shop floor has not only a picture of all the work in each work-center queue, but also information that will enable him to make good decisions on which job to run next. Some companies are already going beyond supplying queue lists in particular work centers. I shall discuss two examples.

DAILY STATUS SYSTEM

A West Coast company which manufactures electronic systems has a dispatching system that captures up-to-the-minute information on job status and works ahead to predict what will happen during the next shift. Two daily reports are prepared. The first (simplified in *Exhibit V*) shows the jobs that are already in each work center at the beginning of the day and

Exhibit VI. Sample report of operations to be performed on "hot" jobs during the day

```
                                    HOT ORDER REPORT
                                    DEPARTMENT 62-00
                                 MANUFACTURING DAY 212

         PART                 ARRIVAL   PREVIOUS  ORDER  PROCESSING  OPERATIONS  PROCESSING  PRIORITY
         NUMBER   LOCATION    TIME      LOCATION  QTY    TIME        LEFT        TIME LEFT

  HOT   324409    62-01       INSTA     61-03     212    2.3         03          8.6         -3.8
                  68-02       8-30      62-01            6.5         02          2.1         -4.2
                  72-08       1-00      68-02            1.8         01          .3          -6.8
  HOT   432186    62-02       INSTA     68-03     57     1.2         06          13.4        -2.1
                  72-08       1-30      62-02            1.4         05          12.0        -6.3
  HOT   448305    62-01       INSTA     60-06     172    3.4         02          5.8         1.9
                  61-03       9-00      62-01            3.2         01          2.6         -0.2
                  72-02       2-30                       .           00          0           -3.6
```

the jobs which are expected to arrive during the day. Jobs classified as "hot" or "rush" are listed before regular jobs. Within these categories, jobs are listed by priority (minimum slack per remaining operation).

Knowing what orders he already has on hand and their relative priorities, and what jobs to expect throughout the day, the foreman can plan his work in an orderly fashion rather than simply react to a continuous stream of requests and demands from expediters, engineers, project managers, and other interested parties. As he plans his day, the foreman can sequence the work in terms of efficiently matching the capacity and skill of his work center to the demands and the priorities of the individual job orders.

The second daily report (simplified in *Exhibit VI*) shows the operations to be performed on "hot" jobs that the computer's dispatching program predicts will be completed during the day. With this "hot order report" in hand, personnel from production control can identify and locate orders that should be expedited, assess their actual versus planned progress throughout the day, and ensure that the high-priority work at the top of the queues moves as rapidly as possible.

In order to generate reports similar to those shown in *Exhibits V* and *VI*, a dispatching program must actually simulate the operation of the shop for one day, keeping track of what jobs are assigned to which machines, move times, queues, priorities, and so forth. This is necessary, since the program must predict not only which orders will arrive in a given work center, but also when during the day they will actually arrive.

JOB SEQUENCE SCHEDULE

The gear company that I mentioned earlier, in the section on short-term scheduling, also has an interesting dispatching system. Its program develops a schedule that specifies a detailed sequence of jobs by simulating the

Exhibit VII. Sample of schedule that specifies detailed sequence of jobs

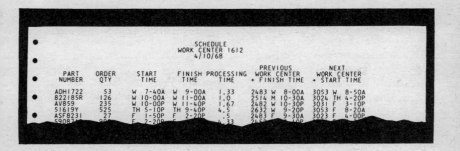

SCHEDULE
WORK CENTER 1612
4/10/68

PART NUMBER	ORDER QTY	START TIME	FINISH TIME	PROCESSING TIME	PREVIOUS WORK CENTER + FINISH TIME		NEXT WORK CENTER + START TIME	
ADH1722	53	W 7-40A	W 9-00A	1.33	2483	W 8-00A	3053	W 8-50A
822185R	126	W 10-00A	W 11-00A	1.0	2514	M 10-30A	3024	TH 4-20P
AV859	235	W 10-00P	W 11-40P	1.67	2482	W 10-30P	3031	F 3-10P
51619Y	525	TH 5-10P	TH 9-40P	4.5	2632	W 9-20P	3053	F 8-20A
ASF8231	27	F 1-50P	F 2-20P	.5	2483	F 9-30A	3023	F 4-00P
59087		F 2-20P		4.33				

operation of the shop three days ahead, according to a minimum-slack dispatching rule. In most of the company's work centers, average setup times are used to develop the schedule, but in certain other work centers, where setup sequences are critically important (e.g., continuous heat treating furnaces), the program develops a schedule that takes into account the cost, in time, of going from one setup to another.

A simplified example of the output of this dispatching program is shown in *Exhibit VII*. Although the foreman can work directly from the schedule without having to sequence the jobs on the available machines, there may be times when he wishes to change the suggested work sequence. If he can obtain savings on setup time, or can better match man or machine capabilities to the available jobs by changing the suggested sequence, he is encouraged to do so.

The question is: How much will such a change affect other parts of the schedule for this job? To answer that question, the foreman is provided with information on where the job is coming from, when it is expected to be completed in the previous work center, where the job is going, and when it is expected to start at the next work center. With these data, the foreman can negotiate backward and forward along the job's route, if necessary, or make a change based on the information at hand that will not affect the scheduling in other work centers.

The sharp-eyed reader may have noted a seeming discrepancy in the first line of the sample schedule in *Exhibit VII*. The job is not only scheduled to start in work center 1612 before it finishes its previous operation in work center 2483, but it is scheduled to start the next operation before it finishes in work center 1612. This is the result of a "line scheduling" feature whereby the first pieces in the lot of a high-priority job are allowed to move ahead to the next operation before the last pieces in the lot are completed in the current operation. This feature requires no outside control and ensures that high-priority work will move through the shop quickly.

In conversations with production managers who have installed successful new production control systems, one big advantage is invariably mentioned: the ability to keep constant tabs on job location and status. The tighter schedules, better delivery performances, and more efficient uses of men and machines that result from such systems are acknowledged and appreciated, but the big breakthrough for most managers is the readily available current information on job location and status.

However, this information does not come at zero cost, and again a supporting system must be considered. Job location and status information is obtained in many companies through the use of remote data-collection devices on the shop floor. Data are entered into a remote device and transmitted to a central location, where they are usually punched into cards or paper tape which can then be read by a computer at frequent intervals to update the job information in the computer's files. While such collection devices speed the process of data acquisition, they are not necessarily essential in all applications. Many companies obtain job location and status information from handwritten cards or forms from the shop that are key punched before entering the computer.

PROFITABLE PAYOFFS

A well-designed dispatching system can:

◻ Greatly reduce the amount of clerical work required to maintain current records.

◻ Implement dynamic priorities which can be updated without laborious hand calculation, sorting, and refiling.

◻ Improve the expediting function.

Nonetheless, the large dollar payoff often comes not from these advantages, but from other areas of activity on the shop floor. One important saving is the control of in-process inventory. Work in process consists largely of jobs in queues waiting for an available machine. These waiting lines are desirable for two reasons: (1) to provide a pool of work from which good setup sequences can be developed; and (2) to provide a cushion of work to prevent machine idleness. But, when the queues get too long, unnecessary investment in inventory is tied up, and the time required to get work through the shop rises.

A study at the New England plant of a large manufacturing company has shown that careful control of the amount of work in waiting lines can have a dramatic impact on overall shop performance. The analysts who conducted the study convinced the shop's management and work force that a backlog on paper is just as real as a backlog in iron on the shop floor. (Several authors have stressed the importance of this step.) Then, many jobs were removed from waiting lines in the shop and later were rereleased to the shop a short time ahead of their due date. In addition, all new work was released in tight relation to due date. This control of work releasing and the use of a shortest-processing-time dispatching rule resulted in a one-third reduction in work-in-process inventory levels. Moreover, manufacturing cycle times were cut in half, much more reliable delivery time performance was obtained, and less finished goods inventory was required to satisfy the customer demand.

Another New England company which uses critical ratios for dispatching decided to hold back on releasing all new orders until the ratio indicated that the job was behind schedule. This action forced priority work ahead of jobs that were already on the shop floor and which were ahead of schedule because of early releasing under the old system, or because of due date and engineering changes. Although, at first, it may seem unwise to hold job orders until they are behind schedule, the critical ratio priorities and the considerably reduced work-in-process inventories have enabled the company to follow and expedite jobs, and still maintain a satisfactory performance on deliveries.

Another area of big payoff as a result of improved dispatching is capacity control. Reliable information on the work and priority content of waiting lines in the shop, and the current location and status of individual jobs, can greatly improve management's ability to make short-term capacity adjustments. The control of overtime is perhaps the best example. One company president recently stated that the yearly cost of the computer required to implement a new production planning and control system in his company has been easily paid by the savings in cutting excess overtime.

Other capacity adjustments that can be made more efficiently with good location and job status information include moving a man from one work center to another, routing a job to an alternate work center for a given operation, and changing the sequence in which the various job operations are performed. All these alternatives are designed to balance the flow of work through the shop and to minimize the number of bottlenecks in work flow at machines where large backlogs have piled up.

We should have clearly in mind, however, that the short-term capacity adjustments under discussion here are the finest of the fine-tuning operations. Remember that initial capacity plans should be laid months, and even years, ahead of actual production, and that opportunities to update and revise those plans to fit actual conditions better should exist at several levels above the shop floor control level.

Viewed in this manner, short-term capacity adjustment becomes a management opportunity (a) to make small moves in reacting to occasional mishaps and requests for unusual service, and (b) to remedy, in some degree, errors in higher-level planning and scheduling. In other words, the

Exhibit VIII. Information flows in a production planning and control system

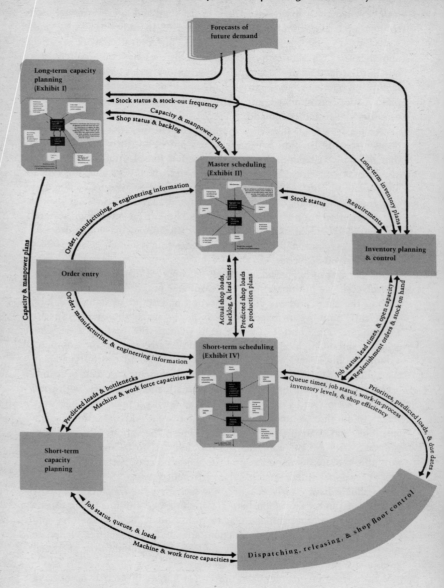

shop will have the flexibility to move a few important jobs quickly, but not enough leeway to overcome the major shortcomings in plans from higher levels.

The Integrated System

At the beginning of this article, I emphasized the goal of tying together the component parts of production planning and control systems. This is done in *Exhibit VIII*, which not only shows the various elements of a production planning and control system (and their relation to the enlarged parts previously illustrated in *Exhibits I, II, and IV*), but also highlights the major information flows that tie the parts together. In studying *Exhibit VIII*, keep in mind my early statement about high-level plans providing guidelines for lower-level planning and the importance of an upward flow of information to ensure that high-level plans are realistic.

Starting at the top of *Exhibit VIII*, long-range forecasts are transformed into capacity plans to guide master scheduling. I use the term "guide" in this instance to mean the setting of approximate limits within which master schedules can be developed. As an example, consider a company whose capacity plans involve an expansion of facilities for turning large work pieces, such as generator shafts or steel mill rolls, with a simultaneous contraction in the milling and heat treating of small forged parts:

□ Master scheduling would be expected to begin to supply a load for the new facilities and gradually build up that load to utilize the new equipment efficiently. At the same time, master scheduling would act as a filter to keep some of the milling and heat treating work out of the system.

If the demand for milling and heat treating job orders continued, strong action would be needed. Either subcontracting could be used, or marketing could be urged to discourage some orders, so as to keep actual production within the guidelines of the capacity plan. In the opposite direction, information describing growing backlogs, lengthening manufacturing cycle times, and increasing difficulty in maintaining adequate inventories could signal the need for more capacity.

Toward the bottom of *Exhibit VIII*, scheduling, dispatching, capacity adjusting, and inventory control are shown to be highly interrelated. Loads from short-term scheduling provide an advance warning of conditions that may develop in the shop, which releasing and short-term capacity planning may be able to heed. Dispatching information on the length, work content, and priority content of queues, and on the status of individual jobs, can signal situations where previous planning has not taken care of all bottlenecks and where immediate action is called for. In addition, dispatching information can be used in short-term scheduling to compare lead times, loads, and the shop's efficiency or actual performance against planned processing times or output expectations, and then to revise them as necessary.

SIGNIFICANT PROGRESS

At this point in the discussion, some managers may well be thinking: If a production planning and control system is so fine a management tool, then why doesn't every production operation use an integrated approach like this?

Actually, from what I can see, recent progress has been significant, and many companies have made great strides in production planning and control. Much of this progress has been due (a) to the development of computer hardware and software that can handle vast quantities of information rapidly and inexpensively, and (b) to practical developments on parts of the system, such as forecasting, capacity planning, and dispatching.

Despite the impressive progress in fixing up the parts, however, few companies have developed systems that tie the parts together as well as they might. There are roadblocks to overcome. The information requirements for a comprehensive system are a major problem. Data on routings, standards, tooling, materials, and engineering changes must be not only available, but also reliable and accurate. The production planning and control system exists in relationship to other systems—financial, accounting, engineering, quality control, material handling, purchasing—and the coordination and standardization required to tie into these other systems is substantial.

But, again based on what I see, progress in the design and implementation of systems that support production planning and control is proceeding faster than progress on production planning and control systems themselves. Thus, as the pressures mount for better planning and tighter control, the roadblocks to a good system are getting easier to overcome.

Conclusion

At the beginning of this article, I stated that the approaches I would discuss would relate to fabrication and assembly operations. Since this term encompasses a variety of organizations, some readers may have found significant differences between my charts and their own operations. Although there are differences in individual situations, each must deal with the basic problems of planning for capacity, such as setting delivery or due dates, developing and interpreting information on shop loads, scheduling the flow of work through the shop, and providing continuous, timely, and accurate reports for the comparison of planned and actual results.

My major point is that managers must look at decision making at all levels in seeking solutions to these problems. They must also recognize that good short-term performance results from an integrated and coherent set of decisions made over a long time span and not solely from more attention to short-term detail. The manager who translates general ideas and approaches into concrete specifications for his plant, and who then launches a well-planned and well-directed systems development effort, will be able to report such things as "on-time delivery performance up from 10% to 90%," "overtime savings which more than pay for the computer," "number of expediters decreased from nine to three," and "productivity jump of one third."

Appendix to Chapter 17

Dispatching Rules

Here are representative examples of the many different dispatching rules currently in use. In each case the rule is used to select the particular job to run next out of a group of jobs waiting for an available machine. Each rule is accompanied by a brief statement about the properties of the schedules that will result from its use.

Simple rules

1. *Earliest Due Date*—Run the job with the earliest due date. Results in good due date performance.
2. *First Come, First Served*—Run the job which arrived in the waiting line first. Results in low variance of manufacturing cycle time.
3. *Shortest Processing Time*—Run the job which has the shortest setup plus machining time for the current work center. One of the best of the simple rules. Results in low in-process inventory, low average manufacturing cycle times, and good due date performance.

Combination rules

1. *Minimum Slack*—Slack equals calendar time remaining minus processing time remaining; or, slack equals due date minus present time minus setup and machining time for all remaining operations. Run the job with the least slack. Results in a very good due date performance.
2. *Critical Ratio*—The critical ratio for made-to-order work is a slack-type rule. Critical ratio equals due date minus present time, divided by number of days required to complete the job order. (The figure for days required to complete the job includes setup, machining, move, and wait times.)

The rule for parts manufactured for inventory is critical ratio equals available stock over reorder point quantity, divided by standard lead time remaining over total manufacturing lead time.

This ratio compares the rate at which stock on hand is being depleted

354

with the rate at which total lead time is being used up. The inventory part ratio is consistent with the made-to-order part ratio; one of its great advantages is that it allows a relative ranking of both kinds of work in any queue.

18. Requirements Planning for Inventory Control

Philip H. Thurston

Specialists on inventory and scheduling and also line managers have succumbed to the lure of statistical tools in managing parts inventories. But, argues this author, the statistically based approach has shortcomings in a number of situations, and its glamour is wearing off. Requirements planning or a combination of the two can lead to substantial savings.

The phrases "safety stock," "reorder point," and "economic order quantity" are commonplace in the management of parts inventories at manufacturing companies. These terms signify that inventory is being controlled on a statistical basis. Certainly, statistics have important applications in inventory management, but during the past two decades specialists on inventory and scheduling and line managers alike have gone overboard—incurring considerable costs—in the excessive use of statistically based tools. An alternate approach called "requirements planning" can, in a number of manufacturing situations, make very substantial savings.

Basically, requirements planning sets aside the "averaging process" of statistics in managing inventory and substitutes a specific enumeration of what parts to place in inventory and when. I shall describe how this is done and offer a more complete definition of requirements planning a little further on. But first, since statistically based tools are so commonly used, let us consider, using an example, what their shortcomings are in a significant number of situations.

My example is that of a company manufacturing machine tools, which had a precise schedule of what machines were to be assembled over the ensuing 15-month period by quantities and weeks. This schedule could be translated, by using bills of material and lead times, into just what parts had to be completed in the factory or purchased in specific quantities and by specific dates. Furthermore, the marketing personnel agreed with the manufacturing personnel on the schedule. Thus uncertainty about what parts to manufacture and purchase for assembly was eliminated.

But, in using the conventional statistical approach to inventory man-

AUTHOR'S NOTE: I acknowledge with thanks the contributions to this article of Robert T. Lund, of the Harvard Business School.

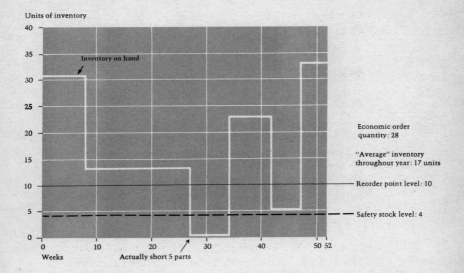

Exhibit I. Actual stock level for one part using statistical approach

agement, what did the company's production control system do? It set safety stocks for parts at four weeks' historical average usage, presumably to allow for variations between actual and average usage rates; it set reorder points to cover safety stocks and to allow for average usage during replenishment lead time; and it established economic order quantities based on historical usage rates.

Implicit in this company's system were the assumptions that (a) the specific demand for parts in any week was unknown, (b) the forces which created the demand in one week could not be distinguished from the forces creating demand in other weeks, and (c) the demand for one part was not tied in a predictable fashion to the demand for other parts. If true, these assumptions would have justified the statistical approach used. The fact is that none of these assumptions was valid; there was a precise schedule of what to manufacture for the following 15 months.

"Statistics" Disadvantages

A little reflection—aided by specific numbers—shows the shortcomings of the *statistical* approach in situations such as in the foregoing example. If lots of, say, 18 milling machines each are scheduled to start assembly in the 8th, 27th, and 42nd weeks of the year, only 18 complete sets of parts and subassemblies are needed at the beginning of each of these weeks. That is all. No stocks are needed for assembly in any of the other 49 weeks of

357

Exhibit II. Optimal stock level for same part using requirements planning approach

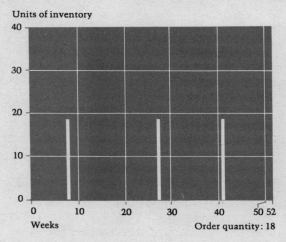

the year. This fact represents a potential for tighter control of inventory and for more purposeful commitment of manufacturing capacity than any statistical system makes possible. Under the conventional approach of using the statistical tools of economic order quantity and reorder point, the stock level for one milling machine part looked like that shown in *Exhibit I.*

Conversely, by working from the 15-month schedule, the inventory of the part could have been greatly reduced. The part *requirements* for the lots of 18 milling machines could be *planned* (hence the name *requirements planning*) to enter inventory just before their need. And the inventory of the part depicted in *Exhibit I* could have approached the pattern illustrated in *Exhibit II.*

Note that under the statistically based system (*Exhibit I*) there was a "stockout." Five parts had to be expedited, delaying assembly. And note particularly that it was not faulty operations within the system that led to the stockout, but the design of the system itself. Further, the average weekly inventory throughout the year was 17—an inventory of parts which was powerless to prevent the stockout. In contrast, the inventory shown in *Exhibit II* can be seen as nearly zero, on an average weekly basis, within a system potentially free of stockouts.

"Requirements" Advantages

It is time now for a more complete definition of *requirements planning.* It covers materials and parts which are not end products themselves, but are fabricated and assembled to become major assemblies and end products.

Requirements planning is the process of working backward from the scheduled completion dates of end products or major assemblies to determine the dates and quantities when the various component parts and materials are to be ordered. Each subassembly level and each part is considered in terms of lead time and scrap expected. The result is a schedule that puts each part or subassembly into stock shortly ahead of the need for that item in the next higher order of assembly.

This approach may seem very logical. Indeed, it is. Requirements planning has been used for more than 40 years by a manufacturer of large electrical motors. Each motor is manufactured to order. The customer and manufacturer agree on the motor specifications and the delivery date, setting the latter by gross yardsticks of factory load. Then the production control department calculates backward from the delivery date to assign the specific requirements for manufactured components to the various factory departments. This takes into consideration lead times and previously assigned work loads, and combines similar parts needed at about the same time. Thus every part is planned and timed for a specific known requirement.

Whereas this manufacturer of electrical motors works from specific, known customers' orders, some manufacturers start with forecasts of demand for *major assemblies*. In the automobile industry, for example, it is virtually impossible to predict the sales of specific end products. The choices given to customers are too numerous. But it is possible to forecast the demand for major assemblies such as a six-cylinder motor.

Other manufacturers start with forecasts of demand for *end products* and work backward from such estimates in requirements planning. A manufacturer of industrial hand tools uses this approach. The company manufactures in anticipation of orders; if its tools are not available on the distributors' shelves, sales are lost. Accordingly, the manufacturer projects sales on a statistical basis, modifies this projection by judgment, and uses this estimate of future demand to decide when lots of each of the hand tools will be assembled. The resulting assembling schedule, showing quantities and dates, is further broken down into the required components to be manufactured with suitable lead times. Thus the original statistical projection becomes the basis for requirements planning.

Earlier, I said that requirements planning is logical; however, this is not the same as saying it is easy. The approach depends on a high order of accuracy in engineering bills of material, in inventory records, in routing and leadtime information, in records of sales and purchase commitments, and in the factory load schedule. Some companies do not appreciate the value of discipline and accuracy in these records. Perhaps it is just as well when such a company controls inventory and manufacturing on a part-by-part basis (using reorder points and lot sizes). Lack of record discipline leads to less trouble there. And the book of accounts at the company with poor control never specifically records two types of hidden but quite substantial costs: those of basing decisions on poor records and those of using a less efficient system for inventory and production control.

Return now, if you will, to the case of the manufacturer of machine tools I described in the example at the outset of this article. If requirements planning is adopted there, the calculations of both the reorder point and the economic order quantity will continue to have some relevance—the reorder point in allowing for uncertainty in demand for repair parts; and the economic order quantity in deciding if some parts should be made in multiples of 18 units.

Reorder point and economic order quantity calculations may also be used for the large number of low-cost parts utilized broadly in the manufacture of many items—e.g., inexpensive hardware and cheap stamped parts—designated "C" in an A-B-C classification of parts. Far outnumbering the expensive items, the "C" items can be stocked more liberally with relatively little investment and controlled by inexpensive means. The tighter control of requirements planning, incurring somewhat greater paper-work costs, is applied to the fewer, more expensive components.

Three men—Joseph A. Orlicky, George W. Plossl, and Oliver W. Wight—who have done much to publicize and help companies with requirements planning have combined their ideas in a single publication entitled *Material Requirements Planning Systems*.[1] In his section of the publication, Orlicky contrasts a statistically based system with requirements planning:

"Order Point is part-based, whereas Requirements Planning is [end] product-oriented. Order Point utilizes data on the historical behavior of a part, while Requirements Planning ignores history and instead works with data on the relationship of components (the bill of material) that make up a product. Order Point looks at the past. Requirements Planning looks toward the future (as defined by a manufacturing master schedule)."

In the same publication, Orlicky also gives his evaluation of requirements planning by calling it "Cinderella's bright prospects for the future."

Critical Indictments

Requirements planning is basically not new. The manufacturer of motors cited earlier and others have used this approach for years. Using various designations for their systems, manufacturers had relied on detailed enumerations of parts to be manufactured and purchased long before statistical approaches to inventory management became widely known.

1. Reproduced by International Business Machines Corporation, Data Processing Division, in publication number G320-1170-0.

Why, then, was the enumeration approach seemingly lost at some companies? What happened? Simply this: the statistical approaches were and still are oversold. Who oversold? Who are the villains? Are they the specialists who sharpen their analytical tools and then point them at what they judge to be appropriate targets?

For working from known statistical tools rather than from understood problems, the specialists are greatly at fault. But the real villains are the line managers who abdicate their responsibilities, not only of understanding the real nature of their scheduling and inventory problems, but also of assessing fully the implications of analytical tools proposed by the specialists.

The (erroneous) substitution of statistically based tools for requirements planning received a big boost from the sheer difficulty that line managers encountered in breaking out and keeping track of thousands of required parts. This necessitated a strong commitment and a high order of information-processing discipline to effectively operate requirements planning systems which used manual or punched card data processing. But for more than a decade now the computer, well suited for the job, has been available to handle the details of requirements planning. The cost is down; the accuracy and speed are up.

Now that I have painted *all* specialists on inventory and scheduling, as well as *all* line managers, with a critical brush, I hasten to qualify these indictments. Some line managers to my knowledge have accurately and steadfastly discriminated between those applications where statistics are useful and those where the statistical approach is not. Likewise, some specialists have not succumbed to the glamorous, faddish, mystical, broad-front shift to statistics.

For instance, at a company manufacturing electrical generating equipment, the line supervisors and specialists jointly installed one of the early computers to improve requirements planning. The former manual system hectographed, from the bills of material and manufacturing planning, thousands of sets of 3x5 shop paper work used in loading the factory with specific parts and assemblies for planned final products. Important parts of this system were computerized. One supervisor described the change in this way:

"Under the manual system, we could load the shop just once with the parts required for each new order. Thereafter, it was too difficult to reschedule a whole job or any major part of a job. We simply had too many pieces of paper. This meant that we sometimes used machining capacity for parts which the passage of time had made less important than other parts. Then we put all our requirements on computer tapes. We could change priorities, our accuracy went up, and we could better pinpoint discrepancies between load and capacity."

It is not within the scope of this Management Memo to cover the planning of factory capacity and load. Suffice it to say that the adoption of requirements planning can be coupled to advantage with improved planning in shop loading.

The glamour of statistics is wearing off just as the glamour of the computer has. We understand both better. And I predict an increasing willingness (a) to chuck the statistical approach in those cases where the requirements planning approach is better suited, or (b) to employ a tailored combination of the two.

19. Sweeping Changes in Distribution

J. L. Heskett

We are at the end of a significant era of technological change in transportation, warehousing, inventory control, and order processing. Now a new era is evolving —one that will be marked by institutional rather than technological change. Greater gains are now possible through such change, in part resulting from the realization of promises made but unfulfilled by technology. This article discusses the nature of institutional change and suggests methods of achieving inter-organizational solutions which will be central to continued improvement of productivity in logistics.

Near the conclusion of World War II, the wartime T-2 tanker, with a rating of 15,600 tons, was thought by many to be too large for expected peacetime petroleum needs and also too large to be handled safely in most ports. Yet just 20 years later, marine architects were designing ships 20 times larger than the T-2, ships exceeding 300,000 deadweight tons which have since been built and now sail the world's oceans.

Only 25 years ago, a respectably advanced rate at which to handle bulk materials was about 500 tons per hour. Recently, a number of installations have been built capable of handling bulk materials at 40 times that rate.

Just a generation ago, there were three basic alternatives for transporting most commodities: rail, water, and truck. Since then, we have witnessed a vast increase in opportunities for transporting commodities other than petroleum by pipeline. Airfreight has become a viable alternative for many shippers. And the development of unitized freight handling and co-ordinated methods of transporting freight has produced a number of new modal combinations, including piggyback and trailers and containers on ships which, for all practical purposes, did not exist 20 years ago.

Since the inauguration of modern-day containerized service, ocean transportation to and from the United States has seen an enormous growth of containerized freight in the general cargo sector. In the North Atlantic trade, it is estimated that 60% of all containerizable freight now moves in containers.

As late as 1950, the Interstate Highway System, although conceived, had yet to be financed for construction.

The computer, whose rapid development was another by-product of World War II, has made possible only within the past 15 years the application of techniques and managerial models so vital to the successful management of logistics activities.

Clearly, the generation just ended has produced remarkable technological advances in transportation, materials handling, and information processing.

Partly in response to technological change, industrial, commercial, and governmental organizations have reorganized to improve the management of logistics activities and to make intelligent use of the newly available technology. Increased breadth, in terms of both the backgrounds of individuals attracted to the field and the scope of responsibilities which they have been given, has facilitated a trend toward the purchase of carrier services, physical facilities, and logistics equipment as elements in a broader system of related activities.

In this sense, the past decade can fairly be termed an era of organizational as well as technological change in logistics.

Toward Institutional Change

If we have witnessed significant technological and organizational change in the recent past, what does the foreseeable future hold? What are the implications of the fact that the U.S. population, and to some degree the size of the market that it represents, appears to be leveling out as emphasis on birth control increases? What will be the effect if pressures for new products and product individuality continue?

Similarly, what types of responses will be required by the growing congestion in city centers and the continuing dispersion and rapid growth of suburban markets? Will new technology continue to provide the primary means with which to deal with logistics problems arising from all these and other trends?

There are signs which suggest that the answer to my last question is *no*. While technological and organizational change will, of course, continue, major challenges will be met primarily by institutional change involving the spatial reordering of functions and facilities within an organization and among cooperating organizations.

This represents a logical progression in logistics from emphasis on decision making based on *internal cost analyses* to emphasis on *internal profit analyses* and on *interorganizational cost and profit analyses* of the sort suggested in *Exhibit I*.

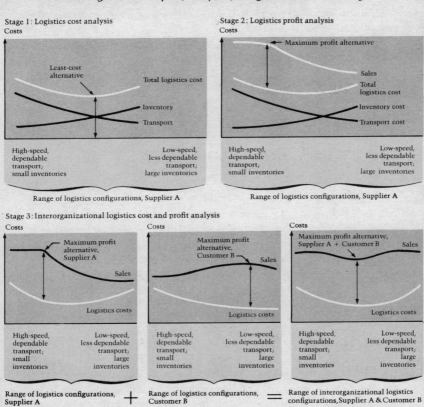

We will turn our interest during the foreseeable future to institutional (as opposed to technological) change, for a variety of reasons. Included among these are the seven possibilities that:

1. There are physical constraints on certain methods of transportation and materials handling, as well as restrictive public attitudes toward the further technological development of others.

2. Certain technological developments appear to be "topping out," at least for the time being.

3. Existing technologies, to an increasing extent, require for their success a rationalization of activity which can be brought about largely through institutional cooperation and new types of institutions.

4. Technological advances have made institutional cooperation not only possible, but in some cases necessary.

5. There are changing attitudes toward interorganizational coordination among individuals in business as well as government.

6. Continued emphasis on logistics management will yield information necessary to justify institutional change.

7. Perhaps of greatest importance, the economic benefits from institutional coordination and change will far exceed any that foreseeable technological developments can offer.

I shall consider each of these factors in the shift of emphasis to institutional change in the course of this article.

1. *Constraints on technology*: Certain transportation modes, such as rail and highway, have natural constraints imposed on them by the existing physical facilities. The height of a rail car can be increased to the point where any further increase would require massive expenditures for greater clearances at bridges, tunnels, and underpass or overpass intersections that have replaced grade-level railroad crossings.

Truckers now speak in terms of a 6-inch increase in the width of a vehicle instead of a 10-foot increase in length, which was more feasible when highway carriers were operating with 27- and 30-foot trailers. And they will have difficulty getting even that small increase in width.

Public attitude now comprises a growing constraint on the further development of other transportation technologies. The refusal to support the development of the supersonic transport, however temporary a victory for such forces it may represent, was an important indicator. It may be significantly more difficult in the future to obtain funds for the development of an ecologically and economically uncertain device such as the SST than for, say, an expanded system of bicycle paths for urban commuters.

When we throw in the growing opposition to supertankers and the fear of the potential disasters they could create, and the issues and arguments over possible ecological impacts of pipelines in the tundra of the Far North, we have a clear indication that technology in the late 1970's and 1980's may be in for close scrutiny.

2. *Temporary "topping out"*: Several years ago, it was popular to look ahead to the "era of the 747," the great hope of airfreight advocates. These "boxcars of the sky" were to eliminate the economic barriers to the use of airfreight. Closer analysis at the time could have shown that the most significant development, the introduction of the DC-8-63F airplane, already had occurred. Furthermore, few anticipated the problems of assembling a sufficient volume of freight in one place at one time to meet the 747's

vastly greater requirements for efficient operation. Finally, with their attention diverted to developments in the sky, most airfreight advocates paid too little heed to the significant improvements needed in the problem area of handling airfreight on the ground.

The same marine architects who produced the 300,000-ton ship designs now tell us that, although designs of 1,000,000 tons are possible, the economics of building and operating such ships quite likely precludes their construction in the foreseeable future, public attitude aside. Certain diseconomies of scale begin to assert themselves.

While ingenious devices for introducing automation in the warehouse have been developed in recent years, the promise of automated warehousing is yet to be realized. In fact, the requirements which it imposes on freight flow for effective utilization may in many cases be achieved only through the type of institutional cooperation I shall discuss later.

We now have the computers and the concepts to achieve significant savings through effective control of inventories. More important, economical computer and communication capacity will make possible the use of models offering more individual attention to product-line items, inventory locations, and customers. But the gains which improved technology in this area could make possible are small compared with the improvements in operations that could be achieved through proper application of currently available machines and methods.

3. *Rationalization of activity*: Typified by improved allocation of effort and responsibility among cooperating and even competing institutions, rationalization of activity has been required by the introduction of certain technologies. Conversely, technological advances have so badly outstripped institutional changes that the absence of the latter now imposes significant constraints on the former.

Perhaps the best example of this is the introduction of containerization on a wholesale basis in North Atlantic shipping several years ago.

Prospective container-ship operators planned for massive capital investment in fast, expensive ships, and the containers they would carry. Even the most forward-looking ship operators, however, did not provide for the numbers of containers which would ultimately be required for the service. They did not properly anticipate the problems of controlling container usage in the hinterlands surrounding the ports which they would serve. And they paid dearly for their traditional lack of interest in, and institutional separation from, freight before it arrived and after it left the docks.

In response to this problem, operators are making extensive efforts to: (a) acquire freight-forwarding, trucking, and other organizations which control freight in the hinterlands; (b) seek out arrangements under which containers can be jointly owned; (c) collect and transmit information in such a way that more effective control can be maintained over container usage.

4. *Necessity for institutional cooperation*: We have already noted that effective utilization of the 747 jetliner requires the assembly of large quantities of freight at a given place and time for shipment to a common destination. It is quite possible that, until airfreight volume increases significantly on a general front, self-organized groups of shippers with common origins and destinations may offer the best potential for providing this kind of volume.

In view of current computer capabilities and concepts, perhaps the most acute need in inventory control activities has been for more accurate data on which to base forecasts of future demand. As we have seen, the data have always existed. They needed to be collected and transmitted in a timely way. This has led to the establishment of direct lines of communications between customers and suppliers.

Production technologies have made possible smaller, lighter products that perform jobs better than their larger, heavier predecessors. At the same time, improvements in our intercity transportation systems have made it easier and less expensive to transport larger quantities of these smaller products, at least to the outskirts of large metropolitan areas.

Yet, in a growing number of cities, we have congestion and chaos.

This is clearly a case in which technology has contributed to a problem that will be solved either by more technological development, perhaps in the form of subterranean freight-access routes, or by institutional cooperation to create more efficient freight flows.

5. *Changing attitudes*: Many forms of organizational coordination not only are legal, but are becoming more and more attractive as problem-solving means to businessmen and government officials alike. The growing interest in coordinating inbound freight movements to congested city centers is just one example of a response by government and industry leaders to a difficult problem. This has led to the organization of the first symposium in this country to explore approaches to the problem of urban freight movements.[1]

Efforts in other countries are more advanced. For example, a recent study of freight movements into Utrecht, Holland, disclosed that the consolidation and systematic delivery of certain types of freight moving typically in small shipments could reduce the number of delivery vehicles in the city center from over 600 to 6.

---

1. Results of this symposium were reported in *Urban Commodity Flow*, Special Report 120 (Washington, D.C., Highway Research Board, National Academy of Sciences, 1971).

The Supermarket Institute has supported investigation into the feasibility of consolidated distribution facilities which might be operated as a joint venture by competing grocery product manufacturers and chain food-store organizations utilizing the same regional distribution centers. Essentially, such facilities would enable manufacturers and retailers to eliminate duplicated warehouse space.

In commenting on the concept of consolidated distribution facilities, the president of a large retail food chain recently remarked that "the idea may not be so farfetched, and it might have advantages to both segments of the industry." Of course, the concept will have arrived when a manufacturer or a store organization closes all or a part of its own warehouse facility to take advantage of a consolidated distribution service.

6. *Continued organizational development*: In the past 15 years there has been a rebirth in the concern for coordinated management of transportation, warehousing, materials handling, inventory-control, order-processing, and procurement activities. Evidence for this can be found in the rapidly increasing number of job titles like Physical Distribution Manager, Materials Manager, and Manager of Logistics, particularly in larger corporations. Further, the growth in membership in organizations such as the 10-year-old National Council of Physical Distribution Management (NCPD) and the even younger Society of Logistics Engineers (SOLE) has mushroomed.

Explanations for this concern and interest range from the competitive advantage that the effective management of logistics activities provides to organizational "me-too" faddism in certain industries. But an analysis of the roster of the NCPD suggests that the base of membership has spread from a few large companies in different industries to many more organizations in those same industries and then to other industries as well. Included among these are grocery and chemical product manufacturers, and manufacturers and distributors of products requiring extensive parts distribution activities. Other industries in which substantial costs of logistics, compared with sales, must be balanced against rigorous demands for customer service will see organizational change and emphasis on logistics.

As a further development in this area, managements will devote more attention to, and change the nature of, responsibility for coordinated product flow. For example, expansions in product lines without commensurate increases in sales produce higher inventory carrying costs as a percentage of sales.

As a result, in order to maintain a given level of customer service, retailers and wholesalers are limiting their speculative risk by reducing stocks of any one item (or by investing a commensurate amount of money in inventory for a broader product line) while at the same time expecting, and in fact depending on, manufacturers making speedy responses to their orders. This customer expectation, stated in the form of a willingness to substitute one manufacturer's product for another's in the event of the latter's inability to meet the customer's demands, in effect raises the incentive for speculation by manufacturers.

Thus caught in a squeeze between broader product lines and increasing demands for faster service from channel institutions, a number of manufacturers have responded by holding larger quantities of stock in semifinished form closer to markets, typically in distribution centers. There they can be cut, assembled, or packaged to order, thus postponing the company's commitment to specific stock-keeping unit locations until the last possible moment while reducing speculation (measured in terms of the elapsed time between customer order and delivery) for the customer.

To an increasing degree, logistics management will involve the operation of light manufacturing as well as distribution facilities. Perhaps the automobile assembly plant offers the most extreme example of this phenomenon. It is the closest thing to a distribution center in the channel of distribution for automobiles produced in the United States; it also houses light manufacturing activities. Because of the complexity of the latter, however, these plants typically fall under the responsibility of production management.

However, in other industries with less complex field requirements—such as the cutting to order of plate glass, paper products, lumber, and so on, and the packaging to order of common commodities—light manufacturing in the field will to an increasing extent fall within the purview of those concerned with logistics.

7. *Increased economic benefits*: Technological change can enable a company in a channel of distribution to perform its functions more efficiently. Typically, institutional change can eliminate the cost of performing a function by shifting the function to another point in the channel, where it can be integrated into other activities. Only occasionally, as with momentous developments such as containerization, can technology accomplish as much. And even then, it can do this only with the institutional change necessary to implement its introduction and growth.

Institutional Responses

Basic functions performed in a channel of distribution, such as selling, buying, storing, transporting, financing, providing information, and others, can only be shifted, not eliminated. They must be performed by some institution at some point in a channel. Distribution opportunities can be pinpointed by identifying the basic functions which can be performed most effectively by each institution in the channel, and the types of institutional change needed to accommodate efficient product flow.

The types of institutional change called for include at least four, arrayed in terms of their organizational impact on companies in a channel of distribution:

1. The coordination of policies and practices to enable cooperating channel members to perform their existing functions more effectively.

2. The shift of functions and responsibilities from one institution to another in a channel.

3. The creation of joint-venture or third-party institutions to eliminate duplication of the performance of functions in such channels.

4. The vertical integration of channel functions which are currently performed by different organizations.

It may be useful to take a closer look at each of these four types of institutional change prompted by the forces I have discussed.

1. COORDINATION OF PRACTICES

The unitized handling of products by means of such devices as pallets is one example of a technological development that has had a profound effect on interorganizational coordination. In order to reap the maximum benefits of palletization, buyers and sellers have to coordinate their materials handling systems to make use of the same size pallet, or at least pallet sizes with modular compatibility.

Thus industry standards for pallet sizes have been established for the shipment of such things as tin cans and paper products. Where standards have not been established, certain wholesalers have adapted their materials handling systems to conform with those of a dominant supplier. Companies electing not to abide by such standards do so at a price which is reflected in increased costs for handling goods.

2. SHIFTING OF RESPONSIBILITIES

A large distributor of personal care and houseware products that employed a network of direct sales personnel desired recently to gain greater control over product delivery to its distributors without actually going into the trucking business. It offered truckers an interesting proposition: a guaranteed, high profit on their investment in return for the full authority to schedule and control their trucks, reductions of up to 40% in existing charges, and access to the truckers' books to verify profit levels.

This case suggests the tremendous potential benefits made possible by a shift of functions between organizations.

A shift of stock-keeping responsibility from inventory-conscious retailers to wholesalers and manufacturers has taken place in recent years. This has resulted in part from the desire of retailers to reduce speculation and unsalable stocks in an age of expanding product lines as well as a realization that warehousing and materials handling costs may be significantly lower per unit for manufacturers and wholesalers than for their retailer customers.

In this case, the shift of responsibility for the performance of these functions in the channel of distribution is a logical result of interorganizational analysis and management.

3. THIRD-PARTY ARRANGEMENTS . . .

Cooperative interorganizational approaches in the form of joint ventures or third parties can provide the objectivity and "arm's length" management often needed when large, proud organizations wish to create a product or service requiring inputs from several participating companies. They are particularly attractive in a field that has been typified by fragmented, duplicated services—logistics.

. . . in distribution utilities: We are now seeing joint ventures and third-party arrangements used in the creation of so-called distribution utilities— companies that are capable of providing a complete range of warehousing, transportation, order-processing, and inventory-control services to shipper customers. A distribution utility contracts with a small to medium-sized manufacturer or a division of a larger company to remove finished stock from the end of the latter's production line and make it available for sale—when, where, and in the quantities desired—with some pre-agreed-on level of customer service. This allows the manufacturer's marketing organization to concentrate on selling.

The distribution utility, to the extent that it takes possession of a product without taking title to it, is the converse of what, in common marketing parlance, is termed a broker—one who buys and sells goods without ever taking possession of them.

However, substantial resources are required to (a) construct or acquire a network of distribution centers (warehouses), (b) support the design and installation of extensive communication and information-processing facilities, and (c) create an organization in which naturally skeptical manufacturer-customers can have confidence. The joint venture provides a convenient means of assembling such resources.

. . . in consolidated regional centers: The movement of carload quantities of stocks directly from the production lines of competing manufacturers into

A. Without consolidated distribution

B. With consolidated distribution

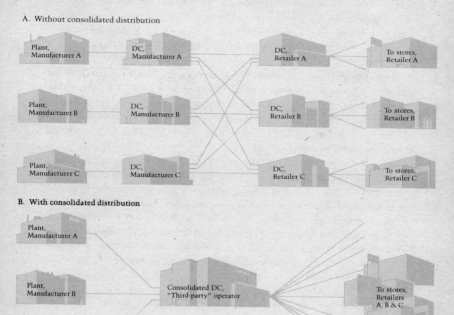

DC = Distribution centers

common regional distribution centers for consolidated delivery direct to retail stores has been under discussion for some time, particularly in the grocery products industry. Until now, objections regarding loss of control over the product, possible disclosure of competitive information, and the elimination of an area of potential competitive advantage have overruled the economic benefits of eliminating the manufacturer-operated and the retailer-operated distribution center as shown in *Exhibit II*. But consolidated distribution of this type is now a reality.

The concept has been recently implemented in Canada with the creation of a distribution center in Vancouver, shared jointly by leading manufacturers and their chain-store customers. The success of this experiment, conducted by a task force of the Canadian Grocery Manufacturers Association, which reports that it has reduced the cost of dry grocery distribution by at least 10%, has led to its rapid expansion to two other provinces of Canada.

. . . in central cooperative facilities: The benefits of consolidating out-
bound freight can usually be enjoyed by a well-managed, medium-sized or
large manufacturer. However, companies typically receiving small shipments from many sources have found that they must establish cooperative
arrangements to enjoy similar benefits.

Thus far, such arrangements have been confined to the formation of
shippers' cooperatives for the consolidation of merchandise purchased by
several companies for delivery to the same destination (a metropolitan
area). Transportation cost savings, in the form of pro rata rebates, from
the replacement of small package shipments by carload and truckload
shipments have been remarkable.

Now, at the urging of city officials, these same companies are beginning to explore the creation of consolidated storage and merchandise-
processing facilities, located in low-cost suburban areas, as well as the
coordination of delivery to retail store sites.

An unpublished feasibility study in which I participated several years
ago indicated that central distribution facilities could be operated at a
satisfactory profit by a third party at a cost to retailer customers of only
80% of their current costs of receiving, processing, and delivering such
goods themselves.

4. VERTICAL INTEGRATIONS

The possibilities I have discussed thus far are interorganizational alternatives to the vertical integration of logistics operations in a channel of distribution by one powerful channel member through the merger with, or
acquisition of, companies with which it deals.

Vertical integration in logistics flourished during the late 1960's as industrial manufacturers began acquiring companies offering complementary
services, such as trucking and warehousing. Interestingly, transportation
companies were not leaders in this trend, possibly because of the Interstate
Commerce Commission's historic tendency to impose stringent controls
on the acquisition of companies offering competing modes of service. Indicators point to more active participation by transport and other companies in ventures involving the vertical integration of logistics services.

However, the rate at which this takes place will depend, among other
things, on (a) the level of pressure exerted on the ICC to relax its control,
(b) the rate at which legal means, such as financial holding companies, are
found for accomplishing vertical integration, and (c) the level of prosperity
in the logistics industries themselves. In the latter regard, adversity may
help rather than hinder the trend.

Implementation Approaches

Perhaps the three most important factors in implementing creative approaches to interorganizational problems and institutional change in logistics are management practices, labor attitudes, and regulatory policies.

MANAGEMENT PRACTICES

Clearly, individuals and companies that can adopt the attitudes and practices necessary to foster creative approaches to interorganizational problems will have an edge on their competitors. What are these attitudes and practices? Early research in the field of interorganizational management has suggested some.[2]

Companies likely to be recognized as leaders during an era of institutional change and interorganizational problem solving will be characterized by:

□ *A tendency to seek what bargaining theorists have termed "nonzero-sum results from negotiations."*

Essentially, a nonzero-sum result is one which reduces the total cost of the negotiating organizations regardless of how they divide the resulting benefits. Nonzero-sum results can be achieved only through a basic change in procedure, such as the design of quantity discounts to reflect efficient handling and shipping or the implementation of incentives to encourage the faster unloading and turnaround of transportation equipment.

In contrast, zero-sum results produce no such net benefits. Price changes made without accompanying changes in procedure only transfer costs and profits from one company's P&L statement to another's, with no net economic benefit to the channel system.

□ *A willingness to absorb risks for the mutual benefit of participants in a channel system.*

A 1968 study examined the common problem of congestion at shippers' truck docks.[3] Its authors estimated that the addition of extra truck bays in several cases would reduce truck waiting time significantly, thereby producing high rates of return on investment.

Unfortunately, to implement these programs, shippers would have to make the investment to alter their facilities, while the benefits would accrue to truckers supplying pickup and delivery services.

Presumably, such situations could be resolved if one or more truckers

2. Much of this section is based on J. L. Heskett, Louis W. Stern, and Frederick J. Beier, "Bases and Uses of Power in Interorganization Relations," in *Vertical Marketing Systems*, edited by Louis P. Bucklin (Glenville, Illinois, Scott, Foresman and Company, 1970), p. 75.

3. Karl M. Ruppental and D. Clay Whybark, "Some Problems in Optimizing Shipping Facilities," *The Logistics Review*, Vol. 4, No. 20, 1968, p. 5.

could reduce rates selectively to encourage the necessary investment, a practice frowned on by the Interstate Commerce Commission. Or the trucker might make the investment with some assurance that he would continue to receive business from the shipper at least over a period sufficient to pay him back for his investment. Again, this practice could be looked on with disfavor by the ICC or a state regulatory body.

Perhaps the only feasible course of action would be for the shipper to absorb the uncertainty by constructing the bay. In return, he might obtain an informal agreement that future consideration, in the form of a rate reduction based on cost improvement, would be given by the carrier. This would only work if one carrier provided all or at least a significant portion of the service.

□ *A willingness to innovate on behalf of the channel.*

Some companies are known as innovators in their respective business spheres, in the testing of new technologies, organizational relationships, or contractual relationships. A company that is first to establish a pool of pallets for the economic handling of goods in a channel of distribution is likely to be regarded as such an innovator, with resulting long-term rewards for successful experiments (and perhaps losses for unsuccessful ones).

□ *The establishment of a mechanism for collecting and transmitting information and skills throughout a channel.*

Information that provides an early warning of inventory build-ups at the retail level can be of use to all participants in a channel system. Manufacturers of such diverse products as drugs and fertilizers have not only provided their distributors with inventory-control systems, but also educated them in the use of these systems. Expectations of long-term improvements in distributor profitability and loyalty motivate such manufacturers with enlightened interorganizational practices.

□ *The exchange of personnel with other parties to interorganizational relationships.*

A factor which distinguishes management in the United States from that in most other parts of the world is executive mobility. U.S. executives expect to make frequent moves; rarely do they expect to spend a lifetime working for a single firm. The exchange of personnel between "business partner" organizations can set the stage for important interorganizational achievements by executives in cooperating organizations who understand each other's problems and economic constraints.

LABOR ATTITUDES

Unionism is typically held up by management as the greatest obstacle to beneficial changes of the type I have discussed. And yet, in situations where managements have recognized the value of providing job (and union membership) security in return for freedom to redesign jobs and introduce technological improvements, labor's attitudes have been positive.

Perhaps the best example of labor's cooperative attitude was reflected in an agreement some years ago between the Pacific Maritime Association, representing ship operating managements, and the International Longshoremen's and Warehousemen's Union. Under the terms of the agreement, the PMA established a trust fund to protect until retirement the salaries of ILWU members expected to be displaced.

As a result of the technology introduced subsequent to the agreement, volume increases made possible by operating economies actually created jobs, leaving the union with a trust fund that it had limited immediate need for. Thus both parties found this transaction beneficial.

REGULATORY POLICIES

The fear of undue advantage or discrimination in dealings between carriers and shippers has proved to be a deterrent to interorganizational problem solving in logistics.

For example, the proposed introduction a few years ago of "Big John" hopper cars with several times the capacity of their predecessors, significantly higher minimum shipping quantities, and rate reductions of 60% on grain transportation from the Midwest to the Southeast by the Southern Railway was delayed for months by the ICC. This period of time was necessary to investigate the effects of the proposed innovation on the traffic of competing inland waterway barge operators. The litigation involved, among other things, a dispute over the question of whether the proposal exaggerated the magnitude of cost reductions which Southern could achieve with the innovation.

In spite of regulatory deterrents, there appears to be a trend toward more creative interorganizational problem solving on the part of carriers and shippers. The trend would be accelerated if, for example, regulatory agencies would emphasize this question in their investigations of carrier rate or service proposals: To what extent will changes resulting from such proposals produce procedural changes necessary to achieve non-zero-sum benefits for negotiants? With this shift in emphasis, proposals scoring high would have a greater chance of being approved and expedited by the concerned regulatory agency.

Conclusion

Institutional changes will, to an increasing extent, replace technological changes as the major sources of continued productivity increases in trans-

378 Production and Operations

portation, warehousing, inventory-control, and order-processing activities in the intermediate future. They both make possible, and are being fostered by, the application of interorganizational management thinking which attempts to produce operating efficiencies for two or more cooperating institutions in a channel of distribution.

This shift in emphasis in logistics threatens to envelop a number of shippers, carriers, and companies in associated industries in problems with which they are not equipped to deal. Significant competitive advantages already have accrued to those fully aware of the favorable competitive positions to be gained by shifting responsibilities for logistics activities from one company to another, creating third-party joint ventures to facilitate the consolidation and coordination of product flows, and seeking non-zero-sum results from interorganizational negotiations.

Such changes promise to inject additional dimensions of excitement to match those provided by recent significant technological developments in logistics. They also promise continued rewards to the executive of sufficiently broad view and flexible mind who is able to change to meet the needs of his chosen field. Clearly, they offer unexplored frontiers in the redevelopment and restructuring of logistics services.

20. Production-Line Approach to Service

Theodore Levitt

We think about service in humanistic terms; we think about manufacturing in technocratic terms. This, according to the author, is why manufacturing industries are forward-looking and efficient while service industries and customer service are, by comparison, primitive and inefficient. He argues that if companies stop thinking of service as servitude and personal ministrations, they will be able to effect drastic improvements in its quality and efficiency. Then he shows companies how to take a manufacturing approach to this activity, one that substitutes "technology and systems for people and serendipity."

The service sector of the economy is growing in size but shrinking in quality. So say a lot of people. Purveyors of service, for their part, think that they and their problems are fundamentally different from other businesses and their problems. They feel that service is people-intensive, while the rest of the economy is capital-intensive. But these distinctions are largely spurious. There are no such things as service industries. There are only industries whose service components are greater or less than those of other industries. Everybody is in service.

Often the less there seems, the more there is. The more technologically sophisticated the generic product (e.g., cars and computers), the more dependent are its sales on the quality and availability of its accompanying customer services (e.g., display rooms, delivery, repairs and maintenance, application aids, operator training, installation advice, warranty fulfillment). In this sense, General Motors is probably more service-intensive than manufacturing-intensive. Without its services its sales would shrivel.

Thus the service sector of the economy is not merely comprised of the so-called service industries, such as banking, airlines, and maintenance. It includes the entire abundance of product-related services supplied by manufacturers and the sales-related services supplied by retailers. Yet we confuse things to our detriment by an outdated taxonomy. For example:

◻ The First National City Bank (Citibank) is one of the biggest worldwide banks. Over half of its employees deal directly with the public, either selling them things (mostly money and deposit services) or helping them with things they have already bought (cashing checks, taking additional deposits, writing letters of credit, opening lockboxes, managing corporate cash). Most of the other employees work back in what is called "the factory"—a massive congeries of people, paper, and computers that processes, records, validates, and scrutinizes everything the first group has done. All the corporate taxonomists, including the U.S. Bureau of the Census, classify Citibank as a service company.

□ IBM is the biggest worldwide manufacturer of computers. More than half of its employees deal directly with the public, either selling them things (mostly machines) or helping them with the things they have already bought (installing and repairing machines, writing computer programs, training customers). Most of the other employees work back in the factory —a massive congeries of wires, microminiature electronic components, engineers, and assemblers. All the corporate taxonomists, including the U.S. Bureau of the Census, classify IBM as a manufacturing company.

Something is wrong, and not just in the Bureau of the Census. The industrial world has changed more rapidly than our taxonomies. If only taxonomy were involved, the consequences of our contradictory classifications would be trivial. After all, man lives perfectly well with his contradictions: his simultaneous faith, for instance, in both God and science; his attachment to facts and logic when making important business decisions, but reliance on feelings and emotion when making far more important life decisions, like marriage.

I hope to show in this article that our contradictory notions about service may have malignant consequences. Not until we clarify the contradictions will companies begin to solve problems that now seem so intractible. In order to do so, they must think of themselves as performing manufacturing functions when it comes to their so-called "service" activities. Only then will they begin to make some significant progress in improving the quality and efficiency of service in the modern economy.

Field vs. Factory

People think of service as quite different from manufacturing. Service is presumed to be performed by individuals for other individuals, generally on a one-to-one basis. Manufacturing is presumed to be performed by machines, generally tended by large clusters of individuals whose sizes and configurations are themselves dictated by the machines' requirements. Service (whether customer service or the services of service industries) is performed "out there in the field" by distant and loosely supervised people working under highly variable, and often volatile, conditions. Manufacturing occurs "here in the factory" under highly centralized, carefully organized, tightly controlled, and elaborately engineered conditions.

People assume, and rightly so, that these differences largely explain why products produced in the factory are generally more uniform in features and quality than the services produced (e.g., life insurance policies, machine repairs) or delivered (e.g., spare parts, milk) in the field. One cannot as easily control one's agents or their performance out there in the field. Besides, different customers want different things. The result is that service and service industries, in comparison with manufacturing industries, are widely and correctly viewed as being primitive, sluggish, and inefficient.

Yet it is doubtful that things need be all that bad. Once conditions in the field get the same kind of attention that conditions inside the factory generally get, a lot of new opportunities become possible. But first management will have to revise its thinking about what service is and what it implies.

LIMITS OF SERVITUDE

The trouble with thinking of oneself as providing services—either in the service industries or in the customer-service sectors of manufacturing and retailing companies—is that one almost inescapably embraces ancient, pre-industrial modes of thinking. Worse still, one gets caught up in rigid attitudes that can have a profoundly paralyzing effect on even the most resolute of rationalists.

The concept of "service" evokes, from the opaque recesses of the mind, time-worn images of personal ministration and attendance. It refers generally to deeds one individual performs personally for another. It carries historical connotations of charity, gallantry, and selflessness, or of obedience, subordination, and subjugation. In these contexts, people serve because they want to (as in the priestly and political professions) or they serve because they are compelled to (as in slavery and such occupations of attendance as waiter, maid, bellboy, cleaning lady).

In the higher-status service occupations, such as in the church and the army, one customarily behaves ritualistically, not rationally. In the lower-status service occupations, one simply obeys. In neither is independent thinking presumed to be a requisite of holding a job. The most that can therefore be expected from service improvements is that, like Avis, a person will try harder. He will just exert more animal effort to do better what he is already doing.

So it was in ancient times, and so it is today. The only difference is that where ancient masters invoked the will of God or the whip of the foreman to spur performance, modern industry uses training programs and motivation sessions. We have not in all these years come very far in either our methods or our results. In short, service thinks humanistically, and that explains its failures.

Now consider manufacturing. Here the orientation is toward the efficient production of results, not toward attendance on others. Relationships are strictly businesslike, devoid of invidious connotations of rank or self.

When we think about how to improve manufacturing, we seldom focus on ways to improve our personal performance of present tasks; rather, it is axiomatic that we try to find entirely new ways of performing present tasks and, better yet, of actually changing the tasks themselves. We do not think of greater exertion of our animal energies (working physically harder, as the slave), of greater expansion of our commitment (being more devout or loyal, as the priest), or of greater assertion of our dependence (being more obsequious, as the butler).

Instead, we apply the greater exertion of our minds to learn how to look at a problem differently. More particularly, we ask what kinds of tools, old or new, and what kinds of skills, processes, organizational rearrangements, incentives, controls, and audits might be enlisted to greatly improve the intended outcomes. In short, manufacturing thinks technocratically, and that explains its successes.

Manufacturing looks for solutions inside the very tasks to be done. The solution to building a low-priced automobile, for example, derives largely from the nature and composition of the automobile itself. (If the automobile were not an assembly of parts, it could not be manufactured on an assembly line.) By contrast, service looks for solutions in the *performer* of the task. This is the paralyzing legacy of our inherited attitudes: the solution to improved service is viewed as being dependent on improvements in the skills and attitudes of the performers of that service.

While it may pain and offend us to say so, thinking in humanistic rather than technocratic terms ensures that the service sector of the modern economy will be forever inefficient and that our satisfactions will be forever marginal. We see service as invariably and undeviatingly personal, as something performed by individuals directly for other individuals.

This humanistic conception of service diverts us from seeking alternatives to the use of people, especially to large, organized groups of people. It does not allow us to reach out for new solutions and new definitions. It obstructs us from redesigning the tasks themselves; from creating new tools, processes, and organizations; and, perhaps, even from eliminating the conditions that created the problems.

In sum, to improve the quality and efficiency of service, companies must apply the kind of technocratic thinking which in other fields has replaced the high-cost and erratic elegance of the artisan with the low-cost, predictable munificence of the manufacturer.

The Technocratic Hamburger

Nowhere in the entire service sector are the possibilities of the manufacturing mode of thinking better illustrated than in fast-food franchising. Nowhere have manufacturing methods been employed more effectively to control the operation of distant and independent agents. Nowhere is "service" better.

Few of today's successful new commercial ventures have antecedents that are more humble and less glamorous than the hamburger. Yet the thriving nationwide chain of hamburger stands called "McDonald's" is a supreme example of the application of manufacturing and technological brilliance to problems that must ultimately be viewed as marketing problems. From 1961 to 1970, McDonald's sales rose from approximately $54 million to $587 million. During this remarkable ascent, the White Tower chain, whose name had theretofore been practically synonymous throughout the land with low-priced, quick-service hamburgers, practically vanished.

The explanation of McDonald's thundering success is not a purely fiscal one—i.e., the argument that it is financed by independent local entrepreneurs who bring to their operations a quality of commitment and energy not commonly found among hired workers. Nor is it a purely geographical one—i.e., the argument that each outlet draws its patronage from a relatively small geographic ring of customers, thus enabling the number of outlets easily and quickly to multiply. The relevant explanation must deal with the central question of why each separate McDonald's outlet is so predictably successful, why each is so certain to attract many repeat customers.

Entrepreneurial financing and careful site selection do help. But most important is the carefully controlled execution of each outlet's central function—the rapid delivery of a uniform, high-quality mix of prepared foods in an environment of obvious cleanliness, order, and cheerful courtesy. The systematic substitution of equipment for people, combined with the carefully planned use and positioning of technology, enables McDonald's to attract and hold patronage in proportions no predecessor or imitator has managed to duplicate. Consider the remarkable ingenuity of the system, which is worth examining in some detail:

To start with the obvious, raw hamburger patties are carefully prepacked and premeasured, which leaves neither the franchisee nor his employees any discretion as to size, quality, or raw-material consistency. This kind of attention is given to all McDonald's products. Storage and preparation space and related facilities are expressly designed for, and limited to, the predetermined mix of products. There is no space for any foods, beverages, or services that were not designed into the system at the outset. There is not even a sandwich knife or, in fact, a decent place to keep one. Thus the owner has no discretion regarding what he can sell—not because of any contractual limitations, but because of facilities limitations. And the employees have virtually no discretion regarding how to prepare and serve things.

Discretion is the enemy of order, standardization, and quality. On an automobile assembly line, for example, a worker who has discretion and latitude might possibly produce a more personalized car, but one that is highly unpredictable. The elaborate care with which an automobile is designed and an assembly line is structured and controlled is what produces quality cars at low prices, and with surprising reliability considering the sheer volume of the output. The same is true at McDonald's, which produces food under highly automated and controlled conditions.

FRENCH-FRIED AUTOMATION

While in Detroit the significance of the technological process lies in production, at McDonald's it lies in marketing. A carefully planned design is built into the elaborate technology of the food-service system in such a fashion as to make it a significant marketing device. This fact is impressively illustrated by McDonald's handling of that uniquely plebeian American delicacy, french-fried potatoes.

French fries become quickly soggy and unappetizing; to be good, they must be freshly made just before serving. Like other fast-food establishments, McDonald's provides its outlets with precut, partially cooked frozen potatoes that can be quickly finished in an on-premises, deep-fry facility. The McDonald's fryer is neither so large that it produces too many french fries at one time (thus allowing them to become soggy) nor so small that it requires frequent and costly frying.

The fryer is emptied onto a wide, flat tray adjacent to the service counter. This location is crucial. Since the McDonald's practice is to create an impression of abundance and generosity by slightly overfilling each bag of french fries, the tray's location next to the service counter prevents the spillage from an overfilled bag from reaching the floor. Spillage creates not only danger underfoot but also an unattractive appearance that causes the employees to become accustomed to an unclean environment. Once a store is unclean in one particular, standards fall very rapidly and the store becomes unclean and the food unappetizing in general.

While McDonald's aims for an impression of abundance, excessive overfilling can be very costly for a company that annually buys potatoes almost by the trainload. A systematic bias that puts into each bag of french fries a half ounce more than is intended can have visible effects on the company's annual earnings. Further, excessive time spent at the tray by each employee can create a cumulative service bottleneck at the counter.

McDonald's has therefore developed a special wide-mouthed scoop with a narrow funnel in its handle. The counter employee picks up the scoop and inserts the handle end into a wall clip containing the bags. One bag adheres to the handle. In a continuous movement the scoop descends into the potatoes, fills the bag to the exact proportions its designers intended, and is lifted, scoop facing the ceiling, so that the potatoes funnel through the handle into the attached bag, which is automatically disengaged from the handle by the weight of the contents. The bag comes to a steady, non-wobbling rest on its flat bottom.

Nothing can go wrong—the employee never soils his hands, the floor remains clean, dry, and safe, and the quantity is controlled. Best of all, the customer gets a visibly generous portion with great speed, the employee remains efficient and cheerful, and the general impression is one of extravagantly good service.

MECHANIZED MARKETING

Consider the other aspects of McDonald's technological approach to marketing. The tissue paper used to wrap each hamburger is color-coded to denote the mix of condiments. Heated reservoirs hold pre-prepared hamburgers for rush demand. Frying surfaces have spatter guards to prevent soiling of the cooks' uniforms. Nothing is left to chance or the employees' discretion.

The entire system is engineered and executed according to a tight technological discipline that ensures fast, clean, reliable service in an atmosphere that gives the modestly paid employees a sense of pride and dignity. In spite of the crunch of eager customers, no employee looks or acts harassed, and therefore no harassment is communicated to the customers.

But McDonald's goes even further. Customers may be discouraged from entering if the building looks unappealing from the outside; hence considerable care goes into the design and appearance of the structure itself.

Some things, however, the architect cannot control, especially at an establishment where people generally eat in their parked cars and are likely to drop hamburger wrappings and empty beverage cartons on the ground. McDonald's has anticipated the requirement: its blacktop parking facilities are dotted like a checkerboard with numerous large, highly visible trash cans. It is impossible to ignore their purpose. Even the most indifferent customer would be struck with guilt if he simply dropped his refuse on the ground. But, just in case he drops it anyway, the larger McDonald's outlets have motorized sweepers for quick and easy cleanup.

What is important to understand about this remarkably successful organization is not only that it has created a highly sophisticated piece of technology, but also that it has done this by applying a manufacturing style of thinking to a people-intensive service situation. If machinery is to be viewed as a piece of equipment with the capability of producing a predictably standardized, customer-satisfying output while minimizing the operating discretion of its attendant, that is what a McDonald's retail outlet is. It is a machine that produces, with the help of totally unskilled machine tenders, a highly polished product. Through painstaking attention to total design and facilities planning, everything is built integrally into the machine itself, into the technology of the system. The only choice available to the attendant is to operate it exactly as the designers intended.

Tooling Up for Service

Although most people are not aware of it, there are many illustrations of manufacturing solutions to people-intensive service problems. For example:

□ Mutual funds substitute one sales call for many; one consultation for dozens; one piece of paper for thousands; and one reasonably informed customer choice for numerous, confused, and often poor choices.

□ Credit cards that are used for making bank loans substitute a single credit decision (issuing the card in the first place) for the many elaborate, costly, people-intensive activities and decisions that bank borrowing generally entails.

□ Supermarkets substitute fast and efficient self-service for the slow, inefficient, and often erratic clerks of the traditional service store.

In each of these examples a technological device or a manufacturing type of process has replaced what had been resolutely thought of as an irrevocably people-requiring service. Similar devices or processes can be used to modify and alleviate the customer-repelling abrasions of other people-intensive service conditions.

Consider the airlines. This industry is highly unusual. It is exceedingly capital-intensive in the creation of the facilitating product (the airplane), but it is extremely people-intensive in the delivery of the product (travel arrangements and the customer's flight experience). The possibilities for revenue production that a \$20-million airplane represents are quickly vitiated by a surly or uncooperative reservations clerk. The potentials of repeat business that the chef so carefully builds into his meals can be destroyed by a dour or sloppy stewardess.

In fact, stewardesses have a particularly difficult job. A hundred passengers, having paid for reasonable service, understandably expect to be treated with some care. While three young ladies are there to serve them, a number of these passengers must inevitably get their drinks and meals later than others. Most experienced travelers are understanding and tolerant of the rushed stewardesses' problems, but a few usually harass them. The pressure and abuse can easily show in the stewardesses' personal appearance and behavior, and are likely to result in nearly all passengers being reciprocally mistreated. This is human. Besides, the ladies may have been on their feet all day, or may have slept only a few hours the night before.

"More and better training" is not likely to help things very much. When the pressure is on, service deteriorates. And so does a stewardess's cheerful manner and appearance, no matter how well schooled she is in personal care and keeping her cool or how attractively her clothes are designed.

But it might help to put mirrors in the airplane galley, so that each time a stewardess goes in she sees herself. There is some reason to expect that she'll look into the mirror each time she passes it, and that she'll straighten her hair, eliminate that lipstick smudge, put on a more cheerful face. Improvement will be instantaneous. No training needed.

Here is another possibility: the stewardess makes a quick trip down the aisle, passing out rum-flavored bonbons and explaining, "For those who can't wait till we get the ice out." This breaks the tension, produces an air of cheerfulness, acknowledges the passengers' eagerness for quick service, and says that the ladies are trying their hurried best. Further, it brings the stewardess into friendly personal contact with the passenger and reduces the likelihood of her being pressured and abused. She, in turn, is less likely to irritate other passengers.

From the manufacturing point of view, these two modest proposals represent the substitution of tools (or, as I prefer, technology) for motivation. Mirrors are a tool for getting self-motivated, automatic results in the stewardesses' appearance and personal behavior. Bonbons are a tool for creating a benign interpersonal ambience that reduces both the likelihood of customer irritation and the reciprocal and contagious stewardess irritation of others. They are small measures, but so is a company president's plant tour.

In each case there is considerable presumption of solid benefits. Yet to get these benefits one must think, as the factory engineer thinks, about what the problems are and what the desired output is; about how to redesign the process and how to install new tools that do the job more automatically; and, whenever people are involved, about how to "control" their personal behavior and channel their choices.

HARD AND SOFT TECHNOLOGIES

There are numerous examples of strictly "hard" technologies (i.e., pieces of equipment) which are used as substitutes for people—coffee vending machines for waitresses, automatic check-cashing machines for bank tellers, self-operated travel-insurance-policy machines for clerks. Although these devices represent a manufacturing approach to service, and while their principles can be extended to other fields, even greater promise lies in the application of "soft" technologies (i.e., technological systems). McDonald's is an example of a soft technology. So are mutual funds. Other examples are all around us, if we just think of them in the right way. Take the life insurance industry:

A life insurance salesman is said to be in a service industry. Yet what does he really do? He researches the prospect's needs by talking with him, designs several policy models for him, and "consumer-use tests" these models by seeking his reactions. Then he redesigns the final model and delivers it for sale to the customer. This is the ultimate example of manufacturing in the field. The factory is in the customer's living room, and the producer is the insurance agent, whom we incorrectly think of as being largely a salesman. Once we think of him as a manufacturer, however, we begin to think of how best to design and manufacture the product rather than how best to sell it.

The agent, for example, could be provided with a booklet of overlay sheets showing the insurance plans of people who are similar to the customer. This gives the customer a more credible and informed basis for making a choice. In time, the agent could be further supported by similar information stored in telephone-access computers.

In short, we begin to think of building a system that will allow the agent to produce his product efficiently and effectively by serving the customer's needs instead of performing a manipulative selling job.

MANUFACTURERS OUTSIDE THE FACTORY

The type of thinking just described applies not only to service industries but also to manufacturing industries. When the computer hardware manufacturer provides installation and maintenance services, debugging dry-runs, software programs, and operator training as part of his hardware sales program, he acknowledges that his "product" consists of considerably more than what he made in the factory. What is done in the field is just as important to the customer as the manufactured equipment itself. Indeed, without these services there would generally be no sale.

The problem in so many cases is that customer service is not viewed by manufacturers as an integral part of what the customer buys, but as something peripheral to landing the sale. However, when it is explicitly accepted as integral to the product itself and, as a consequence, gets the same kind of dedicated attention as the manufacture of the hardware gets, the results can be spectacular. For example:

□ In the greeting card industry, some manufacturer-provided retail display cases have built-in inventory replenishment and reordering features. In effect, these features replace a company salesman with the willing efforts of department managers or store owners. The motivation of the latter to reorder is created by the visible imminence of stockouts, which is achieved with a special color-coded card that shows up as the stock gets low. Order numbers and envelopes are included for reordering. In earlier days a salesman had to call, take inventory, arrange the stock, and write orders. Stockouts were common.

The old process was called customer service and selling. The new process has no name, and probably has never been viewed as constituting a technological substitute for people. But it is. An efficient, automatic, capital-intensive system, supplemented occasionally by people, has replaced an inefficient and unreliable people-intensive system.

□ In a more complex situation, the A.O. Smith Company has introduced the same kind of preplanning, routinizing, people-conserving activity. This company makes, among other things, grain storage silos that must be locally sold, installed, serviced, and financed. There are numerous types of silos with a great variety of accessories for loading, withdrawing, and automatically mixing livestock feed. The selling is carried out by local distributor-erectors and is a lengthy, difficult, sophisticated operation.

Instead of depending solely on the effective training of distributors, who are spread widely in isolated places, A. O. Smith has developed a series of sophisticated, colorful, and interchangeable design-module planning books. These can be easily employed by a distributor to help a farmer decide what he may need, its cost, and its financing requirements. Easy-to-read tables, broken down by the size of farm, numbers and types of animals, and purpose of animals (cattle for meat or cows for milk), show recommended combinations of silo sizes and equipment for maximum effectiveness.

The system is so thorough, so easy to use and understand, and so effective in its selling capability that distributors use it with great eagerness. As a consequence, A.O. Smith, while sitting in Milwaukee, in effect controls every sales presentation made by every one of its far-flung distributors. Instead of constantly sending costly company representatives out to retrain, cajole, wine-and-dine, and possibly antagonize distributors, the supplier sends out a tool that distributors *want* to utilize in their own self-interest.

PRODUCT-LINE PRAGMATICS

Thinking of service as an integral part of what is sold can also result in alteration of the product itself—and with dramatic results. In 1961, the Building Controls and Components Group of Honeywell, Inc., the nation's largest producer of heating and air conditioning thermostats and control devices, did a major part of its business in replacement controls (the after-market). These were sold through heating and air conditioning distributors, who then supplied plumbers and other installation and repair specialists.

At that time, Honeywell's product line consisted of nearly 18,000 separate catalog parts and pieces. The company had nearly 5,000 distributor accounts, none of which could carry a full line of these items economically, and therefore it maintained nearly 100 fully stocked field warehouses that offered immediate delivery to distributors. The result was that, in a large proportion of cases, distributors sold parts to plumbers that they did not themselves have in stock. They either sent plumbers to nearby Honeywell warehouses for pickup or picked up parts themselves and delivered them directly to the plumbers. The costs to Honeywell of carrying these inventories were enormous, but were considered a normal expense of doing business.

Then Honeywell made a daring move—it announced its new Tradeline Policy. It would close all warehouses. All parts would have to be stocked by the distributors. The original equipment, however, had been redesigned into 300 standard, interchangeable parts. These were interchangeable not only for most Honeywell controls, but also for those of its major competitors. Moreover, each package was clearly imprinted to show exactly what Honeywell and competing products were repairable with the contents.

By closing its own warehouses, Honeywell obviously shifted the inventory-carrying costs to its distributors. But instead of imposing new burdens on them, the new product lines, with their interchangeability features, enabled the distributors to carry substantially lower inventories, particularly by cutting down the need for competitive product lines which the distributors could nonetheless continue to service. Thus they were able to offer faster service at lower costs to their customers than before.

But not all distributors were easily persuaded of this possibility, and some dropped the line. Those who were persuaded ultimately proved their wisdom by the enormous expansion of their sales. Honeywell's replacement market share almost doubled, and its original equipment share rose by nearly 50%. Whereas previously nearly 90% of Honeywell's replacement sales were scattered among 4,000 distributors, within ten years after Tradeline's introduction the same proportion (of a doubled volume) was concentrated among only about 900 distributors. Honeywell's cost of servicing these fewer customers was substantially less, its trade inventory carrying costs were cut to zero, and the quality of its distributor services was so substantially improved that only 900 of its distributors captured a larger national market share than did the nearly 4,000 less efficient and more costly distributors.

Again, we see a people-intensive marketing problem being solved by the careful and scrupulous application of manufacturing attitudes. Motivation, hard work, personalization, training, and merchandising incentives were replaced with systematic programming, comprehensive planning, attention to detail, and particularly with imaginative concern for the problems and needs of customers (in this case, the company's distributors).

Stopgaps: Complexity . . .

Exaggeration is not without its merits, especially in love and war. But in business one guards against it with zeal, especially when one tries to persuade oneself. The judicious application of the manufacturing mentality may help the service industries and the customer-service activities of others. Yet this does not necessarily mean the more technology, the better.

Entrepreneurial roadsides are littered with the wrecks of efforts to install Cadillac technologies for people who cannot yet handle the Model T. This point is illustrated by the failure of two exceedingly well-financed joint ventures of highly successful technology companies. These joint ventures attempted to provide computerized medical diagnostic services for doctors and hospitals. The companies developed console hookups to central diagnostic computers, so that everybody could stop sending off samples to pathology laboratories and agonizingly poring through medical texts to diagnose the patients' symptoms.

The ventures failed because of hospital and doctor resistance, not for want of superior or reliable products. The customer was compelled suddenly to make an enormous change in his accustomed way of doing things, and to employ a strange and somewhat formidable piece of equipment that required special training in its use and in the interpretation of its output.

Interactive teaching machines are meeting a similar fate. The learning results they achieve are uniformly spectacular. The need for improved learning is a visible reality. The demand for greater individualization of teaching is widespread. But the equipment has not sold because technologists have created systems employing equipment that is at the cutting edge of technological progress. The teachers and school systems that must use them are far behind, and already feel badly bruised by their failure to comprehend even simple new technologies. For them, the new Cadillac technologies do not solve problems. They create problems.

. . . AND COMPROMISE

On the other hand, failure to exploit technological possibilities can be equally destructive. When a major petroleum company with nearly 30,000 retail outlets in the United States was persuaded to pioneer a revolutionary automobile repair and servicing system, compromises of the original plan ensured the system's failure.

The theory was to build a gigantic service and repair system that could handle heavy volumes of continuous activity by using specialized diagnostic and repair equipment. With this equipment (rather than a harried and overworked man at a gas station) pinpointing the exact problems, cars could be shuttled off to specific stations in the repair center. Experts would work only on one kind of problem and section of a car, with newly designed, fast-action tools. Oil changes would be made in assembly-line fashion by low-paid workers, electrical work would be performed by high-paid technicians doing only that, and a post-diagnostic checkup would be made to guarantee success.

Since profitability would require high volume, the center would have to draw on a vast population area. To facilitate this, the original proposal called for a specially constructed building at a center-city, old warehouse location—the land would be cheaper, the building would be equally accessible throughout the entire metropolitan area, the service center's technological elegance and see-through windows for customers would offset any run-down neighborhood disadvantages, and volume business would come from planned customer decisions rather than random off-street traffic.

The original concept also called for overnight pickup and delivery service; thus a car could be repaired at night while its owner slept, rather than during the day when he would need it. And because the required promotion of this service would tend to alienate the company's franchised service station dealers, perhaps driving them into the hands of competitors, it was recommended that the first center be installed in a major city where the company had no stations.

This sounds like an excellent manufacturing approach to a service situation; but the company made three fatal compromises:

1. It decided to place the center in a costly, high-traffic suburban location, on the grounds that "if the experiment fails, at least the building will be in a location that has an alternative use." The results were an awkward location, a land-acquisition cost five times higher than the original center-city location, and, therefore, a vastly inflated break-even point for the service center.

2. It decided not to offer overnight service, on the grounds that "we'd better crawl before we walk. And besides, we don't think people will leave their cars overnight in a strange and distant garage." The fact that the results would be guaranteed by a reputable, nationally known petroleum company operating an obviously sophisticated new type of consumer service facility was not persuasive to the corporate decision makers.

3. It decided to put the first center in a city occupied by its own franchised dealers, on the grounds that "we know it better." To offset the problem of not being able to advertise aggressively for business, the company offered its dealers a commission to send their repair jobs to the center.

The dealers did this, but only with jobs they could not, or did not want to, do themselves. As a result, the traffic at the big, expensive center was miserably low.

Companies that take a manufacturing approach to service problems are likely to fail if (a) they compromise technological possibilities at the conception and design stage, or (b) they allow technological complexity to contaminate the operating stage. The substitution of technology and systems for people and serendipity is complex in its conception and design; only in its *operation*, as at McDonald's, is it simple.

It is the simplicity of mutual funds that, after all, accounts for their success. But the concept is in fact much more complex than that of selling individual stocks through a single customer man sitting at a desk. Mutual funds are the financial community's equivalent of McDonald's. They are a piece of technology that not only simplifies life for both the seller and the buyer but also creates many more buyers and makes production more profitable.

Mass merchandising is similar. It substitutes a wide selection and fast, efficient self-service for a narrow selection and slow, incompetent salesclerk service. The mass merchandising retail store (e.g., general merchandise supermarket) is a new technology, incorporating into retailing precisely the thinking that goes into the assembly line, except that the customer does his own assembling.

Why Things Go Wrong

The significance of all this is that a "product" is quite different from what it is generally assumed to be. When asked once what he did, Charles Revson, head of Revlon, Inc., made the now well-known reply, "In the factory we make cosmetics, in the store we sell hope." He defined the product in terms of what the consumer wanted, not in terms of what the manufacturer made. McDonald's obviously does the same—not just hamburgers but also speed, cleanliness, reassurance, cheerfulness, and predictable consistency. Honeywell defined it not in terms of replacement parts but, rather, in terms of those needs of its distributors which, if met, would result in substantially larger proportions of patronage for Honeywell. Thus a product is not something people buy, but a tool they use—a tool to solve their problems or to achieve their intentions.

So many things go wrong because companies fail to adequately define what they sell. Companies in so-called service industries generally think of themselves as offering services rather than manufacturing products; hence they fail to think and act as comprehensively as do manufacturing companies concerned with the efficient, low-cost production of customer-satisfying products.

Moreover, manufacturing companies themselves do not generally think of customer service as an integral part of *their* products. It is an afterthought to be handled by the marketing department.

The marketing department, in turn, thinks of itself as providing customer services. There is a hidden and unintentional implication of giving something away for free. One is doing something extra as a favor. When this is the underlying communication to one's own organization, the result is about what one would expect—casual, discretionary attitudes and little attention to detail, and certainly no attention to the possibilities of substituting systems and preplanning for people and pure effort. Hence products are designed that cannot be easily installed, repaired, or modified.

(Motorola's "works in a box" television set, which has been promoted so successfully on the basis of its easy replacement and repairability, is an outstanding example of the sales-getting potential of proper care in design and manufacturing.)

CHILL WINDS FROM ICE CREAM

An excellent example of the confusion between what a company "makes" and what a customer "buys" is provided by a producer of private-label ice cream products for supermarket chains. Since supermarkets need to create low-price impressions in order to attract and hold customers, selling successfully to them means getting down to rock-bottom prices. The company (call it the Edwards Company) became extraordinarily good at producing a wide line of ice cream products at rock-bottom costs. It grew rapidly while others went bankrupt. It covered ten states with direct deliveries to stores out of its factory and factory warehouse, but continued growth eventually required establishing plant, distribution, and marketing centers elsewhere. The result was disaster, even though the company manufactured just as efficiently in the new locations as it did in the old.

Under the direct and constant supervision of the president in the original Edwards location, an exceedingly efficient telephone ordering and delivery system had been working to meet the supermarkets' rather stringent requirements. Because of limited storage and display space, they required several-times-a-week delivery at specified, uncrowded store hours. To make up for low volume in slow periods, they needed regular specials as well as holiday and summer specials. Over time, these needs had become so automatically but efficiently supplied from the original Edwards factory location that this delivery service became routinized and therefore taken for granted.

In building the new plant, the president and his compact management team focused on getting manufacturing costs down to rock bottom. After all, that is what made the sale—low prices. Not being very conscious of the fact that they had created in the original location an enormously customer-satisfying, efficient, automatic ordering and delivery system, they did not know exactly what to look for in evaluating how well they were working out these "service" details at the new plant, distribution, and marketing centers.

In short, they did not know what their product really was (why Edwards had become so successful) and they failed to expand Edwards' success. Service was not considered an integral part of the company's product. It was viewed merely as "something else" you do in the business. Accordingly, service received inadequate attention, and that became the cause of the Edwards Company's failure.

Conclusion

Rarely is customer service discretionary. It is a requisite of getting and holding business, just like the generic product itself. Moreover, if customer service is consciously treated as "manufacturing in the field," it will get the same kind of detailed attention that manufacturing gets. It will be carefully planned, controlled, automated where possible, audited for quality control, and regularly reviewed for performance improvement and customer reaction. More important, the same kinds of technological, labor-saving, and systems approaches that now thrive in manufacturing operations will begin to get a chance to thrive in customer service and service industries.

Once service-industry executives and the creators of customer-service programs begin seriously to think of themselves as actually manufacturing a product, they will begin to think like product manufacturers. They will ask: What technologies and systems are employable here? How can things be designed so we can use machines instead of people, systems instead of serendipity? Instead of thinking about better and more training of their customer-service representatives, insurance agents, branch bank managers, or salesmen "out there," they will think about how to eliminate or supplement them.

If we continue to approach service as something done by individuals rather than by machines or systems, we will continue to suffer from two distortions in thinking:

1. Service will be viewed as something residual to the ultimate reality—to a tangible product, to a specific competence (like evaluating loans, writing insurance policies, giving medical aid, preparing on-premises foods). Hence it will have residual respectability, receive residual attention, and be left, somehow, for residual performers.

2. Service will be treated as purely a human task that must inevitably be

diagnosed and performed by a single individual working alone with no help
or, at best, with the rudimentary help of training and a variety of human-
engineering motivators. It will never get the kind of manufacturing-type
thinking that goes into tangible products.

Until we think of service in more positive and encompassing terms, until
it is enthusiastically viewed as manufacturing in the field, receptive to the
same kinds of technological approaches that are used in the factory, the results are likely to be just as costly and idiosyncratic as the results of the
lonely journeyman carving things laboriously by hand at home.

The Contributors

B. Charles Ames, formerly a Managing Partner in the Cleveland office of McKinsey & Company, is now Chairman–CEO of Acme Cleveland Corp. He has specialized in marketing management, with emphasis on organization and planning.

John C. Chambers is former Manager, Management Science at Xerox Corporation, and was previously associated with the Ford Motor Company, North American Aviation, and Corning Glass Works. His research interests center on strategic planning for new products and development of improved forecasting methods.

Gordon Donaldson is Willard Prescott Smith Professor of Corporate Finance at the Harvard Business School. Besides *Corporate Debt Capacity* (1961), on which his contribution to this book is based, he has written other books and articles on finance.

Cyrus F. Gibson is Vice President of Index Systems, Inc., in Cambridge, Massachusetts. He has recently been studying behavioral and social forces that affect efficient use of computer models in various organizational settings.

Frank F. Gilmore, a pioneer in analyzing executives' planning problems, is now retired. Formerly he was a professor in the Graduate School of Business and Public Administration at Cornell University and director of the Executive Development Program there.

James L. Heskett is 1907 Foundation Professor of Business Logistics at the Harvard Business School. He is the coauthor of *Business Logistics* (1964, 2nd ed. 1973), *Highway Transportation Management* (1963), and *Case Problems in Business Logistics* (1973). He is conducting research in inventory location strategy and interorganizational problem solving.

William K. Holstein is Professor of Management and former Dean of the School of Business at the State University of New York at Albany. His field of interest has been production management, and he has specialized in the development and installation of production scheduling systems. He is the coauthor of *Liberal Education and Engineering* (1960).

Philip Kotler is Harold T. Martin Professor of Marketing at Northwestern University. He has been interested in the development and application of marketing principles in market analysis, new product development, competitive marketing strategies, promotional planning, and information systems. He has written a number of influential books, among them *Marketing Management: Analysis, Planning, and Control* (2nd edition, 1972), and he has received many awards for his contributions to advertising and marketing management.

Theodore Levitt is Edward W. Carter Professor of Business Administration at the Harvard Business School. He has written many articles for the *Harvard Business Review* and several books, the latest of which is *The Marketing Imagination* (1983). His articles have won four McKinsey Awards and a John Hancock Award for Excellence.

Sidney J. Levy is A. Montgomery Ward Professor of Marketing and Chairman of the department at Northwestern University. He has also been staff psychologist since 1948 and director of psychological research since 1952 at Social Research, Inc., where he has been concerned primarily with consumer behavior. His most recent book is *Promotional Behavior* (1970).

John G. McLean taught at the Harvard Business School for sixteen years before joining Continental Oil Company in 1954 as assistant to the president. He became President and Chief Executive Officer at Continental in 1969 and was chairman and chief executive until his death in 1974.

Myles L. Mace is currently a professional corporate director. He has had a long career as corporate executive, teacher, and observer of top management behavior. He was Vice President of Litton Industries, Inc. and Professor of Business Administration at the Harvard Business School. His most recent publication was *Directors: Myth and Reality* (1972).

Dr. Satinder K. Mullick is Director of Economics Planning and Research at Corning Glass Works. He specializes in strategic and tactical planning for new products.

Derek A. Newton is John Tyler Professor of Business Administration at the University of Virginia. He has considerable experience in sales, as a representative, training manager, and sales manager. A book based on the research for the article printed here, *Sales Force Performance and Turnover*, was published in 1970.

Edward G. Niblock was a financial planner with Xerox Corporation when he died at the age of thirty-two, shortly before his article appeared in *HBR*.

Richard L. Nolan is President of Nolan Norton & Co. in Lexington, Massachusetts. He has done research on controlling computer resources through internal pricing, and he has been investigating the conceptual and technical problems of designing internal pricing systems. He has published many articles on EDP issues.

William T. Sandells, Jr. is former assistant treasurer and assistant controller of Baystate Corporation, a bank holding company. He is a certified public accountant and is currently involved in a broad spectrum of financial work, ranging from the development of systems to the analysis of results.

John K. Shank now teaches at the Tuck School of Business, Dartmouth College.

Benson P. Shapiro is Associate Professor of Business Administration at the Harvard Business School, where he teaches courses in sales management and creative marketing strategy. He has done extensive work in the sales management field through consulting and case study preparations.

William W. Sihler is Professor of Business Administration and Executive Director of Special Programs at the University of Virginia. He specializes in corporate finance and is currently at work on a book in that area.

Wickham Skinner is James E. Robison Professor of Business Administration at the Harvard Business School, where he has been since 1958. From 1948 to 1958 he was with Honeywell, Inc., serving in production control, manufacturing management and project supervision, as well as in marketing and general administration.

Donald D. Smith is a former Senior Project Leader in the Operations Research Department at Corning Glass Works. His interests have been the areas of time series analysis and econometrics.

Louis W. Stern is John D. Gray Professor of Marketing at Northwestern University. His primary interest has been in public policy as it applies to antitrust matters, and he is presently studying interorganization management in marketing. He has written on potential competition theory and conglomerate mergers and has published many books and articles, among them *Distribution Channels: Behavioral Dimensions* (1969).

Philip H. Thurston is Professor of Business Administration at the Harvard Business School, where he teaches courses in small business management, strategy formulation, and manufacturing management in the Program for Management Development.

Richard F. Vancil is Lovett-Learned Professor of Business Administration at the Harvard Business School. He is the author of books and articles on finance, control, and organization, including *Decentralization: Managerial Ambiguity by Decision* (1979).

Index